Publication description

Synopsis: Have you ever asked yourself how much Christ charged for his blessings, miracles, and ordinances? Apparently, not many people have thought about that, but we ought to, since, for example, a typical successfully employed LDS member pays out about $500,000 to church headquarters as the cost of a lifetime membership in the LDS church. The truth is that Christ charged nothing for his services, which ought to make one wonder about the extreme expense of belonging to today's LDS church. But, even worse, the present arrangement almost precludes anyone from engaging in serious New Testament-mandated charity work, since all the money one might reasonably have available to do charity work is claimed by the church headquarters, where only about 1% of the money that is received there is actually used for humanitarian aid. So, when was it that Christ came back in person to undo and reverse everything that he did earlier, which included ending the law of Moses and beginning a New Testament charity-based gospel system? Did he or Moses personally come back to re-institute today's law of Moses-style highly profitable professional ministry where a single member might be expected to contribute $500,000 in membership fees in a lifetime? I know of no such momentous event being recorded of Christ reappearing to reverse all that he accomplished during his earthly life.

Christ completely ended the old law of Moses, and that included ending the old law of tithing, and the huge paid ministry of the tribe of Levites that was supported by that tithing. From then on, every man was to be his own priest, so there was no need to have a paid ministry. Christ also did away with any need for any expensive fixed temple such as the Temple of Solomon or the Temple of Herod. Under the new church rules that took effect during and after the life of Christ, the church members had access to all the higher priesthood ordinances, including all the sealing ordinances such as eternal marriage, and yet they had no requirement to build any chapels or any temples. That meant that they could retain all of their personal resources and use them to actually live the New Testament law of charity by taking good care of their friends and neighbors. This also made them very mobile, since they had no need for any particular physical structure to fully engage in their religion.

As a practical matter, the church can have either charity or tithing, but not both. Charity was the only church welfare and finance system in effect for at least 300 years after Christ, as was also true at the beginning of this dispensation under the guidance of Joseph Smith. However, in 1896, Wilford Woodruff decided to begin using tithing for church leadership salaries, and all of Woodruff's contemporary church leader associates (except one) began pressing very hard to reinstitute the old law of Moses version of tithing to increase central church revenue. It took a long time to become fully successful in that policy change as the church members resisted (but apparently offered no organized principled resistance), but now we have almost completely removed charity as a practical church activity and replaced it with the requirement to send 10% of our annual resources to the central church offices where it is poorly used or simply stockpiled.

Additional research materials: I have spent my entire adult life studying the practical effects of the gospel, especially including its important economic freedom effects. Apparently, when a philosophy addresses the entire nature and meaning of life, as does the gospel, then it ends up in direct competition in the marketplace of ideas with every theory of man, most of them inspired by Satan's anti-freedom philosophy. At a young age I sensed the difficulty and importance of the issue of personal freedom as it relates to the gospel, but I had no idea how much time I would spend on the topic or where it might lead me. Vague terms like "all things common," "the united order", etc., have been used as an excuse by the theologians of priestcraft to try to make a profit on the insecurities, idealism, and naïveté of those who are drawn to and accept the general teachings of Christianity. I believe the inevitable distorting of every scriptural and historical nuance to maximize central church revenue is terribly destructive to the true gospel. My previous four books were meant to deal with how the greed and attempts at unrighteous dominion of men have warped the teachings and practices of the LDS church, and by extension, every other human church. Church leaders may have legitimate needs for member resources, but they have no right to command payment or to make payment a condition for receiving priesthood ordinances or blessings. "Freely have ye received, freely give."

The first three books support the proposition in great detail that Joseph Smith and Brigham Young wanted nothing to do with any of man's theories of centralization of power, including communalism, socialism, communism, etc. Nonetheless, the LDS theologians of priestcraft have taken the overwhelming arguments of scripture and church history against priestcraft and turned them completely around to justify the current profitable system of beliefs and practices. The fourth book demonstrates how ineffective the current LDS church program is, and suggests some ways to change the goals and methods. My latest book "Is the Church As True As the Gospel" finally demonstrates in detail how and why the church is failing in its mission today.

Earlier books, all expected to be newly available on Amazon:

1. *Joseph Smith's United Order: A Non-Communalistic Interpretation*
2. *Brigham Young's United Order: A Contextual Interpretation*
3. *Brigham Young's United Order: A Contextual Interpretation; Volume 2, Related Anomalies and Side Issues*
4. *Creating the Millennium: Social Forces and Church Growth in the 21st Century*

Is The Church As True As The Gospel?

Also by Kent Huff

Joseph Smith's United Order: A Non-Communalistic Interpretation
Brigham Young's United Order: A Contextual Interpretation, Vol. 1
Brigham Young's United Order: A Contextual Interpretation, Vol. 2, Related Anomalies and Side Issues
Creating The Millennium: Social Forces and Church Growth in the 21st Century

Is The Church As True As The Gospel?

A Constitutional Approach

Kent W. Huff

This book is not an official publication of The Church of Jesus Christ of Latter-Day Saints.

Paperback
ISBN: 978-0-9755831-2-8

Published by:
Theological ThinkTank
139 West 1720 North
Orem, Utah 84057
801-615-9032

Printed in United States of America.

Cover design:
Jan Wijnants, The Parable of the Good Samaritan, 1670. Oil on canvas, The State Hermitage Museum, St. Petersburg, Russia. Jan Wijnants (1632–1684), a painter from the Dutch Golden Age, painted this interpretation of the biblical parable in 1670.*

*https://www.bibleodyssey.org/tools/image-gallery/g/good-samaritan-wijnants#:~:text=Jan%20Wijnants,%20The%20Parable%20of,soft%20light,%20and%20pastoral%20images.

Is The Church As True As The Gospel? A Constitutional Approach

Table of Contents

Section 3 -- Amending the Gospel

Section 4 -- Creation vs. Evolution

Section 5 -- Some Potential Charitable Activities

Section 6 -- Building Up Zion

Section 7 -- Conclusions

Preface

Is the [LDS] Church as True as the Gospel?
A Constitutional Approach

The immediate intent of this effort is to try to discover whether some portion of those people who are leaving the church (which one estimate puts at about 500 members per day) would be willing to put in a little extra effort to study my analysis of the current LDS church, and decide to use this book text as at least a partial guide to implementing some major changes to the church from the inside. I am hoping that about 20% of those people who "resign" from the church will be willing to consider a new option. Besides the two basic options of staying in the church and leaving the church, there may be a third option which allows people to stay in the church while gently making their views known and promoting change for the better.

I believe most church members do not typically have the time to study church history and church doctrine to the extensive degree necessary to form their own well-considered opinion on all the most basic issues concerning religion and its management. Hopefully, this book will contain enough information for individuals to begin to form their own well-established opinions.

The biggest single problem which I see today is that the church has gradually chosen to end typical vigorous Christian charity activities, and instead to claim all of that member charity money for use at church headquarters, using the old law of Moses term of "tithing." The bulk of that "tithing" money I believe is used very poorly or even completely wasted, where judicious use of that money and the related human resources could be used to make enormous improvements in our society. I believe that if the church were making remarkable improvements to our society and our nation, many of those who are now unhappy with the church would have a reason to change their opinion and their actions.

In summary, I see Christian charity and "tithing" as mutually exclusive concepts: if the "tithing" (taxation to gain salvation) option is chosen, serious charity disappears, meaning that the most important sign of a Christian person disappears. This is especially true when every other level of government is constantly trying to raise taxes or "tithing" to build their own economic empires which compete with what should be more efficient voluntary religious activity.

Suggestions concerning an alternate reading sequence

There may be some people who would prefer to read what has been written in the past on these topics before they read my commentary. In that case, I suggest they read chapters 5 through 8 first, where I mainly quote English writers who have dealt with the tithing issue as it was handled in the United Kingdom at various times during the last 400 years.

Prologue

Human freedom, the first principle of heaven and earth

It may seem very unusual to connect together a famous statement by Joseph Smith and a famous story from Japan to make the main point of this chapter and this book, but the contrast between the two concepts is what this book is all about.

When asked about how he governed the Saints, Joseph Smith answered "I teach them correct principles, and they govern themselves." That is indeed a revolutionary concept – the idea that men can actually be free and make their own decisions! Surely Satan hates that statement and concept more than any other.

I like to put this clash of concepts in terms of the conflict between true religion, which supports freedom completely, and the religions of Satan which foster dependence and slavery, which I call "warlord religions," since they always are specifically designed to benefit some earthly dictator in his misbehavior.

Although Europe certainly had its own versions of feudalism and warlord religions over the centuries, I think there is no better or more extreme example of a warlord religion than could be found in Japan during its feudal period. The feudal period of Japan lasted from 1185 CE to 1868 CE. The Edo period is the period between 1603 and 1867 in Japanese history when the society was under the rule of the shoguns. That seems to be in the most extreme period of feudalism, out of which came many of the most extreme examples of the operation of a "warlord religion." If you have a value system which says who can live, and who can die, and who is in which social class, etc., that should qualify as a very serious religion.

It should not be too difficult to see that Joseph Smith's position is the exact opposite of the Japanese warlord position. And, of course, that Japanese warlord position is the epitome of what Satan would like to do to everyone on the Earth. Luckily, he is only able to do this in some parts of the Earth and in some parts of history.

The famous story of the "47 Ronin" occurs during the Edo period and seems to contain and illustrate all of the bad elements of a "warlord religion." The following material comes largely from Wikipedia.[1]

A rōnin (... "drifter" or "wanderer") was a samurai without a lord or master during the feudal period (1185–1868) of Japan. A samurai became masterless upon the death of his master, or after the loss of his master's favor or privilege. A masterless samurai ... often becomes a mercenary to make ends meet.

The revenge of the forty-seven rōnin (... forty-seven samurai), also known as the Akō incident ... or Akō vendetta, is an 18th-century historical event in Japan in which a band of rōnin (leaderless samurai) avenged the death of their master. The incident has since become legendary.

The story tells of a group of samurai who were left leaderless after their daimyō (feudal lord) Asano Naganori was compelled to perform seppuku (ritual suicide) for assaulting a court official named Kira Yoshinaka.... After waiting and planning for a year, the rōnin avenged their master's honor by killing Kira. They were then themselves obliged to commit seppuku for the crime of murder. The original dispute and attack and suicide occurred in 1701, the revenge attack took place in 1702, and the death of the ronin took place in 1703.

This true story was popularized in Japanese culture as emblematic of the loyalty, sacrifice, persistence, and honor that people should display in their daily lives. The popularity of the tale grew during the Meiji era, during which Japan underwent rapid modernization, and the legend became entrenched within discourses of national heritage and identity.

However, as well as these ideas were received in japan, we might reasonably wonder whether the value system of a pagan feudal society ought to have anything to do with a Christianity-based society.

As the story goes, the ronin were only cut loose because of misbehavior by their master. There is no Christian logic which would hold them accountable for the sins of their master. But, of course, they would become very inconvenient to the other remaining warlords, and those other warlords are certainly going to support an ideology that says that these warriors who have been cut loose ought to kill themselves to simplify the lives of the rest of the feudal warlords. (This seems only to have been true during the extreme Edo period.)

It would certainly seem more simple to have a group of well-trained and hardened warriors kill themselves than to lose perhaps five times that number of troops from your own army to remove them from society. That is the power of propaganda, or at least the power over people which is sought through the means of propaganda or social mind control.

In my opinion, all Christians should consider themselves ronins, in the sense that they are their own priest and need no central organization to receive every priesthood blessing from heaven. Christ intended that men should become their own priests. In other words, they should be independent in every way and have religious, political, and economic freedom. Even though Christ wished everyone to have religious freedom, it appears that most people are unsure of themselves and are easily convinced that their salvation should depend on the approval of some other person, not on God alone.

One will search in vain to find any bureaucracy which Christ set up which required taxes to provide the living for masses of soldiers or other employees acting like disciplined robots to carry out his will. That is what Satan would do, and Christ would have nothing to do with it. That should make one wonder why the church leaders today think that religious bureaucracies are the answer to everything, and of course those bureaucracies require huge amounts of money from the members through tithing and other contributions which are basically wasted as far as carrying out New Testament concepts of charity, individually administered.

The Jews and the Christians and the Muslims all point to Abraham as one of the founders of their religion. Abraham was distinguished by being a nomadic patriarch who owed allegiance to no one and was perhaps as free as any human could be. He certainly was the master of his own family and his own fate. That should be our model and goal, not becoming fanatically faithful followers of some religious warlord bordering on the psychological control of a cult, all to assure oneself of salvation. But, of course, all of that cultish behavior is exactly the opposite of what Christ taught his followers to do.

Christ disbanded the law of Moses with its entire tribe of Levites who were professional priests. Instead, every man was to be his own priest and there was no need for the physical temples and all the associated pomp and ceremony and ritual. Apparently. it is very hard to keep that concept in mind, because as far as I can tell, every restoration of the church has deteriorated into something which looks like the law of Moses or worse, as far as the centralization and monetization of all religious functions and blessings, including the sealing blessings. When the church is operating as it should, those blessings are widely distributed and are free, not metered out from the central offices at an enormous financial cost to those who wish to take advantage of those blessings.

The question then is where do we fit on this scale from perfect heaven-sanctioned freedom on the one hand versus perfect Satan-sanctioned slavery on the other? Logically, as the "one true church" we should be advocating for the perfect freedom of heaven, or a heavenly society on earth, even if that is not always achievable in practice. To the extent that the teachings of church leaders are contaminated with any aspects of the class-creating logic of the samurai warlords, then we can always clearly mark that as wrong. When we claim that church members can only buy their salvation by paying huge amounts to the church headquarters to get access to saving ordinances which should all be free, then at least to that extent we are following the logic of a warlord religion which is really Satan's religion. If we can't get this contrast straight in our minds, then I don't see how we can ever understand what God intends for us to do and to be like.

The LDS church is a fairly mild form of a warlord religion, certainly as compared to the Japanese ronin stories. But to the extent that the LDS church is a freedom-suppressing cult, when it interferes with members performing New Testament-style charitable acts, it has absorbed some of that same ideology.

The church leaders often tell us that "God can do his own work," by which they seem to mean that the church members should send all our resources to Salt Lake City and the bureaucracy there gets to completely decide what to do with the money – whether to keep it or spend it, etc.

One answer to that is to say that God indeed can do his own work, and he can do that work very well through the church members individually, and he prefers to do his work that way. One will search the Scriptures in vain to find arguments that people should create kings and bureaucracies and put themselves in financial bondage to such organizations. Christ always preferred a system of judges, by which He meant a mostly democratic way of choosing leaders.

Notes

1. https://en.wikipedia.org/wiki/Forty-seven_ronin
https://en.wikipedia.org/wiki/Ronin
https://sites.google.com/site/mrvailsclass2/feudal-japan
https://sites.google.com/site/samuraislife/home/history/edo-period
https://en.wiktionary.org/wiki/ronin

Is The Church As True As The Gospel? A Constitutional Approach

Section 1 -- Introduction

Chapter 1

The Problem

Today, simply accurately defining the problems faced by the LDS church may be almost enough to imply the correct answer:

Throughout recorded history, all other restorations of the gospel have begun to seriously deteriorate by the 200-year mark. We are at the 200-year mark, assuming we start counting at 1820. How stands the restoration? In my opinion, we have deteriorated at least as much as the other two restorations carried out by Christ himself in Jerusalem and in the New World. My goal here is to point out the difficulties as I see them, and hope that everyone else who has an interest in maintaining and promoting the gospel will help make any changes necessary to bring us back into conformance with Christ's true gospel as lived by him and his followers in Jerusalem and the New World.

Some people who are not church members, but who have studied the LDS church and its history, have concluded that the LDS church does not have a theology but only a history. That was a shocking and puzzling statement when I first read it. I have been puzzling on that statement for many years. In retrospect, it appears that outside researchers are simply saying that the numerous major changes in doctrine and practice over the life of the LDS church, starting in 1820, must indicate that the church *has* no stable doctrine and practice, but has had a long history of making major changes to the church teachings and practices over the decades. In other words, they conclude that the church has no dependable "constitution," but is whatever the current church leaders choose to say it is on any particular day.

This naturally brings up the question as to whether the gospel consists of a set of eternal unchanging principles and practices, or whether that church's leaders have full authority to make major changes at any time according to their individual viewpoints and preferences.

One might initially expect that the church leaders would be totally bound and constrained by the unusually large amount of scriptures which they have received and presented to the world. But it is easy to show that the church leaders actually feel bound and constrained by almost nothing which is in the written scriptures, but indeed do feel free to make major changes as they see fit.

We might express this thought in another way: What is the purpose of thousands of pages of carefully preserved scripture if every new church president can feel free to ignore all that has gone before and make any changes as might seem convenient, often with little or no explanation for the changes? The words of all the previous prophets, as recorded in scripture, may be interesting as guidelines, but they are not binding in any way? That appears to be the church position today. "Living prophets" might seem like a good idea for maintaining church guidance, but are those "living prophets" authorized to override anything and everything that has gone before as part of their church assignment?

As concerns the U.S. Constitution, we have a few Supreme Court justices who are considered "originalists" who strive to always apply the Constitution as the founding fathers intended, if that is possible. We have other Supreme Court justices who prefer to believe that the Constitution is a "living document," meaning that it can be changed in any way that seems convenient to a small number of activist judges if they simply have enough votes on their side.

The LDS church has exactly the same question come up on a regular basis. Are the writings of all the previous prophets, which we might call the "original intent" of the scriptures, an "original intent" which goes back perhaps 6,000 years (or beyond that to the beginning of eternity?), to be binding in almost every conceivable case, or are those scriptures highly plastic and malleable, to be used or ignored as current leaders prefer?

In national politics today, it is considered important to "follow the money" to understand what is actually going on in political maneuvering. Perhaps the same principle applies just as well to religious matters. The single largest change which has occurred to the LDS church in its 200-year history is the re-adoption of the law of Moses principle of tithing, supposedly making it a part of the gospel of Christ. The original tithing was devoted to supporting an entire tribe of Levites, a professional priesthood. In a similar way, today's tithing supports tens of thousands of "Levites," members of a new professional priesthood consisting of church employees, even though a critical part of Christ's new gospel was to make every man his own priest, so that no professional priesthood was required whatsoever. This new professional priesthood even includes a "Sanhedrin," a large and all-powerful headquarters unit which controls every aspect of the religion, as was done under the law of Moses.

It is interesting to realize that the religion which Christ instituted during his life was extremely efficient, making it suitable to provide guidance for any people at any time in any place, giving them every needful priesthood blessing at no charge. It required no payment of tithing and had no need for any temples or paid clergy or even any chapels. In fact, it did not even require a central headquarters of any kind. There was a requirement that the members look after each other and share each other's burdens, but that was the complete extent of their practical commitments. Being a member of the church thus added no financial burdens at all to those burdens which might already have been imposed by any aggressive tax-and-spend secular government organizations.

This very efficient arrangement leaves room for some large "extra credit" charitable projects specifically designed to repair a damaged society, done with or without the involvement of top church leaders. Often it would be better done without their involvement, again following the pattern Christ set. Such programs would be especially attractive to all charity-minded people if there were zero or minimal program overhead costs to administer them since most administrators would be volunteers.

This latter-day reversion to law of Moses tithing and paid ministry is especially puzzling, since Christ went to such great lengths to end every aspect of the old law of Moses, especially including the principle of tithing, with its paid priests. One might think that if Christ himself thought that his original gospel was faulty in some way, and that it should revert to including many prior law of Moses practices, then he would likely make it extremely clear that he was amending his gospel. One would not expect that this was something that a restored church would merely drift into by incremental administrative steps as opposed to receiving new scripture, probably delivered by Christ himself, concerning such a momentous change to reembrace Old Testament concepts and mix them in with New Testament concepts and expectations, making the new mixture internally inconsistent and incoherent.

One might reasonably expect that the dramatic events surrounding the occasion of Moses giving the children of Israel the law of Moses for the first time would be at least partially recreated on the occasion of reinstituting the law of Moses at a later time. But, as far as I know, none of those bombastic events have ever happened.

But perhaps that reversion to the lucrative law of Moses religious economic system is not really so puzzling when we observe that, at least according to appearances, all prior restorations have gone through the exact same steps of adopting a paid ministry, complete with the creation of a class system, where at least some of the leaders choose and demand to live off the resources of the members. It inevitably ends badly as the entire society is corrupted and disintegrates as it is infected with a pathologically self-centered and non-idealistic view of life, beginning with the church itself, leaving no good examples and leadership for the rest of society. No one is paying the maintenance costs of keeping a vigorous and spontaneously cooperative society intact.

If local church leaders can serve without pay, so can any more general leaders. It is not that they need no resources at all to operate, it is just that they should not demand any, leaving it to the generosity of God and church members to spontaneously supply whatever may be needed. Christ and his disciples demanded nothing of the members by right of their priesthood positions and yet they had what was needed. This system at least prevents any of the waste, fraud, and abuse typically associated with many secular governments' tax-and-spend social programs. Worst of all, and a sure path to complete corruption of the church, is its direct participation in any of those secular government tax-and-spend programs.

Alma 1 points out how dangerous it is to allow the church and its good influence on society to deteriorate as far as it already has:

> 12 But Alma said unto him [Nehor]: Behold, this is the first time that priestcraft has been introduced among this people. And behold, thou art not only guilty of priestcraft, but hast endeavored to enforce it by the sword; and <u>were priestcraft to be enforced among this people it would prove their entire destruction.</u>

(In case someone wishes to quibble that the church uses no force in its demand for tithing, we need only notice that members are completely kept from the benefits of the higher saving ordinances unless a lifetime of full tithes are paid to the central offices. Putting an earthly price on eternal salvation, which everyone naturally desires and deserves, is itself a very improper use of force or prevention, blocking or cutting off free access unless a fee is paid. "Freely ye have received, freely give." Matt. 10:8. One might need to do something to be worthy of receiving those ordinances, but the payment of large sums of money every year to the church central offices cannot be one of those criteria.)

From the account in 4 Nephi, it appears that that particular Alma 1 prophecy was fulfilled completely at about 300 A.D., as not only the church was destroyed, but the entire associated nation disappeared. It seems logical to assume that we face the exact same danger at this point. The church today is very weak and may actually be shrinking in size and influence, and the nation around us is rushing towards its own destruction. Hardly anyone is doing anything about it, or perhaps even *can* do anything about it if they cannot present solutions based on the principles and religion of Christ.

The level of political discord is so striking today that people often wonder about the possibility of another civil war. Of course, it was a civil war that destroyed the New World church. There have been plenty of religious conflicts and wars in Europe, and the true church was also lost there, as it was in the New World, but at least some Christians and Christian principles were able to survive the centuries of conflict, at least in the form of writings, and finally succeeded in creating the remarkable Western Civilization, culminating in the rise of the United States with its inspired Constitution.

It seems obvious at this point that the only way to sustain a permanent and complete restoration of the gospel is to take the "constitutional" approach of carefully defining all the important elements of the gospel, and then coming up with an auditing system which makes sure that no one deviates from that specification without the most rigorous of explanations and verifications. One might protest that this sounds too much like the law of Moses, if we have to specify everything in detail. However, men are by nature foolish and corrupt and self-centered so that, given the opportunity, they will veer off course every time if there is not some system to keep them on the straight and narrow path, and, unfortunately, they will often take many others with them. Every church member should wake up every morning and ask themselves the question, "Is The Church As True As The Gospel?" That should put a brake on inappropriate changes.

The following chart is intended to be a beginning point on what principles the correct gospel includes, plus a comparison with how today's church has modified those basic gospel principles. Making these major repairs would move us a goodly way toward getting back to the true religion of Christ.

A Partial Gospel "Constitutional" Summary and Comparison

Gospel principle/theme	Christ's church	Today's church
Freedom is first principle of heaven. If the institutional church acts in any way to limit any kind of freedom, it is almost certainly wrong.	Observe inspired US Constitution as part of scripture. Maintain consent of governed. Maintain all freedoms -- religious, political, economic.	Ignores US Constitution. Ignores consent of governed. Interferes with freedoms -- religious, political, economic. Constantly promotes exact obedience to central church bureaucracy, limiting member freedom, damaging the spread of the gospel.
Required contributions	None. All ordinances and services are free.	Reinstituted Law of Moses tithing and paid ministry, charges large fees for all higher ordinances
Charity	First practical responsibility of members.	Charity is minimal and is mostly ignored. Tithing and charity are mutually exclusive concepts, and the church consistently chooses tithing.
Creation	God created earth and all life. Man is literal offspring of God	Church accepts and promotes all atheistic organic evolution speculations, including the origin of man, concerning which much ambiguity is maintained.
Grace and works	Grace covers many things concerning salvation, but grace alone is not sufficient to qualify a person for the extensive responsibilities that come with exaltation.	Accepts Protestant formulation of grace and works and its links to the nature of heaven.
Nature of heaven	Qualified, exalted beings continue the eternal advancement of souls. All others have no responsibility for anyone but themselves.	Largely accepts Protestant formulation of heaven, although it adds its own version of universal salvation involving various levels of heaven, and essentially removes the "hell" option. Ignores or waffles on extra duties and opportunities of qualified, exalted

		beings.
Marriage	Joinder of a man and a woman to bring souls into the world and teach them the correct gospel so they can gain valuable experience and serve others in turn.	The definition is becoming more fluid. The church seems to have recently compromised with gay activists on same-sex marriage, opening the path for a new kind of gay-pagan-Mormon to be welcomed into the church to further dilute its ability to be a standard and an influence for good. This is apparently part of a commercially oriented "big tent" strategy to maintain church income.
Amending the gospel	Extremely difficult and rare. Requires direct heavenly intervention with new scripture, formally accepted by church members. Most apparent "changes" are simply the result of getting a better understanding of the original gospel.	Leadership whimsy and convenience is all that is required, as in the case of initiating tithing, charging for priesthood ordinances, ending the literal gathering of Israel, ending vigorous support for freedom, and embracing evolution.

Is The Church As True As The Gospel? A Constitutional Approach

Chapter 2

A Suggested Solution

Although the church problem as outlined above may seem complex and even overwhelming, I believe the general solution is rather simple in concept, however complicated it may be in execution. Here is a high-level treatment of the situation, sent to church headquarters as a suggestion:

November 1, 2019

Elder _________
50 East North Temple
Salt Lake City, Utah 84150

Subject: Member faith crises: a suggestion

Dear Elder _________,

It makes me sad to see people leaving the church for potentially preventable reasons. The question then is, what are the options for encouraging them to want to stay?

Recently, I have been studying the issue of LDS member faith crises. Some materials available on the Internet include a June 2013 study entitled "LDS Personal Faith Crisis," 140 pages in length, which you have probably seen, which surveyed over 3000 people concerning their individual faith crises. In that report, a sense of urgency was expressed as to the importance of resolving this issue. At least two other similar survey studies have been done on this topic, with one set of results reported in a published book, and another set of results reported on an Internet site. I have also been conducting my own informal survey, on a much smaller scale.

Representing a different collection of faith crisis data, in August 2019 a lawsuit was brought in federal court against the LDS church alleging that a large class of people were taught throughout their young lives numerous aspects of early church history, which aspects supposedly have now been shown to be incorrect. These allegedly incorrect teachings are said to have amounted to a fraud, which has caused numerous personal faith crises.

The case is named *Gaddy vs COB (LDS).* It began with a 75-page complaint which outlines the various claimed fraudulent teachings concerning Joseph Smith, the Book of Mormon, etc. The case is only in the beginning stages, but it does appear that the plaintiff and her highly experienced attorney are well prepared to pursue this case as far as possible. The attorney also considers herself to be among the defrauded members or ex-members. No specific numbers are given concerning class size or the expected jury-trial-approved award, but my own quick estimate based on outside data would put the class size at about 26,000, with a potential total award in the range of $250 million.

These kinds of continuing public activities seem to indicate that this "faith crisis" issue will not soon go away, and so should probably be taken seriously and directly addressed. The church statistical data from 2018 seem to show that the church is barely replacing those who die or leave the church, achieving little net growth in active members.

I have been a church member all my life, born and raised in Utah, and at age 78, I have spent most of my life studying various unique aspects of the church, including many aspects of its early history. I have written five books on those topics and have published three of them. I have two law degrees but have spent most of my career as a computer consultant, spending 14 years overseas, which offered three different views of the foreign operations of the church in Saudi Arabia, Mexico, and Russia.

I consider many aspects of church history that are widely objected to today to be based on a profound ignorance of the settings in which many of these events took place. Uninformed and unrestrained "presentism" is seen in almost every one of today's arguments. At the same time, it is often very difficult to find out the exact truth on any particular historical issue because there is so little fully complete and reliable historical evidence available. Joseph Smith made a heroic effort to record the relevant history, but, several generations later, it is not nearly enough to settle all important historical questions that might arise. Most of the data available is nearly all very old and of low quality, and so is a poor basis for any kind of definitive judgment.

I believe several of these historical issues could indeed be settled with broader and better-informed reviews of history, but, at the same time, many more of those kinds of questions may never be fully answered using only historical materials.

Move the discussion to a different kind of history?
Considering overall strategy, we could continue to struggle mightily with these troublesome historical issues, often using nothing more reliable than 200-year-old rumors which are poorly documented and therefore poorly understood. However, I believe in many areas that quest for truth would still prove to be unfruitful.

As an alternative to a constant and sweeping review of innumerable church history topics, I suggest that the church put major resources into creating a new and current "replacement" history, completely positive and verifiable, which would show by its actions that today's LDS church is indeed a copy of the church which Christ himself restored in the meridian of time.

Pres. Nelson has emphasized the need for more personal charitable activity, which is part of the idea of ministering. My main suggestion is that the church simply take some much longer steps down that same road of expanding charity, which was considered the number one focus of the gospel among the early Christians. See 1 Cor. 13.

The essence of my suggestion is that the church consider engaging in some large-scale, society-changing charitable activities as a counterbalance to a less-than-perfect grip on 200-year-old church history, rendering that old history much less relevant.

It should not be too difficult to find suitable social problems in our nation that obviously require enormous charitable efforts to resolve properly, since governments have clearly failed. We have the abortion problem, the homelessness problem, and the immigration and border problem, to name just a few of the more widely recognized situations crying out for solutions. Slightly less obvious are such problems as inner-city education failures, broken families, and social violence. Those particular inner-city activities would also tend to counteract claims of church racism, past or present. (Those claims of racism are incorrect, but I doubt that any amount of public discourse will dispel those claims without some impressive associated actions.)

Most of the surveys mentioned above did not explicitly address this issue of membership opinions of church charitable activity levels. That could have been done through appropriately themed or focused survey questions, designed for easy tabulation, but it was not done. However, I believe the free-form written essay answers, and other similar materials from other sources, do give us some valuable insights into important attitudes. First, we should recognize that most of the respondents were from among the previously most serious and active members -- many of the "best and brightest" -- as indicated by their usually extensive church experience, including demanding positions held. They typically expressed their seeming concern about various historical issues, like so many other people, but I believe they were also, and more importantly, expressing concerns that they were seeing far too little good societal effects, too little "return on investment (ROI)" on church activity in general, based on the extreme levels of individual inputs of time, energy, commitment, and money. These resource factors have not been officially quantified and made public by today's central church, but they certainly amount to many tens of billions of dollars in volunteer payments and volunteer hours, with relatively little to show for it in the realm of improvements to society.

For example, Utah might logically be a social showcase of the best that is possible in the nation and the world, but Utah is not actually very remarkable on many important measures. Perhaps something besides standard secular government methods is needed to achieve impressive excellence.

Based on numerous comments about church financial matters in survey responses, I believe that the underlying logic of many of those disappointed members who were surveyed, however imprecisely that logic may have been stated, is that if the gospel doesn't actively change the world for the better, as it was prophesied it should do, then there must be something wrong with that church's policies and practices. The original church that Christ restored in Jerusalem certainly did go on to almost single-handedly create the cultural richness and technological wonders of Western civilization. Perhaps all we need to do to satisfy some of these serious Christian people is to more staunchly continue that Christian tradition.

A more perceptive membership?

I think we are also glimpsing another interesting, and presumably unexpected problem where the constant reading and studying of the scriptures by bright, highly educated, and committed members, which reading activity is supposed to help keep them committed and doubt-free, can actually serve to highlight the deficiencies in today's church behavior, when compared to the foundational scriptures. This would likely be especially true concerning the topic of charity and general issues of freedom, and could thus create cognitive dissonance and raise doubts, even if only subconsciously, felt as a kind of general unease.

For example, the Book of Mormon, especially in the Book of Alma, vigorously teaches the vital importance of individual political freedom through portraying at length the strenuous lifelong labors of Captain Moroni to keep his religious compatriots free. And the first chapter of Alma describes an extremely efficient system of charity and welfare where there is no expensive central bureaucracy either for government or for church administration, leaving all the resources of the population available to be used in individual charitable acts.

Two remarkably enlightened kings, King Benjamin and King Mosiah, paved the way for a new democratic system of judges, with an absolute minimum of taxes and central administration, matched with the maximum of personal freedom and responsibility. One might conclude that if the church is not vigorously promoting individual freedom and individual charity, as did the original church of Christ, which was actually historically *preceded* by the practices described in the Book of Alma, then something must be wrong.

We also might notice that the saints described in the Book of Alma, and the early saints after the life of Christ, had no requirement to pay into any tithing system, and also built no chapels or temples, leaving essentially all their personal resources available for individual acts of charity, giving them the maximum religious freedom to do good.

I am confident that most of the current history-based objections to the church's legitimacy would disappear from public discussion if the church reverted to those original arrangements established by the original apostles. Under those ideal circumstances, the church grew at about 10% a year for hundreds of years, presumably because of the sense of community and security the members provided each other.

Church-driven limitations on freedom and charity?
From observations made during my international travels, apparently the church has explicitly or implicitly made the determination that it must operate worldwide based on the most restrictive conditions found anywhere, always seeking and applying the lowest common denominator. For example, whatever modicum of individual and church religious freedom is found in Russia must not be exceeded anywhere else in the world, regardless of the vastly different conditions found in other countries. In Russia there are legal limits on any potentially widespread society-changing charity activities. Should the limits on individual religious freedom found in Russia also apply in the United States, where freedom is celebrated and churches are still essentially unconstrained? It seems difficult to justify such widespread, self-imposed religious limitations, even if it might offer some conveniences of consistency of administration to the central church offices.

In other words, should the religious freedom problems of 10,000 members in restrictive countries control the behavior of 10,000,000 members in freer countries, where those freer members could do perhaps hundreds of times more good with their freedom than they do now? As an extra consideration, those good deeds done elsewhere might eventually indirectly help the plight of members in restrictive countries.

I have more information on many of these topics if that seems useful.

Sincerely yours,

Receipt of the letter was acknowledged, but no substantive response was provided.

The suggestion for a solution might have been said more succinctly:

1. Make sure that current church teachings and activities conform with the actual gospel of Christ. It turns out that this is actually very difficult to accomplish, especially after 200 years of doctrinal drift.
2. Make sure that the members actually understand the basic principles of the gospel, which I see as freedom, charity, God as Creator, the nature of the heaven we are striving to reach (since heavenly and earthly principles should be very much the same), what a practical gospel community should look like, etc.

If church members have a clear understanding of these basic philosophies, they can largely compute for themselves what all the other sub-principles of the gospel ought to be. Loving God and loving your neighbor as yourself are two good places to start. A heavy emphasis on personal charity would help get us back into conformity with New Testament and Book of Mormon teachings.

It seems to be a current anti-Mormon fad to find some nit-picking historical issue and use that to convince church members that that proves that the gospel is untrue. But that seems to be the classic problem of not being able to see the forest for the trees, allowing some small point, some shiny object, to obscure the big picture. For example, rather than getting hung up on how many different ways Joseph Smith described his first vision in writing, perhaps we should strive to find out what was learned from that first vision and all other revelations Joseph Smith received, certainly including the Book of Mormon. We have a large mass of scriptures, but our understanding of the most important teachings of the scriptures currently leaves much to be desired.

In my opinion, it is not enough for us to know how to be nice to each other, although that is an important part of the gospel for both children and adults. However, as adults who are managing their own lives and helping others to manage their lives, it is very important to know what an entire Gospel society, what a "Zion," would look like. Only then can we make sure that our actions are always going in the right direction.

A second letter was drafted but never sent:

May 5, 2020

LDS First Presidency
50 East North Temple
Salt Lake City, Utah 84150

Subject: Member faith crises: a suggestion, part 2

Dear Brethren,

I recently sent a rough book manuscript to a publisher, and during the resulting lull in activity it occurred to me that this might be a good time to communicate with church headquarters about an idea. This book is part of a project I want to carry out, but I now realize that there might be other ways to do the project.

The current working title of the book is "Is The Church As True As The Gospel? A Constitutional Approach." The main purpose of the book is to point out that the LDS Church today has gradually become more a reflection of Old Testament teachings than it is of New Testament teachings. The Old Testament was focused on paying tithing, supporting a professional priesthood, and attaining personal purity, while the New Testament ended tithing and any related professional priesthood, and was instead focused almost entirely on carrying out charitable acts that improved the lives of individuals and of society – the Good Samaritan focus. There was less concern about static purity and more concern about active good works. Doing good works vigorously may cause controversy, of course, but Christianity is not supposed to be passive, in my view. I believe Christianity should be an active leaven to society.

Many people may not be sophisticated theologians who can describe and discuss these religious issues and the related ideologies in detail, but a very large number of people nonetheless can sense the strong practical difference between an Old Testament program and a New Testament program. My book simply explains how we got here. I believe these issues have a great deal to do with the missionary and retention success of the church.

I find it interesting that the new information that the LDS Church has at least $100 billion in liquid investments is in the headlines at the same time I am finishing my book that has to do with church policy drift. To my knowledge, the church has not denied the essence of any of these reports, but rather has taken some steps to try to defend its actions, perhaps as being needed preparation for some unclear future events.

This new public knowledge confirms and validates the book I have assembled, since the news makes it clear what the Church's real priorities have been in recent decades – giving charitable works less emphasis and banking the savings. Perhaps we could call this "burying the talent," referring to the New

Testament parable. If church headquarters wanted to do something to change that image, perhaps we could work together.

It seems to me that this might be a good time to offer an alternative suggestion. As part of my publication project I have intended to offer to manage a project which I have called the "Fund for Zion." In my opinion, there are many valuable things that $100 billion could have been spent for during the last many decades, but those actions were not taken. What I am proposing is a separate fund to actually do those things which the Church has chosen to avoid. For example, the church has ended its adoption services, presumably for reasons of avoiding political conflict, but I believe an independent non-church organization would not experience the same political constraints.

I have in mind at least six different "shovel-ready projects" of a charitable nature, at various levels of research and definition, which would make a good beginning in solving a few important social problems that can be easily identified today. Each of these projects needs some seed money to get them started and to introduce and verify some new concepts. The projects could then proceed autonomously and independently in many cases.

Some project examples

1. An abortion/adoption/foster-care project. In my book, I describe in some detail an idea for a demonstration charitable project to deal with the social issues of abortion and adoption on a fairly large scale. I believe the first step in the project would be to get long-term control of the development of perhaps 1200 contiguous acres of suitable undeveloped ground to be used for housing, schools, work experience opportunities, etc., that could be used to support many different aspects of the abortion/adoption project. I am guessing that it would take about $20 million to get the necessary control of that land so that long-term plans could then be made and carried out. The general idea would be to end up with a facility which could support about 20,000 orphans or foster-care kids somewhere in central Utah. The total long-term cost to develop all the facilities might be in the $2 billion range.

2. A genealogy project. I have actually spent the most research time on a genealogy-related project which would have the goal of completing the United States within two years and the entire world within 10 years. Enormous amounts of money and labor have been applied to the genealogy activity already, but the levels of duplication and inefficiency are astronomical. A change in concept and technology would make possible the timeframes I mentioned without any more effort or money being applied than is available now. I hold two software patents whose purpose it is to demonstrate the feasibility of what I have just described. Most technical aspects have been tested already, but a few million dollars could be used to further prove all practical concepts and methods, including user acceptance. My calculations are that $70 million would be required to finish all the basic genealogy for the United States up to about 1940, and that data product should be valuable enough as a starting place, if handled properly, to make possible completing the processing of all records available for the rest of the world.

3. A government integrity project. I have observed through my own sad experiences (described in my book) that the legal and judicial system in the state of Utah is not obviously much better than that in any other state of the Union. If Utah is supposed to represent "Zion," then one of the elements of "Zion" is to have an honest and dependable government administration, something which is not always present in the state of Utah. It seems to me it would be very useful to have an ongoing review and evaluation of most important government and judicial opinions and actions, pointing out the major biases and prejudices that exist in Utah as much as anywhere else. This kind of monitoring of governments is something which news organizations only do on a very sporadic basis. Perhaps a $5 million study project could make major progress in this area.

4. A gathering/migration project. One look at the United States southern border presents a whole list of social problems that need attention – unaccompanied minors, economic refugees, health problems, etc. There are numerous opportunities for charitable activities to help with all the many problems that are highlighted at the border, many of which the state and federal governments are poorly prepared to deal with. As one interesting example, there are people leaving from Venezuela, Honduras, Guatemala, etc., to try to reach the United States. In many cases those people risk their lives many times over using underground-style travel methods while also still paying out enough money to actually be provided safe and easy passage out of their Third World difficulties. One interesting solution, among many, would be to help some of these people relocate to Europe where they would be well received as having much closer values and social ties to the local society than do the majority of the Muslim immigrants who have been flooding Europe and causing many problems. After some further education and experience, those same Hispanic people might be able to move in a logical progression to the United States, if that is their goal. They often have the funds to be able to move from their unpleasant homes to a better place, but they need some guidance and advance preparations to make the transitions pleasant and productive. A few million dollars would go a long way to research and set up practical systems to help these people.

5. An education project. There are many ways in which the current, mostly government-controlled education systems are failing the students and the rest of society. We have the interesting situation where large local companies are willing to invest money in school systems to improve the educational levels of the students those schools produce, but there does not appear to be any really satisfactory place to invest that money effectively. At the same time, the homeschool effort in Utah is doing great things, largely driven by LDS mothers with very high goals and expectations for their children, pointing out that the possibilities for improvement of the state's education systems are numerous. A few million dollars would allow research and practical systems to be set up to help students and families and companies.

6. A health/pension demonstration project. It appears that the New Testament program of individual charitable works amounted to a complete social insurance system for church members and their friends, but without all the rigidity, unfairness, inefficiency, coerciveness, and waste of the typical government tax-and-spend welfare system. That early New Testament charitable system, or any

other charitable system, can be up to five times more efficient than any government program could ever be, meaning that real needs can be met quickly and flexibly as they arise. Today, the lion's share of government budgets, and therefore nearly all political conflict, relates to health care, pensions, and other welfare matters, but a secular government is usually poorly prepared to administer such programs well and wisely. For political reasons, governments almost always promise more than they can deliver, typically eventually bankrupting those systems. Those excessive government promises also tend to result in lowering the growth rate of their population below replacement value. Citizens might wonder why they should bother with raising children of their own to care for them in their old age when the government has promised to always take care of them (by taxing other peoples' children). If everyone follows that logic, then the number of children raised to adulthood drops drastically. This tendency of an overreaching government to initiate a society death spiral through welfare systems seems to be too well-hidden for most people to recognize. A family-oriented, pro-life church might consider advocating strongly against some of our society's current anti-family, anti-life policies.

These few ideas barely begin to deal with the many major problems which are in the world and which need attention, for church members, and for others as well. Also, I'm quite confident that there are many good people in the world, regardless of their church affiliation, who would help with some of these projects if it was clear to them that they were getting a good value for the money they were contributing.

If any of these ideas seem like useful topics for discussion, I hope you will let me know.

Sincerely yours,

Is The Church As True As The Gospel? A Constitutional Approach

Section 2 -- The Overwhelming Historical And Scriptural Case Against A Paid Ministry And Related Tithing

Section introduction

Having briefly outlined the problems faced by the LDS church and its members, and having suggested a general solution, perhaps it is now time to dive deeper into the various issues behind these high-level topics and conclusions. The most critical of all issues is that of tithing and the closely related system of a professional priesthood. I think it is fair to say that every other divergence by the church from the original gospel can be tied in some way to that placing of church income ahead of every other principle of the gospel.

Insisting on treating a restored religion as a for-profit business, complete with retaining massive profits to make equally massive investments in land and other assets, for purposes of supplying pension funds, rainy day funds, and management perks, cannot possibly do anything else except warp essentially every aspect of the original gospel. This makes the LDS church look exactly like the religious empire of the Roman Catholic Church, which it supposedly replaces with supposedly better principles and better intentions.

Selling the gospel is a great deal different from giving it to the world free of charge, as did Christ himself. The current church had no research or development costs in developing this wonderful gospel, but still it wants to seek enormous rents on every aspect of the restored church, changing details and "simplifying it" to optimize income.

We are certainly not the first generation who have suffered because of similar decisions made by church leaders on the issue of tithing. Reading about some of their problems and objections should help put our own situation into better context

Excerpts from about five or six different works from about five or six different time periods should give us a pretty good sampling of past experience. The simple conclusion one might reach from reading all of this history is that the concepts of tithing and charity are mutually exclusive, and always have been. One might easily guess that the "Lamb slain from the foundation of the world" knew all of these things long before he came to earth, and he presented his gospel accordingly, not finding any need to equivocate or be unsure of himself. There was no reason to "test drive" this gospel, making changes on the fly.

After exploring these various histories of tithing we will analyze in some detail a portion of the voluminous scriptural information on this point, plus review our own church history to locate some pivotal events and decisions.

Section Contents
The argument of this book section on the topic of tithing and paid ministry will be established by drawing on

1. introductory topics related to tithing and temples,
2. histories of tithing written by other authors,
3. new historical material compiled using an LDS viewpoint,
4. the presentation of more closely reasoned examinations of all LDS scriptures,
5. a presentation of statistical evidence showing the vast inefficiencies of churches controlled by paid ministries, and
6. more general comments concerning the consequences of the paid ministry choice.

Tithing histories that appear below, in full or in part:
Internet access to these histories:

A very short history of tithing (full text appears below)
"A Brief History Of Tithing After Christ's Crucifixion" by Dr. Fillmer Hevener, 2005, 2 pages
http://www.guthriememorial.org/articles/brief_history_of_tithing.htm
This item is included in the book.

A short history of tithing (full text appears below)
The Great Case of Tithes Truly Stated (1657) by Anthony Pearson, multiple later editions beginning in 1720, 36 pages.
Read the online 1850 edition:
https://play.google.com/books/reader?id=ECTQZZb4LuAC&printsec=frontcover&pg=GBS.PA1
The document opens in a reader application.
This book by Pearson appears below in compact form, but is much easier to read online.
https://play.google.com/books/reader?id=ECTQZZb4LuAC&pg=GBS.PA2

A medium length history of tithing (excerpts appear below)

A history of tithes (1894) by Henry William Clarke, 268 pages, 304 pdf images
Here is the full text of the Clarke book, or the reader can choose other formats:
https://archive.org/stream/historyoftithes00claruoft/historyoftithes00claruoft_djvu.txt
Images of original pages:
https://archive.org/details/historyoftithes00claruoft/page/6
This book is based to a large extent on the earlier Selden book.

A very long history of tithing (excerpts appear below)
John Selden, *History of Tithes*, 1618, 491 pages
Old English text is somewhat difficult to read

Here the full text appears in outline form
https://quod.lib.umich.edu/e/eebo/A68720.0001.001?rgn=main;view=fulltext

Here the reader can see all the original images for the John Selden book
https://play.google.com/books/reader?id=ntZIAQAAMAAJ&hl=en&pg=GBS.PP11

Commentary on the tithing histories used in this book
The first history of tithing appearing below is a modern summary probably written in about 2005 and placed on the internet along with other religious writings by the same author. Since the history of tithing seems to not be widely known by the Christian church populace today, this will give us a simple historical framework to begin with.

Next comes materials from three longer documents: a Quaker tract originally published in 1657 by Anthony Pearson (the 1850 edition is used here for easier reading), a major 1618 work by John Selden which explored this subject in extreme detail (although it is hard to read in middle English), and a later (1894) and more readable compilation based to a large extent on the work of John Selden and others.

As a useful historical reference point, it was in 1517 that Martin Luther posted his 95 theses and inadvertently started the Protestant Reformation. The English Reformation happened a little later:

> The break with Rome was effected by a series of acts of Parliament passed between 1532 and 1534, among them the 1534 Act of Supremacy, which declared that Henry was the "Supreme Head on earth of the Church of England".
> https://en.wikipedia.org/wiki/English_Reformation

Looking at the "history of histories" on the topic of tithing, John Selden was apparently the first to do an enormous amount of original research on the topic and published his work in 1618 in the book entitled *The Historie of Tithes*. Since his research was considered anti-church and anti-monarchy, the two improper beneficiaries of the collection of tithes, it is not surprising that his work was not well received by the social elite at the time.

Other writers later adopted and adapted his material and added their own viewpoints. In 1657 Anthony Pearson composed a lengthy pamphlet to express the Quakers point of view. A Rev. Henry William Clarke prepared a 268-page book in 1894 on the same topic. These writers allude to a larger body of writings from earlier times, presumably mostly referring to John Selden.

These histories tell us how distorted and deteriorated things gradually got under the Roman Catholic Church and why a restoration of the New Testament gospel was needed, at least for the reason of clearing away all the injustices and anti-Christian behavior related to tithing. We certainly should not want to go down that path again, but we seem to be well on our way to reenacting all of the unpleasantness and unfairness related to tithing as we can see it played out in England and Europe.

Chapter 3

The issue of financial classes in the church

The recognized danger of creating doctrinally-required financial classes within the church
A review of the Scriptures and of church history for all available time periods seems to tell us that every time a dispensation of the gospel fails, as all previous ones have failed, and as the current one is failing, it is apparently always for the same reason: the adoption of a paid ministry by the church itself. That inevitably results in the corrupting and paralyzing of the main source of good in the world and gives Satan free reign, uncontested by any vigorously competing group or organization promoting classic Christianity.

1. The church which Christ restored in Jerusalem existed for about 300 years before the twin visible corrupting features of tithing and a paid ministry largely finished off and corrupted that initial restoration.
2. In the New World, the Scriptures tell us that the church lasted about 320 years before falling apart, most likely after adopting the tithing/paid ministry heresy.
3. In our day, it was only 66 years after the church was organized that the tithing/paid ministry heresy was brought in to neutralize and paralyze the church. It took a few more years for that heresy to establish a complete grip on the church, and it has been all downhill since then.

The concept of creating classes among the people is always an issue in the falling away process. And the main way which the church itself participates in this class-creating process, and thus encourages other class-creating processes concerning other aspects of the society, is to bring in the tithing/paid ministry heresy. If the church has adopted this corrupt class-creating process itself, you can be sure that every other Satan-inspired, freedom-weakening government centralization process will be essentially approved by the church and thus greatly accelerated, to the great detriment of the entire society.

It is easy to see the effects of the class system that was the inherent nature of the law of Moses system that later invaded the Christ-restored Jerusalem church which ended up producing the highly political, heavily bureaucratic monarchical Roman Catholic Church, which invented all manner of paid positions and policies and practices which have no justification in the scriptures. It is easy to see the class system which has been created in the modern-day LDS church, where an enormous and wasteful central bureaucracy lives off the tithing the church now demands before anyone can use the temples. The old "freely ye have received, freely give" (Matt. 10:8) counsel concerning all priesthood blessings and ordinances has been completely overridden concerning all the higher ordinances, essentially monetizing all those religiously valuable higher ordinances.

It is not quite so easy to verify that that is what happened in the New World church that was created after Christ's resurrection. However, I think we can infer that the exact same process occurred and produced the exact same results. I think we can call this essentially a nearly inevitable religious law of degradation. The scriptures in 4 Nephi tell us that classes were created among the people. That is the definition of adopting the tithing/paid ministry heresy. We might recall that King Mosiah (who gave up his kingship and ended kings among his people, consciously adopting a democratic system) had carefully ended all "paid ministries," whether they were religious or governmental. Those unusually wise people of Mosiah called themselves "Christians" while apparently essentially abolishing nearly all aspects of the law of Moses, almost certainly ending anything that looked like the tithing/paid ministry heresy.

This all seems to suggest a very specific way to purify a restoration and keep it pure, allowing it to have the effect on the world that was intended. The most important thing an organization needs to do is to make sure that it never adopts the tithing/paid ministry heresy, which is the "pathway drug" which leads to all other deviations and heresies, all introduced to make life even easier for a paid ministry which has gained control of the church. The entire point of a paid ministry is to achieve wealth and ease with nothing more than a skill with ideology and rhetoric. Actual valuable service is not required, but only the feigning of it.

Although Christ did everything in his power to make it clear that the law of Moses tithing/paid ministry heresy was to be ended with his act of atonement, the natural man and the greed factor, with constant cheerleading from Satan, is relentless in trying to reestablish that heresy in every possible situation. We need to make it clear that the temptations of Christ, where he refused to accept any of the temptations Satan set before him concerning wealth and fame and power, are all critical prerequisites for the gospel to remain uncorrupted. The number of ordinary men is extremely small who are similarly willing to pass the same temptation tests and deny themselves wealth and fame and power even though they have been given important gospel authorities which give them innumerable opportunities to fail those temptation tests. Giving men the opportunity to profit from religious leadership almost inevitably dooms them to be corrupted by that opportunity. Only by permanently obliterating that opportunity is there a chance that men will remain pure.

In our own time, we can see exactly how that process played out, as Joseph Smith, Brigham Young, and John Taylor faithfully followed the principles and practices of Christ, and consistently resisted all the same temptations that Christ resisted, but when Wilford Woodruff became the president of the church, he and all his associates and successors quickly failed that set of temptations and started the church on the standard downward spiral. Once one person in leadership makes that choice, apparently no succeeding leader can ever understand the long-term problem that has been created, or has the grit and determination to undo what was wrongly done. Apparently, once one is called a "prophet," it is just too embarrassing, inconvenient, and unthinkable to "prophesy" that a previous prophet made a serious doctrinal and practical error concerning church finance that needs to be rectified. This seems to create a one-way ratchet downward, where no one in the leadership sequence dares interfere with the very process that gave them their existing power and authority, however illegitimate it may be when compared with original principles.

In order to maintain a good reason for the church's existence, the church members and affiliated organizations should work hard to END the class-infected society, NOT contribute to classes for self-interest's sake, like everyone else is doing.

The church leaders first deplored and then created financial classes
In the 1800s, numerous church leaders worried about the problem of social and economic classes forming among the church members. It is somewhat ironic that a little bit later, very specifically beginning in 1896 at the instigation of Wilford Woodruff (who seems not to have spoken out publicly on this issue), it was the church leaders themselves who invented a class system based upon the church leaders living on the religious contributions of the members.

As a curiosity, of those who spoke in public on this topic, it may be that only George Q. Cannon lived to see the church invent its own version of a class society with church leaders being supported by the labor of the members.

Here are a few rhetorical text samples from the Journal of Discourses:

> JD 15:209, George Q. Cannon, October 8, 1872
> Before co-operation started, you doubtless saw and deplored the increase of wealth in some few hands. There was rapidly growing in our midst a class of monetary men composing an aristocracy of wealth. Our community was menaced by serious dangers through this, because if a community is separated into two

classes, one poor and the other rich, their interests are diverse. Poverty and wealth do no[t] work together well – one lords it over the other; one becomes the prey of the other. This is apt to be the case in all societies, in ours as well as others; probably not to so great an extent, but still it was sufficiently serious to menace us as a people with danger. God inspired his servant to counsel the people to enter into co-operation, and it has now been practiced for some years in our midst with the best results. Those who have put in a little means have had that more than doubled since Z. C. M. I. started – three years last March. And so it is with co-operative herds, co-operative factories, and co-operative institutions of all kinds which have been established in our midst, and all the people can partake of the benefits of this system. You can see the effect of co-operation on the people. But this is only a limited system, it does not extend as far as needed, although it required faith to enter into this; yet it will require more to enter upon the other of which I have spoken.

JD 15:335, Orson Pratt, January 26, 1873
The Lord means what he says, He has told us in one of the first revelations published in this book, that though the heavens and the earth should pass away, not one of the prophecies and predictions contained in these revelations should go unfulfilled; therefore if Zion sin, if her people suffer pride to arise in their hearts, and follow after the foolish fashions of the Gentiles who come into their midst, and are lifted up one above another, the rich and wealthy looking down upon the poor with scorn and derision because they cannot clothe themselves in the same costly apparel as the rich, and begin to make distinctions of classes among themselves, behold the Lord will visit Zion according to all her works, and he will purge her and pour forth his judgments upon her, according to that which he has spoken.

I hope that we shall take a course to prevent these things coming upon us. It is better to be chastened and receive judgment in this world, even if it be sword, pestilence, famine and the flame of a devouring fire, if we can be brought to repentance thereby, than to remain unchastised and go down swiftly to the pit. If we, because of our sins, need chastising by the Almighty, let the chastisement come while we are in the flesh, that we may repent; and I would say still further, and pray in the name of the Lord, "Oh Lord, if chastisement must come, may it come from thine hands." When the Lord through the Prophet gave David the choice of one of three terrible judgments – first to fall into the hands of his enemies, and for the people of Israel to be afflicted many years; second, a lengthy famine, and third, three days' pestilence, he chose the three days' pestilence, for he said it was better to fall into the hands of the Lord, who was full of tender mercy, and who might repent and withdraw the chastisement, than to fall into the hands of the wicked who have no mercy. I would say the same so far as my feelings are concerned, and if it be needful let the Lord chasten those who need it, and not suffer us to continue in our sin, and to grow and flourish like the green bay tree, as the wicked do until we are cut off finally from the earth and cast away in the eternal worlds. It is better for us to be saved there if we are punished here.

Here are a few more similar references in the Journal of Discourses:

JD 15:210 1872 GQC --class distinctions;
15:335 OP 1873 --make distinctions of classes among themselves
15:358 OP 1873 --distinctions of classes arise
16:7 OP 1873 --may prove the overthrow of many
16:19-20 1873 BY --distinctions will cease
16:57 OP 1873 --different classes
16:117 GQC 1873 --puffed up in pride
17:31 OP 1874 --classes introduced
21:6-7 JT 1879 --treat all men alike
25:352 JT 1884 --desperate classes
26:186 GQC 1884 --divide humanity into classes

Life spans of speakers:
GQC Lived: Jan 11, 1827 - Apr 12, 1901 (age 74)
OP Lived: September 19, 1811 - October 3, 1881 (aged 70)
BY Lived June 1, 1801 - August 29, 1877 (aged 76)
JT Lived: November 1, 1808 - July 25, 1887 (aged 78)

Abbreviations: GQC George Q. Cannon, OP Orson Pratt, BY Brigham Young, JT John Taylor

Chapter 4

Temples, Altars, and Work for the Dead

Profiting from the dead
This might be a convenient place to point out a common practice of a degenerate church used to extract the largest possible amount of money from its members. From the Pearson book on tithing that appears below in this book:

> If any man claim tithes by my ancestor's gift, may I not ask him, To whom, and for what my ancestors gave them? And it is plain beyond denial, that all those gifts of lands or tithes in England, since Augustin the monk* planted the Roman Catholic faith, and preached up the payment of tithes, were given to priests, for saying prayers for the souls of the givers, and <u>their deceased ancestors</u>, as old consecrations do witness: And therefore in reason, if the consideration and service be ceased, so ought also the wages; for no man in law or equity, ought to claim wages when he will not do the work for which it was given; and seeing those priests and prayers are laid aside, the gift ought to return to the donor, and may not without his consent be perverted to another use. See Page 27 of the Pearson book (emphasis added)
>
> *Presumably Augustine of Canterbury (Not to be confused with Augustine of Hippo.). Augustine of Canterbury (born first third of the 6th century – died probably 26 May 604) was a Benedictine monk who became the first Archbishop of Canterbury in the year 597. He is considered the "Apostle to the English" and a founder of the English Church. https://en.wikipedia.org/wiki/Augustine_of_Canterbury

Here we learn that Augustine initiated in England the practice of paying priests "for saying prayers for the souls of the givers, and their deceased ancestors." Of course, the beginning assumption here is that a professional priesthood has been established, and it has been determined that one of their salaried duties can be praying for the living and the dead (and perhaps providing special facilities for carrying out such prayers). It appears that the LDS church has learned well this administrative lesson from the past, and it seems likely that its largest source of income, and the largest impetus for its members continuing to pay tithing every year, has to do with building extravagant temples and maintaining individual licenses ("recommends") to use those temples to do work for themselves and their dead. We should point out that the early Christians had no need for any kind of temples and therefore no need for any related contributions. The work they did for themselves and for the dead was all completely without charge.

We might notice that many other religions have adopted the same monetizing technique. Buying and burning candles for the dead appears to be a major franchise in the Russian Orthodox Church, for example. At least buying a few candles would certainly be less expensive than paying out a tenth of one's income every year. One of the purposes for the "indulgences" which were a major source of money to the Roman Catholic Church at the time of Martin Luther was supposedly to free souls from purgatory. Never mind that it is unknown just how the Catholic Church signaled the heavens that those individual souls in purgatory should be released. Similarly, it is not perfectly clear that the massive expenditures of time and money on behalf of the dead under LDS administration is effective or even necessary.

We have the case of Alvin Smith who was resurrected and exalted before any temples were built or any regular LDS work for the dead could be initiated. There is also a basic fairness question which is unresolved: does it really make sense for the perhaps 70 billion souls, or more, who have lived on this earth to wait hundreds or thousands of years for the relatively tiny LDS church to finally get around to releasing them from spirit prison by finally doing their temple work? After nearly 200 years of effort we have still not finished the work just for those who have lived in the United States, let alone everyone else who has lived in our big world. If all this work must be done by proxy on earth, which seems questionable, then perhaps it can only be done on an industrial scale during the millennium when all these people can come to the earth themselves to do their own work, if that is necessary. I would argue that we ought to do all that we can to move towards a millennial condition where all of these things could be taken care of quickly and properly rather than continuing to move at an extremely expensive and slow snail's pace under current conditions.

Temples and altars

There is a related issue concerning the need for temples. The LDS Bible dictionary presents an entry which perfectly fits the current church's definitions, doctrines, and practices:

> **Temple**
>
> A temple is literally a house of the Lord, a holy sanctuary in which sacred ceremonies and ordinances of the gospel are performed by and for the living and also in behalf of the dead. A place where the Lord may come, it is the most holy of any place of worship on the earth. Only the home can compare with the temple in sacredness.
>
> Whenever the Lord has had a people on the earth who will obey His word, they have been commanded to build temples in which the ordinances of the gospel and other spiritual manifestations that pertain to exaltation and eternal life may be administered. In cases of extreme poverty or emergency, these ordinances may sometimes be done on a mountaintop (see D&C 124:37–55).

> This may be the case with Mount Sinai and the Mount of Transfiguration. The tabernacle erected by Moses was a type of portable temple, since the Israelites were traveling in the wilderness.
>
> From Adam to the time of Jesus, ordinances were performed in temples for the living only. After Jesus opened the way for the gospel to be preached in the world of spirits, ceremonial work for the dead, as well as for the living, has been done in temples on the earth by faithful members of the Church. Building and properly using a temple is one of the marks of the true Church in any dispensation, and is especially so in the present day.
>
> The best known temple mentioned in the Bible is that which was built in Jerusalem in the days of Solomon. This was destroyed in 587 B.C. and rebuilt by Zerubbabel about 70 years later. The restored structure was partially burned in 37 B.C. and was partially rebuilt by Herod the Great, although the rebuilding continued until A.D. 64. It was destroyed by the Romans in A.D. 70. See also Tabernacle.
> https://www.churchofjesuschrist.org/study/scriptures/bd/temple?lang=eng

The basic problem here, as in so many other places, is that the current church indiscriminately mixes Old Testament Law of Moses principles and practices with New Testament Christian principles and practices, as though they were all the same and had the same authority and application today. The critical statement "Whenever the Lord has had a people on the earth who will obey his word, they have been commanded to build temples…" is demonstrably untrue. It would be correct to say that Adam and Noah and Abraham built altars to the Lord, but those altars were just a pile of rocks put together perhaps with a few hours work, hardly something which could be called a temple on the scale of the Temple in Jerusalem or one of the modern day temples. These rocks were required to be whole and untouched by iron and could not be piled high enough to require climbing any steps. (See Topical Guide entry for "altar.")

> Exodus 20:25 And if thou wilt make me an altar of stone, thou shalt not build it of hewn stone: for if thou lift up thy tool upon it, thou hast polluted it.
> 26 Neither shalt thou go up by steps unto mine altar, that thy nakedness be not discovered [revealed -- in footnote] thereon.
>
> Deut. 27:5 And there shalt thou build an altar unto the Lord thy God, an altar of stones: thou shalt not lift up any iron tool upon them.
> 6 Thou shalt build the altar of the Lord thy God of whole stones: and thou shalt offer burnt offerings thereon unto the Lord thy God:

These alters were much less permanent and stationary than the portable tabernacle constructed under the law of Moses. In fact, those early Christians from Adam to Abraham were forbidden to use any modern construction techniques which might result in a permanent temple, and yet they had access to all the higher ordinances they had need of for themselves. After the life of Christ (if not before his death), the church members were able to do work for the dead on a regular basis, again without the need for any special structures.

Although we are told that **Adam** built at least one of these unhewn rock altars, apparently it does not explicitly affirm that in the Scriptures. Things are a little bit more specific in the case of Noah.

> Gen 8:20 And Noah builded an altar unto the Lord; and took of every clean beast, and of every clean fowl, and offered burnt offerings on the altar.

One bit of church history humor, which may or not may not be true, is that many people that go to Adam-ondi-Ahman in Missouri take away a rock, hoping it was one of the rocks that made up the altar of Adam, so that the church has to keep bringing in trucks full of rocks to replace those carried off by visitors.

More thoughts on the history of temples

If large, permanent, ornate temples were always really so important, surely we would have heard of the great and wondrous Temple of Adam, the Temple of Enoch, the Temple of Noah, the Temple of Abraham, the Temple of Melchizedek, etc. Unless we want to describe the giant ark built by Noah as a "temple," there seems to be no scriptural evidence of any kind of large permanent temple before the children of Israel left Egypt. In fact, one might argue that having a large, permanent, ornate temple is direct evidence of general religious degeneration. The example of the Tower of Babel comes to mind, where the intent was to defy God.

King David gathered the materials for the Jerusalem Temple but was not allowed to construct it. King Solomon, his son, oversaw the building of that Temple, but I don't think that anyone would say that Solomon represented the peak of righteousness. Having that Temple to the one true God was better than having a Temple to some pagan idol, but not by much.

It is the pagans who build the large, permanent, ornate temples and groves at which they worship idols. The pretentious temples of the Israelites are too much like those of the pagans. For example, the Roman government built numerous temples to various gods and for their cult of the Emperor. Building ostentatious public buildings signaled the merger of the corrupted Christian church with the pagan Emperor Constantine and the beginning of the collection of tithes to support such construction.

Apparently, avoiding building temples is one way to avoid idolatry. It is actually a little bit difficult to differentiate the law of Moses temple in Jerusalem, and all its sacrificial rules and activities, from the pagan practices of the Romans around them. We might notice that the New Testament has many warnings about the new Christians getting caught up in the old practices of the Roman pagan temples, including food offerings. That seems to indicate that the law of Moses and the pagan practices were really not all that different. Perhaps the only real difference was the specific named god they were supposedly worshiping. This brings to mind Paul's reference to the "unknown god" worshiped by the Greeks, where the religious practices were not all that different, but getting the name right was the important thing. Acts 17:23.

> Acts 17:22 Then Paul stood in the midst of Mars' hill, and said, Ye men of
> Athens, I perceive that in all things ye are too superstitious.
> 23 For as I passed by, and beheld your devotions, I found an altar with this
> inscription, TO THE UNKNOWN GOD. Whom therefore ye ignorantly worship,
> him declare I unto you.
> 24 God that made the world and all things therein, seeing that he is Lord of
> heaven and earth, <u>dwelleth not in temples made with hands;</u>
> 25 Neither is worshipped with men's hands, as though he needed any thing,
> seeing he giveth to all life, and breath, and all things;
> 26 And hath made of one blood all nations of men for to dwell on all the face of
> the earth, and hath determined the times before appointed, and the bounds of
> their habitation;
> 27 That they should seek the Lord, if haply they might feel after him, and find
> him, though he be not far from every one of us:
> 28 For in him we alive, and move, and have our being; as certain also of your
> own poets have said, For we are also his offspring.
> 29 Forasmuch then as we are the offspring of God, we ought not to think that the
> Godhead is like unto gold, or silver, or stone, graven by art and man's device.
> 30 And the times of this ignorance God winked at; but now commandeth all men
> every where to repent:
> 31 Because he hath appointed a day, in the which he will judge the world in
> righteousness by that man whom he hath ordained; whereof he hath given
> assurance unto all men, in that he hath raised him from the dead.

I think it is significant that the early Saints had just broken off all connections with the temple in Jerusalem, having no need for any temples of stone, and that complete disconnect from any physical temple remained in effect for at least 300 years. That should tell us that a physical temple is simply not part of the New Testament gospel, and all saving ordinances can be conducted in other places, and apparently were so conducted after the life of Christ. This does leave us a small bit of ambiguity to resolve sometime. The Kirtland Temple, Nauvoo Temple, Salt Lake Temple, St. George Temple, etc., seem to be unexplained exceptions to this general rule. The approximately 200 extravagant temples, which have been either built or are planned in our own time, raise a number of questions.

There are even serious questions about the need for ANY work for the dead except perhaps to help the living better understand the plan of salvation. We have the interesting case of Alvin Smith who apparently died, was resurrected, and exalted, before any priesthood was on the Earth to conduct any ordinance work for either the living or the dead.

> Section 137
> *A vision given to Joseph Smith the Prophet, in the temple at Kirtland, Ohio, January 21, 1836. The occasion was the administration of ordinances in preparation for the dedication of the temple.*
> *1–6, The Prophet sees his brother Alvin in the celestial kingdom; 7–9, The doctrine of salvation for the dead is revealed; 10, All children are saved in the celestial kingdom.*
> 1 The heavens were opened upon us, and I beheld the celestial kingdom of God, and the glory thereof, whether in the body or out I cannot tell.
> 2 I saw the transcendent beauty of the gate through which the heirs of that kingdom will enter, which was like unto circling flames of fire;
> 3 Also the blazing throne of God, whereon was seated the Father and the Son.
> 4 I saw the beautiful streets of that kingdom, which had the appearance of being paved with gold.
> 5 I saw Father Adam and Abraham; and my father and my mother; my brother Alvin, that has long since slept;
> 6 And marveled how it was that he had obtained an inheritance in that kingdom, seeing that he had departed this life before the Lord had set his hand to gather Israel the second time, and had not been baptized for the remission of sins.
> 7 Thus came the voice of the Lord unto me, saying: All who have died without a knowledge of this gospel, who would have received it if they had been permitted to tarry, shall be heirs of the celestial kingdom of God;
> 8 Also all that shall die henceforth without a knowledge of it, who would have received it with all their hearts, shall be heirs of that kingdom;
> 9 For I, the Lord, will judge all men according to their works, according to the desire of their hearts.
> 10 And I also beheld that all children who die before they arrive at the years of accountability are saved in the celestial kingdom of heaven.

Since it is obviously impossible to do all the Temple work on earth for the more than 70 billion people who have lived on the Earth, especially since we have individual records for only a tiny fraction of those people, perhaps no more than 5%, with perhaps no more than 0.5% completed so far after 200 years of effort, one might expect that heaven has a far more efficient plan for taking care of these matters. I would argue that our first duty should be to the living, and we should devote only a small part of our effort to work for the dead. We can see exactly what is happening in our help of living people, and all we really have is speculation about whatever help we might be offering those who are dead.

All the marvelous New Testament manifestations of the day of Pentecost occurred without any special buildings being available as a prerequisite. One might wonder why the Kirtland Temple was required for similar manifestations. The Salt Lake City saints functioned without a completed temple for 40 years and seemed to do well enough using the Endowment House for that time period, making the need for a magnificent temple a bit questionable. Perhaps an actual structure is a partial throwback to a law of Moses "schoolmaster" time, hopefully not a permanent need.

As another consideration, building and maintaining a highly visible temple will always require some compromise with the local governments controlling that land, and any such compromise could damage the religious, political, and economic freedom of the Saints who live there, unless the Saints actually control the political government.

TEMPORARY TEMPLES

Historically, the Lord has asked relatively little of His followers as far as the need for building large expensive fixed structures for religious purposes. In fact, the existence of a large expensive temple as a center of worship is normally a sign of corruption. Below is displayed some past and possible future history on this point.

Some Temporary Temple Images

Top – Two Old Testament-style alters of uncut stone.

Center – The Endowment House, used for about 40 years until the Salt Lake City Temple was completed.

Bottom – Some possible local architectural themes that might conceivably be found in the Shanghai Temple announced in April 2020. The assumption here is that the building, if ever built, will alternate between temple status and chapel status.

(If the images of temporary temples shown here are not in color in this edition of the book, then you can go to one of the following web locations to see them in full color. You miss the sense of extravagance without the color: IsTheChurchAsTrueAsTheGospel.blogspot.com, https://tinyurl.com/y75mefej, https://tinyurl.com/ybyhvuoe, http://kenthuff.com/ All locations may not be set up at publication time. Third URL is to Dropbox,)

Chapter 5

A Brief History of Tithing After Christ's Crucifixion

The most basic church history
Everyone in our nation, and certainly in our church, should know a few simple, well-documented facts about the history of the early Christian church, especially on the topic of tithing, but for some reason these very basic elements of information have been forgotten and blotted out, presumably for the sake of widespread church administrative self-interest.

The short article quoted below, apparently published in 2005, gives us the essence of what we need to know. As the article points out, for at least 300 years after Christ, there was no such thing as doctrinally-required payment of tithing to any church organization or leaders. The people voluntarily took care of each other and contributed to other church needs that arose. There were no chapels or temples built during that 300 years, leaving all of those material resources available to aid the poor. That is the simple essence of the gospel, but enormous amounts of thought and effort seem to always be going into trying to confuse that simple essence, for the purpose of self-aggrandizement, profit-taking, and creating a class structure. This is the "mystery of iniquity" we will read more about later from the Quaker pamphlet.

Since I assume there are many people who will be very surprised to hear this ancient but previously well-known news about the history of tithing, and will therefore be very skeptical, I am also supplying excerpts from and links to other materials in the following chapters to flesh out that basic concept for many hundreds of pages, certainly to the extent any reasonable person might want to read more about it.

A BRIEF HISTORY OF TITHING AFTER CHRIST'S CRUCIFIXION

by Dr. Fillmer Hevener

Most Christians understand that with the death of Christ on the cross, the Ceremonial Laws, requiring such practices as the sacrificing of animals, circumcision, and tithing, were abrogated. The animal sacrifices pointed to the coming Messiah, whose spilling of His blood, would annul the sacrificing of animals and all other requirements associated with the Ceremonial laws.

After the crucifixion of our Savior, therefore, the New Testament Church was supported by free-will gifts. Since there was no longer tithing, how did the Church survive financially?

For several hundred years after Christ's death, churches were not institutions with large buildings or paid leaders supported by the members. Instead, the churches were similar to modern-day home groups. They met in homes with leaders who supported themselves through such labor as carpentry, fishing, farming, etc. Therefore, the early church groups had few expenses. The vast majority of the funds given could be used for missionary purposes, for spreading the gospel at home and in distant places.

The Apostle Paul, a tentmaker, notes that although he had the right to receive support from the congregation, he refused to accept this support. Why, because he did not want to take money from mission needs and because he did not want anyone suspecting that he was preaching the gospel out of a desire for money. (1 Cor. 9.) He did not wish to hinder the spreading of the gospel of salvation through Christ. The churches did frequently support widows, the poor, and orphans. (1 Tim. 5.) Paul did at times accept gratuities from friends (food, shelter, and friendship). Paul, being of the tribe of Benjamin, could not have legally accepted tithe; only the Levites could have done this.

THE CHURCH CONTINUED WITH THIS VOLUNTARY APPROACH TO GIVING AND TO THE SUPPORT OF THE CHURCH FOR OVER 300 YEARS.

In the fourth century, the Roman Emperor, Constantine, converted to Christianity. He is credited with bringing status to Christianity and with starting the first large church building program. (Note: he is also credited with instituting the first Sunday law in 321; his edict required the people to rest on the "venerable day of the sun.") Constantine wanted the church to have impressive buildings that would honor his name and his contributions to the church. Consequently, the church groups moved out of homes and into finer buildings and began employing full-time ministers. Therefore, there was a need to support these buildings and these salaried bishops. The New Catholic Encyclopedia summarizes the situation:

"The early Christian church had no tithing system. The tithes of the Old Testament were regarded as abrogated" by Christ's death. However, as the church's material needs grew because of its vast building program and paying of bishops, it adopted the pre-cross, Ceremonial Law-method of support, tithing. Therefore, "the Council of Macon in 585, ordered the payment of tithes and threatened excommunication to those who refused to comply."

From the sixth century forward, tithing was adopted by the Catholic Church and later accepted into many protestant churches from the 1500's onward.

The Encyclopedia Britannica notes: "Despite serious resistance, tithing became obligatory as Christianity spread across Europe. It was enjoined by ecclesiastical law from the sixth century...." In the 14th century, Pope Gregory VII, outlawed ...lay ownership of tithes." In other words, Pope Gregory VII, concluded that only paid clergy could receive and direct the use of tithe, not lay, unpaid, Christians. (Note: A similar position is taken by E. G. White when she states that the tithe is to be used for ministers, only. Testimonies, Vol. 9, 248-249. This position is contrary to Deut. 14, which teaches that tithe was, among other things, to be used for strangers (refugees), orphans, and widows.) The following statement is made by the Archdiocese of St. Louis: "TITHING IS ABSOLUTELY STILL NECESSARY IN THE CATHOLIC CHURCH TODAY. (See their: Office of Stewardship and Development statement on the www.)

In 765, the Carolingian King Pepin III (the Short) sent a letter to all bishops making the payment of tithe by each individual to his parish church a legal obligation. Also, everyone was forced to tithe 800 years after Christ when Charlemagne founded the Holy Roman Empire, blending church and state and making tithing a state law.

Unfortunately, when the Protestant reformers of the 1500's broke with the Catholic Church over such issues as "salvation by grace, rather than by works," they did not reject the spurious Sabbath, Sunday, nor the Ceremonial Law's practice of tithing. These reformers could have had much greater credibility if they had adopted the post-cross method of support of the church through free-will giving. See: Matthew 10:8; Luke 6:38; Acts 20:35; II Cor. 9: 6-7; I Tim. 5:8.

In summary, this is what we know:

1. Tithing was a part of the Ceremonial Law, which was abrogated by Christ's death.

2. The early Christian church was supported by free-will giving for at least 300 years.

3. Tithing first came into the Christian church when Constantine was converted; he needed money for fine buildings and for bishops' salaries.

4. The Catholic Church made tithing a law nearly six centuries after Christ's crucifixion.

5. Some 800 years after Christ, Charlemagne required the paying of tithe under the penalty of imprisonment.

6. Priests cursed for their tithe, telling those who didn't tithe that they would lose their salvation and go to hell.

7. In the 1500's, Protestant churches preached "salvation by grace," but they continued to preach and practice tithing and the false Sabbath, Sunday.

Friend, reject erroneous traditions! Prepare for eternity by accepting Christ as your Savior and by following His teachings in Holy Scripture, the Bible.

May our Lord bless and keep each of you!

Pastor Fillmer Hevener, Ed. D.

http://www.guthriememorial.org/articles/brief_history_of_tithing.htm

Other sources

In the next few chapters, I will present excerpts from and links to other longer historical works on the general subject of tithing.

Chapter 6

The 1657 Quaker position on the evils of forced tithing – partly based on the earlier work of John Selden.

Having presented a very short history of tithing in the prior chapter, as a brief introduction to this whole important topic, I now want to present in its entirety a pamphlet on the topic of tithing written by a Quaker in 1657. It was 36 pages in the original, which makes for a rather lengthy quote, but the material he covers seems very important to show how corrupted the history and doctrine of tithing had become by 1657 and how corrupt the actual handling of tithing had become at his time, including jailing people indefinitely for not paying up to three times what was imagined to be their "tithing." As a justice of the peace himself, he would be only too aware of the misbehavior of other courts. Some of his descriptions may be meaningless to people who have lived exclusively in cities, but those who own and work the land, as farmers or ranchers, might find some of his detailed treatment of land uses quite interesting. Part of his pamphlet is based on the earlier work of John Selden, who will be discussed below. This pamphlet has been republished many times over the years, in 1850 in this case, which has allowed the language to be updated to be something closer to what we can easily understand today.

I view this Quaker pamphlet partly as a cautionary tale to indicate how deviant and corrupt church and government organizations can become on religious topics. The LDS church today has not yet resorted to confiscating property and jailing people to collect a full tithing, but the pressures to do these kinds of extraordinary things are present at all times once the church has started down the path of doctrinally making tithing paid to a central organization mandatory to gaining salvation. Every time I hear someone repeat the phrase "Will a man rob God?" I wince. Remember that that quote comes from Malachi 3:8 in the Old Testament. That kind of thinking, where non-payment of tithing is made a crime, is the path to the kind of trouble discussed in the Quaker pamphlet. Today we ought to have nothing to do with the old law of Moses or any of the pronouncements that come from that time, as in the Book of Malachi. So, when someone starts quoting the law of Moses and thus perhaps inadvertently trying to reinstitute the law of Moses, my alarm bells go off.

There are many interesting points made in this pamphlet, but one small segment struck me as especially interesting, almost poetic.

> 5th, That as the mystery of iniquity began to work, and men's imaginations were taught, instead of the doctrine of Christ, divers men, taking their ground from Moses, began to preach that tithes again ought to be paid. [emphasis added.]

This is the gospel-killing process that has happened over and over throughout the history of the earth. The "mystery of iniquity" phrase is used by Paul in 2 Thess. 2:7.

The last statement from this pamphlet is so profound that it deserves to be read first. After the many explanations of the pamphlet,

> And let no man henceforth think it strange, that any should refuse to pay tithes; but rather wonder, that any will pay them.

THE
GREAT CASE OF TITHES
TRULY STATED, CLEARLY OPENED,
AND FULLY RESOLVED.

BY ANTHONY PEARSON,

A JUSTICE OF PEACE IN WESTMORELAND IN THE TIME OF THE COMMONWEALTH.

LONDON:
Printed for the TRACT ASSOCIATION of the SOCIETY of FRIENDS.
Sold at the DEPOSITORY, 84, Houndsditch.
-
1850.

No. 63. [Price 1s. 6d. per dozen.]

ADVERTISEMENT.

The ensuing treatise was first published in the year 1657, and was so well received, that a subsequent Editor says, it passed through three editions in about two years; the present is a reprint of the former editions, with the exception of most of the Latin notes and phrases, and a few omissions and corrections, which are not intended to alter the sense. The Author was a zealous advocate for liberty of conscience in those days, and it appears he was induced to write on this subject, by the many complaints of the people, then labouring under severe prosecutions for tithes. By way of preface, he introduces his work with the following short address.

To the Countrymen, Farmers, and Husbandmen of England.

It is for your sakes that this small treatise is sent abroad, that in a matter wherein you are so much concerned, you might be truly informed: and because there are many differing opinions, and of late years have been great disputes, concerning *the right of Tithes*, which makes the case seem difficult to be resolved, I have given you the substance of all that ever I could find written, or hear discoursed, touching that point; and for more than two years last past, I have made much enquiry into it.

First, *I have begun with tithing among the Jews, which, either in precept or example, is the foundation of all others.*

Secondly, *I have given you a short view of the opinions and practices of the primitive church concerning them, and from thence downward until this day.*

After which, having made some short observations, I state the case as it concerns us in England. And then hearing what every one hath to say for them, I proceed to satisfy some great objections, and so conclude the whole, in as much brevity as the variety of the subject would permit.

A. PEARSON.

THE GREAT CASE OF TITHES.

OF TITHING AMONGST THE JEWS.

God having chosen Aaron and his sons for the office of the Priesthood, and the rest of the tribe of Levi for the service of the Tabernacle, he gave unto the Levites all the tenth in Israel for an inheritance for their service, and they were to have no inheritance among the children of Israel.

And the Levites out of their tithe, were to offer up a tenth part unto the Lord and give it unto Aaron the priest for him self and his sons; and no other portion had the priests out of the tithes, but they were for the Levites that did the common services of the tabernacle, for the strangers, for the fatherless, and the widows.

Besides the tenth of the tithe, (Deut. xviii. 4) the priests had the first ripe fruits of the ground, of wheat, of barley, of figs, of grapes, of olives, of pomegranates and dates, at what quantity the owner pleased; an offering also of corn, wine, oil, fleece, and the like, was given to the priests at the sixtieth part, sometimes at the fiftieth or more, at the devotion of the owner. Ezek. xlv. 13.

Of cattle also the first-born were the Lord's, paid to the priests, of clean beasts in kind, of unclean in money, with a fifth part added: also divers parts of the sacrifices were appointed for the priests. Exod. xiii. 2.

But no tithes did the priests receive of the people: for those belonged to the Levites that were appointed over the tabernacle, and the instruments thereof, to bear it, to take it down, and set it up, to serve Aaron and his sons, and to do the services of the tabernacle, and keep the instruments thereof; and their service chiefly was upon removing of the host; for better ordering whereof, and every one's service, they were divided into three parts, the Koathites, the Gershonites, and the Merarites, and these received tithes of the people, and out of them, a tenth part they delivered to the priests.

Afterwards, when Solomon built the temple, and placed the ark therein, other offices were appointed for the Levites; (1 Chron. xxvi., xxx., and xxxii.) one part of them were to be singers; another to be porters, and take the charge of the gates of the temple; another to be keepers of the treasury; others of them also were placed abroad in the country, on the west side of Jordon one thousand seven hundred, and on the east side two thousand seven hundred.

By this time also, the posterity of Aaron being much increased, the priests were divided into twenty-four ranks or courses, according to the names of their families, and every one's attendance [page 4] was required by turns; and hereupon Zacharias is said to be of the course of Abia, and to execute the priest's office, and burn incense as his turn came, (Luke i.) and the first of the first rank had the pre-eminence, and was the High Priest, and so every one according to their precedency.

The Levites that were singers were divided, as the priests, into twenty-four ranks or courses; the porters into five parts, one part to every of the four gates of the temple, and the fifth to Asuppim, i.e., the Council-house.

The treasury was generally committed to one, as the chief, but under him to two sorts of other officers; one to keep the treasures of the house of the Lord, and those things that were offered to the Lord; and the other to keep the dedicate things. In these treasuries were put the second tithes, the offerings of all sorts of people, which were for the uses and services of the temple, for the fatherless, the stranger, and the widow.

After the captivity, and new dedication of the temple, it appears that, in many particulars, their laws, ordinances, and customs were much changed, especially in this of tithing: but not being pertinent to this discourse, I shall pass them over; only let the reader understand, that though the priests and Levites were both of the tribe of Levi, yet was the priesthood settled in the sons of Aaron, and the offices of the priests were quite different from the Levites, and so was their maintenance distinct.

These priests and Levites being separated for the work of the Lord in the tabernacle and in the temple, they ministered according to the ordinances of the first covenant which were figures for the time then present, and shadows of good things to come.

A VIEW OF THE DOCTRINES, DECREES, AND PRACTICES OF TITHING, FROM THE INFANCY OF THE CHRISTIAN CHURCH UNTIL THIS DAY.

But in the fulness of time, God raised up another priest, CHRIST JESUS, who was not of the tribe of Levi, nor consecrated after the order of Aaron: for he pertained to another tribe, of which no man gave attendance at the altar, who, (having obtained a more excellent ministry, of a greater and more perfect tabernacle, not of the former building, being the sum and substance of all the patterns of things under the first covenant) put an end to the first priesthood, with all its shadows, figures, and carnal ordinances, and changing the priesthood, which had a command to take tithes of their brethren, there was made of necessity also a change of the law, and a disannulling of the commandment going before, which was but imposed until the time of reformation.

And the apostles and ministers of Christ Jesus, when he had [page 5] finished his office upon earth, by offering up himself through the eternal Spirit, a sacrifice without spot unto God, did not look back to the ordinances of the former priesthood, but testified that *an end was put unto them;* and witnessed against the temple, wherein the priests ministered, for which Stephen was stoned to death: against circumcision, saying, *it was not that of the flesh;* against the Passover, priests, &c.; and preached up Christ Jesus and his doctrine, the new and living way, which was not made manifest while as the first tabernacle was standing. Nor did they go about to establish the law by which tithes were given in the former priesthood, but freely they preached the Gospel which they had received, and did not require any settled maintenance, but lived of the free offerings and contributions of the saints, who by their ministry were turned to Christ Jesus.

At Jerusalem, and thereabouts, such was the unity of heart among the saints in the apostles' time, that all things were in common, and none wanted (Acts iv. 34); and as many as were possessors of lands or houses, sold them, and brought the price, and laid it down at the apostles' feet, and it was distributed unto every man according as he had need.

So the church gathered by Mark at Alexandria in Egypt, followed the same rule as the Saints did at Jerusalem, having all things in common. And Philo Judaeus, a famous author of that time, reporteth, that not only there, but in many other provinces, the Christians lived together in societies.

In the churches at Antioch, the saints possessed every man his own estate (Acts xi. 29); so likewise in Galatia and Corinth, where the apostle ordained, that weekly offerings for the saints should be made by every one as God had blessed him (1 Cor. xvi. 2); and by these offerings (which were put into the hands of the deacons of the churches) were all the services and need of the church supplied.

By example of these, the course of monthly-offerings succeeded in the next ages, not exacted, but freely given at the bounty of every man, as appears plainly by Turtullian in Apolog. cap. 39, where, upbraiding the Gentiles with the piety and devotion of Christians, he saith "Whatsoever we have in the treasury of our churches, is not raised by taxation, as though we put men to ransom their religion; but every man once a month, or when it pleaseth himself, bestoweth what he thinks good, and not without he listeth; for no man is compelled, but left free to his own discretion: and that which is given, is not bestowed in vanity, but in relieving the poor, and upon children destitute of parents, and maintenance of aged and feeble persons, men wrecked by sea, and such as are condemned to the metal mines, banished into islands, or cast into prison, professing the true God, and the Christian faith." [page 6]

And this way of contribution continued in the church till the great persecution under Maximinian and Dioclesian, about the year 304, as

Eusebius testifieth, which also appears by the writings of Turtullian, Origen, Cyprian, and others.

About this time also, some lands began to be given to the church, and the revenue of them was brought into its treasury; belonged to the church in common, and was distributed, as other offerings, by the deacons, and elders; but the bishops or ministers meddled not therewith: for Origen saith, "It is not lawful for any minister of the church to possess lands (given to the church) to his own use." And called to the ministers, "Let us depart from the priests of Pharoah, who enjoy earthly possessions, to the priests of the Lord, who have no portion in the earth." And in another place he saith, "It behoveth us to be faithful in disposing the rents of the church, that we ourselves devour not those things which belong to the widows and the poor; and let us be content with simple diet and necessary apparel." And Urban, bishop of Rome, anno 227, did declare, "That the church might receive lands and possessions offered by the faithful, but not to any particular man's benefit, but that the revenues thereof should be distributed as other offerings, as need required."

Cyprian, bishop of Carthage, about the year 250, also testifieth the same, and sheweth, that "the church maintained many poor," and that "her own diet was sparing and plain, and all her expenses full of frugality."

Prosper also saith that, "a minister able to live of himself, ought not to participate of the goods of the church; for," saith he, "they that have of their own, and yet desire to have somewhat given them, do not receive it without great sin."

The council at Antioch, in the year 340, (finding that much fault had been among the deacons, to whom it properly belonged,) ordained that "the bishops might distribute the goods of the church," but required, "that they took not any part to themselves," or "to the use of the priests and brethren that lived with them, unless necessity did justly require it," using the words of the apostle, "having food and raiment be therewith content."

In these times, in many places, the Christian converts joined themselves in societies, and chose a separate life, selling what they had, and living together in common, after the example of the former saints about Jerusalem, as Chrysostom notes, who lived about the year 400, by whose writings it also appears that there was not the least practice of the payment of tithes in those ages.

The church now living altogether by free offerings of lands, money, and goods, the people were much pressed to bountiful contributions for holy uses, as may be seen by the writings of [page 7] Hierom and Chrysostom, who brought the Jewish liberality in their payments of tenths for an example, beneath which they would not have Christians determine their charity; where Chrysostom says, "he speaks these things not as commanding or forbidding, that they should give more, yet as thinking it fit, that they should not give less than the tenth part." Hierom also doth earnestly admonish them "to give bountifully to the poor, and double honour to him that labours in the Lord's work;" not binding at all to offer this or that part, leaving them to their own liberty, but pressing "they might not do less than the Jews did."

Ambrose, who was bishop of Milan, about the year 400, preached up tenths to be offered up for holy uses, as may be seen in his Sermon on Repentance; but his authority he produceth wholly from Moses, and quotes divers sentences, and threatens the people, that "if they would not pay their tenths, God would reduce them to a tenth."

In like manner Augustin, Bishop of Hippo, hath a whole homily for the right of tithes, and calls upon those that have no fruits of the earth to pay the tenth of whatsoever they live by; and saith, "the neglect of payment of tithes is the cause of sterility and blasting;" and agrees with Ambrose in his threats, that, "God would reduce them to a tenth;" and tells them, "that not paying their tithes they shall be found guilty, at God's tribunal, of the death of all the poor that perish through want, in the places where they dwell;" and bids them "that would either get reward, or desire the pardon of their sins, to pay their tithes." These two great bishops agree, and from the law given to the Israelites, take their whole doctrine, and impose their own opinion with heavy penalties. But take notice to what end they require them, that the poor might not want, saying that God had reserved them for their use.

Leo, who was pope from 440 to 460, was likewise very earnest in stirring up every man's devotion to offer to the church part of his received fruits, but speaks not a word of any certain quantity, as may appear by his sermons.

Severin also, about the year 470, stirred up the Christians in Panonia, who in example of his bounty, gave the tenth of their fruits to the poor.

Gregory not only admonisheth the payment of tithes from Moses's law, but also the observing the time of lent, consisting of six weeks, out of which take the Sundays, and there remain thirty-six days, the tenth part of the year, fractions of days omitted; this tenth of time he would have given to God, saying, "we are commanded in the law to give the tenth of all things unto God."

And from the opinions of these and other ancient fathers, who [page 8] took their ground from the law, tithes, Easter, Pentecost, and other things, came to be introduced into the church.

But notwithstanding the doctrine and hard threats of some of the great bishops of that time, it was not a generally received opinion, [as is testified by Agobard, bishop of Lyons,] that *tithes ought to be paid;* nor till about the year 800 was anything by the then church determined, touching the quantity that should be given; though, no doubt, in many places, amongst the offerings of the devouter sort, tenths, or greater parts of their annual increase were given according to the doctrine of Ambrose and others.

The offerings of the people in those ages were received and disposed of in maintenance of the priests, and relief of those that were distressed; neither had the priests such a particular interest in the profits received, as of late time they have usurped; all that was received, wheresoever in the bishoprick, was a common treasury, and was dispensed, one fourth part to the priests, out of which every one had his portion; another fourth part to the relief of the poor, sick, and strangers; a third to the building and repairing of churches; and the fourth to the bishop. And generally then, the bishop lived in some monastery, and his clergy with him, from whence he sent them out to preach within the counties in his diocese, and there they received such offerings as were made, and brought them to the treasury.

And though divers of the fathers, popes, and bishops, did declare *that tithes were due,* and *ought to be paid,* none of the first eight general councils of the church did ever so much as mention the name of tithes, or declare them a duty. The ninth, held at Lateran, under Pope Calixtus II., about the year 1119, mentions tithes, but speaks only of those which had been given to the church by special consecration; so doth also the council held under Pope Alexander III., anno 1180, but that only prohibits appropriations to religious houses without assent of a bishop; for, at that time, people being led to believe that their tithes ought to be given for the use of the poor, did chiefly dispose of them to the governors of religious houses, who kept open hospitality for the poor, and entertainment of strangers, and were esteemed holy, as good treasurers for the needy, who took care of the distribution of them, as is testified by Cassian the hermit. But that council seeing much given to the poor, little to the priests, made that decree to restrain the people's freedom; and indeed, by this time much wickedness had crept into these houses, as histories relate.

Nor was any law, canon, or constitution of any general council as yet found, that purposely commanded the payment of tithes, nor any that expressly supposed them a duty of common right, before the council of Lateran, held in the year 1215, [page 9] under Pope Innocent III.; about which time the pope's authority was grown powerful, and the canons more received into practice, that before were little, especially herein, obeyed.

About the years 800, 900, 1000, and after, tithes were called the *Lord's goods, the patrimony of the poor, &c.* Whence also the council at Nants declared, the "clergy were not to use them as their own, but as commended to their trust;" and they were not then given for the clergy, but to be disposed of for the uses of the poor.

And at this time no regard was had to the nature of the increase; but whatsoever did arise in profit, whether by trade, merchandize, or husbandry, the tenth was required to be paid for tithes.

But still the people had more mind to give them for the poor than the priests, as may be understood by the complaint of Pope Innocent III., who preaching on Zaccheus's charity, cried out against those that gave their tithes and first-fruits to the poor, and not to the priests, as heinous offenders.

Also, in a general council held at Lyons, under Pope Gregory X., in the year 1274, it was constituted, "That it should not thenceforth be lawful for men to give their tithes of their own pleasure, where they would, as it had been before, but pay all their tithes to the mother church." By these it may be seen that though the people, who then generally were Papists, did believe they ought to pay them, yet were they free to dispose them where they pleased, till these councils restrained their liberty.

But the great decree which speaks most plain, and till which nothing was given forth which did directly constitute them, but rather still supposed them as due by some former right, was made at the council of Trent, under Pope Pius IV., about the year 1560. And yet that great council followed the doctrine of their father, and said, they *were due to God*, and had no new authority for their great decree, which they command to be obeyed under the penalty of excommunication.

Having thus briefly run over the ecclesiastical state abroad, from the infant purity of the church to the height of the papal dominion, and taken a glance through every age to the point in hand, I shall now return to what may concern this nation.

I shall not trouble the reader with a relation of Joseph of Arimathea, and his eleven disciples coming into Britain, sent by Philip the apostle, in the reign of Arviragus, as histories report nor of the conversion of King Lucius afterwards, who is said to have given great endowments to the church; nor of the British Christians. Nothing at all appearing of the payment of tithes in their days. But passing by them, and those many years wherein the Saxons overran this nation, exercising most cruel [page 10] persecutions, till the very name of Christian was blotted out, and those heathens seated in the quiet possession of a sevenfold kingdom in this land.

About the year 600, Gregory I., then Pope of Rome, sent over Augustin the monk into England, by whom Ethelbert, king of Kent, was converted; and by him and his followers, in process of time, other parts of the nation, and others of the kings were also brought to their faith. This Augustin was a canon regular, and both he and his clergy, for a long time after, followed the example of former ages, living in common upon the offerings of their converts; and those that received them were joined in societies, in imitation of the primitive practice, having such direction sent him by Pope Gregory, that in the tenderness of the Saxon church, he and his clergy should still imitate the community of all things used in the primitive times under the apostles, that they might not make their religion burthensome.

But afterwards, having brought a great part of the nation to their faith, they began to preach up the old Roman doctrine, that *tithes ought to be paid;* and having taught the people that the pardon of sin might be merited by good works, and the torments of hell be avoided by their charitable deeds, it was no hard matter, when that was believed, to persuade them not only to give their tithes, but also their lands, as the riches of those called religious houses may testify: for in this nation, they and the clergy had almost gotten the third part of the whole land; and so besotted were the poor ignorant people, that, had not a law against Mortmain prevented it, a far greater part of the nation had been in their hands.

As concerning laws and canons for tithes among the Saxons, it is reported that, in the year 786, two legates were sent from Pope Hadrian I. to

Offa, King of Mercland, and AElfwolfe, king of Northumberland, who made a decree, "That the people of those two kingdoms should pay tithes."

Also that Ætheluph, king of the West Saxons, in the year 855, made a law, that the tithe of all his own lands should be given to God and his servants, and should be enjoyed free from all taxes. Great difference is among historians about this grant, few agreeing in the words or substance of it, as Selden shews, some restraining it to the tithe of his own demesne lands; others to the tenth part of his lands; others to the tithe of the whole nation. At that time, the nation being under great and heavy pressures by Danish irruptions, intestine wars, great spoils, and miseries, he called a council, where were present Bernredus, king of Mercia, and Edmond, king of East Angles, and they, to remove the heavy judgments then over them, granted the "tithe of all their land to God and his servants."

King Athelstone, about the year 930, king Edmond, about [page 11] ! the year 940, king Edgar, about the year 970, king Ethelred, about the year 1010, king Kanute, about the year 1020, Edward the Confessor, and others of the Saxon kings, made several laws for tithes, as histories report.

The Normans afterwards entering this kingdom, and subduing it to themselves, William the Conqueror confirmed the liberties of the church; so did Henry I., Henry II, king Stephen, and it may be, others of the succeeding kings did the like.

Some episcopal constitutions also have been made to the same effect by Robert Winchelsey, Archbishop of Canterbury, and others.

That the reader may understand the principles upon which these men acted, and the doctrine then preached amongst them, and received and believed, I have inserted the preamble of a grant of king Stephen, which runs thus—"Because through the providence of Divine mercy, we know it to be so ordered, and by the churches publishing it far and near, every body has heard that, by the distribution of alms, persons may be absolved from the bonds of sin, and acquire the rewards of heavenly joys, I, Stephen, by the grace of God, king of England, being willing to have a part with them, who by an happy kind of trading, exchange heavenly things for earthly; and smitten with the love of God, and for the salvation of my own soul, and the souls of my father and mother, and all my forefathers and ancestors," &c. And so he goes on and confirms divers things that had been granted to the church, as tithes and other things.

But notwithstanding the many laws, canons, and decrees of kings, popes, councils, and bishops, "that every man ought to pay the tenth part of his increase;" yet was it left to the owner to confer it where he pleased, which made so many rich abbeys and monasteries; and till the year 1200, or thereabouts, every one gave their tithes at their own pleasure, which made Pope Innocent III. send his decretal epistle to the Bishop of Canterbury, commanding him to enjoin every man to pay his temporal goods to those that ministered spiritual things to them, which was enforced by ecclesiastical censures; and this was the beginning of general parochial payment of tithes in England—see the second part of Coke's Institutes, "And because the pope's decree seemed reasonable, it was admitted and enjoined by the law of the nation, king and people being then papists."

This decree of the pope, receiving all possible assistance from the bishops and the priests, in whose behalf it was made, did not only in a short time take away the people's then claimed right to give their tithes to those that best deserved them, but did also so much corrupt the clergy, that, in the time of Richard II., Wickliffe, our famous reformer, made heavy complaint to the Parliament, which I have inserted in his own words, for the [page 12] reader's satisfaction—"Ah, Lord God! where this be reason to constrain the poor people to find a worldly priest, sometimes unable both of life and cunning, in pomp and pride, covetisse and envy, gluttonness, drunkenness, and lechery, in simony and heresie, with fat horse and jolly, and gay saddles and bridles ringing by the way, and himself in costly clothes and pelure, and to suffer their wives and children, and their poor neighbours perish for hunger, thirst, and cold, and other mischiefs of the world: ah, Lord Jesu Christ! sith within few years men paid their tithes and offerings at their own will, free to good men, and able to great worship of God, to profit and fairness of holy church fighting in earth, why it were lawful and needful that a worldly priest should destroy this holy and approved custom, constraining men to leave this freedom, turning tithes and offerings unto wicked uses."

That the meaning of this, and the practice of the nation in this matter, may the better be understood, it is needful to inform the reader, that when the pope's doctrine was received in a nation, that nation was divided into so many bishoprics as were needful, and every bishopric into so many, parishes as were thought convenient, and till then, most preachers were sent out of the monasteries and religious houses, and the people did at their own free will give their tithes and offerings where they pleased, which liberty they enjoyed till about the year 1200. And though it was generally believed that tithes ought to be paid, yet did no man claim any property therein, but every owner of the nine parts was required to give the tenth part to the priest and the poor, as due unto God.

But now the pope, having set up parishes, did enjoin, that a secular priest canonically instituted, should attend the service of each parish, and that where tithes were not already settled, they should be paid to the parish priest, notwithstanding any custom to the contrary; the people then generally being papists, did yield obedience, as they durst not do otherwise; and it may easily be supposed that, having persuaded the people to pay tithes, it was no hard matter to appoint the persons to whom they should be given.

Parishes being set up, priests appointed, and tithes paid to them, after forty years' possession, what before was owned as a gift, was now claimed as a debt; and *prescription* was pleaded by the priests as their just title; the people then seeing themselves in a snare, began to contend, but the pope, to uphold his clergy, thundered out his interdict against this nation, excommunicated the king, frighted the subjects, with his bulls against the arbitrary disposal of tithes: and Rome, now grown formidable, did highly insult over kings and princes: witness Frederick Barbarossa, Henry VI., and other princes of the [page 13] empire; and the stories of our Henry II. and king John; also our Richard I., to gratify the clergy for their liberality, in contributing to his ransom from captivity, gave them an indulgent charter of their liberties, and in this advantageous time, the Canon laws gained such force, that parochial payments became general. Notwithstanding, our English parliaments, unwilling wholly to forget the poor, for whose sake tithes were chiefly given, made divers laws, "That a convenient portion of the tithes should be set apart for the maintenance of the poor of the parish for ever." Richard II., 15. 6. 4. Henry IV.

The pope having by these means brought in tithes, and made a pretended title by prescription, set up courts to recover them, which were called ecclesiastical courts, where his own creatures were judges, and thus the poor people might easily know what they had to expect from them; yet no greater punishment could they inflict on those that did not pay, than excommunication out of their church.

The pope always willing to favour his chief props, notwithstanding his general decree, could tell how to dispense with his own lands at his pleasure, and therefore frequently granted exemptions to divers orders, to free them from payment of tithes; witness the Hospitallers, Cistercians, Templars, and generally to all lands held in the occupation of those called religious persons and houses, which is the ground of all their claims, who have bought the lands of dissolved monasteries, &c., and say they are tithe-free.

When the pope, by colour of the Jewish laws, had gained an universal payment of tithes to all his clergy, in further imitation of that earthly tabernacle, set up a new building after the former pattern, and therefore to himself claimed first-fruits and tenths, as a successor of the Jewish high-priest; sins also he undertook to pardon; cardinals also he appointed as leaders of their families; mitres they wore on their heads, as Aaron did; synagogues they built, with singers, porters, &c., and into the form of the levitical priesthood they transformed themselves, thereby denying Christ Jesus, (the end of types and figures,) to be come in the flesh.

Afterwards, Henry VIII, king of England, being a papist, and believing the pope's doctrine, as also did his parliament, "that tithes were due to God and holy church," made a law that every one should set out and pay his tithes.

And seeing this is the great law, and the first of our parliamentary laws for tithes, and that upon which the rest are grounded, I shall here insert the preamble of it.

"Forasmuch as divers numbers of evil-disposed persons, having no respect to their duties to Almighty God, but against right and good conscience have attempted to substract and withhold, [page 14] in some places the whole, and in some places great part of their tithes and oblations, as well personal as predial, due unto God and holy church," &c.

A second law in his time was also made to the like purpose, and in pursuance of the former: and great reason he had, and need there was for them; for having dissolved many monasteries which had many tithes and rectories appropriated to them, and either had them in his own hands, or sold them to others, to be held as lay-possessions, and they having no law whereby to recover them, the pope's laws not reaching the lay persons, he was necessitated to make new laws to enforce the payment of them, which, the better to colour over the matter, he made in general terms, but still restrained the trial of tithes to the ecclesiastical courts.

After him, Edward VI., in pursuance of his father's laws, and upon the same ground, made another law for the payment of predial and personal tithes, under penalty of treble damages, who also restrained the trial to the ecclesiastical courts. These laws suppose that tithes were due to God and holy church, and therefore they require, "That every man do yield and set out his tithes as had been accustomed."

In pursuance of these laws, some ordinances were made in the time of the long parliament, in the exigencies of the war, because the courts of justice were obstructed.—And these are the substance of all our English laws concerning tithes.

Having thus briefly run over the laws and practices of tithing, both abroad and in this nation, I shall give some hints of the opinions of former times concerning tithes. About the year 1000 and 1200 after Christ, when tithes were generally preached up and claimed, great controversy arose between the canonists and the clergy, by what immediate law tithes were payable.

The canonists generally ground themselves upon the decrees and canons of the church, and on the writings of Augustin, Ambrose, and the rest of the ancient fathers, who say they are due by divine right.

The clergy of those times were at a difference among them selves, some of them saying that tithes, as a determined part, are due only by positive and ecclesiastic law; but as a competent part to be allowed for the maintenance of the ministry, are due by divine law; and that the tenth part was decreed by the church, in imitation of the Jewish state, and not by any continuing force of it under the Gospel; and that the church was not bound to this part, but freely might as well have ordained the payment of a ninth or eighth, according to the various opportunity. This was taught by Hales, Aquinas, Henricus de Grandavo, R. de Midiâ villâ, Cardinal Cajetan, Io. Mayer, Suarez, Malder, and others, who say, "It is the common opinion of [page 15] the greatest part of the clergy of that time," and that the "tenth part was rather ceremonial than moral." -

Here also was made a distinction, and many said that predial and mixed tithes were due by the divine ecclesiastical law; but personal tithes only by the decrees of the church; and therefore in Venice and other cities, where no predial tithes are, a personal tithe is required by the positive law of the church, by virtue of the substance (not ceremony) of the command.

Another opinion (and that owned by many) was drawn from the former doctrine, which concluded that, seeing tithes were not enjoined by the command of God, therefore they were mere alms, and to be dispensed as what was justly due to charity. Of this opinion were the Dominicans and Franciscans, who both began about the year 1210, and by their doctrine got many tithes to be given to their monasteries, and that whatsoever was given to the four orders of mendicant friars, was a sufficient discharge from the priests.

And our famous reformers, John Wickliffe, Walter Brute, William Thorpe, and others, whose arguments are at large in Fox's Acts and Monuments, did in their days bear their testimony against tithes, for which some of them suffered in the flames.

Agreeing herewith are the articles of the Bohemians, published nearly three hundred years since, wherein a divine right to tithes since the Gospel is denied; whereupon also long since they took all their temporalities from their ministers; and before Wickliffe's time, Gerardus Sagarellus was of the same mind. And the great Erasmus also said, that the common exacting of tithes by the clergy of his time was no better than tyranny.

Having thus briefly run over the doctrines, decrees, practices, and opinions concerning tithes; I shall make some short observations thereupon, that the reader may understand whereunto they tend, and then proceed to the matter as it concerns us at this day, wherein he will find the knowledge of these things will be useful.

1st, That amongst the Jews, tithes were paid to the Levites that did the common services of the tabernacle and temple, and not to the sons of Aaron, the priests; for they had only a tenth part out of the tithes, and therefore he that pleads for tithes from the Mosaical laws for tithing, had need consider how the payment of tithes to ministers, succeeds to the payment of tithes to the Levites, who were not priests, nor were to touch or meddle with that holy office, lest they died.

2d, That among the Jews, no outward law was appointed for the recovery of tithes; but he that did not pay them robbed God, and by him only was punished. -

3d, That the tithes were not for the Levites only, but for the stranger, the fatherless, and the widow, who were to eat thereof, and be satisfied. [page 16]

4th, That when the Levitical priesthood was changed by the coming of Christ Jesus, the law for tithing was also changed, as Paul wrote to the Hebrews: for it is evident, that in the beginning of the church, for the first three hundred years, while the purity and simplicity of the Gospel was retained, no tithes were paid among Christians.

5th, That as the mystery of iniquity began to work, and men's imaginations were taught, instead of the doctrine of Christ, divers men, taking their ground from Moses, began to preach that tithes again ought to be paid.

6th, That those that first preached up tithes, pressed the payment of them, not for the maintenance of a ministry only, but chiefly for provision for the poor and needy.

7th, That in the first practice of the payment of tithes, they were not paid as tithes, but as free offerings, at the bounty of the giver, and not as answering any law that required the tenth part, and so more properly were called offerings than tithes.

8th, That notwithstanding any doctrines preached, it was not a received doctrine, that tithes ought to be paid, till about the year 1000, that the pope had then sent up his authority, and usurped dominion over the greatest part of Europe, and almost all emperors, kings, and princes were brought into subjection to him, and his superstitions. -

9th, That notwithstanding the strict commands of the pope, no compulsory law was made by the pope or his councils, to enforce any to pay tithes, but only their excommunication.

10th, That tithes were always accounted an ecclesiastical duty, and therefore by ecclesiastical courts were tried and judged; and till the dissolution of abbeys, &c., were never called a civil right.

11th, That tithes were brought in as a duty owing unto God, and were so required and enforced, and therefore all laws made for the payment of tithes, take that for their ground, and not any civil property or right in him that claims them.

12th, That till the year 1200, or thereabouts, it was the common practice for every one to bestow his tithes where he pleased.

13th, That from such arbitrary dispositions, abbeys and monasteries came to be so richly endowed with tithes and rectories.

14th, That all exemptions from payment of tithes, came from the pope.

15th, That first-fruits and tenths are but a late innovation, and claimed by the pope as successor to the Jewish high-priest, as Coke in the third part of his Institutes also testifies.

16th, That tithes are the same thing, whether claimed by an abbey, or impropriator, or a priest, and stand upon the same ground and foundation, and differ nothing but in the person that possesseth them. [page 17]

17th, Here also the declining state of the church to corruption and error may be clearly discerned and traced: for as the power of truth was lost, so was the fruit thereof, which caused such earnest pressing to needful contributions, and when that would not serve, laws and decrees were made to enforce them; but in the beginning it was not so; for while the purity and simplicity of the Gospel was retained, they needed no pressing, for their charity then abounded not only to the tenth part, but even greater parts, as the need of the church required.

18th, That the right of tithes was never cleared, but remained in controversy, even among the greatest papists, and in all ages there were those that withstood the payment of them; and many of the martyrs for that, among other things, suffered in flames.

These things thus premised, I shall briefly state the great CASE and Question, at this day chiefly controverted concerning tithes, as claimed and paid in England, viz.–

Whether any person have a true and legal property in the tenth part of another man's increase, now called Tithes?

The terms are plain, and need no opening: yet it is needful to declare why the case is thus stated; for the great question rather seems to be, Whether Tithes be not due at this day?

That may be due to another, wherein yet he may have no legal property, as custom, tribute, taxes, which are to be paid because commanded by the state; and though law and equity obliges the payment, yet is no distinct property in him that commands; and so tithes may be supposed to be due, because so many laws have been made for payment of them, though the person that claims them may have no particular interest or property therein, other than is derived from the command.

But now in England, tithes are not only claimed by virtue of divers laws, but also as being a distinct property, severed from the property of the nine parts. -

And if this could clearly be evinced, all scruples of conscience were answered: for if a true and legal property be in another person to the tenth part of my increase, I ought in conscience to yield and set it forth, because it is not mine; and then the name of tithe, as having in any measure relation to the Jewish priesthood, or popish clergy, were at an end, but as a debt it ought to be truly paid to the proprietor.

Many things have been said, and much written, to prove such a property, the substance whereof, as far as hath come to my knowledge, I shall briefly sum up under these general heads; as also the grounds of those who claim them to be due, and yet plead no property, which being the lesser, may be fully included and answered in the other. [page 18]

THE SEVERAL CLAIMS MADE FOR TITHES, AND A LEGAL PROPERTY THEREIN ANSWERED.

1. The first claim tithes to be due, *jure divino,* and produce the law of Moses for it.

2. Others say that tithes are not now due by the law of God; only the equity of the law is still of force, which obligeth to afford a competent maintenance for the ministry, but doth not bind to the certain quantity.

3. Others plead the decrees, canons, and constitutions of general councils, popes, bishops, convocations, and these say, that tithes are due *jure ecclesiastico.*

Under these several claims, or some of them, have tithes been demanded and paid, since the dark night of apostacy overspread the earth under the papal power, till the pope's supremacy and religion was cast off in England; and where the popish religion is professed, they are now by the same demanded and paid.

But now of late in England new claims are made, and a human right is pleaded, which I shall briefly bring under these few heads.

1. The gifts of kings and princes who were rulers of the people, as Ethelwolph, &c.

2. The temporal laws of kings, parliaments, &c.

3. The particular gifts, appropriation, consecration, or donation, of those who were former owners of the land.

4. Prescription, and a legal right by their possession.

5. A legal right by purchase.

And besides these, I never heard or read of any other pretence for tithes, though I have diligently, for two years and more, laboured to inform myself fully what could be alleged for them.

To begin with the first, those that say tithes are due by divine right. -

Some of them say, That the law given to Israel for payment of tenths to the tribe of Levi, doth also oblige Christians to pay tenths to their ministers, as succeeding in the priest's office.

Answ. To such it is clearly answered, that the priesthood which had a commandment to take tithes being changed by Christ Jesus, there is made of necessity also a change of the law; and now the priesthood is no more committed to the offspring of Levi, or any other tribe, but to Christ Jesus the unchangeable priesthood, whose kingdom stands not in figures and carnal ordinances, but is the substance of what that was but a figure. And it is clear the primitive churches were assured of it, who for some hundreds of years never called for the payment of tithes, as is before plainly proved.

And how doth a Gospel ministry succeed to the Levites, who [page 19] received tithes, but were not priests? Much more colour had the choristers, singing men, and the rest of the rabble brought into the late cathedrals, to claim them, and only to pay out a tenth part to the priests as the Levites did.

Others say, That Abraham paid tithes to Melchisedec, which was before the levitical priesthood; and Christ Jesus is made a priest after the order of Melchisedec.

Abraham returning from the slaughter of the kings, was met by Melchisedec, who brought him bread and wine, and Abraham gave him the tenth of the spoil. But what is this to the payment of tithes, unless it oblige the soldiers? For it doth not appear that Abraham paid the tenth part of his own increase; nor doth it appear that Abraham gave the tenth part at any other time; and how will this prove a yearly payment of tithes to ministers?

And what if Jacob gave tithes? How are either of these examples more binding than any other of the good acts that either of these holy men did?

Object. If it be said that Jesus Christ said, "Ye tithe mint, &c., these things ye ought not to leave undone:"

It is answered, that Jesus Christ then spoke to the Jews, in the time when the levitical priesthood was not ended, who were bound by the law, so long as it was of force, till he was offered up, and said, *it is finished*.

But though divine right hath been long pretended, few are now left who will stand to it, and the generality, both of lawyers, priests, and people, are of a contrary mind.

For if tithes be absolutely due by the law of God, no custom, usage, prescription, privilege, or popish dispensation, can acquit from payment of the utmost penny of the tenth part; but scarce the tenth person in England payeth tithe in kind, and many plead they are tithe free, and pay none at all, and others very small matters; and so the greatest part of the people of England deny tithes to be due by God's law.

Again, if tithes be due by the law of God, then it is to the end for which they were commanded, for the Levites, the strangers, the fatherless, and the widows; all therefore who plead for tithes by divine right, must not pay them to an impropriator; for by God's law he cannot claim, neither ought any impropriator, of that mind, to receive them.

And of late years, it was by Rolls, chief justice, adjudged in the upper bench, that tithes are not now due by the law of God.

2. Those that plead the equity of the law is still of force.

These plead not for tithes properly, but for a comfortable maintenance, and by way of tithes, as they suppose most convenient, &c. And these bring many Scriptures in the New Testament. "That he that labours is worthy of his hire: he that [page 20] preacheth the Gospel ought to live of the Gospel; let him that is taught communicate to him that teacheth;" and the like.

And to such I say, that not only the equity of the levitical law for tithing, the doctrine of Christ Jesus and his apostles do bind, but even from natural things we are largely taught our duty therein; "No man muzzleth the mouth of the ox; and no man goeth a warfare at his own charge; and he that plants a vineyard eats the fruit thereof." And herein it is agreed, that the ministers of Christ Jesus, who are called to his service, and labour in the word, ought to be comfortably provided for, that they go not a warfare at their own charge.

But this doth not require that the worldly should contribute, much less be compelled, to give a certain portion of the fruits of their labours towards the maintenance of Christ's ministers.

And these grant, that every man is the sole owner of his own labour and possession; and though by another he may not be compelled, for such sacrifice God abhors, yet ought every one freely to glorify God with his substance, to strengthen the weak hands and feeble knees, and to give to him that teacheth those things that are needful, and such cheerful givers God accepts.

And this leaves every one free to give to him that teacheth, not binding to the maintenance of those who have less need than the giver, or of those who are transformed as apostles and ministers of Christ, who have the form, but want the power, who teach for filthy lucre, keeping ever learning, but cannot bring to the knowledge of the truth.

And of such as Christ Jesus sent forth, he always took care, and they never wanted, but they reaped the fruits of their labour, and eat the fruits of their own vineyards, which they had planted, and by the churches who were gathered out of the world, were they maintained to preach the Gospel to the world, unto whom they would not make the Gospel chargeable or burdensome, which was their glory and their crown. For in this it is assented, that the ministers of Christ Jesus, who sow unto us spiritual things, should reap of our temporals. But here is the difference, 1st, That our consciences must be our judge, who those ministers are; for to the conscience were Christ's ministers always made manifest. 2dly, That our gift must be free, and by no man's compulsion.

3. A third sort plead the decrees, canons, constitutions of general councils, popes, bishops, convocations.

To such I shall only say that, for the first eight hundred years after Christ, no canon, or decree was made by general council, nor was it then determined by the church what part every man should pay. And the first eight general councils do not so much as speak of the name of tithes, and that was till about a thousand years: and then about that time it came to be [page 21] received and believed that *tithes ought to be paid;* yet in England, as well as other nations, every man might have given his tithe where he pleased, till about the year 1200, as is already proved. But I need not say much to these, few being of this mind but those that own the pope for their head, we having in England denied and cast off his supremacy, though in this matter of tithes, and many other things, we still feel his power among us.

And now having briefly gone over the substance of what is pleaded for a divine or ecclesiastic right, I come next to what is pretended for a human right. -

And first, the gift of kings, as Ethelwolph, &c.

To this I answer, if they could prove the whole land had been the particular possession of any such king, they said something; though that would not justify the taking tithes from all the people, as shall be more fully proved hereafter. But by what right could he give the tenth part of the increase and fruits of the labours of all the people of his dominions, who had no legal property therein? It was an easy matter, when the pope's emissaries had taught the people, "that tithes were due to God and them;" and had persuaded kings and nobles "that heaven might be purchased by their works," to procure from them the gift of that which was not their's, the poor people's tithes; especially considering the people were of the same mind, and as zealous of all the popish superstitions as themselves, and every one striving who should therein most excel; witness those many rich abbeys and monasteries, lately in this land. But if that king Ethelwolph's grant be the foundation of tithes, then how many succeeding kings and bishops, and others, have violated his deed, by appropriating them to abbeys, monasteries, and such like houses? And how have all ages since Ethelwolph's time taken upon themselves the disposal of tithes, without any relation to what he did? Which shews clearly, that neither kings, parliaments, nor people, did ever hold themselves bound by his grant. But the folly of this argument will more plainly appear hereafter.

The next, and those which seem to have the strongest plea, do urge the temporal laws of kings and parliaments, and say, By the law they have as good property in tithes as any man hath in his lands.

Answ. To such I say, the law doth not *give* any man a property, either in land or tithes, or any other thing, but only doth *conserve* to every man his property, which he hath in his land and possessions, either by gift, purchase, or descent, and secure him from the injury or violence of another.

But let us not be deceived with a new pretence, lately taken up to delude simple minds, of a legal property and a civil right; [page 22] for that is but a shift when they see their other claims will not serve; but hear what the makers of the laws say of them; and passing by the Saxons' times, and king Stephen, let us come to Henry VIII., who cast off the pope, and upon whose law all others that were since made are built; and in the preamble of the act it is declared, "That tithes are due to God and holy church," and they blame men for being so wicked as not to pay them, and therefore that law is made; and here is the ground of the law, not any property or civil right in priests or others, and therefore if the law require them as due by divine right, he that saith they are only due by human right cannot claim them, nor ought to recover them by that law, for he claims them by another right; and for any man to claim that by human right from human law, which commands them as due by divine right, is but a mere deceit. And that law of Henry VIII., and the rest, did not upon any civil ground set up, or constitute the payment of tithes, but takes it for granted, that "tithes are due to God and holy church;" and therefore the foundation of the law being taken away, "that they are due to God and holy church," the law falls to the ground; for the law not making them due, but supposing them due by a former right, if they were not so due, the law cannot be binding.

That tithes were never, till now of late, claimed of civil right is plain; for as they were imposed by the pope, so they were triable in his courts; and those very laws made by late parliaments did appoint them to be tried in the ecclesiastical courts, and restrained the temporal jurisdiction, as the acts themselves testify.

But what is the property that is now claimed? Is it in a person? That cannot be, for the priest hath them not till he enters his office, and when he parts with that he loseth his tithes. So the priest hath no property but his office; and what is that? It was a popish office when tithes were first paid to it; and how comes the property to continue now the office is laid aside, and the pope that set them up? But how can a civil right or property be pretended, when the author was the pope? the end for a spiritual office, and recovered in an ecclesiastical court?

In the act of 32nd Henry VIII., tithes are called spiritual gifts. And there of impropriate tithes sold after the dissolution, it is said they are now made temporal. And before that time it was never heard that tithes were called a temporal right.

But it is farther said, these laws were made by Parliaments, the representatives of the people: and though tithes were not due before, yet they might give tithes, because their own, they being the body of the people.

This would suppose a particular consecration, or donation of the people, not only as in their legislative capacity to bind [page 23] themselves by a law, but by a particular act of free gift: But it is plain, the act never intended any such thing, for it gives nothing, but commands what was before.

And as to the law itself, and all other laws of kings, parliaments, popes, councils and bishops, for the payment of tithes, since Christ Jesus came in the flesh, how do they all or any of them bind the conscience? For if tithes be not due by the law of God, as is herein proved, and almost generally granted, who hath set them up? the law of man at best: And who is man, that makes a law in the place where God disannulled his own command? Is it better to obey man than God? or is man grown wiser than his maker? Who put this power into the hand of man, to raise a compulsory maintenance for ministers? it may be to set up and maintain those who are contrary to Christ, instead of Christ's ministers, who never looked for, nor durst own such a way of provision. Will any say they have power? From whom had they it? Is it derived from the people? That cannot be. Have they any power committed to them as magistrates? if so, the Turk, and all infidel magistrates have the like: Or is it as they are Christian magistrates? Then may not France, Spain, &c., claim the same? For what nation in Europe will not say they have a Christian magistracy. And may not they by as good right require and compel maintenance for their ministers, as Henry VIII., or any other? But that I may not be mistaken, as if I went about to take away the magistrate's power to raise taxes, assessments, or other charges, for the service and defence of the nation, it is needful to distinguish between those things that are civil, and such as are spiritual: For civil ends and uses, the people may give power to their representatives to raise moneys, or any other civil thing, because in such things they are their own masters: But in matters of religion, no man can give power unto another, to impose any thing upon himself, or his neighbour; for in those things every one is to be accountable unto God. And thus "we give unto God the things that are God's; and unto Caesar the things that are his;" paying tribute to whom tribute is due. But as for all laws made in the will of man, in the things of God, they reach not the conscience, and therefore make no sin against God.

And as concerning the laws of King Henry VIII., and Edward VI., it may be considered, some of them were made by a popish king and parliament, and the rest, in the glimmerings of light, when men were but seen as trees; and therefore, to make their laws a rule for this day of clear and sunshine light, is a shame to our Reformation. And if it be said, papists might and did make good laws; it is true, in temporal things they did, but not in things of religion.

But were the law just in commanding tithes, can it be equal to [page 24] give double or treble damage, where they are not paid? If any man owe a just and due debt, no more by law can be recovered, but what the debt is, besides the charges of the law: How cruel, therefore, are these laws and ordinances, which in a matter of so much just scruple, require and impose the double or treble value? And how unrighteous are all such persons, as by force of such laws receive them? For if tithes were due, is therefore the treble value due, because the law hath made that penalty? Where is equity or justice in either? The pope and his adherents did only excommunicate the refuser till he conformed; and till these late laws, such penalties as imprisonment, and treble damage were never known. And here what was by our forefathers begun in ignorance, we build up, and confirm with tyranny, and instead of their rods, make to ourselves scorpions.

But herein is not all, but the law requires every man to set out the tenth, and so makes him a voluntary agent in that, against which his conscience testifies, which is most cruel and unrighteous; and him that cannot do so, they sue and hale before courts and magistrates, and there they get judgment of treble damage, and by that judgment, frequently take five-fold, yea sometimes ten-fold the value. Shall not these things render this age, which so much pretends to reformation, contemptible to future generations? And for these things, shall not even papists rise up in judgment against us and condemn us?

But how is it that any law for tithes is now executed? Do not all laws and statutes for tithes restrain the trial of them to the ecclesiastical courts, and prohibit the temporal courts from meddling with them? [This was in the time of the commonwealth.] And since the ecclesiastical courts are destroyed, Who have power to give judgment for tithes? No temporal judge proceeding according to the laws for tithing. How, is it then, that so many persons are sued, prosecuted, and unjustly vexed for tithes in all the courts at Westminster; and not only so, but in the Sheriff's court, and other petty courts in the country?

Object. If it be said, The statute gives double damages and costs, and no court being appointed where that shall be recovered, it must be supposed to be the common law courts.

I answer by asking, of what must they give the double or treble damage, seeing they are restrained from trying for the single value? If they cannot judge the one, how can they award the other? Will they condemn an accessory before they try the principal? What is this but to make the law a nose of wax, to uphold unrighteousness.

Object. It will be said, justices of peace have power. It may be so by an ordinance, but no act of parliament, which is the law of England; and that they do it many poor people feel; for generally they give treble damages for all manner of tithes, [page 25] whereas the statute gave but double and costs, and that only for predial tithes. And they usually execute their precepts by such persons as will do it effectually, who take generally five times more than the value, which they appraise and sell far under the worth. I write what I can prove by manifold instances.

Though these oppressions be many and great, yet are they not all that this age exercises; for by a new device, under pretence that priests are not able to pay tenths to the protector, unless every man pay them their tithes, they sue men for all manner of tithes by English bill in the Exchequer, and there force them upon their oaths to declare what tithes they have; whereas in the ecclesiastical courts the ordinary might not examine a man upon his own oath concerning his own tithe. And here such as either make conscience of swearing, which Christ forbids, or cannot themselves tell what tithe they had, are cast into prison for contempt, where they may lie as long as they live, no law in the nation reaching them any relief. And divers upon this account have long lain in the Fleet, and yet are there: [this was in the year 1655. See the Suff. of the Quakers]; and I believe above an hundred suits are in the Exchequer depending, and proceedings stopt at this point; the hearts of the very officers of the court relenting with pity towards such numbers of poor men brought thither every term, from the most remote parts of the nation, and some of them not for above twelve pence.

O shameful reformation! What! compel a man himself to set out the tithe of his own goods to maintain a priest, it may be one openly profane, and so make him sin against his own conscience! And not only so, but to force him to swear what tithes he had, or commit him to prison, there to lie without hope of relief. Must we still have priests and tithes? Then may we not wish for old priests, and old ecclesiastical courts? For much more moderation was in them, that even Papists would blush at our cruelties. Did but the magistrate see what havock is made in the north, what driving of oxen out of the plough, the cows from poor and indigent children, what carrying of pots and kettles, yea, and fetching the very clothes off poor people's beds, he would either be ashamed of such justices, or such priests or tithes, or of them all. Such instances I could give as would make the reader's ears to tingle; and he that cannot believe me, let him send into Cumberland, and he shall meet with few that cannot inform him of it; or do but let him go a little after harvest, and he may find the justices as busy as if they had little other work. But whither have I digressed? Let me return to hear what the next can say.

3. And these plead the gift of those that were formerly possessors of the land, and say, Those that pay tithes do but that which their ancestors justly charged upon them. [page 26]

To such I answer, that it is true many ancestors gave tithes, which of them were required, as before hath been declared; but what is that to us? Or how are we thereby bound? Did ever any man, in any deed or conveyance of his land, express any such gift, or make any exception of tithes? I never saw or heard of such a thing; and let those who can find such reservations make their claim; but I believe it will not be in England. That which this sort pleads, seems to make a ground for a distinct property; for if there be a property, it must of necessity arise from him that was the true owner, and had power to charge himself and his posterity; and these say, They have as good right to the tenth part as the owner hath to the nine, and that he never purchased it, and the like. Unto all which I answer, that though it were true, and could be proved that mine ancestors gave tithes, and that for ever, yet am I not thereby bound to pay them or stand any way chargeable with them. It is true, when they were owners of land, they might themselves yield and set forth what part of their increase they pleased, or might have given the tenth, or any other part of their land, as they would, or they might have charged upon the land what rent they liked; but they could not charge their posterity with that which was no-way their's, nor which in any true sense or construction they could be said to have any property in, and which is not paid by reason of that which is derived from them; for tithe is neither paid of land, nor by reason of the land, but is paid by reason of the *increase* of renewing; and therefore the doctrines of the old fathers, the statute of Edward VI., and so the popish laws for tithes do as well require the payment of the tenth part of men's profits and gain, whether by trade, commerce, or merchandize, as of the fruits of the earth, yea, the tenth part of wages, and all personal increase. And surely no man will say, that he pays tithe of these because his ancestors charged him with it; nor will any man allow that another person, by any gift of ancestors, can have distinct property in the tenth part of the fruit of his labours; and the case is the same as to all tithes, whether predial, personal, or mixt. If I sit still and plough not, no corn will grow. If I sit still, and work not, no profit will rise; so that it is my labour, my diligence, and industry, that raiseth the tithe, and in my power it is to make it less, or more; and sometimes, yea, often it falls out, that the tithe of corn is thrice more worth than the yearly value of the land on which it grows; and herein tithe of corn is far more hard and unequal than personal tithes; for the one pays but the tenth, all charges deducted; the other pays the tenth of charges and all. Mine ancestor could not charge me with that which doth not accrue by reason of that which I have from him; nor am I bound, because mine ancestor left me land, to pay tithe, which [page 27] is not paid by reason of the land, but of the increase, unto which I am no more tied by law, than he is who hath increase without land. If I have land and no increase, I pay no tithes; if I have increase, though no land, I ought by law to pay tithes. If I husband my land, so that the increase of it is not to be severed, no tithe can be recovered of it; and, therefore, if I pasture my land, no tithe shall be paid for the grass, which is eaten unsevered, but only a rate-tithe for that which doth depasture on it; which makes it plain, that tithe is not paid by reason of the land, but of the stock; and in that also, it lies in my power to make the tithe much, little, or nothing; if I plough and sow corn, the tenth part of the increase is generally more worth than the land on which it grows, which comes not by the land which descends from the ancestor, but because of the increase, won by the great charge, industry, and labour of the husbandman. If I pasture my ground with sheep that yield a fleece, the tithe will be considerable, though not so much as by corn. If I pasture with cows or breeding cattle, a much less tithe is paid. And if I pasture with horses and barren cattle, a very small rate only is required, though in few places of the nation would that have been recovered in the times of the papacy. But if I plant wood, and let it stand for timber; or if I store my land with beasts, wherein there is no personal property, no tithe shall be paid. Or, if I let my land lie waste, (which may be supposed because it may be done) or will eat my meadow, or corn standing, no tithe can be required. All these instances manifest that tithe hath still relation to the stock and personal estate, and not to the land: and is paid by reason of the stock and not the land; and so no ancestor could lay and perpetuate such a charge as tithe upon it, nor could he bind his successors to it. If by my ancestor I am bound to pay tithes in consideration of the land which he leaves me, to what value must it be? I may yearly pay more than the land he leaves me is worth, if I keep it in tillage; and if I pasture it, I need not pay the twentieth part: have I not herein, without fraud to my ancestors, power to pay much or little? How is this like a rent-charge certain, which is by some objected? If tithes were paid by reason of the land, surely there is most reason, that the tenth part of the grass renewing upon all pasture-grounds should be paid; for the land still brings that with it, and it is easily divideable by rent, or let by month. If another hath as good right to the tenth part of the increase as the owner hath to the nine, why can he not take it without the owner's setting it out, or recover it by action of debt or trespass? But it is clear, there is no title till it be set forth, and then if the owner carry it away, an action of trespass lies, because he had set it out, and given it to another, and so altered his property, as one man doth, by marking his cattle for another man; and therefore it is, [page 28] that the law which commands tithes, doth not give power to any to take the tithe, because he had no title, but enjoins the owner to set it forth, and so make it another's by his own consent.

If any man claim tithes by my ancestor's gift, may I not ask him, To whom, and for what my ancestors gave them? And it is plain beyond denial, that all those gifts of lands or tithes in England, since Augustin the monk planted the Roman Catholic faith, and preached up the payment of tithes, were given to priests, for saying prayers for the souls of the givers, and their deceased ancestors, as old consecrations do witness: And therefore in reason, if the consideration and service be ceased, so ought also the wages; for no man in law or equity, ought to claim wages when he will not do the work for which it was given; and seeing those priests and prayers are laid aside, the gift ought to return to the donor, and may not without his consent be perverted to another use.

“Tithe was never claimed in respect of any ownership in the land, but *ex debito,* by the law of God, for substraction whereof, no remedy lay at the common law; and, therefore, if a parson let a lease of his glebe to another, with all the appurtenances, yet he himself shall have tithe of it."—SHEPPERD.

"Terra non sunt decimabiles; and, therefore, neither mines nor quarries of iron, brass, tin, lead, coals, stones, tile, brick, or lime, are titheable, nor houses, nor trees, nor grass, nor corn, till they be severed from the land, the real estate which descends by inheritance from the ancestor, and made a distinct personal possession."—COKE.

And therefore tithe is not paid of land, nor by reason of the land, nor is it a charge upon land, like a rent-charge, nor was it ever so claimed, till of late.

But some object and say, When I bought my land, I bought not the tithe, nor paid any thing for it.

I answer, that I and all men bought all our land, and that without any charge of tithe upon it; and, therefore, in all conveyances it is still said, "All that, &c." and never any covenant for, or exemption of a tenth part, either of land or increase; and to him that saith, the "seller or his ancestor, charged it with tithes as a rent," I say, where a rent is charged, it is still expressed; and find any such exemption or covenant, and I will freely pay them as a just debt. And is it not ridiculous for any to talk of purchasing his tithe? for with his labour, charge, and husbandry, he pays dear enough for his whole increase.

Another objects, That though I bought all my land, yet I bought it cheaper than I could have bought such land as was known to be tithe-free; and therefore having a cheaper bargain, I am bound in equity to pay tithes.

I answer, that I have already proved all land is tithe-free, [page 29] and the charge of tithe is upon the stock and personal estate, and not upon the land. And the strength of this objection lies, in comparing those who pay tithes with those that are free; they that buy lands tithe-free, are eased of this oppression, and are in no hazard; and though all others ought to be so, yet it being a question, whether they can ease themselves of the burden, they buy under a hazard, and as subject to such a charge; but if they can cast off the yoke, they get but what is their own. And seeing we have denied the pope's authority and supremacy, we may so soon as we can, wholly cast off the burdens which he laid on us. And thus, he that buys lands in the years of trouble and heavy taxes, may perhaps buy much cheaper than when none, or little, is paid: Shall he therefore always be required to pay taxes when others are discharged? Or shall he that bought cheap land on the borders, between England and Scotland, when those parts were infested with mosse-troopers, always maintain, or pay tribute to thieves and robbers? We bought land when the pope's yoke was upon our necks, and if we cast it from us, we may, by as good reason, be eased of our tithes, as they are of their taxes. But if I bought cheaper, what is that to the state, or to a priest? If in equity I be bound to pay any more, it is most just, that he have it of whom I bought my land, and not another.

There are others who plead a legal right by prescription, and that they have a good right, because they have so long possessed them.

This was the old device, first to preach that tithes were due, and then to limit them to the parishes, and when forty years were past, to claim them as a debt, which before was paid as charity, or at most as a free-will offering of the owner. And thus the pope got first-fruits and tenths, and Peter-pence, and many great sums out of this and other nations, which long continued; and he might as well have pleaded his prescription, as any of his branches now can do. [In the reign of Henry III., the pope had above 120,000*l*. per annum, out of this nation, which was then more worth than the king's revenue.] But shall the continuance of an oppression give right to perpetuate the grievance? How many great and heavy pressures, in other things, did long lie on this nation, which still have been abolished, as light did increase; notwithstanding the usages and customs of former ages. But yet this is a great mistake, for by the common law no man can prescribe to have tithes, though many may prescribe to be free from tithes, or part thereof; for he that claims tithes (except impropriators, to whom I shall speak hereafter) must claim them as a parson, vicar, or other called ecclesiastic officer, and, as I have hinted before, he claims them not as such a person, but as such an officer, and the prescription (if any were) is to his office. Now if no such office be in being, his claim is at an end: That there is now no such office is plain; for when Henry VIII. renounced the pope, he was declared by act of parliament to be the head of the church; and all archbishops, bishops, and all others in ecclesiastical orders, were no longer to hold of the pope, but of the king, and not to claim their benefices by title from the pope, but of the king, by virtue of that act of parliament. And here the succession from the pope was cut off; and the king, by his new authority as head of the church, made bishops, and gave them power to make parsons, vicars, and others called ecclesiastic officers. Afterwards, as the king renounced the pope, so the parliament of England laid aside kings, who had assumed the title and style of head of the church, and also abolished archbishops and bishops, and all their dependencies, root and branch: And here the whole ecclesiastic state was dissolved, and the body fell with the head, and the branches with the root; both parsons, vicars, and curates, and so all their right, title, and claim to tithes was at an end, as is more plainly, and fully, set forth in a late printed paper, by Jer. Benson, to which I refer.

And now I come to the last, those that claim by purchase, and these are the impropriators, and they say, "They have bought them of the state, and have paid great sums of money for them, and many of them have no other subsistence."

To these I answer, That I have showed before, that in the root all tithe is alike, whether it be now claimed by a priest or an impropriator, and both must fall together. And seeing those that sold them had no good title, neither can theirs be made good which is derived from them. But seeing it was the state that sold them, and that the whole nation had the benefit of their moneys, it is equal and just, when they cannot have what is sold, that their moneys be repaid; to which point I shall speak more fully hereafter, in answer to an objection which I meet with in my way, needful to be resolved.

And thus I have briefly gone over the whole matter, and considered what every one can say, by which it plainly appears that no man at this day can claim tithe of another, either by divine or human right; and that tithes are neither due by the express law of God, nor by the equity of that law; nor by the decrees of the church, nor grants of kings, nor laws of parliaments, nor gifts of the people, nor prescription of the possessors, nor the purchase of impropriators. -

It now only remains, that I answer some general objections, which I shall do in as much brevity as I can, and so leave the whole to the reader. |

The first is made by the state.

The second by impropriators.

And the third by parish ministers. [page 31]

And all these together object and say, That though it should be granted, that the right of tithes cannot be proved, yet if it be found that taking them away will bring great loss to the public revenue, much damage, if not ruin, to many particular persons and families, and great hazard of bringing confusion to the nation, by such a great alteration, after so long a settlement, and endanger the very public profession of religion, by taking away ministers' maintenance, and consequently ministry itself; it is not prudence, for satisfying some, to bring so many and great inconveniences upon the nation.

These objections plead not for the right of tithes, but against the removing of them, to prevent inconvenience; and if it be granted that tithes are an exaction and oppression, and neither due by the law of God nor man, such considerations as these ought not to obstruct the removal of so great a grievance, but that which is just ought to be done, for the general good to the whole body; and then such parts as are found oppressed, may be afterwards relieved; and even if these should in some measure suffer it were but just, seeing their compliance with the oppressor hath brought such a burden upon the whole body, and are now become the only obstructions of the general relief and freedom.

And yet a few words I shall answer to every one separately, and first to the state, which complains of a great loss by taking away first-fruits and tenths, which are paid out of tithes.

When the pope had established the payment of tithes, and set up a new hierarchy, after the pattern of the Jewish priesthood, (Ezek. xliv, 28, &c.) he took upon himself to be successor to the Jewish high-priest, and claimed tenths from all his inferior priests; and in process of time he got to himself, by the like colour, first-fruits also; and though it was long ere he brought his work to pass in England, yet at last it was effected: you may by these following instances know, how much our English nation struggled against them.

The king forbade H. P., the pope's nuncio, to collect firstfruits, 2 Ed. III. Rol. Claus. M.

The pope's collector, "was willed no longer to gather the first fruits, it being a very novelty, and no person was any longer to pay them."

The commons petition, "that provision may be made against the pope's collectors for levying of first-fruits." 4 Par. 1, Ri, II. Nu. 66.

The king in parliament answers, "There shall be granted a prohibition in all such cases, where the pope's collectors shall attempt any such novelties." Rol. Parl. 4 R. II. Nu. 50.

Upon complaint made by the commons in parliament, the [page 32] king willeth, "that prohibitions be granted to the pope's collectors, for receiving of first-fruits." Rol. Parl. 6 R. II. Nu. 50.

First-fruits, by archbishops and bishops to the pope, were termed "an horrible mischief, and damnable custom." 6. H. IV.

The pope's collectors "were required from thenceforth not to levy any money within the realm, for first-fruits." Rol. Parl. 9 H. IV. N. 43.

The pope thus claiming first-fruits and tenths as annexed to his chair, successor to the Jewish high-priest, and head of the church, continued to collect them, till Henry VIII., discontented with the pope, renounced the pope's supremacy, and assumed it to himself; and by act of parliament, in the twenty-sixth year of his reign, got first-fruits and tenths annexed to his crown, as head of the church; and so himself became worse than the pope, taking the wages, but not doing the pope's work: and that which before by parliaments, under the papacy, was declared as a damnable custom, was now, in the beginning of reformation, made a foundation-stone to support the greatness of the new-made head. - -

Afterwards, queen Mary, not daring to assume the headship of the church, did relinquish, and by act of parliament, wholly took away first-fruits and tenths, she doing no work to deserve such wages. And what a shame is this to our nation, after so long talk of reformation, now to plead for such wages, first exacted by the pope, and then by such as assumed to themselves the style of head of the church, who upon that very account had them annexed to the crown? And shall we now, who pretend to have cast off the pope, uphold such oppressions. For the pretence of paying tenths is the ground of the many suits for tithes in the Exchequer, where otherwise by law they could not, nor ought to be recovered. And as to the public revenue, I am informed they add not much thereto, but all, or a great part of them, are given in augmentations to priests; though I know, many of them, not long since, complained against them as a popish oppression. But take away tithes, and there are as many glebe lands will fall to the state, as will fully make up that loss, which they may as well take away, as their predecessors did the revenues of abbeys and monasteries; and when the people are eased of tithes, they will be better able, and more willing, to enlarge the public treasury, if it be found wanting.

But it is hoped, our state rather looks at the freedom of the people than the increase of the revenue; seeing so lately they took away the profits of the Court of Wards, which was a much better income, and granted many great men such freedom for nothing, as they could neither in right claim, nor in reason expect; and surely, they will not deny the poorer sort of people their own and dear-bought increase. [page 33]

Secondly, *To impropriators, and such as have more lately bought tithe-rents.*

And to these I say, though it be a general rule, *caveat emptor*, yet seeing the ignorance of former days, did take it for granted, both buyer and seller, that the title was good; and since the purchasers did pay great sums of money for them to the state, which went to defray the public charge of the nation, it is just that they have a moderate price for them, with which I believe most of them would be well pleased and content; only in the estimate of that rate they must consider, that they have bought no more, but what the abbey, monastery, or other dissolved house had; and these houses, out of their appropriate tithes, were to find a sufficient priest or curate, canonically instituted, which was to have allowance at the discretion of the bishop of the diocese, and also a convenient portion of the tithe was to be set apart for the yearly maintenance of the poor of the parish for ever, as is provided by divers acts of parliament. And after the dissolution and sale of tithes, the like charge was, and ought to be continued upon them, as at large is proved in a treatise called "The Poor Vicar's Plea;" and let but such purchasers look to their original grants, and they shall find that the yearly value was but little, and the rate small, after which they paid for them; and in regard of the charges and hazards upon them, they were seldom, or never esteemed more worth than ten years' purchase, and that rate, at a moderate yearly value, may well be accepted for them.

This answer will please the impropriator well, who hath not been without his fears to lose his tithes, and get little or nothing for them; and it cannot much displease others, because it is equal and just, that seeing he cannot have what is bought, he may have his money returned.

But the great difficulty seems, the raising of so great a sum of money, and who is to pay it? For, first, there are many who plead, Our lands are wholly tithe free: others say, "We pay a rate, or small prescription-rate, or have a *modus decimandi,* and our tithe is very small, though our lands be of good value:" others say, "We have converted our lands into pastures, and pay little tithe; and therefore it seems not equal, that we should pay as much as those, whose lands consist of tillage, whose tithes are often as much worth as the land."

I answer, That the raising of this sum, is not to follow the rate of tithe, nor hath it any relation to tithe; for if it had, many would as justly scruple the payment of anything towards it, as they do the payment of tithes; but the case must be thus considered: at the dissolution, tithes of abbeys, monasteries, &c., [page 34] were taken into the hands of the state, they sold them, and the money raised went to defray the great charge then upon the nation, as it was of late in our days, when tithe-rents were sold; and at that day, there were wars with France and Scotland, and many great exigencies of state, as the statutes for the dissolution show; and in the service and use of these moneys, the whole nation, and every man therein, had his share, and so far as those moneys went, the people were spared, as the case was with us of late; and so he that had land tithe-free, and he that paid only a small rate for tithes, and he that had pastures and no tillage, all these shared in the sum, yea, and the very impropriator| himself, and not according to the proportion of tithing, but according to the value of their estates in lands or goods, and by which they had been otherwise chargeable; and so the impropriator depositing so much money upon a pledge, the one being required, the other must be returned, and by a general tax it must be raised, wherein every one must bear his proportion, the very impropriator himself.

But then in comes he that bought the lands of abbeys, &c., which, he saith, the pope had made tithe-free, and that when he bought his land, he also paid for the tithe, and so he must either be freed from paying to the impropriator, or must have his money returned as well as he.

I answer, Though there are many such purchasers, yet I believe, to the freeing the nation from this great and long-continued oppression, they, or most part of them, would be content to contribute without any such demand. But if any stand upon it, let him show *what he paid for his tithe,* and he shall have it, which was not a penny; for, search the Court of Augmentations, and it will be found, that there was not in the value of land, the least difference made between tithe-free, and that which paid tithes; as there was not of late, in the sale of bishops', and dean and chapters' lands, many of which also were as much tithe-free; and so if they bought land tithe-free, as cheap as if they had paid tithes, they have had profit enough, and may now well afford to pay with their neighbours.

Thirdly, *To parish ministers.*

And with these I desire a little to expostulate, both as touching the *end of their work;* and as to the way of their maintenance. Their work, as they profess, is to preach the Gospel, and to propagate religion. Now I would ask them, why they suffer not only villages, country towns, and parishes, but even great and populous cities and market towns, and whole corners of counties, to lie destitute, who never could get any other minister, than a poor vicar or reading curate; they will presently answer me, There is no maintenance, and without that they cannot live. [page 35] If I ask them further, why there is no maintenance? they will tell me, it is either a city or market town, to which there belongs no land, and so no tithes; or it is an impropriation and pays only a small stipend; or the lands are tithe-free, or claim customs and prescriptions, and only pay small rates for tithes; or otherwise the people have converted their arable lands into pastures, and their tithe is of small value, and will not afford a maintenance. I would yet ask them again, Is not a third part of the nation in this condition? And must they never have an able minister? Have they no share in your Gospel, because they have no maintenance? Are none of you called to such places? or hath Christ no seed of election amongst them? If this be not your doctrine, yet your practice preacheth it. And if you were really for spreading the Gospel, you would forthwith throw up your tithes; for so long as they continue, there can never be any possibility of raising maintenance in such places.

And secondly, as to *their maintenance*; is their any indifferency, equality, proportion, or justice in their present way of tithing? One man pleads he is to pay nothing to a minister, because the pope hath given him a dispensation, and made his land tithe-free. Another man saith, he hath a prescription to pay but a penny (it may be) for the value of a shilling. Another saith he hath converted his lands into pastures, and hath by his artifice so ordered it, that little is due for tithes. Another saith, he dwells in a city or market town, and hath no land, though it is like he gains more by trade, than ten poor countrymen that pay tithes do by their lands. Another saith, he pays tithe to an impropriator, and he cannot afford to pay both him and a minister. Is this your equal way of maintenance, and have you not a more righteous rule? The rich pay little, and the poor husbandman bears the burden, even he that supplies the nation with bread, who is, notwithstanding, at more charge in his husbandry than any other; and out of the tithes of such country parishes of tillage, great sums are often paid for augmentations, to cities and market towns, when the inhabitants, that have far greater gains by trading go free. Be persuaded, then, to follow the example of your neighbouring reformed churches, and throw up tithes as a relic of popery; and betake yourselves to a more Gospel-like way of maintenance.

It is like you will answer, -- We confess, the present way of a maintenance by tithes is very unequal, unless the whole nation could be brought to quit all their customs and prescriptions, and pay tithe in kind; and also all merchants and tradesmen would pay the tenth part of their gains, as was by the pope enjoined, but that will never be done, and therefore it is better to hold some, than lose all; for we know not what better way would be provided: but show us how we may have a comfortable [page 36] and certain maintenance, and more like the Gospel, and we shall most willingly quit the one and embrace the other.

To this I answer, that there is a way, which, as it would establish the nation upon a sure foundation of true freedom, as to conscience, and give content to all separated congregations, societies, and persons; so would it upon the same basis of liberty, hold forth full satisfaction to all people of the nation, both as to ministry and maintenance, and would be as acceptable to every one, as the taking away tithes. But I have said enough at once, and when this is a little digested, the other will be more fit to be proposed.

Only to such as fear confusion, or trouble, or loss to the nation, by taking away tithes, I would say a few words: Do but look into almost every country town, and there shall you find debate, strife, and variance, either between man and man, or between parishes and their ministers, either about tithe itself, the quantity, or the setting it out; look into courts, and there you shall find suit upon suit; and at assizes and before justices of peace, multitudes of trials and judgments about them: Look into prisons, and there you shall find not a few restrained, and lying under great oppressions, because they cannot pay them: And these suits and troubles are daily increasing, and these are no small confusions in our state: for it is evident, there are more differences about tithes, than any one thing whatsoever in the nation; and how soon might all these be ended, and every one satisfied, by taking away tithes? And then do but look upon the many moors, commons, and wastes in the nation, amounting to a full third part of the whole, as hath been computed, to the many counties which are turned into pastures and meadows, because of the unreasonable payment of a clear tenth part, which in most places is half the profit; and it will be found, nothing does so much hinder the improvement of the nation, which would ease the public burdens, and would soon be of more advantage than first-fruits and tenths. Nothing so much hinders tillage, and forceth us to seek bread out of other countries; whereas this nation is generally so fit for corn, that it might be as a rich granary, not only for our own supply, but the relief of our neighbours. I might say a great deal more upon this subject, but much to this purpose hath been said by others, and therefore I shall conclude. And let no man henceforth think it strange, that any should refuse to pay tithes; but rather wonder, that any will pay them.

END.

~~~~~~~~~~~~~~~~~~~~~~~~~~

Printed by E. Couchman, 10. Throgmorton Street, London.
~~~~~~~~~~~~~~~~~~~~~~~~~~

Chapter 7

A 1894 History of Tithing, Emphasizing Christian Free-Will Offerings

Here are a few quotes to give the reader the general trend of his arguments:

> I hold strongly to the view that free-will offerings are the only scriptural mode for the maintenance of the Christian ministry, and these are the same kind of offerings to which Pope Gregory referred in his answers to Augustine's questions.
> ...
> THE first law making the payment of tithes legally imperative was enacted in 779 by Charles, King of France, in a general assembly of his estates, spiritual and temporal, viz., "Concerning tithes, it is ordained that every man give his tithe, and that they be distributed by the bishop's command." ...[1]
>
> Charles's civil law had only enforced by coercion the existing ecclesiastical law or custom of payment of tithes; and the ecclesiastical law was founded upon the Levitical law; but I hold that the Levitical law, as regards tithes, was not binding on Christians. In the New Testament there is no reference whatever to tithes to be given to the Christian priesthood. None of the apostles claimed tithes from their followers.

What follows are most of two chapters from the Clarke book:

CHAPTER II.

FROM THE CHRISTIAN ERA TO THE COUNCIL OF MASÇON

IN Apostolical times the Christian ministers were supported by voluntary contributions out of a common fund, and this practice prevailed for four hundred years.[1] Those who preached the Gospel lived by the Gospel, but this Scriptural statement did not mean, as some assert, that they were to live on the payment of tithes, otherwise it would have been stated. St. Paul ordered weekly collections to be made for the saints in the Churches of Galatia and Corinth (1 Cor. xvi. 1, 2). The voluntary contributions of the faithful were collected and put into a common treasure (Acts ii. 44; iv. 34). The liberality of the Christians then far exceeded anything which could have been collected from tithes. And even if tithes had been exacted, it is exceedingly doubtful whether the progress of Christianity would not have been materially checked at its outset.

The Jewish Law, as regards the payment of tithes, was not binding on Christians, no more than the custom of bigamy and polygamy adopted by the Israelites is binding on the Christian Church. There is no injunction in the New Testament binding Christians to pay tithes to their ministers. And when the payment was first urged in the Christian Church, it was supported by references to the Mosaic Law and not to St. Paul's words, viz., " That those who preach the Gospel should live of the Gospel."

[1] Van Espen, "jus Univ. Canon," pars. ii. sec. 4. [page 5]

There was a growing habit of looking upon the clergy as the successors and representatives of the Levites under the Old Law, and this habit had given an impulse to that claim which they set up to the payment of tithes by the laity.[1]

The Apostolical Constitutions for the Christian Church, collected, as it is alleged, by Pope Clement I., the successor as is said of St. Peter, first bishop of Rome, were fabricated more than eight centuries after apostolical times. Cardinal Bellarmine is honest enough to ignore them. But they imposed on the credulous and were accepted without criticism as genuine, even by canonists, in the tenth and eleventh centuries. Selden thinks they were concocted about A.D. 1000; others think in 1042. In these Constitutions tithes are stated to have been paid by the Christians to the Apostles. Sir H. Spelman (p. 108) thinks the first thirty-five canons are very ancient. "Dionysius Exiguus," he says, "who lived within 400 years after the Apostles, translated them out of Greek."

The fifth canon ordained that first fruits and tithes should be sent to the house of the bishops and priests, and not to be offered upon the altar. The Greek word in the copy is not [SeKacr/xovs]. No solid argument for the payment of tithes can be founded on this canon, for if we take the custom of the Anglo-Saxon Churches at the end of the sixth century, which was in accordance with that in primitive times, we find no account for the payment of tithes. "There is no mention of tithes," says Lord Selborne, "in any part of the ancient canon law of the Roman Church, collected towards the end of the fifth century by Dionysius (called Exiguus or the Little), a Scythian monk who collected 401 Oriental and African canons."[2]

[1] See Kemble's "Anglo-Saxons," New Ed.: 1876, vol. ii. 473.
[2] "Facts and Fictions," pp. 9, 47. [page 6]

The monks in their cells had sufficient leisure to concoct these Constitutions, and palm them on the credulous as the genuine production of the Apostles. The concocted Constitutions were copied and handed down from century to century without any attempt being made to test their genuineness and authenticity. It seems exceedingly strange that African divines and laymen should refer to the Apostolical Constitutions as an authority for the payment of tithes in apostolic times, although Cardinal Bellarmine, a great champion of "Holy Church," ignored them.[1]

Churchmen like Archdeacon Tillesley, many of whom are in the receipt of tithes or tithe-rent charges, will naturally act like drowning men, and snatch even at passing straws to save the tithes. Could anything, for example, be more childish and absurd than the story of tracing the payment of tithes to Adam? And what makes the case worse is to distort Scripture so as to deceive the people who could neither read nor write, and even those who could read had no open Bible to consult to see for themselves whether these things were so.

Members of the Anglican Church forget when using such weapons as the "Constitutions" in support of tithes, that the very cause of the English Reformation in the sixteenth century was the adoption into the English Church of the traditions and errors of the Church of Rome, which were said to have been handed down by the Apostles in the so-called Apostolical Constitutions, although many of them can be shown to be contrary to the Scriptures. Archdeacon Tillesley does not defend the whole volume of the socalled Constitutions of Clement I., but he does that part which deals with the payment of tithes. He evidently had forgotten the mechanical axiom, that nothing is stronger than its weakest part.

[1] See the Animadversions on Selden's "History of Tithes," in 1621, by Dr. R. Tillesley, Archdeacon of Rochester. [page 7]

"Because the early Christians," he says, "were liberal to the Church, therefore it was reasonable that tithes in the 'Constitutional Apostolical' were true." Nothing of the sort, because it does not follow as a logical sequence.

After apostolical times, monthly offerings and oblations, we are informed, were made in all the churches, and were used for three purposes, (1) In maintaining the clergy; (2) in supporting the sick and needy; and (3) in repairing the church fabric. These monthly contributions were in the third century augmented by grants of lands, which were annexed to churches, the revenues derived from which were appropriated to the same three purposes. In A.D. 322 Constantine, the first Christian emperor, published an edict which gave full liberty to his subjects to bestow as large a proportion of their property to the clergy as they should think proper. From all these sources of revenue the Christian Church was rapidly increasing in wealth. But for more than four hundred years after the Christian era there was no authoritative Church canon made for the payment of tithes; and then such canon was founded upon the Mosaic Law. The question then is, are Christians justified in adopting the Mosaic Law for the payment of tithes? This law had no force outside Jewish territory. There is no order in the New Testament for their payment. Among the Jews we fail to find such anomalies, rather scandals and misappropriations, in respect to the distribution of tithes, as are found in England and Wales. The gross amount of tithe-rent charge is slightly over four millions per annum. Add to this the extraordinary rent charges on hops, the corn rents and extensive lands awarded in lieu of tithes by the large number of Inclosure Acts. Among the Jews we find no record of lay impropriators, schools, colleges, charities and hospitals receiving tithes. Granted, for argument's sake, that the Christian priesthood [page 8] as succeeding the Mosaic priesthood, claimed the tithes according to the Mosaic Law, then it is a misappropriation of tithes to give them to those outside the priesthood, and who perform no spiritual functions. We must therefore go back to very early times, to the history of tithes in the Christian Church, for the beginning of the scandalous misappropriations of tithe endowment for spiritual purposes. In England the scandal commenced after the Norman Conquest with the Norman monks who were in English monasteries.

About one-fourth of the whole tithe rent charge is appropriated or rather misappropriated to lay purposes by laymen, many of whom are quite unconnected with the religious duties of those parishes from which the tithes arise. Then, again, we have a large extent of land -- formerly monastic -- which is tithe free. There are also lands in the vicinity of large cities and towns built upon, for which the landlords receive enormous ground rents, and when the leases expire they take possession of the house property. But they pay nothing to the Church for the increased value of their land, which may be one hundred times the yearly value per acre before it was built upon.

In the Christian Church tithes were *at first* given by the faithful as spontaneous offerings, at the urgent solicitations of the clergy. "Nam nemo compellitur," says Tertullian, "sed sponte confert." These spontaneous tithe free-will offerings were not given in cash but in kind. Some gave a tithe of sheep, others of wool, or of corn, etc., just according to the free-will of the donor. This was the germ of tithes in the Christian Church, which commenced in the fourth century, and were ordered to be paid by canon law about the beginning of the fifth century. These canons were framed and passed by ecclesiastics. The people who paid had no voice in the matter. The canons which were framed [page 9] afterwards had ordered them to be paid as a right, as a divine law of the Old Testament, and were not to be considered as free-will offerings. Here is just that specimen of arbitrary conduct on the part of the ecclesiastics which would only be tolerated in the dark and middle ages. Tithes were too profitable a source of revenue to be ignored in the Christian Church. A book entitled, "The Englishman's Brief on behalf of his National Church," has been published by the Society for the Promotion of Christian Knowledge. A good cause needs no fiction to bolster it up. In that book there is quite twice as much fiction as fact. The extensive circulation of this mixture has embarrassed many in gaining a correct knowledge of the tithe question from the earliest period to the present time. It is written in the style adopted by special pleaders. It gives a one-sided account of the subject. It asks questions and then furnishes the answers. The answers are most misleading and also erroneous, and it carefully omits a great deal which could be said on the other side. I strongly object to this way in dealing with so important a subject as the history of tithes in this country. To be appreciated, the "Brief" should be impartial, which it is not. It is not my object to review the book here *seriatim*, and to point out what is fiction and what is fact. In my statements a good deal of the fiction is refuted indirectly without reference to the "Brief." But I may just indicate one remarkable feat of fiction which appears in it. When the Christian religion was first propagated, the writer of the "Brief" would have us to believe that the converted Jews transferred the payment of their tithes from the Jewish to the Christian ministers, just as easily and as quietly as one could transfer the payment of a cheque from one bank to another. Here is the statement, "So that when the Jews and heathen became Christian, throwing off their old religion and adopting the new religion of Christianity, [page 10] they never dreamt of being less liberal to that form of religion which they loved the more and had adopted, than they had been towards that which they had loved the less and had discarded. Hence the transfer of tithes from the old religion to the new religion."[1] We are not informed upon what authority this statement is made. There is nothing about it in Josephus. There is no order in the New Testament for the payment of tithes. No order of a general or provincial council. We read nothing of this in the writings of the first and second centuries. We read of exhortations to pay tithes in the writings of the third and fourth centuries. We read of canons having been made for their payment in the fifth century. But I have failed to find any evidence to support the statement quoted above from the "Brief."

The Provincial Council of French bishops, held at Masçon in A.D. 586, is commonly considered to have been *the earliest council* which ordained the payment of tithes. It ordained, "Ut decimas ecclesiasticas omnis populus inferat, quibus sacerdotes aut in pauperum usum, aut in captivorum redemptionem erogatis, suis orationibus pacem populo ac salutem impetrent." {Google Tranlate's approximation of the meaning: "To impose a tenth of all the people of the church, in which priests or in poor use or redemption of prisoners extend their prayers for peace and safety of the people to be effective."} Isidore, in his compilation of decrees of councils, makes no reference to this council. Friar Crab is the first to have mentioned it in his edition of the councils under Charles V.

Lord Selborne considers the canon of this council as spurious, because it proves too much, for it wanted to prove that the Mosaic Law, as regards the payments of tithes, was regarded in A.D. 586 not only as binding from the first upon Christians, but also as having been for centuries universally observed. This was going too far, in his lordship's opinion, and therefore he stamped it as spurious. Selden was the first to throw considerable doubt

[1] Page 34. [page 11]

upon the genuineness of this canon at the Council at Masçgon.[1] The mistake originated in calling the offerings and oblations tithes. The same mistake is repeated by writers at the present time. For instance, Dr. J. S. Brewer, in his "Endowments and Establishment of the Church of England," 2nd Edition, 1885, translates "portiones" (quoted from Bede), *tithes*. Pope Gregory says in his reply to Archbishop Augustine's question, "Communi autem vita viventibus jam de faciendis *portionibus*, vel exhibenda hospitalite et adimplenda misericordia, nobis quid erit loquendum." "But as for those who live in common, why should we say anything now of making *portions*?" etc. Brewer translates the passage thus, "As for those who are living in common, I need give no advice about dividing *tithes,*" etc. Now, the Latin word for tithe is decima, and is so used in all the monastic charters. The same writer states, and he is followed by writers of leaflets for the Church Defence Institution, that the scriptural precept, "To live of the Gospel" (1 Cor. ix. 14), refers to the payment of tithes. I am certain that St. Paul never intended anything of the sort. I fully admit that the passage may cover a tithe free-will offering, as it would any other free-will offering, but I cannot admit that it implies a compulsory payment of tithes, that is, to carry it to its logical sequence, a distraint on the goods of a person who is unable or unwilling to pay tithe. Such compulsion would be contrary to the spirit of the Gospel of Christ.

I hold strongly to the view that free-will offerings are the only scriptural mode for the maintenance of the Christian ministry, and these are the same kind of offerings to which Pope Gregory referred in his answers to Augustine's questions.

The instances are many in which words of old authors and passages of Scripture are not only strained but intentionally dis- [page 12]

[1] "Ancient Facts and Fictions," Edition 1888, pp. 47, 48. Selden, p. 58.

torted, in order to show the early origin of tithes. There is nothing gained, but much confidence lost, in this critical age by distorting the meaning of, or giving a forced interpretation to, plain words of Scripture, or of secular and religious writers.

The Christian religion had been introduced into Britain at a very early date, and from Britain it passed over to Ireland. Ireland was specially remarkable for her evangelical missionary monks, who visited Scotland, England, and the Continent, for the purpose of converting the heathen. Its geographical position favoured a quiet, retired and contemplative life. Britain served as a *buffer* for many centuries against the piratical devastations of the northern hordes. The inhabitants of Ireland were therefore left in quiet and undisturbed possession of their lands, churches, and monasteries at a time when the inhabitants of Britain were driven from the east and south to the west of the island; their lands were taken from them, their churches and monasteries were pillaged, and then burnt down by the invaders.

...

CHAPTER VI.

THE FIRST PUBLIC LAY LAW FOR THE PAYMENT OF TITHES.

THE first law making the payment of tithes legally imperative was enacted in 779 by Charles, King of France, in a general assembly of his estates, spiritual and temporal, viz., "Concerning tithes, it is ordained that every man give his tithe, and that they be distributed by the bishop's command." [De decimis, ut unusquisque suam decimam donet, atque per jussionem pontificis dispensentur.][1]

Charles's civil law had only enforced by coercion the existing ecclesiastical law or custom of payment of tithes; and the ecclesiastical law was founded upon the Levitical law; but I hold that the Levitical law, as regards tithes, was not binding on Christians. In the New Testament there is no reference whatever to tithes to be given to the Christian priesthood. None of the apostles claimed tithes from their followers.

"The growing habit," says Kemble, "of looking upon the clergy as the successors and representatives of the Levites under the old law may very likely have given the impulse to that claim which they set up to the payment of tithes by the laity."[2]

The establishment of the right in England followed the same course as that in France.

[1] Baluze, i. 141, 142; Selden, c. vi. s. 7.
[2] "The Saxons in England," ii. 473. [page 34]

It is important to give Milman's observations on the working of the above law.

"On the whole body," he says, "of the clergy, Charlemagne bestowed the legal claim to tithes. Already, under the Merovingians, the clergy had given significant hints that the law of Leviticus was the perpetual law of God. Pepin had commanded the payment of tithes for the celebration of peculiar litanies during a period of famine. Charlemagne made it a law of the empire; he enacted it in its most strict and comprehensive form as *investing the clergy in a right to the tenth of the substance and of the labour alike of freemen and serf."*

"The collection of tithes was regulated by compulsory statutes; the clergy took note of all who paid or refused to pay; four or eight, or more, jurymen were summoned from each parish as witnesses for the claims disputed; the contumacious were three times summoned; if still obstinate, they were excluded from the Church; if they still refused to pay, they were fined over and above the whole tithe, six solidi; if further contumacious, the recusant's house was shut up; if he attempted to enter it, he was cast into prison to await the judgment of the next plea of the Crown. The tithe was due on all produce, even on animals. The tithe was usually divided into three portions, one for the maintenance of the Church, the second for the poor, the third for the clergy; the bishop sometimes claimed a fourth. He was the arbiter of the distribution; he assigned the necessary portion for the Church, and appointed that of the clergy. This tithe was by no means a spontaneous votive offering of the whole Christian people. *It was a tax imposed by imperial authority and enforced by imperial power.* It had caused one, if not more than one, sanguinary insurrection among the Saxons. It was submitted to in other parts of the empire, not without strong reluctance. Even [page 35] Alcuin ventured to suggest that if the apostles of Christ had demanded tithes, they would not have been so successful in the propagation of the Gospel."[1]

[1] Milman, ii. 292, etc.

Chapter Notes

1. Publication details:
A History of Tithes, by The Rev. Henry William Clarke, B.A., Second Edition, London, Swan Sonnenschein & Co; A History of Tithes, 2nd ed., (1894) by Henry William Clarke, New York: Charles Scribner's Sons 1894

2. Related history:
Alcuin of York (/ˈælkwɪn/;[1] Latin: Flaccus Albinus Alcuinus; c. 735 – 19 May 804 AD) – also called Ealhwine, Alhwin or Alchoin – was an English scholar, clergyman, poet and teacher from York, Northumbria. He was born around 735 and became the

student of Archbishop Ecgbert at York. At the invitation of Charlemagne, he became a leading scholar and teacher at the Carolingian court, where he remained a figure in the 780s and '90s. During this period he invented Carolingian minuscule, an easily read manuscript hand using a mixture of upper and lower case letters.[2]
Alcuin wrote many theological and dogmatic treatises, as well as a few grammatical works and a number of poems. He was made Abbot of Tours in 796, where he remained until his death. "The most learned man anywhere to be found", according to Einhard's Life of Charlemagne[3] (ca. 817-833), he is considered among the most important architects of the Carolingian Renaissance. Among his pupils were many of the dominant intellectuals of the Carolingian era. https://en.wikipedia.org/wiki/Alcuin

Charlemagne (English: /ˈʃɑːrləmeɪn, ˌʃɑːrləˈmeɪn/; French: [ʃaʁləmaɲ])[3] or Charles the Great[a] (2 April 748[4][b] – 28 January 814), numbered Charles I, was King of the Franks from 768, King of the Lombards from 774, and Emperor of the Romans from 800. During the Early Middle Ages, he united the majority of western and central Europe. He was the first recognized emperor to rule from western Europe since the fall of the Western Roman Empire three centuries earlier.[5] The expanded Frankish state that Charlemagne founded is called the Carolingian Empire. He was later canonized by Antipope Paschal III. https://en.wikipedia.org/wiki/Charlemagne

3. All things common

The Rev. Henry William Clarke has supplied some good information in his book, but the very fact that he has the title Reverend in front of his name, makes me a little bit suspicious when it comes to items of speculation. He might have a tendency to favor the church receiving tithing money if he can do so without directly contradicting known history. Quoting from the first paragraph of Clarke's second chapter:

> St. Paul ordered weekly collections to be made for the saints in the Churches of Galatia and Corinth (1 Cor. xvi. 1, 2). The voluntary contributions of the faithful were collected and put into a common treasure (Acts ii. 44; iv. 34). The liberality of the Christians then far exceeded anything which could have been collected from tithes. And even if tithes had been exacted, it is exceedingly doubtful whether the progress of Christianity would not have been materially checked at its outset.

He references 1 Cor 16:1-3:

> 1 Cor. 16:1 Now concerning the collection for the saints, as I have given order to the churches of Galatia, even so do ye.
> 2 Upon the first day of the week let every one of you lay by him in store, as God hath prospered him, that there be no gatherings when I come.
> 3 And when I come, whomsoever ye shall approve by your letters, them will I send to bring your liberality unto Jerusalem.
> 4 And if it be meet that I go also, they shall go with me.

I don't have any specific history on that exact point, but I read those verses differently than he does. I read those verses as being part of an effort to send charity supplies to Jerusalem where presumably they are in need of assistance. This sounds like a one-time charitable event, having nothing to do with any required on-going communal behavior. He also cites Acts 2:44, 4:34:

> Acts 2:44 And all that believed were together, and had all things common;
> ...
> Acts 4:32 And the multitude of them that believed were of one heart and of one soul: neither said any of them that bought of the things which he possessed was his own; but they had all things common.
> 33 And with great power gave the apostles witness of the resurrection of the Lord Jesus: and great grace was upon them all.
> 34 Neither was there any among them that lacked: for as many as were possessors of lands or houses sold them, and brought the prices of the things that were sold,
> 35 And laid them down at the apostles' feet: and distribution was made unto every man according as he had need.

There is some embedded New Testament history that can help us reach a different interpretation of these words and events. I have previously researched this issue, and here is what I found:

> Acts 8:1 tells us that because of persecution, all the saints except the apostles left Jerusalem shortly after the death and resurrection of Christ. First, they fled to other Judean and Samarian cities, and then on to Cyprus, Antioch, Damascus, and Alexandria. This had essentially been accomplished before the conversion of Saul. The Bible chronology tells us that Saul's conversion occurred in 35 A.D. If we use the date of 33 A.D. as the year of the death and resurrection of Christ, then the large growth spurt of the Church and the exodus from Jerusalem all took place within two years. The Ananias and Sapphira episode occurred somewhere during that time, probably near the beginning of the two-year period. [Notice that Joseph Smith provides a very different interpretation of the Ananias and Sapphira episode, which will be explained in detail later.]
>
> The persecutions would mean that people would have to flee their homes and lands to avoid imprisonment or death. Selling those possessions where possible would be the most sensible thing to do. ["Use them or lose them."] The money received could be used to help finance a trip to a new location and the establishment of a new home and occupation. Part of those funds could go to assist those who had no means, perhaps because their belongings had been confiscated or destroyed. Brigham Young's United Order, p.108.

I will provide other fascinating evidence later on, but I see no reason to imply some rigorous set of rules, a return to the law of Moses and an ending of the maximum religious freedom of the New Testament, simply because the term "all things common" appears in the text. That term can be true if everything is done on a totally free-will basis. It does not need to imply some administrative overlay to reach a certain predetermined result.

Clarke also speaks of

> The liberality of the Christians then far exceeded anything which could have been collected from tithes. And even if tithes had been exacted, it is exceedingly doubtful whether the progress of Christianity would not have been materially checked at its outset.

I disagree with both of his speculations here I don't know how he could possibly know that the Christians' liberality greatly exceeded 10%. I don't know of any appropriate individual accounting records from that time period that have survived. And I happen to believe that requiring tithing would have damaged the infant church a great deal. Just making that a formal requirement would be a direct return to the law of Moses, adding the temptation of a self-seeking paid ministry, etc., etc., greatly accelerating the almost inevitable apostasy.

Chapter 8

The Historie of Tithes (1618) by John Seldon
– The predecessor to all later positions on tithing

The 1618 book by John Selden *The Historie of Tithes* (491 numbered pages, 47 unnumbered pages) was important for many reasons. It caused some political uproar because of its attack on tithing and all those who received that tithing. Apparently, Selden's approach to history was also different enough to change the general approach to historical research by other researchers. The book is important to us today because it was an early and very thorough treatment of all of the historical and practical foolishness that had been added to the original topic of tithing. Selden made it clear that there was no religious or historical basis for the laws concerning tithing at his time. The later book by Rev. Henry William Clarke relies heavily on the Selden book and quotes from it. Conveniently, the Clarke book was published much later and so is much more readable for modern readers.

Rather than attempt the enormous task of fully translating the Selden work into modern English, including translating Latin and Greek as well as middle English words, I'm just going to present a small segment from his book which makes clear his disgust for the possible outcomes of having corrupt priests receiving the tithes that should go to the poor, and his support for the idea of "arbitrary consecrations" which was his term for free-will offerings presented without any coercion from church or government. Selden is quoting John Wycliffe and is in turn quoted by Clarke:

> [page 290]
> ...
> For notwithstanding all those Ordinances, both Secular and Synodal, anciently here made for due payment, it is clear, that in the time before about that [Pope] *Innocent* [the third], it was not only usual, in fact, for Laymen to convey the right of their Tithes, as Rents-charge, or the like, to what Church or Monastery they made choice of, but by the course and practice of the Law also of that time (both Common and Canon, as it was here in use) such conveyances were clearly good, and what was through them so acquired, was continually, and is to this day (except some particulars, which either the Popes authority of later time, or new Compositions or Grants, or the like, have altered) enjoyed by the Churches, that, yet remaining, had portions so anciently given them, or

by the King or his Grantees of impropriated Tithes; very many of which, had their chief original from those arbitrary Consecrations
[page 291]
(which you may well call Appropriations of Tithes) and not from the appropriating only of Parish Churches, as some out of gross ignorance, with too much confidence, deliver. But thereof you may see more in the examples of the next Chapter. where, for most apparent proof of the practice of arbitrary Consecrations [free-will offerings, sometimes called tithing] in those times, Moniments [records, references] enough are collected. This arbitrary disposition, used by the Laity as well de jure (as the Positive Law, then received and practiced, was) as *de facto*, is that which *Wicclef* [see note below] remembered in his complaint to the King and Parliament under *Richard* the second. His words are: *A Lord God, where this be reason, to constrain the poor people to find a worldly Priest, sometime unable both of life and cunning, in pomp and pride, covetous and envy, gluttony, drunkenness and lechery, in simony [see note below] and heresy, with fat Horse, and jolly and gay Saddles and Bridles, ringing by the way, and himself in costly Clothes and Pelure [French: literally skin, perhaps meaning adornments, appearance], and to suffer their wives and children, and their poor neighbors, perish for hunger, thirst, and cold, and other mischiefs of the world. A Lord Jesu Christ, sith [since] within few years, men payed their Tithes and Offerings at their own will free to good men, and able to great worship of God, to profit and fairness of holy Church fighting in earth Where it were lawful and needful, that a worldly Priest should destroy this holy and approved custom, constraining men to*
[page 292]
leave this freedom, turning Tithes and Offerings into wicked uses. But what he calls a few years, will fall out to be about CC. [200] for he wrote about the year M.CCC.XC. [1390] With him well agrees some passages in our Year-books of the times before him. [Latin quotations]
...
some later Books tells us, that from the Council of *Lateran* [1215 in Rome] the first alteration of that course of arbitrary disposition came. But plainly, no Council of *Lateran* hath any Canon that altered the Law in it, except that under *Alexander* the third, before spoken of in the end of the sixth Chapter, may have place here: which, indeed, the Canonists will not endure, unless you restrain it only to ancient Feudal Tithes. And they suppose, every man might have arbitrarily conveyed, before that Council, his Feudal Tithes to what Church he would.

The terms "arbitrary consecrations" or "arbitrary conveyances" also appear at pages 362, 365, 395, 400, 468, and 491 in the book and are further discussed.

Chapter Notes

1. John Wycliffe (/ˈwɪklɪf/; also spelled Wyclif, Wycliff, Wiclef, Wicliffe, Wickliffe; c. 1320s – 31 December 1384),[2] was an English scholastic philosopher, theologian, Biblical translator, reformer, priest, and a seminary professor at the University of Oxford. He became an influential dissident within the Roman Catholic priesthood during the 14th century and is considered an important predecessor to Protestantism.

Wycliffe attacked the privileged status of the clergy, which had bolstered their powerful role in England. He then attacked the luxury and pomp of local parishes and their ceremonies.

Wycliffe also advocated translation of the Bible into the vernacular. In 1382 he completed a translation directly from the Vulgate into Middle English – a version now known as Wycliffe's Bible. It is probable that he personally translated the Gospels of Matthew, Mark, Luke, and John; and it is possible he translated the entire New Testament, while his associates translated the Old Testament. Wycliffe's Bible appears to have been completed by 1384, additional updated versions being done by Wycliffe's assistant John Purvey and others in 1388 and 1395.

Wycliffe's followers, known as Lollards, followed his lead in advocating predestination, iconoclasm, and the notion of caesaropapism, while attacking the veneration of saints, the sacraments, requiem masses, transubstantiation, monasticism, and the very existence of the Papacy.

In the 16th century and beyond, the Lollard movement was sometimes regarded as the precursor to the Protestant Reformation. Wycliffe was accordingly characterised as the evening star of scholasticism and as the morning star of the English Reformation. Wycliffe's writings in Latin greatly influenced the philosophy and teaching of the Czech reformer Jan Hus (c. 1369–1415), whose execution in 1415 sparked a revolt and led to the Hussite Wars of 1419–1434.
https://en.wikipedia.org/wiki/John_Wycliffe

2. sith -- archaic variant of SINCE
https://www.merriam-webster.com/dictionary/sith

3. pelure f (plural pelures), Noun: 1. peel, rind (of a fruit), 2. skin (of an onion)
https://en.wiktionary.org/wiki/pelure

4. simony
the buying or selling of ecclesiastical privileges, for example pardons or benefices.
https://www.lexico.com/en/definition/simony

5. What is the sin of simony?
Simony, buying or selling of something spiritual or closely connected with the spiritual. More widely, it is any contract of this kind forbidden by divine or ecclesiastical law.

The name is taken from Simon Magus (Acts 8:18), who endeavoured to buy from the Apostles the power of conferring the gifts of the Holy Spirit. https://www.britannica.com/topic/simony

Simony /ˈsɪməni/ is the act of selling church offices and roles. It is named after Simon Magus,[1] who is described in the Acts of the Apostles as having offered two disciples of Jesus payment in exchange for their empowering him to impart the power of the Holy Spirit to anyone on whom he would place his hands. The term extends to other forms of trafficking for money in "spiritual things."[2][3]

The appointment of ecclesiastical officials, such as bishops and abbots, by a secular authority came to be considered simoniacal and this became a key issue during the Investiture Controversy. https://en.wikipedia.org/wiki/Simony

6. Because the Selden book is difficult to read in its entirety for a modern person, perhaps, for our purposes, some of the most interesting aspects of his book are the way his book was treated by others at his time. In this public argument started by John Selden, it should not be difficult for each of us to decide which side of that argument we would like to be on.

Histories of Tithes: Religious Controversy and Changing Methodologies

by Madeline McMahon
February 18, 2015 Intellectual history / Think pieces

In December 1618, the talented scholar John Selden was called before King James to answer for the publication of his *Historie of tithes* (London: William Stansby, 1618). Selden's work on tithes (literally, the "tenth" of all goods due to the church) had instantly incited controversy. Selden was made to apologize to the High Commission of bishops and forbidden to respond to the royally commissioned attacks against his book (G. J. Toomer, "Selden's 'Historie of Tithes': Genesis, Publication, Aftermath"). Reflecting back on this moment several decades later in his *Vindiciae*, Selden recalled that

> *Although it had been licensed…by the signature of one of the priestly tribe, yet once it had been printed, it offended very many of them, and also all the bishops then about the court, with the exception of the then Bishop of Winchester, that most learned and peerless Lancelot Andrewes, who was quite pleased by it as being in agreement with the most accepted practices amongst us…Hence those fierce hornets [i.e. bishops at court]…incited the mind of the king… (Selden, Vindiciae, 16 –*

17. English translation from G. J. Toomer, "Selden's 'Historie of Tithes': Genesis, Publication, Aftermath" 361-2.]

Selden's account reveals the influence of what Kenneth Fincham called "court prelates"—the bishops who made their home at King James's court. It also raises questions. Why did Selden's already licensed book offend? And why, alone of all the court prelates, was Lancelot Andrewes instead "quite pleased" by the *Historie of tithes*?

Under James, the status and collection of tithes had not improved since the reformation reallocated church property to the state and prominent private citizens: as support for parish clergy, tithes were inadequate, unreliable, and often went to leading laymen anyway. In the later years under Elizabeth, clergy began to argue what had been "politically unacceptable" following the reformation: that tithes were due *jure divino*—by divine right (E. A. Bershadsky, "Politics, Erudition and Ecclesiology: John Selden's 'Historie of Tithes' and its contexts and ramifications", 4; Toomer, *John Selden: A Life in Scholarship*, 257-8).

Andrewes was one of the first to make this argument in his dissertation for his Doctorate of Divinity at Cambridge in 1590, when he was thirty-five years old. Like many writing a dissertation, he claimed (justifiably in his case) that his argument was new: "nor is there any by whose candle I shall light mine" (*Of the Right of Tithes. A Divinity Determination*... (London: Andrew Hebb, 1647), 5). This "avant-garde defence of clerical tithes" which "ran counter to advanced protestant opinion" was a risk that paid off: Andrewes was immediately made chaplain to both the Archbishop of Canterbury and the Queen (Peter McCullough, *Lancelot Andrewes: Selected Sermons and Lectures*, lviii; McCullough, ODNB). Andrewes was one of the first of a movement that pushed back against the earlier Protestant reformers, especially the Calvinism prominent in the Church of England (see Peter Lake's essay in *The Mental World of the Jacobean Court*). It was true, he admitted, that before the reformation "the desire to increase the Revenue of the *Clergy* proceeded to such a height, that it was greatly to be feared, lest the *Church* should swallow up the *Common-wealth*" (*Right of Tithes*, 3). The reformers had addressed this and other abuses, but Andrewes wished they had "taken care not only of *increasing the light*, but also of *allowing oil*"—providing means for the church they had reformed (*Right of Tithes*, 5). Andrewes sought to defend tithes from abrogation by proving that they were "provided for by the *Sacred Law*" (*jure divino*) by "*God*, the *Lawyer himself*" (5).

Andrewes drew on a range of evidence. He turned to two passages of scripture as the cruxes of his argument: Abraham giving tithes to the priest Melchizedek in Genesis 14:20 and, ironically, Jesus's critique of tithes in Matthew 23:23. Melchizedek blessed Abraham and Abraham in return gave a tenth of his goods (*Right of Tithes*, 6). This, for Andrewes, was the moment that established tithes by sacred law, as the return due to the priesthood for its services.

Andrewes went on to prove that tithes had been considered due *jure divino* throughout history—and not just in the Jewish and Christian religions. Greco-Roman religions mandated tithes as well, which meant that not only sacred but also natural law required such payments (24). He pointed out tithes' protection by canon and civil law, including English common law (13) and cited different church fathers to illustrate the ubiquity of tithes across the early Christian world. He also argued from "Reason" that clergymen's dependence on the fruits of the earth made them more sympathetic to their agrarian parishioners—tithes made for a better community (22). At the end, though, Andrewes returned to "the example of *Melchisedek*, who surpasseth the antiquity and faith of all *Histories*" (26).

Under James, it became *de rigueur* to argue that tithes were owed according to sacred law. Andrewes' once subversive argument had become the norm. While Selden did not write against tithes, his approach and rationale was opposite to Andrewes', despite the fact that he touched on similar topics and even structured his book in much the same way. For Selden, the Jewish practice of tithes was neither continuous nor relevant to that of the Christian church. Besides, Selden pointed out with philological and historical bravado, technically Abraham had paid Melchizedek spoils of war (*The Historie of Tithes*, 1-3). The early church was supported by charity rather than legal requirement. Only in the late medieval church were tithes enforced.

In his defense to the king, Selden wrote that he had "resolved wholly to leave the point of divine right of tythes, and keep myself wholly to the historical part" ("Of my Purpose and End in writing the History of Tythes", quoted in Toomer, *John Selden*, 259). The title of his work—the *Historie*, rather than *Right* of tithes—signaled Selden's real departure from previous approaches. Perhaps Andrewes saw something of his own in Selden's work: another subversive and innovative treatment of tithes. Both Andrewes' and Selden's works were coopted several decades later when the case for an established church itself was at stake. Andrewes' dissertation was translated and published in 1647, while Selden noted in the 1650s that clergymen then sought

> *where they might find the best argument for their tithes, setting aside the* jus divinum*; they were advised to my History of Tithes, a book so much cried down by them formerly (in which, I dare boldly say, there are more arguments for them than are extant together anywhere)… (Selden,* Table Talk, *quoted in Toomer, "Selden's 'Historie of Tithes'," 374-5)*

https://jhiblog.org/2015/02/18/histories-of-tithes-religious-controversy-and-changing-methodologies/

Sub-Notes to note 6:

Note 6-1
The author McMahon notes that Andrewes cites Matthew 23:23 as proof of the eternal validity of tithing:

> **23** Woe unto you, scribes and Pharisees, hypocrites! for ye pay tithe of mint and anise and cummin, and have omitted the weightier *matters* of the law, judgment, mercy, and faith: these ought ye to have done, and not to leave the other undone.

Presumably the argument made by Andrewes was that the phrase "and not to leave the other undone" is a command to live the law of tithing for all time. However, that seems like a silly argument, since one of the great purposes of Christ's life and ministry was to end the law of Moses, including its very intrusive and burdensome law of tithing. Obviously, one must argue that Christ did not end the law of Moses in order to make this argument that tithing remained in effect after Christ.

Note 6-2
Presumably, one of the "royally commissioned attacks against his book" was the "Animadversions on Selden's "History of Tithes," in 1621, by Dr. R. Tillesley, Archdeacon of Rochester." as cited in A History of *Tithes*, 2nd ed., (1894) by Rev. Henry William Clarke.

Note 6-3
Even though he was told not to, apparently Selden did answer the *Animadversions* book with an essay of his own, but I have yet to find the text of Selden's answer. See following mention of the answer:

> These numerous attacks Selden was for the time forced to suffer in silence, for King James had told him that he would put him in prison if he or any of his friends made any answer to them. But as he insists, when he was at length able to reply to Dr. Tillesley's ' Animadversions,' he had been careful in making his submission to retract nothing. ' I was and am,' he says, ' sorry that I published it, and that I so gave occasion to others to abuse my history, by their false application of some

arguments.' A full account of the whole matter will be found in Works, vol. i. Vita Authoris, p. v-viii. See also vol. iii. pp. 1370, 1394 and 1452 ff.
Table Talk of John Selden by Samuel Harvey Reynolds, Oxford Press. 1892, p.180

Chapter 9

The 95 theses of Martin Luther of 1517 apply today for the same reasons they did then, concerning the charity versus tithing issue

The last six chapters above have mostly to do with the issue of tithing. I am assuming that most people would not associate the 95 Theses of Martin Luther with the general subject of tithing, but my goal here is to point out how much Martin Luther's 95 Theses and the above six chapters are speaking to the same issues, and therefore the 95 Theses document is a relevant addition to this book which is largely about tithing.

As I read the 95 Theses, Martin Luther is pointing out in some detail why the concept of tithing, the collection of vast amounts of money from church members using some kind of spiritual or temporal coercion to support a huge church bureaucracy and to build extravagant structures, is inconsistent with the first duty of the church which is to care for the poor and provide charitable aid as necessary. Basically, Christian charity and tithing are mutually exclusive. Resources are typically very limited, and charity should get clear preference.

I also believe there is at least a general historical link between the work of Martin Luther and the work of John Selden and Anthony Pearson in the chapters above. Martin Luther published his 95 Theses in 1517 and inadvertently helped begin the Protestant Reformation. In 1532, Henry VIII started his breakaway from the Catholic Church. John Selden published in 1618 his extensive work on documenting and criticizing the history of tithing, roughly 100 years after the 95 Theses of Martin Luther. We could say that John Selden was further protesting the holdover principle of tithing from the Catholic Church. The work on tithing of Anthony Pearson in 1657 was another push in that direction. (The official collection of tithing by the Catholic Church might be counted from either 800 years after Christ, under the rule of Charlemagne, or 1215 A.D. at the direction of the Council of Lateran in Rome. Unofficially, the collection of tithing started about 300 AD.)[1]

It is worth the time to carefully read and analyze each one of the 95 Theses and consider their interactions, but I will present a few here to get things started. Most of the 95 Theses are focused on the issue of indulgences by which people pay the church to have various sins forgiven for the living and the dead.

Perhaps among the most graphic and entertaining are numbers 27 and 28:

> 27. They preach only human doctrines who say that as soon as the money clinks into the money chest, the soul flies out of purgatory.
> 28. It is certain that when money clinks in the money chest, greed and avarice can be increased; but when the church intercedes, the result is in the hands of God alone.[2]

It should not be too difficult to relate indulgences in 1517 to tithing payments in 2019. Both involve paying large amounts of money to receive salvation and ordinances which should all be free. The tithing system today is slightly more administratively complex and indirect (involving a little sleight of hand), but it is based on the same principle and reaches exactly the same result as the indulgences paid for under Pope Leo X. In both cases, the church is holding both the living and the dead hostage to church action, which action is not the legitimate activity of the church in the first place.

Here are a few more of the theses with some comments.

> 32. Those who believe that they can be certain of their salvation because they have indulgence letters will be eternally damned, together with their teachers.
> ...
> 41. Papal indulgences must be preached with caution, lest people erroneously think that they are preferable to other good works of love.
> 42. Christians are to be taught that the pope does not intend that the buying of indulgences should in any way be compared with works of mercy.
> 43. Christians are to be taught that he who gives to the poor or lends to the needy does a better deed than he who buys indulgences.
> 44. Because love grows by works of love, man thereby becomes better. Man does not, however, become better by means of indulgences but is merely freed from penalties.
> 45. Christians are to be taught that he who sees a needy man and passes him by, yet gives his money for indulgences, does not buy papal indulgences but God's wrath.
> 46. Christians are to be taught that, unless they have more than they need, they must reserve enough for their family needs and by no means squander it on indulgences.
> 47. Christians are to be taught that they buying of indulgences is a matter of free choice, not commanded.

Comments: I believe having a temple recommend today and having an indulgence letter at the time of Martin Luther are very much the same. (See thesis 32.), The way one learns to be a real Christian, and proves one is a real Christian, is by being an actual vigorous Good Samaritan, not by merely reading about other charity-minded people or getting a "purity" certificate from a church administrator at the cost of thousands of dollars. (See thesis 44.)

In my view, the above listed theses bring to mind the uncertain LDS doctrine of the "second endowment" by which supposedly one can be assured during this life of exaltation after death. (I recall reading somewhere that Wilford Woodruff, I believe, suggested that the second endowment was particularly appropriate for old men. Perhaps it was purely coincidental that old men might have the means and the motive to pay into church coffers large amounts to receive that assurance of exaltation in the afterlife. That would be serious and lucrative death-bed repentance, very like the concept of indulgences, and just as questionable. At least those old men might want to keep up their tithing subscriptions to the tune of perhaps $500,000 in a lifetime if they hoped to qualify at some point for guaranteed salvation.)[3]

One might suspect that all these "final judgment" matters will be settled by someone who has all the facts and all the wisdom -- Christ himself -- rather than by any mortal church official, not possessing the required knowledge and wisdom. I consider it bad doctrine that current church officials offer the so-called "second endowment" to selected members of the church, apparently mostly limited to stake presidents and above in the hierarchy (which practice also seems to point to a conscious intention by church leaders to create a multiclass system within the church for political and financial reasons).

Luther's mention of freedom here (see thesis 47) seems to be significant and demonstrates that he agrees that religion should not involve ANY forced contributions of any kind, perhaps especially including tithing.

> 50. Christians are to be taught that if the pope knew the exactions of the indulgence preachers, he would rather that the basilica of St. Peter were burned to ashes than built up with the skin, flesh, and bones of his sheep.

Comments: Luther here greatly gives the benefit of the doubt to the Pope. I assume that in reality, although the Pope *should* indeed greatly prefer seeing the poor being properly taken care of than to construct a grand basilica, I assume that he is part of the problem and is the source of the indulgence doctrine and the resulting neglect of the poor.

I hear that up to 1.5 million people have resigned from the LDS church since 1995 because of various disagreements they have with the church and its teachings and actions. Perhaps we can say that they are a new wave of the Protestants following the path of Martin Luther away from a church which has been corrupted in much the same way that the Catholic Church had been corrupted in the time of Martin Luther.

In the time of Martin Luther, the Catholic Church made no efforts to change its ways and readopt the ways of the original church of Christ. That may be the outcome in our presence situation, but we should at least hope that the church can be placed back on the right track.

The unrepentant Catholic Church, after attempting to use warfare to bring those protesting members back under their control, eventually tried a new technique of building more attractive churches to draw dissenting members back in. That architectural ploy is also a major technique in today's LDS church, again at the direct expense of much more valuable and charitable works. https://quizlet.com/23773065/the-reformation-flash-cards/

On the issues of charity and tithing and obsession with architecture, history has repeated itself, presumably for the reason that history always repeats itself because the motivations and inclinations of humans are always the same. Given enough time, they reach the same destinations. The tragedies may be just as bad in each case, but the later repetitions are also more farcical, since they should have knowledge of what went before.

> **The 95 Theses (1517)**
>
> Out of love for the truth and from desire to elucidate it, the Reverend Father Martin Luther, Master of Arts and Sacred Theology, and ordinary lecturer therein at Wittenberg, intends to defend the following statements and to dispute on them in that place. Therefore he asks that those who cannot be present and dispute with him orally shall do so in their absence by letter. In the name of our Lord Jesus Christ, Amen.
>
> 1. When our Lord and Master Jesus Christ said, ``Repent" (Mt 4:17), he willed the entire life of believers to be one of repentance.
> 2. This word cannot be understood as referring to the sacrament of penance, that is, confession and satisfaction, as administered by the clergy.
> 3. Yet it does not mean solely inner repentance; such inner repentance is worthless unless it produces various outward mortification of the flesh.
> 4. The penalty of sin remains as long as the hatred of self (that is, true inner repentance), namely till our entrance into the kingdom of heaven.
> 5. The pope neither desires nor is able to remit any penalties except those imposed by his own authority or that of the canons.
> 6. The pope cannot remit any guilt, except by declaring and showing that it has been remitted by God; or, to be sure, by remitting guilt in cases reserved to his judgment. If his right to grant remission in these
> cases were disregarded, the guilt would certainly remain unforgiven.
> 7. God remits guilt to no one unless at the same time he humbles him in all things and makes him submissive to the vicar, the priest.

8. The penitential canons are imposed only on the living, and, according to the canons themselves, nothing should be imposed on the dying.
9. Therefore the Holy Spirit through the pope is kind to us insofar as the pope in his decrees always makes exception of the article of death and of necessity.
10. Those priests act ignorantly and wickedly who, in the case of the dying, reserve canonical penalties for purgatory.
11. Those tares of changing the canonical penalty to the penalty of purgatory were evidently sown while the bishops slept (Mt 13:25).
12. In former times canonical penalties were imposed, not after, but before absolution, as tests of true contrition.
13. The dying are freed by death from all penalties, are already dead as far as the canon laws are concerned, and have a right to be released from them.
14. Imperfect piety or love on the part of the dying person necessarily brings with it great fear; and the smaller the love, the greater the fear.
15. This fear or horror is sufficient in itself, to say nothing of other things, to constitute the penalty of purgatory, since it is very near to the horror of despair.
16. Hell, purgatory, and heaven seem to differ the same as despair, fear, and assurance of salvation.
17. It seems as though for the souls in purgatory fear should necessarily decrease and love increase.
18. Furthermore, it does not seem proved, either by reason or by Scripture, that souls in purgatory are outside the state of merit, that is, unable to grow in love.
19. Nor does it seem proved that souls in purgatory, at least not all of them, are certain and assured of their own salvation, even if we ourselves may be entirely certain of it.
20. Therefore the pope, when he uses the words ``plenary remission of all penalties," does not actually mean ``all penalties," but only those imposed by himself.
21. Thus those indulgence preachers are in error who say that a man is absolved from every penalty and saved by papal indulgences.
22. As a matter of fact, the pope remits to souls in purgatory no penalty which, according to canon law, they should have paid in this life.
23. If remission of all penalties whatsoever could be granted to anyone at all, certainly it would be granted only to the most perfect, that is, to very few.
24. For this reason most people are necessarily deceived by that indiscriminate and high-sounding promise of release from penalty.
25. That power which the pope has in general over purgatory corresponds to the power which any bishop or curate has in a particular way in his own diocese and parish.
26. The pope does very well when he grants remission to souls in purgatory, not by the power of the keys, which he does not have, but by way of intercession for them.
27. They preach only human doctrines who say that as soon as the money clinks into the money chest, the soul flies out of purgatory.
28. It is certain that when money clinks in the money chest, greed and avarice can be increased; but when the church intercedes, the result is in the hands of God alone.
29. Who knows whether all souls in purgatory wish to be redeemed, since we have exceptions in St. Severinus and St. Paschal, as related in a legend.

30. No one is sure of the integrity of his own contrition, much less of having received plenary remission.
31. The man who actually buys indulgences is as rare as he who is really penitent; indeed, he is exceedingly rare.
32. Those who believe that they can be certain of their salvation because they have indulgence letters will be eternally damned, together with their teachers.
33. Men must especially be on guard against those who say that the pope's pardons are that inestimable gift of God by which man is reconciled to him.
34. For the graces of indulgences are concerned only with the penalties of sacramental satisfaction established by man.
35. They who teach that contrition is not necessary on the part of those who intend to buy souls out of purgatory or to buy confessional privileges preach unchristian doctrine.
36. Any truly repentant Christian has a right to full remission of penalty and guilt, even without indulgence letters.
37. Any true Christian, whether living or dead, participates in all the blessings of Christ and the church; and this is granted him by God, even without indulgence letters.
38. Nevertheless, papal remission and blessing are by no means to be disregarded, for they are, as I have said (Thesis 6), the proclamation of the divine remission.
39. It is very difficult, even for the most learned theologians, at one and the same time to commend to the people the bounty of indulgences and the need of true contrition.
40. A Christian who is truly contrite seeks and loves to pay penalties for his sins; the bounty of indulgences, however, relaxes penalties and causes men to hate them -- at least it furnishes occasion for hating them.
41. Papal indulgences must be preached with caution, lest people erroneously think that they are preferable to other good works of love.
42. Christians are to be taught that the pope does not intend that the buying of indulgences should in any way be compared with works of mercy.
43. Christians are to be taught that he who gives to the poor or lends to the needy does a better deed than he who buys indulgences.
44. Because love grows by works of love, man thereby becomes better. Man does not, however, become better by means of indulgences but is merely freed from penalties.
45. Christians are to be taught that he who sees a needy man and passes him by, yet gives his money for indulgences, does not buy papal indulgences but God's wrath.
46. Christians are to be taught that, unless they have more than they need, they must reserve enough for their family needs and by no means squander it on indulgences.
47. Christians are to be taught that they buying of indulgences is a matter of free choice, not commanded.
48. Christians are to be taught that the pope, in granting indulgences, needs and thus desires their devout prayer more than their money.

49. Christians are to be taught that papal indulgences are useful only if they do not put their trust in them, but very harmful if they lose their fear of God because of them.
50. Christians are to be taught that if the pope knew the exactions of the indulgence preachers, he would rather that the basilica of St. Peter were burned to ashes than built up with the skin, flesh, and bones of his sheep.
51. Christians are to be taught that the pope would and should wish to give of his own money, even though he had to sell the basilica of St. Peter, to many of those from whom certain hawkers of indulgences cajole money.
52. It is vain to trust in salvation by indulgence letters, even though the indulgence commissary, or even the pope, were to offer his soul as security.
53. They are the enemies of Christ and the pope who forbid altogether the preaching of the Word of God in some churches in order that indulgences may be preached in others.
54. Injury is done to the Word of God when, in the same sermon, an equal or larger amount of time is devoted to indulgences than to the Word.
55. It is certainly the pope's sentiment that if indulgences, which are a very insignificant thing, are celebrated with one bell, one procession, and one ceremony, then the gospel, which is the very greatest thing, should be preached with a hundred bells, a hundred processions, a hundred ceremonies.
56. The true treasures of the church, out of which the pope distributes indulgences, are not sufficiently discussed or known among the people of Christ.
57. That indulgences are not temporal treasures is certainly clear, for many indulgence sellers do not distribute them freely but only gather them.
58. Nor are they the merits of Christ and the saints, for, even without the pope, the latter always work grace for the inner man, and the cross, death, and hell for the outer man.
59. St. Lawrence said that the poor of the church were the treasures of the church, but he spoke according to the usage of the word in his own time.
60. Without want of consideration we say that the keys of the church, given by the merits of Christ, are that treasure.
61. For it is clear that the pope's power is of itself sufficient for the remission of penalties and cases reserved by himself.
62. The true treasure of the church is the most holy gospel of the glory and grace of God.
63. But this treasure is naturally most odious, for it makes the first to be last (Mt. 20:16).
64. On the other hand, the treasure of indulgences is naturally most acceptable, for it makes the last to be first.
65. Therefore the treasures of the gospel are nets with which one formerly fished for men of wealth.
66. The treasures of indulgences are nets with which one now fishes for the wealth of men.
67. The indulgences which the demagogues acclaim as the greatest graces are actually understood to be such only insofar as they promote gain.
68. They are nevertheless in truth the most insignificant graces when compared with the grace of God and the piety of the cross.
69. Bishops and curates are bound to admit the commissaries of papal indulgences with all reverence.

70. But they are much more bound to strain their eyes and ears lest these men preach their own dreams instead of what the pope has commissioned.
71. Let him who speaks against the truth concerning papal indulgences be anathema and accursed.
72. But let him who guards against the lust and license of the indulgence preachers be blessed.
73. Just as the pope justly thunders against those who by any means whatever contrive harm to the sale of indulgences.
74. Much more does he intend to thunder against those who use indulgences as a pretext to contrive harm to holy love and truth.
75. To consider papal indulgences so great that they could absolve a man even if he had done the impossible and had violated the mother of God is madness.
76. We say on the contrary that papal indulgences cannot remove the very least of venial sins as far as guilt is concerned.
77. To say that even St. Peter if he were now pope, could not grant greater graces is blasphemy against St. Peter and the pope.
78. We say on the contrary that even the present pope, or any pope whatsoever, has greater graces at his disposal, that is, the gospel, spiritual powers, gifts of healing, etc., as it is written. (1 Co 12[:28])
79. To say that the cross emblazoned with the papal coat of arms, and set up by the indulgence preachers is equal in worth to the cross of Christ is blasphemy.
80. The bishops, curates, and theologians who permit such talk to be spread among the people will have to answer for this.
81. This unbridled preaching of indulgences makes it difficult even for learned men to rescue the reverence which is due the pope from slander or from the shrewd questions of the laity.
82. Such as: ``Why does not the pope empty purgatory for the sake of holy love and the dire need of the souls that are there if he redeems an infinite number of souls for the sake of miserable money with
which to build a church?" The former reason would be most just; the latter is most trivial.
83. Again, ``Why are funeral and anniversary masses for the dead continued and why does he not return or permit the withdrawal of the endowments founded for them, since it is wrong to pray for the
redeemed?"
84. Again, ``What is this new piety of God and the pope that for a consideration of money they permit a man who is impious and their enemy to buy out of purgatory the pious soul of a friend of God and do not rather, because of the need of that pious and beloved soul, free it for pure love's sake?"
85. Again, ``Why are the penitential canons, long since abrogated and dead in actual fact and through disuse, now satisfied by the granting of indulgences as though they were still alive and in force?"
86. Again, ``Why does not the pope, whose wealth is today greater than the wealth of the richest Crassus, build this one basilica of St. Peter with his own money rather than with the money of poor believers?"
87. Again, ``What does the pope remit or grant to those who by perfect contrition already have a right to full remission and blessings?"
88. Again, ``What greater blessing could come to the church than if the pope were to bestow these remissions and blessings on every believer a hundred times a day, as he now does but once?"

89. ``Since the pope seeks the salvation of souls rather than money by his indulgences, why does he suspend the indulgences and pardons previously granted when they have equal efficacy?"
90. To repress these very sharp arguments of the laity by force alone, and not to resolve them by giving reasons, is to expose the church and the pope to the ridicule of their enemies and to make Christians unhappy.
91. If, therefore, indulgences were preached according to the spirit and intention of the pope, all these doubts would be readily resolved. Indeed, they would not exist.
92. Away, then, with all those prophets who say to the people of Christ, ``Peace, peace," and there is no peace! (Jer 6:14)
93. Blessed be all those prophets who say to the people of Christ, ``Cross, cross," and there is no cross!
94. Christians should be exhorted to be diligent in following Christ, their Head, through penalties, death and hell.
95. And thus be confident of entering into heaven through many tribulations rather than through the false security of peace (Acts 14:22).

Baroque architecture was an integral part of the Catholic counterreformation efforts to win back the lost protestants with more lavish structures. The LDS church seems to have the same strategy today for very similar reasons. Two versions of a short article on "Baroque architecture" should give us some of this valuable background.

Baroque architecture (current article)

Baroque architecture is a highly decorative and theatrical style which appeared in Italy in the early 17th century and gradually spread across Europe. It was originally introduced by the Catholic Church, particularly by the Jesuits, as a means to combat the Reformation and the Protestant church with a new architecture that inspired surprise and awe. It reached its peak in the High Baroque (1625–1675), when it was used in churches and palaces in Italy, Spain, Portugal and France, and Austria. In the Late Baroque period (1675–1750), it reached as far as Russia and the Spanish and Portuguese colonies in Latin America, Beginning in about 1730, an even more elaborately decorative variant called Rococo appeared and flourished in Central Europe.

Baroque architects took the basic elements of Renaissance architecture, including domes and colonnades, and made them higher, grander, more decorated, and more dramatic. The interior effects were often achieved with the use of Quadratura, or trompe-l'oeil painting combined with sculpture; The eye is drawn upward, giving the illusion that one is looking into the heavens. Clusters of sculpted angels and painted figures crowd the ceiling. Light was also used for dramatic effect; it streamed down from cupolas, and was reflected from an abundance of gilding. Twisted columns were also often used, to give an illusion of upwards motion, and cartouches and other decorative elements occupied every available space. In Baroque palaces, grand stairways became a central element.

Baroque Architecture (article from past years)

Baroque architecture is the building style of the Baroque era, begun in late 16th-century Italy, that took the Roman vocabulary of Renaissance architecture and used it in a new rhetorical and theatrical fashion, often to express the triumph of the Catholic Church. It was characterized by new explorations of form, light and shadow, and dramatic intensity. Common features of Baroque architecture included gigantism of proportions; a large open central space where everyone could see the altar; twisting columns, theatrical effects, including light coming from a cupola above; dramatic interior effects created with bronze and gilding; clusters of sculpted angels and other figures high overhead; and an extensive use of trompe-l'oeil, also called "quadratura," with painted architectural details and figures on the walls and ceiling, to increase the dramatic and theatrical effect.[1]

Whereas the Renaissance drew on the wealth and power of the Italian courts and was a blend of secular and religious forces, the Baroque was, initially at least, directly linked to the Counter-Reformation, a movement within the Catholic Church to reform itself in response to the Protestant Reformation.[2] Baroque architecture and its embellishments were on the one hand more accessible to the emotions and on the other hand, a visible statement of the wealth and power of the Catholic Church. The new style manifested itself in particular in the context of the new religious orders, like the Theatines and the Jesuits who aimed to improve popular piety.

Lutheran Baroque art, such as the example of Dresden Frauenkirche (1726-1743), developed as a confessional marker of identity, in response to the Great Iconoclasm of Calvinists.[3][4]

The architecture of the High Roman Baroque can be assigned to the papal reigns of Urban VIII, Innocent X and Alexander VII, spanning from 1623 to 1667. The three principal architects of this period were the sculptor Gianlorenzo Bernini, Francesco Borromini and the painter Pietro da Cortona and each evolved his own distinctively individual architectural expression.[4]

Below are a few examples of Baroque architecture, first in a compact collection, and then with two shown in greater detail:

Baroque architecture

Clockwise from top: Church of Saint Ignatius of Loyola in Italy, Santa Prisca de Taxco in Mexico, Smolny Cathedral in Russia, St-Gervais-et-St-Protais in France

Years active late 16th–18th centuries

Church of Saint Ignatius of Loyola, Rome, Lazio, Italy. The three frescoes around the high altar are the 17th Century works of the Jesuit Andrea Pozzo. They show Saint Ignatius Loyola during his vision at La Storta, sending Saint Francis Xavier to the Indies, and greeting Saint Francesco Borgia.

Smolny Cathedral in Russia

Notes

1. https://en.wikipedia.org/wiki/Fourth_Council_of_the_Lateran
2. https://www.luther.de/en/95thesen.html
3. "'The Fullness of the Priesthood:' The Second Anointing in Latter-day Saint Theology and Practice" by David John Buerger, Dialogue Vol. 16 No 1, p.10, 33
4. https://en.wikipedia.org/wiki/Baroque_architecture

Chapter 10

James E. Talmage and *The Great Apostasy* – An argument for replacing one divergent religious empire with another

What was the nature and purpose of the book *The Great Apostasy* when it was first published in 1909 by James E. Talmage? One might think that, simply by reading the full title, the answer would be easy. That full title is: *The Great Apostasy Considered in The Light of Scriptural and Secular History.* One might reasonably expect to read a textbook blow-by-blow account of how the great apostasy happened, as the original church which Christ restored gradually degenerated into the highly corrupt Roman Catholic Church, perhaps indicating the exact point at which the ability to pass on legitimate priesthood authority was lost, and pointing out the errors that were made so that they could be avoided during the next restoration process.

But, as it turns out, one would be quite disappointed if that was the expectation. After a lifetime of study on my part, it now becomes clear that what was left out of that book is far more significant than what was included.

As a young missionary I read the book and noted the conclusions Talmage reached, but was not wise enough myself to realize all that had been left out, all of the actual history of the apostasy and the steps that the church went through in those days. My very limited take-away was that the original apostles were all killed, and that caused the church to quickly deteriorate. Of course, that was the impression that I was supposed to take from the book, even though that was very far from the actual truth. A more accurate title might have read something like "The Great Apostasy Considered in The Light of Limited Elements of Scriptural and Secular History Carefully Cherry-Picked for Polemical Purposes."

Even the credentials which Talmage presents as his qualifications for writing the book are confusing and perhaps questionable, perhaps intentionally so. Perhaps there is a complete explanation for what is presented, but I am unable to put it together. One might reasonably expect that someone writing about theology and the history of religion in a way that was intended to change the entire world of religion would be well-qualified in that field. Perhaps the term "D. Sc. D." might mistakenly be read by the casual reader as being the equivalent of a Dr. of Divinity (DD), perhaps acquired through lengthy study at Harvard or Oxford or some other such famous school. But, as far as I can tell, the two terms "D. Sc. D." and "Ph. D." mean exactly the same thing, that is, terminal or doctoral level studies in a scientific field. In other words, Talmage seems to be claiming to have the equivalent of two PhD's. Whether it is for the same set of science studies, which consisted of chemistry and geology, that he managed to get two degrees, or whether he actually earned two completely separate doctoral degrees in science is not clear. But that is not the sort of thing which should be left open to speculation. https://en.wikipedia.org/wiki/Doctor_of_Divinity

The last part of the string of qualifications "F. R. S. E." refers to his being a Fellow of the Royal Society of Edinburgh.

> **Fellowship of the Royal Society of Edinburgh (FRSE)** is an award granted to individuals that the Royal Society of Edinburgh, Scotland's national academy of science and letters, judges to be "eminently distinguished in their subject". This society had received a royal charter in 1783, allowing for its expansion. https://en.wikipedia.org/wiki/Royal_Society_of_Edinburgh

That final professional title amounts to a recognition of his educational attainments, so that one might conclude that he is claiming something like the equivalent of three different PhD's, all for the same work, none of which had anything to do with theology and religious history. Obviously, he was a very bright fellow, having written the book *Jesus the Christ* (1915) by church assignment after writing *The Great Apostasy* (1909), but the reader should not assume that any of his advanced studies in formal institutions had anything to do with theology or church history. In one sense, that was a good thing, because he could then say anything he wanted to without worrying about going against anything contrary he may have learned in formal studies. But, at the same time, the results of his studies should be considered to be his own private work without reliance on or reference to the vast knowledge located at any particular religious University.

The nature of the book is more clearly explained in the preface than one might expect for a book of polemics and apologetics, such as it is, but one would have to be much more sophisticated than a typical high school graduate, as I was, to immediately grasp the nuances of what was being said. One might reasonably expect that, as a religious work, it would contain "the truth, the whole truth, and nothing but the truth," as opposed to being a highly partisan work of polemics, carefully selecting the materials it contained based on the "spin" one wants to put on things. These days, in the world of political discourse, we even have such things as "spin rooms" where highly partisan political issues are discussed in highly partisan ways and everyone fully expects that they are only going to hear a tiny part of the real truth, if there is, indeed, any truth at all contained in any statements made. That is not the sort of presentation one would expect when one is proclaiming the gospel to the world, but that is what we have here.

What follows is the preface material:

> Press of Zion's Printing and Publishing Company
> Independence, Jackson County, Missouri.
>
> Published by the Missions of the Church of Jesus Christ of Latter-day Saints in America
>
> BUREAU OF INFORMATION—Temple Block, Salt Lake City, Utah.
> CALIFORNIA MISSION—153 W. Adams St., Los Angeles, Calif.
> CANADIAN MISSION—36 Ferndale Avenue, Toronto, Ontario, Canada.
> CENTRAL STATES MISSION—302 S. Pleasant St., Independence, Mo.
> EASTERN STATES MISSION—273 Gates Ave., Brooklyn, N. Y.
> HAWAIIAN MISSION—P. O. Box 3228, Honolulu, Hawaii.
> MEXICAN MISSION—3531 Fort Blvd., El Paso, Texas, U. S. A.
> NORTHERN STATES MISSION—2555 N. Sawyer Ave., Chicago, Ill.
> NORTHCENTRAL STATES MISSION—2725 3d Ave.S., Minneapolis, Minn.
> NORTHWESTERN STATES MISSION—264 East 25th St., Portland, Ore.
> SOUTHERN STATES MISSION—371 E. North Ave., Atlanta. Ga.
> WESTERN STATES MISSION—538 East 7th Ave., Denver, Colo.
>
> PREFACE.
> The Church of Jesus Christ of Latter-day Saints proclaims the restoration of the Gospel and the re-establishment of the Church as of old, in this, the Dispensation of the Fulness of Times. Such restoration and re-establishment, with the modern bestowal of the Holy Priesthood, would be unnecessary and indeed impossible had the Church of Christ continued among men with unbroken succession of Priesthood and power, since the "meridian of time."
>
> The restored Church affirms that a general apostasy developed during and after the apostolic period, and that the primitive Church lost its power, authority, and graces as a divine institution, and degenerated into an earthly organization only. The significance and importance of the great apostasy, as a condition precedent to the re-establishment of the Church in modern times, is obvious. If the alleged apostasy of the primitive Church was not a reality, the Church of Jesus Christ of Latter-day Saints is not the divine institution its name proclaims.
>
> The evidence of the decline and final extinction of the primitive Church among men is found in scriptural record and in secular history. In the following pages the author has undertaken to present a summary of the most important of these evidences. In so doing he has drawn liberally from many sources of information, with due acknowledgment of all citations. This little work has been written in the hope that it may prove of service to our missionary elders in the field, to classes and quorum organizations engaged in the study of theological subjects at home, and to earnest investigators of the teachings and claims of the restored Church of Jesus Christ.

Salt Lake City, Utah, James E. Talmage.
November 1, 1909.

PREFACE TO THE SECOND EDITION.

The first edition of "The Great Apostasy" was issued by the Deseret News, Salt Lake City, in November, 1909, and comprised ten thousand copies. The author has learned, with a pleasure that is perhaps pardonable, of the favorable reception accorded the little work by the missionary elders of the Church, and by the people among whom these devoted servants are called to labor. The present issue of twenty thousand copies constitutes the second edition, and is published primarily for use in the missionary field. The text of the second edition is practically identical with that of the first.

Salt Lake City, Utah, James E. Talmage.
February, 1910.

Incidentally, it is hard to imagine that there was actually a church publishing and printing office physically located in Independence, Jackson County, Missouri at the time of this printing, as set forth and claimed in the preface. This sounds to me like a history-based affectation that only adds more whimsy to this entire document. The preface to the second edition seems to clarify this situational detail: "The first edition of 'The Great Apostasy' was issued by the Deseret News, Salt Lake City, in November, 1909, and comprised ten thousand copies," indicating that this was really a Salt Lake City publication, as one might have expected.

So, what is missing from the book? As the reader might notice, the materials presented in earlier chapters of this present book -- the early writings of Selden, Pearson, and Clark, as summarized by Hevener -- give a brief introduction to the large body of historical knowledge and writings on the subject of church history, especially focusing on the issue of tithing as it appeared throughout the centuries of gradual disintegration of the original church which Christ restored. As far as I can tell, none of this important material was known by Talmage, or at least it was not referred to by him in any way.

In other words, we can say with some confidence, that James E Talmage actually had no idea about the various steps the church went through in its process of gradual disintegration, or at least he demonstrated a high level of incuriousness about many important issues relating to the apostasy of the original Christian church. All he was really focused on in his argument was the desired end result which is that the Roman Catholic Church had lost the "mandate of heaven" somewhere along the way before the LDS church was restored. That was all that mattered to him, and all that ought to matter to anyone else, he would probably assert. One might say that he merely assumed and asserted or declared the final desired answer, and then went about to put together some related but not dispositive information.

By closely reviewing the preface material from the Talmage book, we can see that this was very explicitly written as a missionary tract with the message that the ancient Roman Catholic Church was now defunct, and that the time was ripe for its replacement to come forward, that replacement being the LDS church.

Unfortunately, to be completely candid, Talmage would have needed to reveal that the new church of Christ had already decided to follow the exact same path which had been followed by the Roman Catholic Church as it began its intertwined processes of both earthly empire-building and doctrinal deterioration and had already taken or was planning several important steps down that path. The leaders of the LDS church had already decided to try to create an international religious empire on the scale of the old Roman Catholic Church, using the exact same means for the exact same purpose. That is, where it had taken over 300 years for the original church of Christ to start abandoning the concept of individual charity and embracing the concept of doctrinally-required tithing payments to the explicitly empire-building central church, the relatively new LDS church, seemingly a little drunk on its new-found religious organizational momentum and power, had only waited 66 years before it made that critical decision in about 1896 which began the inexorable decline of the church to something functionally equivalent to the Roman Catholic Church.

It is somewhat speculative to say this, of course, but it appears that in 2019, about 110 years after what we might call the "Talmage manifesto" to the world in the form of his book *The Great Apostasy,* the LDS church seems to feel that it has finally arrived at the point where it can directly challenge the Roman Catholic Church as its full worldwide replacement by spending perhaps as much as $5 billion to create its own basilica in Rome to compete in grandeur and artistic excellence and extravagance with the Baroque architecture of that city and other cities. The following article tells us that the architecture for the Rome temple was inspired by San Carlino, a Roman Catholic church in Rome. The article also gives a partial description of the expensive extravagance of the temple:

> 14 January 2019 - Rome, Italy News Release
>
> **Rome Italy Temple to Begin Public Tours**
>
> **Ancient Italian architecture reflected in edifice design**
>
> Public tours begin this month for the Rome Italy Temple of The Church of Jesus Christ of Latter-day Saints in Italy, the Church's 162nd operating temple in the world.

"It is beautiful," said Elder David A. Bednar of the Quorum of the Twelve Apostles, who serves as chairman of the Temple and Family History Department. "The craftmanship is expert and perfect."

After years of construction, Italy's first Latter-day Saint temple will be open for a free public open house from Monday, January 28, 2019, to Saturday, February 16, 2019, excluding Sundays.

The Rome Italy Temple is in northeast Rome near the village of La Cinquina Bufalotta. The temple's architecture was inspired by ancient Rome. Its exterior is constructed from Bianco Sardo granite.

Design
"This had to be one that when you walked onto this site, every person should feel like they were on an Italian site," said architect Niels Valentiner. "They would recognize it because of the materials, because of the design, and because of the surrounding."

Valentiner said the temple's design was inspired by San Carlino, a Roman Catholic church in Rome. "The curved ceilings, the curved walls, the expression of the colonnades and columns. And that started this very early concept of a curved church, a curved temple and temple building both on the exterior as well as on the interior."

The Rome Italy Temple is part of a 15-acre religious and cultural center that includes a multifunctional meetinghouse, a visitors' center, a family history center and housing for visitors.

Interior
At the temple's entrance, a floor-to-ceiling stained-glass wall depicts a scene from the life of the Savior Jesus Christ. Stained-glass windows are inspired by the olive tree.

Warm earth tones and blue, bronze and gold hues can be seen throughout the interior. Top artisans and craftsmen have installed the high-quality materials, which includes Perlato Svevo stone flooring quarried in northern Tuscany; Cenia marble from Spain; deep reddish brown Sapele, burl and cherry wood millwork; and Murano glass fixtures from Venice.

"We use the finest materials because it is the house of the Lord," said Elder Bednar. "The temple is an expression of our love and devotion to the Savior, the Lord Jesus Christ. Nothing is too good for the Lord."

"We hold our craftsmen to the highest possible standards," explained Bret Woods, project supervisor.

Woods said the temple's grand lobby staircase is an engineering feat. "It's connected just at the top and the bottom, so it's essentially a free-floating staircase — and of course, an elliptical shape." The oval design of the staircase is reminiscent of Michelangelo's Piazza del Campidoglio masterpiece near Capitoline Hill in Rome.

Original paintings hang in all areas of the temple, reminding temple guests of Jesus Christ and His teachings to follow Him. A picture in the baptistry depicts the Savior's baptism by John the Baptist.

The baptistry's purpose is in keeping with the Savior's example to enter the waters of baptism and His commandment that all must be baptized. In the temple, patrons can act on behalf of those who did not have the chance to be baptized in this life.

The oval motif continues in the baptistry, where inlaid stone wraps around an elliptical font adorned with Roman-style acanthus leaves. The font is held up by 12 oxen representing the 12 tribes of Israel.

In the instruction room where Church members learn about God's love, the creation and the purpose of life, a mural reveals a magnificent setting depicting Italy's landscape ranging from the hills to the sea.

The Baroque-era feel of the bridal room is enhanced by the crystalline sconces and hand-painted chairs.

A seemingly endless reflection from the mirrors in the sealing rooms symbolizes eternity. In those rooms, Latter-day Saint faithful participate in sacred ceremonies that join families together forever.

An exquisite chandelier containing thousands of crystal prisms serves as the centerpiece of the celestial room, a space that represents the progression of reaching heaven. The room is also filled with elegant furnishings made by Italian artisans.

Visitors' Center

In the visitors' center, a life-size statue of the Christus accompanied by the original Twelve Apostles faces the temple through full-length windows. The statues are replicas of sculptor Bertel Thorvaldsen's works displayed in the Church of Our Lady in Denmark, except the Judas Iscariot figure has been replaced by a statue of the Apostle Paul. Special permission was received from the Lutheran Church to digitally scan the original figures. Carrara marble for the three-quarter scale statues was taken from the same quarry in Tuscany as the marble for Michelangelo's David.

"When I saw the statues of the Savior, the Christus, and the Twelve Apostles, it was just a spiritually stunning moment for me," said Elder Bednar.

The statues are complimented by an original mural of olive trees in an Italian countryside that serves as a backdrop.

Piazza

The visitors' center, temple patron housing and a meetinghouse connect to the temple through an Italian-style piazza or square constructed from native travertine.

"These artisan stone layers have been working for seven generations," said Alberto Malara, senior assistant of Temple Facilities Management, who said the master stone layers spend 400 hours in the classroom.

The Church also salvaged 110-year-old Basalt cobblestones from the streets of Rome for the temple roundabout.

"If you look closely at some of these stones, you can see the grooves worn in by the passage of old wagon wheels," described Malara.

Open House and Dedication

Church leaders will meet with the media and take them on tours of the Rome Italy Temple on Monday, January 14, 2019. VIP tours for leaders of government, business, legal, interfaith and humanitarian organizations will be held at the temple from Tuesday, January 15, through Tuesday, January 22, before the public open house begins on Monday, January 28.

Reservations for the public temple open house can be made online at templeopenhouse.lds.org.

The temple will be formally dedicated Sunday, March 10, 2019, through Tuesday, March 12.

Members will be able to perform ordinances in the new temple beginning Tuesday, March 19.

Background

Construction began on the three-story, 40,000-square-foot temple on October 23, 2010, two years after the Rome Italy Temple was announced by Church President Thomas S. Monson. He and local Church and community leaders participated in the groundbreaking ceremony.

"It's difficult to explain my feeling," expressed Christian Bruno, a former Latter-day Saint missionary. "The Spirit was all around us. It was a great day for me, for my family and for all the Saints in Italy."

Latter-day Saints and other Christians consider Rome to be one of the most historic locations in the world, a biblical city where the ancient apostles Peter and Paul preached the gospel of Jesus Christ.

In 1997, the Church purchased the temple site, an abandoned 15-acre farm, which included a villa, small olive orchard and outside pizza oven.

"I used to come here as a youth, and we used to organize small soccer games," said Stephano Mosco, a local Latter-day Saint. "And there was a stone over there where we used to cook pizzas."

Trees

Olive trees from the old farm were preserved, and ancient olive trees from northern Italy, ranging in age from 400 to 500 years old, are planted in the piazza.

"There's tremendous symbolism in olives and in olive trees," said Elder Bednar, who said the trees' roots sink deep into the ground. "Whenever you cut the roots of an olive tree, they'll sprout. They don't die; they will continue to sprout. Some have suggested that perhaps that's symbolic of the hope of the resurrection."

The Church also preserved Italian stone pine trees on the property that line the stairs leading to the temple.

Temples

The temple will serve over 23,000 Church members living in Italy and in neighboring countries. Currently there are more than 160 operating temples worldwide, including 12 in Europe.

"In our holy temples, available are the most sacred and important sacrament or ordinances that we receive as members of our Church," taught Elder Bednar.

> "And those ordinances bring peace. They bring purpose. They're a source of remarkable joy."
>
> The Latter-day Saint apostle continued: "All temples are significant because a temple is a point of intersection between the earth and heaven. A temple is the house of the Lord. It's His house where we learn about Him, and we worship Him."
>
> Latter-day Saint temples differ from churches where members meet for Sunday worship services. Temples are considered "houses of the Lord" where the teachings of Jesus Christ are reaffirmed through marriage, baptism and other ceremonies that unite families for eternity.

When we hear President Russell M. Nelson speak of a positive "hinge point" in the church's growth, as a direct result of this extravagant temple complex in Rome, it is perfectly reasonable to wonder whether the unstated purpose of the church is as I suggest here. Obviously, I have no access to any inside information about the church's thinking on these matters, and can only speculate based on what I see and hear publicly. But, as we saw when we discussed the "95 Theses" of Martin Luther, the church today has exactly the same policies in place that Martin Luther was complaining about that were being sponsored and supported by the Catholic Church of his time. It should not be too outrageous to speculate that it is time for a "Protestant Reformation" within the LDS church for all the same reasons expressed by Martin Luther. A near-total abandonment of the concept of charity and caring for the poor, in favor of a mandatory sending of all of those resources to be consumed by church bureaucracies and building projects was the problem then, and we have the exact same problem today.

if the church had made a legislative-style presentation to its membership, asking whether that particular $5 billion in tithing funds ought to be spent on an outrageously expensive remote temple project which would likely never be of any practical value to any of the people who involuntarily funded it and would likely never even see it except in press releases (as the German poor and middle class had their money sent to Rome for the construction of the basilica, which they would likely never use or even see) as opposed to a long list of projects that might be done using that $5 billion to take care of the needs of the LDS poor or to improve the lives and especially the education of millions of desperate people in US cities, what do you suppose the members would choose? They would likely see the Rome temple project as an act of ultimate pridefulness on the part of the church leaders, drunk on the wealth provided them by the members with no strings attached and no responsibility for the value of the results, the leaders having taken to themselves the unbridled power to do as they whimsically wished with those consecrated resources.

Only the top church leaders would ever be able use it or even see it in person, making its construction an act of pure self-centeredness, creating a far-away monument to themselves. Are they planning to move the church headquarters to Rome, leaving behind the dilapidated and old-fashioned 120-year-old Salt Lake City temple which they may now view with disdain as not being worthy to house their exalted selves? Do they move to Rome while the Salt Lake temple is updated?

Their actual thought processes are a mystery of course, but some of the elements I suggest may in fact exist. Otherwise, why would such an expensive and extravagant temple complex be built in such a remote and inaccessible location to serve only 23,000 members directly? Why wouldn't they choose to build it somewhere in Utah where so many members are located, or at least build it somewhere in the United States, perhaps in Jackson County were Zion is to be built? (Are the Utah members not worthy enough for the temple to be built there, even though they paid for it?) Did someone decide that ALL the old prophecies and goals for the church have suddenly been canceled and replaced, including where Zion is to be built, and some version of the old Roman Empire is to be rekindled again in the Mediterranean area, with Rome as its capital? Whatever the answer is, it is probably equally as bizarre as anything I have imagined here. Perhaps they would have built the new temple in the Jerusalem area to replace the old temple of Herod if that had been politically possible. Perhaps Rome was as close as they could arrange for at the current time.

Rome Italy Temple

The worldview and philosophy of James E Talmage
It is difficult to know the actual thinking processes of historical figures such as James Talmage, but one can sometimes infer their pattern of thinking by their actions and the causes they espouse. At least we can say that Talmage did not completely accept all the teachings of Christ, and had moved part way along the ideological path toward Nimrod who defied God and oversaw the building of the tower of Babel, which we might see as man's attempt to

declare himself independent of God. Talmage appears to have accepted some of the teachings of men (who are always influenced by Satan), including some atheism and some humanism, even though he was, at the same time, holding the office of an apostle of Jesus Christ. It is likely that most of his cohort of church leaders agreed with him on many issues.

Talmage accepted atheistic organic evolution, which competes directly with the concept that God created the world and everything on it including his human offspring. This is atheism versus theism in its starkest form. I know of no good way to fully reconcile the two opposite positions.

During the three temptations of Christ, Christ definitively rejected Satan's offers of earthly wealth and fame. (Strangely enough, the earth and its inhabitants were his already as long as he didn't make that direct claim during his life.) Christ also rejected any form of paid earthly bureaucracy as part of his central church organization. Christ's directions to his followers were to spend nothing on temples or chapels or a paid ministry and to devote all of their resources to caring for each other and for the poor. In contrast, Talmage was willing to be part of a paid ministry which was working to build up an earthly empire including a large central bureaucracy and, in order to fund these ambitions, charge fees for priesthood ordinances which were intended to be free in Christ's church.

It may seem strange for anyone to teach of Christ as a part of a process of self-aggrandizement, but millions have managed to make their fortune by appearing to defer to and worship Christ when they are really just thinking of themselves. We have a new category of people known as televangelists who have turned this form of priestcraft into an art form. That is basically what the LDS church has done, although they have managed to appear to maintain a better sense of decorum and solemnity. I don't believe Christ would accept any of these forms of priestcraft, but many of his self-proclaimed followers join in gladly.

In summary, James E Talmage seems to think that the priests of the Roman Catholic Church had the right solution to what an earthly church should look like, and he is willing to simply declare the LDS church as the Roman Catholic Church version 2.0, with a few added Scriptures to make it seem like the new church is better supported by revelation and therefore more legitimate. The truth, of course, is that this new form of the LDS church does indeed have extra Scripture, but it consciously ignores some of the most important principles taught in those Scriptures. The Scriptures become more like a valuable religious relic, like the finger bones of some long-dead apostle, then a source of knowledge for teaching us to live the gospel correctly.

Chapter 11

Incidents of shock and awe to introduce Christ's new gospel, powerful enough to change the world for 2000 years

As Joseph Smith demonstrated, with his diligent efforts to compile what ended up as a multivolume history of the church, the context in which new gospel information was given to us is often very important in order for us to answer many detailed questions about what exactly was intended, and what the exact lesson was we were supposed to learn. I think Joseph Smith would have said that there is no such thing as too much church history. Apparently, historical events do not always come with a complete theoretical and theological explanation attached telling us their full significance.

Many of the church history issues that trouble so many people today were apparently incompletely recorded, leaving innumerable loose ends that can eventually confuse and torment people. (Maybe we need a current version of the Jewish Torah, the extensive commentaries on the Scriptures.) The ancient tribal concept of polygamy is one issue; the requirements for "tithing" and other contributions is another; and so on. Rather than let these issues fester until it drives a few people crazy, the correct interpretation needs to be discovered and described, with that study and decision-making process itself being a new segment of recorded church history.

It is certainly beneficial to have projects such as the Joseph Smith Papers, where materials are collected which provide more detail than might have been available before, but then the question arises as to what can ultimately be derived from those materials and presented as new wisdom. It is not obvious that we have an adequate analysis and interpretation system to go along with the new printed information.

Wouldn't it be nice if Christ had resolved every conceivable question while he was alive? Maybe he did, but we don't have the data. I have always been intrigued by these comments in the Book of John:

> John 21:23 Then went this saying abroad among the brethren, that that disciple should not die: yet Jesus said not unto him, He shall not die; but, If I will that he tarry till I come, what is that to thee?
> 24 This is the disciple which testifieth of these things, and wrote these things: and we know that his testimony is true.

> 25 And there are also many other things which Jesus did, the which, if they should be written every one, I suppose that even the world itself could not contain the books that should be written. Amen.

But then, if we did have that comprehensive level of information about Christ's sayings and doings, we might then have the risk of eventually setting up an even more oppressive version of the law of Moses. Instead of about 600 rules for controlling our daily behavior under the original law of Moses, we might then have 6000 rules for controlling our daily behavior. That could again impinge on our intended freedom to choose the right based on inadequate information, as was intended to be our situation on this side of the veil.

Valuable startup information

One of the most fascinating kinds of history which I find terribly lacking and incomplete is the processes of how the church was restored in other times. We have more information about the experiences of Joseph Smith and the restoration that came through him, although there are still vast amounts of information about that process that we have not captured and do not understand. There have been any number of "dispensations" or restorations, but it is only the largest and most important ones that we know anything about at all. Heavenly values and thinking on numerous issues were surely revealed in all these cases, if we could only assemble and analyze the necessary information.

One way of looking at the final set of actions taken by Christ to finish all the steps of his restoration of the gospel is that he went out of his way to make sure that the new gospel had no connection whatsoever with the old law of Moses, which also meant that the members of the new church had no reason to have contact with Jerusalem, and in fact it was in their personal security interest to stay as far away from Jerusalem as possible. The fanatical Pharisees in Jerusalem were trying to kill them and were actually managing to jail and kill church members, giving the members extremely good reasons to get as far away from Jerusalem as possible. In one sense, the Pharisees were doing the church members a favor by helping convince them that they should get as far away as possible from Jerusalem and its old ways of thinking and behaving.

Christ seems to have stirred up a hornets' nest on purpose, to make sure that he would be killed and that all his followers would be driven out of Jerusalem and thus far away from the old law of Moses culture, both of those unpleasant steps apparently being necessary to make the gospel progress that was desirable on a much larger front.

Joseph Smith seems to have accomplished almost the exact same thing through his martyrdom and the saints fleeing and being driven westward. ("We wanted to go West because we had to.") Joseph Smith suggested going West much earlier, but no one would go with him. They called him a coward for not staying and fighting for their land and freedom, even though they could not possibly win that battle, either physically or culturally. (Perhaps human psychology requires the death of the irreplaceable leader before members will finally act on their own as they should have in the first place if they had been wise.) If the Saints would not follow Joseph Smith willingly, and do the sensible thing when it would have been relatively easy and orderly to do, then they had to be driven out, and that is what actually happened.

It would be fascinating to know if Christ tried to designate a gathering place, a "Zion," somewhere far away from Jerusalem, and the Saints were not willing to move there, possibly helping to make his death necessary to get everyone moved. It appears to me that Christ was indeed checking out Samaria as one of the good places for his future church members, the new Christians, to go in the future, when the predicted persecutions had started in earnest. It seems he was doing some preparation for them to be well received when they arrived there. Unfortunately, I don't know of any information being available on this speculative "Zion" point, although Christ did teach the Samaritans, apparently before any other "Gentiles" were contacted. John 4:39-42.

(Maybe Samaria would be a good Zion place, since he spoke so highly of the good Samaritan, and the Jews wanted to stay away from Samaria, a place where the people of a slightly different religion were scorned and shunned and there was no full law of Moses Temple. Note that for the new Christians, having no law of Moses Temple available was a good thing, since they had no need for any such Temple and needed to wean themselves completely from the temple and the related society. The new church could conceivably advance quickly in Samaria, since the populace already knew a great deal about Israelite and gospel history and theology.)

It is interesting that Christ cleansed the temple his last week while complaining that the Pharisees had made his father's house a den of thieves, but, at the same time, Christ had no intention whatsoever that either he or any of the members of his new church would have any need for that Jerusalem temple anymore in the future. One of the ironies of the church today is that the church leaders have done everything they can to bind members today to regular temple attendance when the gospel of Christ has no requirement for any temple structure anywhere whatsoever. It is really a return to the procedure-bound thinking and behavior of the Old Testament law of Moses for us to become so emotionally and practically (and financially) attached to some particular piece of architecture and real estate, almost allowing some of these structures to have some of the emotional and sociological functions of pagan Baroque idols and pagan temples, worshipped for their extravagant beauty or political significance. This is analogous to the extravagant structures built by the pope to try to win back Protestants through architecture, not through actual effective faith. It is a little bit challenging and even frightening how independent-minded Christ wanted his people to be, leaving behind all the ideological and psychological snares of rote behavior.

The members of Christ's original church thrived and grew quickly for 300 years without any chapels or temples, living widely scattered in completely autonomous groups where the entirety of the gospel was available, including all the higher priesthood ordinances. (There was at least one "Melchizedek" in each church charity group, so to speak.) There was no such thing as a central headquarters, because there was no need for one. (In fact, as another lesson from religious history, we can say that having a central headquarters, and an associated paid bureaucracy like a Sanhedrin, is itself a sign of church decay and apostasy, a sign of the return to law of Moses thinking, where the economics of empire-building and profit overshadow spiritual matters, which are the "weightier matters of the law," so to speak.)

It would probably be a great shock to many people today to realize that the stake patriarchs at one point were the ones who had all of the higher priesthood ordinances. Under Joseph Smith, Brigham Young, and John Taylor, the various stakes and their patriarchs operated autonomously wherever they were located. It was only under Wilford Woodruff and later presidents that these priesthood ordinances, and those who had the authority to administer them, were centralized and controlled and monetized through the recommend system which required payment of a full tithing to the central offices before anyone could attend the temple as the only place to receive any of the higher ordinances. To repeat, this law of Moses-style money extraction system was not operating for at least the first 300 years in the original church of Christ, and it was not operating for the first 66 years of the church in our time. If tithing is really the first principle of the gospel as it is today, considered to be the critical feature and limiting factor in expanding the gospel, why is it not found in our Articles of Faith which were written during Joseph Smith's lifetime?

There were many seeming parallels between the saints living at the time of Christ and those living at the time of Joseph Smith. The Saints of Joseph Smith's time found it impossible to stay in the "promised land" of Missouri, because of the Saints' anti-slavery views. Christ and the new church members were against the slightly less intense version of slavery which was the law of Moses.

The big issue of Joseph Smith's day was whether Missouri would stay a slave state or become a non-slave state through a statewide vote to end slavery. Since there were already thousands of slaves on plantations in Missouri along the Missouri River, the immigration into Missouri of thousands of anti-slavery-voting Northerners like the Mormons was a huge threat to the property and economy of the slaveholders in the "Little Dixie" part of Missouri. Driving out or exterminating the quickly-assembling Mormons was the sensible thing to do from the standpoint of the slaveholders. No one cared a whit about what we believed, beyond the fact that we did not believe in slavery and would vote against it. The first significant contact between the Mormons and the old settlers was during a time of voting. The slaveholders tried to drive off the Mormons from the voting areas, but the Mormons were tougher than the slaveholders and won that skirmish. That made it even worse, because the Mormons made it clear that they would not be easily intimidated, requiring the slaveholders to escalate their attacks to rid themselves of the anti-slavery Mormon vote. We can certainly say that the early Mormons were far more stalwart for freedom than we are today.

Surely God knew from the beginning 1) that the Saints could not remain in Missouri, and 2) that they had to be driven to Utah. The Lord used the Mormons to end slavery while also using slavery issues to get the Mormons moved to the safe space of Utah where they were spared the ravages of the Civil War. Without that insight into the big picture, hardly anything that happened during those times makes any sense.

As it turned out, the Saints were not safe until they had passed through several situations such as Nauvoo and Winter Quarters to get to Utah where they were finally safe. The slavery issue was what determined where the Saints were able to live. The mobs drove out the Saints, against their will, naturally, until they were in the safe place which they were supposed to be in. Joseph Smith had earlier told the members that they needed to move to the Western states to be safe, but no one was willing to do it until their lives literally depended on it. This seems like an almost 100% parallel of the earlier Saints having to be driven by fears for their own lives to end up where they needed to be, somewhere outside of Jerusalem and out of the grip of the law of Moses culture. They might have understood where they needed to be, but almost no one was willing to go unless there were severe threats driving them forward.

One of the lessons learned from all of this is that, on a long-term basis, a church can choose between having temples and having Christian charity, but it can't have both. (This sounds like the old "guns or butter" choice in nation-level economics.) If you let the "camel's nose" of extravagant semi-pagan temples under the tent, then before long it will be taking all the extra resources and there will be essentially no resources devoted to Christian charity. ("If a religion cannot save you temporally, it cannot save you spiritually." – The gospel is intended to address and take care of all of our human needs, not just our fear of death, but also our fear of suffering in this life.) That is the way it was in Christ's time, as illustrated by the parable of the good Samaritan, where the priests had their living from tithing and they were not going to share with anyone, and no one else (except someone outside of the law of Moses strictures such as the good Samaritan) felt they had any money (or duty) left over to do it themselves.

With this law of Moses temple focus in control of the church, instead of the charity focus, everyone is concerned about themselves and their "personal purity," and, in general, striving to display symbols of their current worthiness for exaltation, rather than focusing their concerns on the practical welfare of everyone else.

That is the way it is today. All of our money, which would otherwise go to charity, goes to the central offices where they spend it on themselves and on temples and structures and questionable projects, while the amount of money spent on actual charity or humanitarian aid is nearly zero. Only about one-fourth of 1% of the total amount received by Salt Lake City appears to be devoted to such valuable charitable things. The church could make huge positive changes to the world through wise use of charity, but it prefers to keep all that money for its own internal use.

In the 1890s, the issue of church debts was used as a lever and an excuse to restart the law of Moses tithing system among the Saints, permanently redirecting their Christian charity to the use of the centralizing paid ministry "Judaizers" who saw the reintroduction of the law of Moses as a good thing for themselves personally. Fortunately, at least as far as I know, they did not try to re-institute circumcision, although I believe there has been significant confusion on even that small point.

A recurring problem throughout the 2000-year history of the Christian church has been the reappearance of "Judaizers" who thought the old law of Moses had some features which appealed to them, usually something having to do with collecting tithing to establish a paid ministry. This includes Roman Catholic priests beginning to wear a miter, the hat which Aaron wore to complete his priestly duties. The possibility of collecting unearned money using nothing but ideology and rhetoric is almost always an irresistible temptation, it appears.

So, what were those church debts that were used as an excuse to reintroduce law of Moses tithing? It seems that no one ever described them in public. If they were nothing more than promises of salaries to church leaders, then they were not valid. If they were left-over Perpetual Emigration Fund debts, then they were really individual debts, but it would be nice for the church to help pay them off to outsiders, but not to use that incident as way to set up a constant illegitimate inflow of money to the central offices. Normal charity processes apparently could have taken care of the PEF debts without involving the central church at all. Perhaps this was a case of standard leftist ideology and practice: No one should let a good crisis go to waste when leftist (anti-gospel) social engineering can occur.

Some more observations on this "sweep of history" view of restorations: the main reason the Saints had all the trouble they had in the United States was because of their anti-slavery position. It was realized at the time by the political representatives of the southern slave owners that an organized group such as the LDS who were anti-slavery, and amounted to about 30,000 individuals, could single-handedly determine the slave/no slave status of all the remaining western territories, if they chose to do so. That is why there were about six different "extermination orders" at different stages of the Saints' progress West, not just the one in Missouri. It happened in Nauvoo and Winter Quarters and in Utah itself, twice.

The preferred solution was simply to kill or scatter the Saints so that they were neutralized as a political influence. It was the nightmare of the southern slave plotters to allow the Saints to get out West where they could control the fate of Colorado, Utah, and California (a great place for plantations), and perhaps some other places.

Although we usually skip over this part, the southern slave strategists hoped that the "Mormon Battalion" maneuver would be a way to separate and kill off a large number of able Mormon men and thereby break up the whole movement and prevent the Mormons' migration West to interfere with slavery plans there. Our church history usually leaves out the significant point that the members of the Mormon Battalion were pressed into service at gunpoint and were treated as a prisoner battalion, with two other battalions sent along to be their guards.

However, fortunately, the evil plans of Southerners (who controlled most of the US government) backfired, because those Saints actually made it alive to California, and not only survived to make it to Utah, but also apparently were instrumental in starting the gold rush which brought tens of thousands of anti-slavery entrepreneurs to California to make sure that there could never be a successful state vote to legitimize slavery within the state of California.

Those same Mormon Battalion members made it back to Utah with their weapons and military experience in plenty of time to "stand like a stone wall" against the Army sent there, commanded by a Texas slave-holding general and manned mostly by proslavery Missourians. The Army had been sent there to first make Utah a slave state and then claim the associated seats in the US House of Representatives to help get control of that federal governing body, and then to move on to California and make it a slave state as well and claim its House seats. The southern states already controlled the federal Presidency, the Senate, and the Supreme Court, but not the House of Representatives, so the southern states were just a whisker away from total control of the federal government so that they could declare slavery legal nationwide, as was their goal, winning that war almost without firing a shot.

But those machinations were stopped in their tracks by the 20,000 sturdy and determined Mormon mountain men who by then were inhabiting Utah, and were not about to be scattered or crushed by a hostile proslavery Army, as had happened at least twice before. Since the army could not accomplish its task in Utah, just as it had not been able to accomplish that exact same assignment in 1857 in Kansas, the army was stopped. And, a short time later, with the southern strategists having been stymied on their plan to turn the western territories into slave states, those southern leaders made the desperate and foolish decision that the only option they had left to spread slavery nationwide was war. That meant that some of the southern strategists and a goodly number of their proslavery followers were wiped out and their slave-based civilization almost completely destroyed. The Mormons had already done more than their share of fighting in the pre-Civil War conflicts, and were able to sit out most of the big war itself.

The Mormons were central to all of these activities of freeing the slaves. I'm sure the leftist propagandists today, Mormons or not, who claim that Brigham Young was a racist, have not even a tiny speck of information about what was going on in those pre-Civil War times, and how the ideological strength and determination of the Mormons brought down the entire proslavery movement in United States. I would call that a pretty good accomplishment. In truth, the Mormons were among the first warriors in the Civil War, and, because of their steadfastness, they were the linchpin force which brought down the whole history of national disgrace over the question of slavery. Even if today the Mormons themselves have forgotten and become confused about what happened concerning slavery, that does not lessen the great things that were accomplished by earlier Mormons.

Being a powerful pro-freedom force is what the gospel is all about. After the time of Christ, even with all the problems it developed, the Christian church was the basis for Western civilization with its emphasis on freedom and individual rights, found nowhere else in the world. Unfortunately, today the LDS church headquarters cares nothing about actively defending freedom, and so has intentionally and willfully "included itself out" of the long tradition of Christian-supported freedom.

The Saints at the time of Christ were surely a powerful force for freedom, although we don't seem to know very much about what they accomplished, except for the fact that they threw off the chains of the old law of Moses. Similar logic to the law of Moses has been used over and over again to impose slavery on peoples based on a twisted form of religion. So, getting rid of the law of Moses was itself a major step forward. That also meant that some of the associated structures such as the kingdoms of David and Solomon which were based on similar religious principles, such as "the divine right of Kings," etc., were denigrated.

(As a footnote observation, many people would say that the law of Moses concept of society reached its zenith under King David, but we might notice that the tax rate under King David has been estimated to be about 50%, demonstrating how far the Israelites were from freedom. It is interesting to read how persecuted the Nephites often felt in the Book of Mormon when they were being taxed at only a 20% rate. Mosiah 11:3. (King Noah). We can say that Christ was anti-tax of almost any kind, since taxation is a measure of the practical level of bondage and lack of freedom, and a limit on charity. Demanding that members pay tithing puts the church halfway to persecuting its own members without even considering any secular taxes.)

The early Saints probably had something to do with ending the Roman empire and allowing greater freedom, but I have not as yet accumulated specific information on that particular point.

The opening blast

Another fascinating aspect of restorations are that some of them involve a few miracles, including the violence of natural forces. We hear of Enoch being able to move mountains and rivers to defend his gospel sanctuary city of Zion. In the New World, at the death of Christ, we hear of earthquakes and volcanoes that changed the face of the land and destroyed the cities of the wicked. This presumably made it very easy for the true Christians to live freely without threats from their now-missing enemies and to expand without restraints for a time.

Concerning the Saints moving west to safety, there are tales of the mighty Mississippi River freezing over so that the Saints could make a quick escape from their enemies and not be trapped and possibly killed. When Johnson's Army was working so hard to pick a fight with the Mormons in Utah, so they could claim they had been attacked, and start a shooting war, there was an unusual snowstorm which kept that Army isolated and inactive so that literally their "hotheads" were cooled off. When Zion's Camp returned to Missouri to attempt to reclaim the Saints' property, it might have been destroyed by superior forces, except for a furious wind and rain and thunderstorm and flood which thoroughly convinced many of the would-be mobbers that the heavens were on the side of the Mormons.

It has occurred to me more than once that Christ could easily have made Jerusalem as much of a smoking crater as any of the destroyed cities in the New World, but obviously he had other plans for that place and those people. The new church members were mixed in with the old autocrats and it would have made no sense to destroy everything on a wholesale basis. It was not yet like the unmitigated sin and tyranny that led to a Noah situation where the entire world had to start over.

We might recall that Sodom and Gomorrah were wiped out completely, but only after the last few believers had escaped. Perhaps there is a connection here with Jerusalem, which was totally destroyed about 30 years after the death of Christ. That is quite a long time to delay such wrath, but, surely by that time, there were indeed no Christians left in Jerusalem.

Nonetheless, I believe there was some indication through clouds and earthquakes that the heavens disapproved of the actions of the local Jews. We might remember that Jerusalem was eventually completely obliterated, nearly as completely as some of the cities in the New World. There was a time delay of about 30 years between crime and punishment, but it still suffered a similar fate in 70 AD. Surely there is historical information available on the connection between the rejection of the Savior and the destruction of Jerusalem, but I don't personally know what it is yet. We know that Jesus predicted the destruction of Jerusalem, but, again, we don't know the doctrinal or sociological reason for his making that prophecy. The people around him could probably see the connection, but we cannot.

The effect of the destruction of Jerusalem could have been something as simple as a way to signify the total end of the law of Moses and the destruction of the hopelessly corrupt Jewish state which had been continually harassing the saints, causing a Jewish diaspora which was in effect for 2000 years, and only now is experiencing a revival of a new version of Jewish culture. Unfortunately, today, we seem to have confused ourselves about Christ's intentions about the law of Moses. We somehow imagine that bringing back the law of Moses and quoting scriptures from the Old Testament in support of the law of Moses tithing system is a way to make us more holy today. But I believe that this is having the exact opposite effect.

I believe we can say with certainty that for the members of the church at the time, they were very happy to be long gone from Jerusalem when the Roman soldiers showed up to destroy it in 70 AD, and presumably they understood the symbolic significance of an unequivocal end to the law of Moses and the Temple associated with it, with the whole society and all the related structures ground to powder. If they still had tendencies to listen to the Judaizers and keep going back to the law of Moses rules of tithing, circumcision, sacrifice, etc., that should have put all of those questions to rest.

When John the Revelator wrote his epistle known as the Book of Revelation to the seven churches in Asia in about 90 A.D., we can be fairly sure that all of the old errors and "traditions of the fathers" had been pretty well stamped out among the widely scattered Christians. Perhaps that was the high point of the early church having everything understood and figured out and applied in practice, especially including the vigorous application of individual charity and the complete lack of a religious/spiritual need for chapels and, especially, temples. They were "free at last" of the taxes and chains of the law of Moses, although they were not completely free of Roman influence.

Generations of priestcraft

When we read about the characters of Nehor and Korihor in the Book of Mormon, where Nehor was willing to kill to defend priestcraft, we might want to tie them in more closely with other aspects of similar religious history. We learn about Abraham almost being sacrificed in some pagan temple. We read of the priests of Pharaoh who were presumably behind the killing of the Israelite babies, plus later bringing on the many deadly plagues on Egypt because of their stubbornness . We continually read about the "fires of Moloch" where pagan Israelites and others discarded/sacrificed unwanted babies. We read about Christians in Rome rescuing discarded babies from the refuse piles.

Perhaps it would be useful to compare the corrupt priestcraft operatives of the time of Christ, the Pharisees and all their allies, with this very undistinguished group of actively evil people appearing throughout history. That comparison should be useful, because it should help emphasize how thoroughly and completely Christ wished to grind out of existence every last vestige of the law of Moses. Today we have readopted large portions of the law of Moses, including the rigid application of tithing, the re-emphasized importance of constant on-site temple worship, and expensive temple contributions, and we have a new Levite class that is supported by the tithing of the masses – all the essential accoutrements of the law of Moses, including the Sanhedrin, a central bureaucracy for governing that religion. Strangely enough, our Sanhedrin is probably 10 times or 100 times larger than was the original Sanhedrin, although perhaps we have just replaced the decentralized Levites with a more centralized version of that parasitic tribe. None of that has any place in the gospel Christ introduced. It only had a place in the old thinking of the law of Moses. The more we are drawn to it, the more we are drawn away from what Christ intended us to learn from New Testament concepts.

Just as the priests of Pharaoh killed the babies of the Israelites, Herod later killed the children of the people of Bethlehem, grisly murders for the sake of retaining political power. It is hard to imagine a more evil heart than that. But these are samples of powerful feelings and actions of evil which priestcraft creates and supports. The mass slaughter of infants in the womb, and infanticide after birth, supported today by pagan forces, is much the same.

Perhaps we specifically avoid today the studying of these aspects of priestcraft at the time of Christ simply because it would then be easy to see the parallels between what was done then and what is being done today, bringing all those old issues up on a recurring basis.

Priestcraft and Samaria

I was browsing through a book entitled *The Parables Of Jesus: Revealing The Plan Of Salvation** and something caught my eye which related to the danger of priestcraft to a society. It appeared to me to be a possible old world application of the Alma 1 assertion that priestcraft will mean the end of a society:

> Alma 1:12 "... And were priestcraft to be enforced among this people it would prove their entire destruction."

Here is the story:

> Leaving Judea, where He had spoken with Nicodemus by night, Jesus and His disciples returned to Galilee by way of the high-country road through Samaria. Near the village that John called Sychar was the place given by the patriarch Jacob to His beloved son Joseph. Joseph's tomb was nearby, as was Jacob's well. Cut into the solid rock (possibly 100 to 170 feet deep), this is one of the best attested sites mentioned in the New Testament.
>
> This spot is located east of the mountain valley pass that runs east and west between Mount Gerizim (on the south) and its twin, Mount Ebal (on the north). These two mountains were especially holy to the Samaritans.
>
> There was no love lost between the Jews and the Samaritans. In 111-110 B.C.E., the Jews under John Hyrcanus (the Jewish high priest and son of Simon Maccabaeus) had destroyed the Samaritan temple on Mount Gerizim and had reduced the nearby ancient city of Shechem to a mere village as part of his expansive conquests in the regions around Jerusalem. At the time of Jesus, that village was called Sychar, and the people living there were still reminded of those losses by the remaining ruins. Even though all that was left of the temple on Mount Gerizim was rubble, the Samaritans continued to worship and sacrifice at that spot, a place that was rich in tradition for all the tribes of Israel. The Samaritans followed their version of the law of Moses as found in the first five books of their Bible.

Perhaps we could say that the high priest at Jerusalem had enforced his priestcraft with the sword. Perhaps there was a link between this unpleasant event and the destruction of Jerusalem in 70 A.D., resulting in the end of the Jewish society.
* John W. And Jeannie S. Welch, *The Parables Of Jesus: Revealing The Plan Of* Salvation (American Fork, Utah: Covenant Communications, Inc., 2019)

Some more historical background for the story:

Samaritans

The title is used to describe the people who inhabited Samaria after the captivity of the northern kingdom of Israel. They were the descendants of (1) foreign colonists placed there by kings of Assyria and Babylonia (2 Kgs. 17:24; Ezra 4:2, 10); (2) Israelites who escaped at the time of the captivity. The population was therefore partly Israelite and partly gentile. Their religion was also of a mixed character (see 2 Kgs. 17:24–41), though they claimed, as worshippers of Jehovah, to have a share in the rebuilding of the temple at Jerusalem (Ezra 4:1–3). This claim not being allowed, they became, as the books of Ezra and Nehemiah show, bitter opponents of the Jews, and started a rival temple of their own on Mount Gerizim. When Nehemiah ejected from Jerusalem a grandson of the high priest Eliashib on account of his marriage with a heathen woman (Neh. 13:28), he took refuge with the Samaritans, taking with him a copy of the Pentateuch, and according to Josephus became high priest at Gerizim. There are several references in the New Testament to the antagonism between the Jews and Samaritans (see Matt. 10:5; Luke 9:52–53; 10:33; 17:16; John 4:9, 39; 8:48); but the people of Samaria were included among those to whom the Apostles were directed to preach the gospel (Acts 1:8), and a very successful work was done there by Philip (Acts 8:4–25).

Temple on Mount Gerizim

Josephus gives the following account of the erection of this temple: Manasseh, brother of Jaddua the high priest, was threatened by the Jews with deprivation of his priestly office because of a marriage he had contracted with a foreign woman. His father-in-law, Sanballat, obtained permission from Alexander the Great, then besieging Tyre, to build a temple on Mount Gerizim. Manasseh was its first high priest. It became the refuge of all Jews who had violated the precepts of the Mosaic law. With this account must be compared Neh. 13:28, which from the names and circumstances probably relates to the same event. Josephus places the event 90 years later than the Bible. The establishment of the counterfeit worship on Gerizim embittered and perpetuated the schism between the Jews and the Samaritans. The Samaritans altered their copies of the Pentateuch by substituting Gerizim for Ebal in Deut. 27:4 and by making an interpolation in Ex. 20 and so claimed divine authority for the site of their temple. Antiochus Epiphanes, at the request of the Samaritans, consecrated it to Jupiter, the defender of strangers. John Hyrcanus destroyed it (109 B.C.). Though the Emperor Zeno (A.D. 474–491) ejected the Samaritans from Gerizim, it has continued to be the chief sacred place of the Samaritan community. There the Paschal Lamb has been almost continuously offered by them up to the present day.

Shock and Awe

We might imagine that the only restoration that was attended by massive displays of shock and awe was the one in the New World after Christ's resurrection, where the entire landscape was changed, cities were totally destroyed, being pushed up or buried, and the sun was unable to shine for three days. But that was not the only spectacular preparation for introducing the gospel. Apparently, these unusual events are actually common at times of restoration, if we know what to look for. The Book of Acts contains many amazing things:

> Acts 1
> *Jesus ministers for forty days after His resurrection...*
> 1 The former treatise have I made, O Theophilus, of all that Jesus began both to do and teach,
> 2 Until the day in which he was taken up, after that he through the Holy Ghost had given commandments unto the apostles whom he had chosen:
> 3 To whom also he shewed himself alive after his passion by many infallible proofs, being seen of them forty days, and speaking of the things pertaining to the kingdom of God:
> 4 And, being assembled together with them, commanded them that they should not depart from Jerusalem, but wait for the promise of the Father, which, saith he, ye have heard of me.
> 5 For John truly baptized with water; but ye shall be baptized with the Holy Ghost not many days hence.

The Acts 1 headnotes tell us that "Jesus ministers for 40 days after his resurrection." Although the Book of Acts only mentions Christ appearing to his apostles, unless all those meetings were held in secret rooms, and no one ever spoke to others about it, it seems very possible that Christ was seen in person by thousands of people, which would naturally include spies for the Pharisees. If the Pharisees weren't sure who they had just killed, and whether that had been a good idea or not, they would now be perfectly sure, since there could be no confusion about what happened. That sounds like some serious shock and awe all by itself. For a short time there was some consternation about the empty tomb, guarded by soldiers, but we never hear about later reactions by the Pharisees, but there must surely have been some reactions, as in the case of Gamaliel.

In verse four, Christ tells his apostles that they should not immediately "depart from Jerusalem, but wait for the promise of the father..." Perhaps we can assume that the apostles told a few thousand people what Christ had said about not leaving Jerusalem, making sure that there would be a large crowd gathered on the Day of Pentecost to be "baptized with the Holy Ghost," something rather exciting to look forward to.

Some details on the Day of Pentecost:

> "Pentecost" is actually the Greek name for a festival known in the Old Testament as the Feast of Weeks... The Greek word [Pentecost] means 'fifty' and refers to the fifty days that have elapsed since the wave offering of Passover." https://www.gotquestions.org/day-Pentecost.html

Apparently, the Saints were very anxious to leave Jerusalem, for good reason, because of Jewish reactions, and were only held back by the instructions of the Savior so that they could receive the Holy Ghost before they left and became scattered far and wide. It's not clear to me whether any of them had received the Holy Ghost before, along with baptism, or if that particular ordinance was delayed until after the death of Christ, which seems to be the most likely situation. Perhaps it was done in that sequence for the very purpose of having a spectacular event with many in attendance. We can probably assume that a large, presumably open-air event of this magnitude would be well known to the Pharisees.

Acts 2 tells us the Pentecost story. This great event with "a sound from heaven as of a rushing mighty wind" and "cloven tongues like as of fire," with every attendee hearing the words in his own language, being spoken by Galileans, was presumably attended by many more than 3000 people, since about 3000 souls were baptized and added to the church that day. These men were from every nation and could be ambassadors and missionaries to the known world and carry the gospel quickly as they returned to their homes after this great meeting. It would be interesting to know if all these people came for Passover and were able to stay the 50 days until the Feast of Weeks, or whether they might have arrived separately for this Feast of Weeks.

The events of the Day of Pentecost may be the most outwardly spectacular occasion at the time of the restoration of the gospel, but there were certainly many others only slightly less notable.

Events at the death of Christ

Matthew 27:50-54 deals with a time period about seven weeks before Pentecost. It contains a great deal of information about events surrounding Christ's death and the independent startup of the church without his constant physical presence and leadership, and is a good place to start this particular narrative.

> Matthew 27:
> 50 Jesus, when he had cried again with a loud voice, yielded up the ghost.
> 51 And, behold, the veil of the temple was rent in twain from the top to the bottom; and the earth did quake, and the rocks rent;

> 52 And the graves were opened; and many bodies of the saints which slept arose,
> 53 And came out of the graves after his resurrection, and went into the holy city, and appeared unto many.
> 54 Now when the centurion, and they that were with him, watching Jesus, saw the earthquake, and those things that were done, they feared greatly, saying, Truly this was the Son of God.

In evaluating the statement "the veil of the temple was rent in twain from the top to the bottom" perhaps we can say that that rent which opened the holy of holies to the impure outside world so that anyone could see it, not just the supposedly highly purified Temple priests, and possibly signaled that all the holiness was gone from the Temple, to the extent that there had been any holiness there recently. It certainly signaled that Christ was done with that structure (and any other structure like it) for a very long time. We might additionally wonder if the centurion saw any resurrected beings, as is hinted at here.

We might note that this Temple was first built in the days of Solomon, sometime during his reign from 970 to 931 BC.

> This [temple] was destroyed in 587 BC and rebuilt by Zerubbabal about 70 years later. The restored structure was partially burned in 37 BC and was partially rebuilt by Herod the Great, although the rebuilding continued until A.D. 64. It was destroyed by the Romans in A.D. 70. (Bible Dictionary "Temple")

Unfortunately, the Bible dictionary article about the Temple is inaccurate on several related points. That article does reflect current 21st century church teachings and practice, but it does not reflect the practice of the Christians for the 300 years after the death of Christ, which seems like it ought to be controlling on how to do things correctly. Those people had no temples and did not require any. They had all the necessary priesthood powers available at the local level without charge, as did the Saints in the time of Joseph Smith, up until the presidency of Wilford Woodruff. The article claims that "In cases of extreme poverty or emergency, these ordinances may sometimes be done on a mountaintop," but that is not correct. We know that work for the dead was done on a regular basis outside of any temples after the atonement of Christ initiated that process. 1 Cor. 15:29. This latter-day drive to return to the law of Moses policies concerning temples is apparently part of the more general drive to return the entire church to a law Moses operating basis, which is so beneficial to a paid ministry, especially including the rigorous central collection of tithing.

At the moment of Christ's death "the earth did quake, and the rocks rent." (There was a lot of "renting" of veils and rocks going on in the Jerusalem area.) This sounds an awful lot like the volcanic activity that went on at about the same time in the New World, although the New World activity was much more severe. This physical activity was surely noted by the centurion in charge of Christ's crucifixion:

> 54 Now when the centurion, and they that were with him, watching Jesus, saw the earthquake, and those things that were done, they feared greatly, saying, Truly this was the Son of God.

In a more modern vernacular, those soldiers might have said "It looks like we dodged a bullet. We could have been blown apart or boiled in lava by the tiniest twitch of Christ's little finger." Indeed, I have wondered about how easy it would have been to convert the Jerusalem area into a very large smoking crater just as happened in the New World, and Christ had some reason to do that, although he, as always, used wisdom and foresight and kept everything within appropriate bounds.

Continuing with the Bible Dictionary article on temples:

> "From Adam to the time of Jesus, ordinances were performed in temples for the living only. After Jesus opened the way for the gospel to be preached in the world of spirits, ceremonial work for the dead, as well as for the living, has been done in temples on the earth by faithful members of the Church. Building and properly using a temple is one of the marks of the true church in any dispensation, and is especially so in the present day."

Again, we know that work for the dead was carried on after the death of Christ, and there were no temples available and none were required. Even the statement concerning Adam is not completely accurate. Living ordinances were clearly done on a regular basis without any temples at nearly every period of time, except perhaps during the time when the law of Moses was in effect. We might ask "Did Adam have to first build a magnificent "Temple of Solomon" before any of his many children and grandchildren could be married?" I believe the answer is no.

Resurrected saints

If the earthquakes were not enough to get everyone's attention, one might guess that a New Testament "Christian zombie apocalypse" surely got the attention of every living soul, especially including the Pharisees, who probably had spies everywhere to make sure that they did not miss anything of importance.

> 52 And the graves were opened; and many bodies of the saints which slept arose,
> 53 And came out of the graves after his resurrection, and went into the holy city, and appeared unto many.

I remember hearing that there were those who were resurrected at the time when Christ was resurrected, but I had not mentally registered the fact that these people "went into the holy city, and appeared unto many." The raising of Lazarus from the dead was a very recent event, which probably caused quite a stir in the Jerusalem area, especially among the Pharisees. So then we should try to imagine what perhaps 1000 Lazarus resurrections, all at once, as widely publicized as possible, with everyone in Jerusalem seeing those people walking around and talking to people, would do to the mental state of the Pharisees and everyone else in Jerusalem. We should not be too surprised to learn from history that some of the Pharisees had a mental breakdown about this time and were reduced to quivering and drooling in a fetal position.

We might recall that one of the Pharisees, Gamaliel, had suggested taking a low-key position and letting these things play out. He may have been wise and contemplative in his suggestion of conservative behavior, but he might also have been frightened out of his wits, and was suggesting that things might go very badly for the Pharisees if they aggressively intervened.

I am assuming that Gamaliel gave his advice after the death and resurrection of Christ, but it may not be clear whether he gave his advice before or after the deaths of Ananias and Sapphira. In the Book of Acts chapter 5, the story of the Gamaliel comes after the story of Ananias and Sapphira. Surely, after the deaths of Ananias and Sapphira, his worst fears would have been verified that if the Pharisees tried to intervene in any way to deflect or compromise or infiltrate this huge new religious movement, they might all end up dead through a similar process. The Savior had made it extremely clear throughout his life, and especially during the last week of his life, and also the weeks thereafter, that he was the Lord of life and death, and, in fact, the priests of the law of Moses were only allowed to live by his good graces, and perhaps they understood that rather personally. (Other prophets had killed all opposing priests on similar occasions. Elijah in 1 Kings 18:40)

We might mention the very public curse on the barren fig tree as Christ entered Jerusalem where that tree immediately died. Matt 21:19. It was just another one of hundreds of indicators of the vast powers that were at play here.

Priests joined the church
It must have been very disconcerting to the law of Moses paid ministry that many of their own, probably including such men as Nicodemus, joined this new church and left their previous station in society and ministry.

> Acts 6:7 And the word of God increased; and the number of the disciples multiplied in Jerusalem greatly; and <u>a great company of the priests were obedient</u>

to the faith.

Presumably those priests who joined would have included Zacharias, father of John the Baptist, assuming he lived long enough. It is likely that he learned the gospel from his own son, and presumably was baptized, and also learned of Christ. But the Scriptures don't seem to tell us exactly when he was murdered by the evil priests. One might wonder on what basis was his murder justified? Was he being interrogated by the evil priests about his son John, where those priests were probably intent on capturing and killing John?

> Matt 23:34 ¶ Wherefore, behold, I send unto you prophets, and wise men, and scribes: and some of them ye shall kill and crucify; and some of them shall ye scourge in your synagogues, and persecute them from city to city:
> 35 That upon you may come all the righteous blood shed upon the earth, from the blood of righteous Abel unto the blood of Zacharias son of Barachias, whom ye slew between the temple and the altar.
> 36 Verily I say unto you, All these things shall come upon this generation.

This indicates that the Pharisees were very upset about the new religion and were willing to kill anyone who threatened their priestcraft way of life, making them as bad as Nehor. Besides Christ himself, we have John the Baptist, John's father Zacharias, Stephen, etc. We might wonder if church leaders today will be as incensed against any who challenge their self-appointed privileged positions.

Effects of "shock and awe"

I think some of this "shock and awe," even though it was not quite on the same scale as occurred in the New World, would still be quite enough to warn everyone who mattered that they should proceed very carefully, because their very lives were on the line. (We might recall that all the firstborn Egyptians were singled out for death in the last plague. Perhaps the Pharisees recalled the same frightening story.) It is possible that it would have an even more powerful effect on an individual psyche than seeing a distant and highly destructive earthquake or volcanic eruption. In the New World, if you lived through the cataclysms, that meant you were a good person. In the old world, you could never be sure which way the personal axe of destruction was going to fall, but most people were probably painfully aware that it could indeed fall on them at any moment.

In this setting of turmoil and uncertainty, it's a little bit surprising that someone like Saul the Pharisee was still so fanatical that he continued to persecute Christians. However, we might note that on one occasion he merely held the coats of those who killed Stephen as opposed to directly participating. Perhaps he was wisely testing the system to see whether they would all immediately die or whether they would be allowed to live. Since they were allowed to live, he probably took heart and decided to continue on the road to Damascus to persecute some more Christians. However, the system caught up with him there and dealt with him rather roughly, blinding and frightening him. Damascus, Syria, was about 135 miles away from Jerusalem, and presumably operated under a very different set of laws than existed in Jerusalem of Judea.

There might have been multiple messages in this event. Perhaps Saul's experience indicated that the Savior was encouraging the Saints to leave Jerusalem and go to other places, such as Damascus, preferably as far away from Jerusalem is possible. And, at the same time, any attempts by the Pharisees to follow the church members and continue the persecution would be dealt with harshly. We do read that the Saints had gathered to some new places, and apparently were not harassed there by the Jews, tending to demonstrate that there were heaven-protected sanctuary cities outside of Jerusalem. This would leave the Saints with enormous negative incentives to leave Jerusalem and with similarly positive welcoming incentives to relocate, knowing that they could find safe spaces.

We read that within two years, there simply were no more church members in Jerusalem, all of them having left town. "[A]nd they were all scattered abroad throughout the regions of Judea and Samaria, except the apostles." Acts 8:1. That becomes important a little bit later when we talk about the very revealing case of Ananias and Sapphira. If we understand correctly the setting in which that story took place, then these people in Jerusalem who were helping each other were in an unusual "use it or lose it" situation. They were all planning to leave anyway, so if some could sell their property so that they could use some of their wealth to get themselves to a new town, and if they could help their friends get to a new town, then that would be as ideal as was possible at the time. Otherwise, they would just have to leave these things behind with no gain whatsoever. The wisest and most sensible thing then would be to sell the property, if possible, and use that money to get yourself and your friends out of town, because if you waited any longer, you might not be able to sell the property and you would simply lose it, perhaps along with your freedom or your life.

This high-pressure gathering scenario is very much the same as happened in the time of Joseph Smith. People were excited to hear about the gospel and anxious to join with other Saints, but many of them simply picked up stakes from their farms in New York or wherever, and went to Kirtland or Missouri and arrived penniless. They left behind valuable property simply because they didn't have the patience to wait to sell it. This became a nightmare in Kirtland and Missouri because a very large portion of the people who arrived there had nothing but the clothes on their back, even though they could have contributed thousands of dollars to the cause of Zion if they had been a little more wise in their dealings.

The strange situation that put these people in during the time of Joseph Smith was almost exactly the same thing which happened to the Saints right after the death of Christ. Behaving tribally and sharing everything makes a great deal of sense in the case where if you don't share it then everybody loses. (For example, if someone has a good hunt, they might as well share their good fortune with everyone, because they can't eat it all and they can't preserve it, so they might as well share it so that they can be eligible to share in someone else's successful hunt later on.) It is not a matter of being selfish or not being selfish. It is a matter of being practical in an obvious way.

It makes perfect practical sense to treat this initial restoration gathering situation much like a wagon train operation, where you rationally pool all your resources and get on with what needs to be done, doing as well as you can. No one in their right mind would think that this was an ideal situation that should go on for the rest of your life. It is simply a practical way to get through a critical hard spot so that normal life can resume in another location. People seem to continually make the shortsighted and foolish observation that just because one has to "join the Army" for a year or two as a way to save the whole group, that the ideal way to live life is to be in the army the rest of your life. That is just nonsense, and has no relationship to practicalities or people's feelings. Most certainly it is not something required by the gospel beyond the need to help others survive these hard times.

More on volcanoes, earthquakes, and destruction

I think it is interesting to know that there are 30 volcanoes in Italy, some of which have been active on and off. At the time of Christ's death, the most recent Italian eruption of note had occurred in 104 BC. In other words, it seems likely that the soldiers could easily imagine some very serious volcanic eruptions, the kind which they perhaps sensed that they had just barely escaped.

It is also interesting that in the year 79 A.D., Mount Vesuvius exploded and completely destroyed the cities of Pompeii, Herculaneum, and others. The historical notes concerning Pompeii mention that many people from Rome regularly ventured there on holiday. It is interesting to speculate whether there were certain important Roman citizens who died in that horrendous blast who might have been tempted to increase the persecution of Christians in Rome and the Roman Empire. (I believe the movie "Pompeii" implies that that was true.) That might have been one way to tamp down the persecutions against the Christians. We might wonder whether some people took that devastating blast as an indication that there was something wrong with the way the Romans were operating their country.

There might be an interesting connection here between the destruction of Jerusalem in 70 A.D., perhaps brought on by very unwise behavior by the Jews. That 70 A.D. event basically ended the kingdom of the Jews and their ability to have a major organized political influence anywhere in the world for the next 2000 years. Likely that had something to do with protecting the Saints from any long-term Jewish persecution.

To have an event on the scale of the Mount Vesuvius explosion just a few years later in 79 A.D., where possibly a large number of important Romans were wiped out, seems to offer the historical possibility that the Romans were being repaid for their fanatical attack on Jerusalem, even though it would have a good effect for many Christians, and that the loss of those Romans in Pompeii would also help to protect Christians from even more aggressive Roman persecution. It would be interesting if someone could review any detailed historical records of these times to see if any of my speculations contain any truth.

Various articles indicate the level of continuing Jewish persecution of the new Christians. Here is one:

> Main article: Persecution of Christians in the New Testament
> Early Christianity began as a sect among Second Temple Jews, and according to the New Testament account, Pharisees, including Paul of Tarsus prior to his conversion to Christianity, persecuted early Christians. The early Christians preached the second coming of a Messiah which did not conform to their religious teachings. However, feeling that their beliefs were supported by Jewish scripture, Christians had been hopeful that their countrymen would accept their faith. Despite individual conversions, the vast majority of Judean Jews did not become Christians.
>
> Claudia Setzer asserts that, "Jews did not see Christians as clearly separate from their own community until at least the middle of the second century." Thus, acts of Jewish persecution of Christians fall within the boundaries of synagogue discipline and were so perceived by Jews acting and thinking as the established community. The Christians, on the other hand, saw themselves as persecuted rather than "disciplined."
> https://en.wikipedia.org/wiki/Persecution_of_Christians

It would be interesting to know if by considering persecution of Christians an internal matter, "synagogue discipline," that allowed the Jews to kill Christians where they would not be authorized to do so under Roman law. Why were the Jews allowed to kill Stephen but not Christ? Was it merely because they stoned him instead of crucifying him?

We do know that the Jerusalem church lasted much longer than the church in the New World, which was completely wiped out after 300 years, where the old world church was still doing reasonably well after 300 years, and continued on to basically create Western civilization where individual freedom was considered extremely valuable and necessary to human life.

The size of the early church

Is there any way to guess at the size of the church perhaps within a year of the death of the Savior? If we tally up the impressions Christ and his apostles made on many men, and, through them, their families, the numbers add up very quickly. We can probably assume that there were many events that were not recorded in the scriptures, so that would lead us to further multiply the available numbers. Here are a few examples:

> Acts 4:1 And as they spake unto the people, the priests, and the captain of the temple, and the Sadducees, came upon them,
> 2 Being grieved that they taught the people, and preached through Jesus the resurrection from the dead.
> 3 And they laid hands on them, and put them in hold unto the next day: for it was now eventide.
> 4 Howbeit many of them which heard the word believed; and the number of the men was about five thousand.

Here the apostles boldly used an area near the Temple, it appears, and added 5000 men. If they were all heads of families of five people, that would be 25,000 in one instance.

> Matt. 14:19 And he commanded the multitude to sit down on the grass, and took the five loaves, and the two fishes, and looking up to heaven, he blessed, and brake, and gave the loaves to his disciples, and the disciples to the multitude.
> 20 And they did all eat, and were filled: and they took up of the fragments that remained twelve baskets full.
> 21 And they that had eaten were about five thousand men, beside women and children.

So, another 5,000 men, or 25,000 people were added in all.

> Matt. 15:29 And Jesus departed from thence, and came nigh unto the sea of Galilee; and went up into a mountain, and sat down there.
> 30 And great multitudes came unto him, having with them those that were lame, blind, dumb, maimed, and many others, and cast them down at Jesus' feet; and he healed them:
> 31 Insomuch that the multitude wondered, when they saw the dumb to speak, the maimed to be whole, the lame to walk, and the blind to see: and they glorified the God of Israel.
> 32 ¶ Then Jesus called his disciples unto him, and said, I have compassion on the multitude, because they continue with me now three days, and have nothing to eat: and I will not send them away fasting, lest they faint in the way.
> 33 And his disciples say unto him, Whence should we have so much bread in the wilderness, as to fill so great a multitude?

> 34 And Jesus saith unto them, How many loaves have ye? And they said, Seven, and a few little fishes.
> 35 And he commanded the multitude to sit down on the ground.
> 36 And he took the seven loaves and the fishes, and gave thanks, and brake them, and gave to his disciples, and the disciples to the multitude.
> 37 And they did all eat, and were filled: and they took up of the broken meat that was left seven baskets full.
> 38 And they that did eat were four thousand men, beside women and children.

This time another 4,000 men, or 20,000 people were added in all.

We don't often talk about where the multitudes appeared from to celebrate Christ's triumphal entry into Jerusalem, but surely there were thousands of them if they could pave a long path for the king with their garments. It seems reasonable to assume that many of them were church members at that point.

> Matt. 21:8 And a very great multitude spread their garments in the way; others cut down branches from the trees, and strawed them in the way.
> 9 And the multitudes that went before, and that followed, cried, saying, Hosanna to the Son of David: Blessed is he that cometh in the name of the Lord; Hosanna in the highest.
> 10 And when he was come into Jerusalem, all the city was moved, saying, Who is this?
> 11 And the multitude said, This is Jesus the prophet of Nazareth of Galilee.
> 12 And Jesus went into the temple of God, and cast out all them that sold and bought in the temple, and overthrew the tables of the moneychangers, and the seats of them that sold doves,
> 13 And said unto them, It is written, My house shall be called the house of prayer; but ye have made it a den of thieves.
> 14 And the blind and the lame came to him in the temple; and he healed them.
> 15 And when the chief priests and scribes saw the wonderful things that he did, and the children crying in the temple, and saying, Hosanna to the Son of David; they were sore displeased,

Christ was certainly doing all he could to stir up a hornet's nest by cleansing the temple and then healing the blind and lame in the Temple and then hearing his followers shout Hosanna in the Temple. We don't have an estimate of crowd size for this event, but based on the crowd sizes he typically drew together and healed and converted, that might amount to another 5,000 men or 25,000 total family members.

Here we might take note of another interesting provocation on the part of Christ: Basically, on the first day that he announced his role as the Messiah, by speaking at the synagogue in Nazareth, he also infuriated most of the listeners so that they tried to kill him, and apparently, he never returned there again. Luke 4:16-30. He obviously often stirred up very strong feelings among his observers. It is too bad in this case that his neighbors who knew him well could not perceive the good he had come to do.

The Day of Pentecost events added 3,000 men or 15,000 in all:

> Acts 2:41 Then they that gladly received his [Peter's] word were baptized: and the same day there were added unto them <u>about three thousand souls</u>.
> 42 And they continued steadfastly in the apostles' doctrine and fellowship, and in breaking of bread, and in prayers.
> 43 And fear came upon every soul: and many wonders and signs were done by the apostles.
> 44 And all that believed were together, and had all things common;
> 45 And sold their possessions and goods, and parted them to all men, as every man had need. [Recall that the Christians were quickly leaving Jerusalem to escape persecution.]
> 46 And they, continuing daily with one accord in the temple, and breaking bread from house to house, did eat their meat with gladness and singleness of heart,
> 47 Praising God, and having favour with all the people. And the Lord added to the church daily such as should be saved.

So, we have estimated so far 25,000+25,000+20,000+25,000+15,000 = 110,000 and we have only described a few day's work for the Savior and his apostles. Based on this small sample of data about early church growth, I am going to guess that there were at least 200,000 church members within a few months of Christ's death, and at least 400,000 church members within a year of his death.

We need to say something about the members' economic arrangements:

> Acts 2:44 And all that believed were together, and had all things common;
> 45 And sold their possessions and goods, and parted them to all men, as every man had need.

We should recall that the Christians were quickly leaving Jerusalem to escape persecution. They had only delayed their leaving because Christ himself had requested they remain until the Day of Pentecost for a special experience. One example of their desire to quickly leave Jerusalem seems to come from the story about how Saul became Paul. I don't recall that any of the travels of Christ or the travels of the apostles had taken them anywhere near Damascus, Syria where they might have converted some local residents. (The scriptures seem to tell us that Caesarea Philippi was the northernmost extent of Christ's journeys, still quite a distance from Damascus, and no specific missionary work seems to have happened at that time.) We should probably assume that a large group of church members in Damascus was there because they had left the Jerusalem area where nearly all conversions had taken place. We might also wonder whether Saul was headed for Damascus, simply because his own actions, including the death of Stephen, Acts 7:54-60, had driven thousands of church members out of Jerusalem. Acts 11:19. If there were still many thousands of church members in Jerusalem, why wouldn't Saul be attacking them there rather than making the strenuous journey of about 135 miles from Jerusalem to Damascus where the outcome of his efforts could not be known in advance?

Ananias and Sapphira and Christian civilization

I wanted to cover some of this New Testament "shock and awe" material in preparation for perhaps the most powerful "shock and awe" incident recorded in the New Testament concerning the story of Ananias and Sapphira. It may not actually exceed in significance having perhaps 1000 resurrected beings wandering the streets of Jerusalem a few days after Christ's resurrection, but it did have an enormous impact when it happened, and its correct interpretation has an overwhelming logical impact today, bringing some of that early "shock and awe" into our times.

It is important to revisit this incident because the usual account and interpretation of the story is not only wrong, but is exactly the opposite of the content and significance of the real event, and its constant incorrect retelling has been used for a damaging purpose in teaching the Gospel.

What a Christian civilization is and is not

The story of Ananias and Sapphira has been used millions of times as part of an argument that one's religious salvation requires giving up large amounts of personal freedom, even though, I would argue, personal freedom is the first principle of the gospel, without which the gospel of Christ becomes the gospel of Satan.

In the ideal civilization, recommended and commanded by God in many different ways, there are no more important principles than that of maximum personal freedom concerning religion and politics. That naturally includes the maximum freedom of individual ownership and management of property, and that maximum freedom of property can only occur when a society leaves the maximum amount of discretion to the individual as to how he administers his resources through nongovernment charitable processes concerning his family and others. Today's aggressively socialist countries throughout the world do all in their power to extract through taxes on the people all the necessary resources for operating a secular government, but they also go perhaps 10 times beyond that minimum needed amount for good government and also try to take over all legitimate charitable and welfare functions as well, forcing a practical and secular religion of atheism on their people for the very purpose of crushing out the competing loyalties and mechanisms of Christianity.

It appears that the first and most powerful argument of Satan against Christianity is the biggest of "big lies" that the only way to be acceptable to Christ is to live perfectly the laws of Satan which always involve maximum force and control and maximum centralization of everything under principles which are variously known as socialism/Marxism/communism. The presence of the slightest hint of any of that set of principles is a sure sign that Satanism is being preached to a greater or lesser degree. Satan wants total control of everyone in his celestial slave state, with everyone marching in nice little rows and giving him all of their allegiance and all of their resources.

Ananias and Sapphira

Perhaps the single biggest piece of propaganda on this topic, the greatest single story and argument in the endless preaching of the various communalism/communism/Satanism perversions of Christianity comes to us from a conscious distortion and lie of the blackest and most egregious sort extracted from a single story in the New Testament.

This is the story about Ananias and Sapphira which appears in Acts 5. Ostensibly, as it is so often told, it is a story about how all the members of the church at that time were required, as a condition of membership, to convert all their goods into money and give it all to the church, making them paupers and giving themselves over to the complete temporal control of their church leaders. Based on that Acts 5 story, today we are told that tithing, which only requires 10% of our resources annually, instead of the supposedly original 100%, is the literally "lesser" law that has been given to us because we are too weak and foolish and faithless to live the 100% consecration law. If members complain that paying 10% is too much, they are then threatened with a reversion to the 100% level as a kind of punishment for their rebellion.

However, all of this propaganda about a church's right to control its members and all their property as a condition of achieving salvation is totally wrong, nothing but the manipulations and contrivances of evil people who wish to control and exploit the larger mass of people who have good intentions but are naïve and thus are easily exploited, making their leaders even more culpable for taking advantage of their trust.

Actually, I believe what we have here is Peter, in effect, denying that as a church leader he makes any claim on whatever property they may have. It was their property to do with as they wished. Although this is certainly a confusing situation, I take this all to mean that there was something else going on here besides "having all things in common." The fatal lie was not that Ananias and Sapphira were not turning over the full amount of the proceeds of their sale, or that they had any duty to do so, but that they were spending some particular amount of money to try to ingratiate themselves into the church organization, perhaps as a way to gain control of it and subvert it to some extent. To repeat, it's not even clear that these two people had been baptized – most likely not. In the spirit of "following the money," which affects all public activity, this looks like a good place for a transcribing priest to have modified the story slightly to make it more likely that he and others like him could collect money from ordinary members.

> Acts 5:1 But a certain man named Ananias, with Sapphira his wife, sold a possession,
> 2 And kept back part of the price, his wife also being privy to it, and brought a certain part, and laid it at the apostles' feet.
> 3 But Peter said, Ananias, why hath Satan filled thine heart to lie to the Holy Ghost, and to keep back part of the price of the land?
> 4 Whiles it remained, was it not thine own? and after it was sold, was it not in thine own power? why hast thou conceived this thing in thine heart? thou hast not lied unto men, but unto God.
> 5 And Ananias hearing these words fell down, and gave up the ghost: and great fear came on all them that heard these things.

As will be explained in much more detail later on, I think the interpretation I am giving here is accurate. As mentioned in verse 13 and 14, the ordinary members rushed to join the church in multitudes. That would be quite irrational if they feared that the tiniest accounting mistake on their part could end up in their deaths. That bit of logic should tell us that something else was indeed going on here.

> Acts 5:12 And by the hands of the apostles were many signs and wonders wrought among the people; (and they were all with one accord in Solomon's porch.
> 13 And of the rest [*rulers*] durst no man join himself to them: but the people magnified them.
> 14 And believers were the more added to the Lord, multitudes both of men and women.)

It seems that the first thing that is forgotten in religious matters is that men are meant to be as free as Adam, who had no man who even COULD claim to rule over him. The book entitled *The World In The Grip Of An Idea* presents in great detail the constant attacks on man's freedom using sophistry and propaganda to convince man to accept his own bondage as actually desirable. Everyone knows about the war in heaven, but not everyone seems to realize that the intensity of that war has not receded in the least, and is still raging, now merely relocated to an earthly realm where real pain and real death can be used as further means of persuasion – forces presumably far beyond the means of argument available to competing advocates in the spirit world.

We can be sure that the use of any means of force, whether extreme arguments or threats or intimidation or mockery, or more direct physical attacks, are all counter to God's will for us and need to be resisted resolutely, even when they come from sources that seem to be within the church itself. This especially includes its leaders, who have the greatest temptation to take the wrong ideological position because they are the ones who stand to immediately benefit from impinging on individual freedom and receiving the world's goods in return.

Christ passed a series of critical temptations at the beginning of his earthly ministry, but most other men fail those tests. Such great men as Lehi, Nephi, King Benjamin, King Mosiah, Alma, Joseph Smith, Brigham Young, and John Taylor all passed the test, even while under great pressure, but Wilford Woodruff, and all his contemporary and subsequent "prophets, seers, and revelators," have succumbed to those temptations and now defend their choices as matters of THEIR personal freedom and calling and "keys," even if other members are very specifically not treated the same way.

The temptations of Christ concerned earthly fame, power, and riches. Luke 4:1-13. He rejected them all, and instructed his disciples to do the same, but the results have been mixed in times since. Unfortunately, today, acceptance of these corrupt and anti-scriptural principles of earthly organization is now a prerequisite for being ordained to the apostleship, starting at the time of Wilford Woodruff and his doctrinal and policy disputes with Moses Thatcher and B. H. Roberts.

We might note that early in church history it was voted that Joseph Smith and Oliver Cowdery should receive each receive a salary (of about $3000, I believe, a very large sum at the time, certainly equal to at least ($3,000*28.50=) $85,500 in today's currency.). Later that vote was rescinded, and I know of no repeated votes on the subject. I assume that kind of salary was far beyond the means of the church members at that time. They could barely survive themselves, let alone pay someone else's salary. https://www.officialdata.org/1832-dollars-in-2017

I think it is significant that the Articles of Faith document prepared by Joseph Smith makes no mention of tithing or of any other church contributions as part of this summary "creed." As an indicator of church policy change on this point over the years, we might notice that the church-prepared materials on "Self-reliance" place tithing (paid to the central offices) as the number one goal to be achieved by those wishing to achieve self-reliance. This may indeed be a church goal, but member-level goals should be much different, since they should be grounded in real charity. If Joseph Smith gave "tithing" the overwhelming importance assigned to it by the current church for members to be in good standing, he would surely have included tithing paid to the central offices as among the first articles of faith.

The most fascinating thing about the story of Ananias and Sapphira which appears in Acts 5 is that it was meant to teach, and did teach, at the time, the exact opposite of the lesson that it is used to teach today in a church where the first principle of salvation is paying tithing, and all other factors are clustered at a distant second level of importance. (Tithing as necessary fire insurance, etc.) Obviously, a paid ministry clergy WOULD make tithing the number one doctrine since their desired generous livelihood depends on that constant income, independent of what their personal resources or needs might be. And, speaking sarcastically, how could the members possibly get along with only the Scriptures and personal revelation to guide them on every imaginable gospel question? Wouldn't they naturally need a huge set of Levites to help keep them in line?

Here is the article that provided the insight that all of our usual interpretations of the story of Ananias and Sapphira completely miss the point and are directly backwards from the truth. I don't think I could improve on his presentation or even shorten it much, by rewriting it, so I will just quote almost the entire thing:

> Preachers for years have told us that Ananias and Sapphira were believers because they wanted to see it that way and they wanted their hearers to understand it that way. Fear of judgment on the believer is one of the false teachings out there that many use to keep the saints walking in obedience. It doesn't work, but they try it any way. But the New Covenant knows nothing of a fear of judgment on the believer. The very "idea" is a misnomer. As John wrote, "We have confidence in the day of judgment and we have no fear for as Jesus is so are we in this world."
>
> In fact, the most glaring fact found in Chapter 5 of the Book of Acts that proves Ananias and Sapphira were not believers is the very event of judgment itself that fell on these two people. It should be our first reaction to say that they must have not been believers, but because we are not confident in the bold assertion of God Himself that "He will be merciful to all our iniquities and remember our sin no more" in this New Covenant because of the death of His Son, Jesus, we wonder about this scene.
>
> The chapter does not state clearly that Ananias and Sapphira were believers, nor does it say that they were unbelievers. The reader must read the context with an understanding that judgment simply cannot fall on a believer, not a true believer, otherwise we don't have a New Covenant and all the promises of God relative to the work of His Son are meaningless. So, what clues can we find in the passage that indicate they were not believers. To begin with, every time Luke refers to a believer in the book of Acts, he prefaces it by saying, "a certain disciple named . . ." But in the case of Ananias and Sapphira Luke writes, "A man named Annanias, with his wife Sapphira . . ." Because of this one statement one could say Luke is clearly saying that they were not believers. Also, Peter refers to Ananias as one in whom "Satan has filled his heart." [Acts 5:3] The same phrase used of Judas and certainly not a phrase you can use when referring to any believer for the

> believer has a new heart and is filled with the Holy Spirit. As Peter says in the meeting in Jerusalem, recorded by Luke in chapter 15 of Acts, God "cleanses the heart" of all who believe on Jesus. Another clue is the reference to "the rest of the group" that Ananias and Sapphira came out of being in fear. The "rest of that group" that Ananias and Sapphira came out of "dared not try" the same thing. Ananias and Sapphira saw a good thing and tried to buy themselves a place among the believers.
>
> Also, Luke writes that all the more people were constantly being added to the church. People were flocking to the church. True believers. There was no fear that they would suffer the same fate as Ananias and Sapphira if they committed some sin, but rather they had heard the joyful news that all their sins were placed on the Christ and through Him they could receive the complete forgiveness of all sin so that sin would no longer even be imputed to them ever again. And they also understood that there was a God in heaven, a Heavenly Father, who was going to watch over His sheep and protect His sheep from those who would try to enter in to the flock by another door, other than through faith in Jesus. This kind of drastic action is not something God does to unbelievers on a regular basis because He has provided forgiveness for all people and He is constantly reaching out to the unbeliever in great patience and mercy, but at the inception of the tiny church He was zealous to make clear that the only currency He recognizes in His kingdom is the currency of faith, not money.
>
> The only fact in the entire passage that may indicate that Ananias and Sapphira were believers is the fact that they were trying to join the church. That's it. That's the only fact that might lead someone to see them as believers. All the other facts and clues in the passage clearly argue that they are unbelievers without doubt. Think of all the people in our society that join churches across the world every day for whatever reason (social, business, moral, etc.) and they are no more a true believer than, as it has been said, being in a garage makes you a car. Hopefully those people will become believers as they hear the good news but to say that Ananias and Sapphira were believers based on this one fact alone is not only intellectually dishonest but a sloppy reading of the text. It is sad to me to think of the millions of believers through the centuries that have been put in fear of judgment because of preachers who preached this passage wrongly. Without realizing it, they were doing the work of Satan himself. For as Paul said, think it not strange that Satan himself is able to make himself appear as an angel of light and his ministers as ministers of righteousness.
>
> I'm so glad we can with all confidence proclaim the good news to all that whosoever believes on Jesus shall receive the forgiveness of all sin, past, present and future, and be given the gift of the Holy Spirit, joining them to God Himself through Christ. As Jesus said so clearly, "He who believes on Me shall not come into judgment but has already passed from death and into life!"
> "Reconciling the Story of Ananias and Sapphira with the New Covenant of Grace"
> http://seeinggrace.com/blog/?p=25

We should note that this discussion is about the Protestant concept of the boundless nature of the Savior's grace, not about whether or not one should pay tithing or other resources to some religious official as a matter of religious duty required to gain salvation. However, the logic applies almost equally well in either case. Many Protestants do not teach or accept the concept of tithing, the Quakers being one group which is adamantly against it, based on their analysis of the Scriptures and of church history, but these Protestant commentators are concerned just as strongly about religious freedom and freedom from bondage to preachers who try to frighten people into contributing to their personal cause, their one-man priestcraft ambitions. So, I believe the argument works quite well either way.

This story of Ananias and Sapphira raises many other issues and has many other consequences for today's LDS religion, and all those other factors need to be spelled out.

Just as with the law of Moses or any other of many paid ministry situations, from the very beginning of the church in our time it was plagued with constant attempts to turn it into a source of profit for ambitious preachers. Enemies of the gospel within the church were constantly trying to turn it into corrupt but profitable priestcraft, while at the same time enemies on the outside of the church were charging Mormons with the evils of preaching required communalism in hopes of frightening people into not joining the church (which would likely lower the priestcraft income of the outsiders making false allegations).

There were innumerable discussions of the proper rules of religious life, with many asserting over and over again that only a strong communalism could meet the requirements for salvation (while also incidentally providing those advocates with a convenient temporal salvation or living of their own).

Joseph Smith constantly fought that strong tendency toward required communalism (alias paid ministry).

> Here is another quotation defining the economic relationship of the members to the church:
>
> > Tuesday, 8. - I spent the day with Elder Rigdon in visiting Elder Cahoon at the place he selected for his residence, and in attending to some of our private, personal affairs; also in the afternoon I answered the questions which were frequently asked me, while on my last journey but one from Kirtland to Missouri, as printed in the *Elders Journal,* Vol. I, Number II, pages 28 and 29, as follows:
> > ...Sixth - "Do the Mormons believe in having all things in common?"
> > No.
> > ...Twelfth - "Do the people have to give up their money when they join his Church?" No other requirement than to bear their proportion of the expenses of the Church, and support the poor.

> ...I published the forgoing answers to save myself the trouble of repeating the same a thousand times over and over again.[10] (HC 3:28-29. May 8, 1838, Far West.)

The comment "no other requirement than to bear their proportion of the expenses of the church, and support the poor," makes it clear that no complicated joinder of property was required. The "thousand times over" comment shows that the whole topic was one which people tediously refused to understand.
Kent W. Huff, *Joseph Smith's United Order: A Non-Communalistic Interpretation* (Orem, Ut., Cedar Fort, Inc., 1988), p.26.

This brings up the undying theme of the story of Ananias and Sapphira.

We might notice that the topic of tithing is not even mentioned here. There were indeed some financial transactions going on to care for the poor and help with the expenses of the church, but none of those were mandatory and none of them came under the category of religiously required tithing. As the headnote to Doctrine and Covenants 119 points out, the term "tithing" was used occasionally, but it meant nothing more than general free will contributions. Somehow, beginning with the fourth president of the church, old scriptural entries that were interpreted one way for 66 years, were suddenly reversed to mean the opposite for the convenience of the current leaders.

Brigham Young had also continued to resist these never-ending suggestions of religiously required financial advantages over others (some are always more equal than others in these strange communalist arrangements). He very specifically rejected the usual interpretation of Acts 5, but apparently did not have the historical background to explain the exact series of errors embodied in the story as usually told. Here is Brigham Young's treatment of the question. It was clear to him that whatever the doctrinal or historical issues may be, it would be a complete disaster as a practical matter and so should not be considered:

> Those who are in favor of an equality in property say that that is the doctrine taught in the New Testament. True, the Savior said to the young man, "Go and sell that thou hast, and give to the poor, and thou shalt have treasure in heaven, and come and follow me," in order to try him and prove whether he had faith or not.
>
> In the days of the Apostles, the brethren sold their possessions and laid them at the Apostles' feet. And where did many of those brethren go to? To naught, to confusion and destruction. Could those Apostles keep the Church together, on those principles? No. Could they build up the kingdom on those principles? No, they never could. Many of those persons were good men, but they were filled with enthusiasm,

> insomuch that if they owned a little possession they would place it at the feet of the Apostles.
>
> Will such a course sustain the kingdom? No. Did it, in the days of the Apostles? No. Such a policy would be the ruin of this people, and scatter them to the four winds. We are to be guided by superior knowledge, by a higher influence and power. JD 4:29 BY Aug. 17, 1856 SLC. Discussed in Kent W. Huff, *Brigham Young's United Order: A Contextual Interpretation* (Springville, Utah, Cedar Fort, Inc., 1992), p.127-8

We can at least say that Brigham Young got part of his scriptural history correct when he notes that the early Jerusalem members were scattered to the four winds, something he definitely wanted to avoid in Utah, although he doesn't describe here all the underlying factors in the Jerusalem situation.

I can't claim credit for these insights into Acts 5, although I can take credit for realizing during most of my life that there was a critical question contained in the normal telling of the story, and then asking an important question about other possible interpretations of this story which might have a contrary lesson to teach, and then confirming that Joseph Smith knew the right answer and was not misled by this story, as is indicated by a single word change in the Joseph Smith Translation of the Bible. That single word substitution by Joseph Smith can serve as a powerful "smoking gun" level of evidence to indicate that those who came after him and taught a contrary interpretation of this New Testament story, as began with Wilford Woodruff and his two counselors and the 10 apostles holding office at the time, were at least extremely negligent in their studies of the most important principles of the gospel or, more likely, since this has always been a source of lively discussion and strong disagreement among members and leaders, they were conscious and intentional participants in a serious distortion of the gospel for their own personal benefit.

Brigham Young worries about prosperous saints

Brigham Young expressed his concern more than once that the Saints would only follow the gospel carefully as long as they were poor and persecuted. He feared that as soon as they had a few extra worldly resources, they would start to rely on the arm of flesh and forget their faith in the Lord who had taken them through so much. However, I think he was worrying about the wrong thing, as things turned out. As church members improved their economic situation, the church members stayed faithful generally, but it is the church leaders who went rogue. When the church members were poor, there was nothing that could be extracted from them to build a lucrative paid ministry system. The leaders would "make a virtue of necessity" by not trying to collect money enough to allow them to have a salary, so that they could be proud of themselves for being so humble. However, as soon as the members' economic situation improved, that meant that there was some excess which the church leaders could then siphon off to create their own class society with them being the beneficiaries. And that is where we are today.

Ideally, the extra resources which the Saints were able to collect together should have been used for charitable purposes to make the Mormon society all that it ought to be and also use those resources to spread charity and prosperity and success to the rest of the nation. But instead, the church leaders saw this small amount of excess as a chance for them to take that excess and spend it on themselves, including doing some prideful empire building and building up a permanent bureaucracy, a faithful staff of retainers, a king's court, who would offer them continual adulation. The idea of vastly expanding charitable operations seems never to have occurred to them, but that is apparently typical of all priestcraft situations. The only charity they recognized was themselves.

Joseph Smith's trillion-dollar one-word retranslation of Acts 5:13
I recently discovered something extremely fascinating about Acts 5 and the story about Ananias and Sapphira. I have presented above an interpretation which is the complete opposite of what most LDS people have probably heard about this story and its historical and doctrinal and economic meaning. Simply because we have heard this interpretation of the story possibly presented thousands of times as the exact opposite of what was actually true, a few people might not be willing to easily accept this opposite interpretation. The fascinating thing is that Joseph Smith appears to have completely understood the correct interpretation and even left some important evidence of his correct interpretation by changing one critical word in the Book of Acts.

More accurately, Joseph Smith's trillion dollar one-word retranslation of Acts 5:13 could have *saved* us about $1 trillion in mostly wasted and even counterproductive tithing collections if church members and leaders had not forgotten or misrepresented the correct interpretation of the Ananias and Sapphira story.

The one-word change
Joseph Smith certainly was adamant about presenting the correct interpretation of this story about Ananias and Sapphira, or at least the important related doctrinal points, and he did so many times throughout his life, never wavering. Brigham Young perfectly agreed with him on the relevant doctrinal points, although Brigham Young seems not to have been as well-informed as Joseph Smith on the actual scriptural history and interpretation. Here is the relevant text from the New Testament:

Acts 5:13 And of the [a]rest durst no man join himself to them: but the people magnified them.
Note 13a JST Acts 5:13 … *rulers* …

New reading:
Acts 5:13 And of the rulers durst no man join himself to them: but the people magnified them.

Based on an apparently self-interested and intentional misunderstanding of the New Testament text, over the last 120 years the LDS church has collected and redirected at least $1 trillion of membership money into uses that were never authorized under the policies of Jesus Christ. Over that 120 year period the church leadership gradually build up a mythology based on misinterpreting the Scriptures and the history and the general doctrine of the Church of Christ, all for the purpose of creating a burgeoning paid ministry at the expense of the membership, where that process basically ended the original policies of individual charity and required the redirecting of all that money to support a very expensive and wasteful paid ministry.

Probably since about 1900, the church has consistently misrepresented the meaning of the story of Ananias and Sapphira found in Acts chapter 5 of the New Testament. Numerous misinterpretations of that story are continually propagated. The story is read as indicating that the early Saints lived in a form of required communalism, where everyone was required to put all their property into a single pool. But that requirement never existed. People had their own private property and only ever contributed to the needs of others as they saw fit. Without that complete and continual religious and political freedom, the concept of charity has no meaning at all.

Multiple major misinterpretations have been continually propagated. The logic goes like this: The true state of the gospel is to be in complete bondage to someone else. (Wasn't that Lucifer's plan?) To be acceptable to God one has to give up all private property and donate it to the church and become a pauper. Since that is difficult to do, the Lord has given us the lesser law of tithing which says we only have to give 10% to the church to earn a watered-down salvation. The threat is always in the air that if anyone complains about paying 10%, then the rule will be instituted of everyone having to pay 100%. Not only that, but if someone lies about paying their 100%, they might be struck down like Ananias and Sapphira were. But all of the elements of this narrative are lies and are gross misinterpretations of every involved factor.

If today's typical LDS interpretation is correct, one might wonder why, after the Ananias and Sapphira events, everyone wasn't instantly frightened out of their wits about the thought of joining the church instead of joining it joyfully in large numbers, as they did. I believe the answer is that the lesson they took from this event was completely different from the one today's leaders try to impose on it. This fatal incident was strong evidence that impostors were not to be tolerated and that there was good reason to believe that those who joined the church did so without fear that this church organization would be corrupted by the same people who had corrupted the law of Moses version of the gospel. That promise of purity would cause the true believers to join more quickly and more joyously than before as opposed to filling them with dread that they would be struck down at the slightest provocation.

Simon Magus
There was another case that might have ended in a way similar to that of Ananias and Sapphira, but instead ended happily, with a new and better-informed church member keeping his money and his life:

> Acts 8:9 But there was a certain man, called Simon [Magus], which beforetime in the same city used sorcery, and bewitched the people of Samaria, giving out that himself was some great one:
> 10 To whom they all gave heed, from the least to the greatest, saying, This man is the great power of God.
> 11 And to him they had regard, because that of long time he had bewitched them with sorceries.
> 12 But when they believed Philip preaching the things concerning the kingdom of God, and the name of Jesus Christ, they were baptized, both men and women.
> 13 Then Simon himself believed also: and when he was baptized, he continued with Philip, and wondered, beholding the miracles and signs which were done.
> 14 Now when the apostles which were at Jerusalem heard that Samaria had received the word of God, they sent unto them Peter and John:
> 15 Who, when they were come down, prayed for them, that they might receive the Holy Ghost:
> 16 (For as yet he was fallen upon none of them: only they were baptized in the name of the Lord Jesus.)
> 17 Then laid they their hands on them, and they received the Holy Ghost.
> 18 And when Simon saw that through laying on of the apostles' hands the Holy Ghost was given, he offered them money,
> 19 Saying, Give me also this power, that on whomsoever I lay hands, he may receive the Holy Ghost.
> 20 But Peter said unto him, Thy money perish with thee, because thou hast thought that the gift of God may be purchased with money.
> 21 Thou hast neither part nor lot in this matter: for thy heart is not aright in the sight of God.
> 22 Repent therefore of this thy wickedness, and pray God, if perhaps the thought of thine heart may be forgiven thee.
> 23 For I perceive that thou art in the gall of bitterness, and in the bond of iniquity.
> 24 Then answered Simon, and said, Pray ye to the Lord for me, that none of these things which ye have spoken come upon me.

Barnabas the Cyprian Levite
Here we have another case mentioned in close proximity to the Ananias and Sapphira case. In this case, it was all done without any problems. The

Scriptures are again preaching "all things common," but also typically leaving out the rather critical information that the Saints were all leaving town this fast as they could:

> Acts 4:32 And the multitude of them that believed were of one heart and of one soul: neither said any of them that bought of the things which he possessed was his own; but they had all things common.
> 33 And with great power gave the apostles witness of the resurrection of the Lord Jesus: and great grace was upon them all.
> 34 Neither was there any among them that lacked: for as many as were possessors of lands or houses sold them, and brought the prices of the things that were sold,
> 35 And laid them down at the apostles' feet: and distribution was made unto every man according as he had need.
> 36 And Joses, who by the apostles was surnamed Barnabas, (which is, being interpreted, The son of consolation,) a Levite, and of the country of Cyprus,
> 37 Having land, sold it, and brought the money, and laid it at the apostles' feet.

One puzzling element of this story is that Joses/Barnabas was apparently a Levite, who might thus be living off the tithing of the church members, but who also lived in Cyprus which might mean that the law of Moses did not function that way in Cyprus, meaning that he might have had no special position as a member of the professional priesthood. That would certainly make it easier for him to make the transition to being a church member who earned his own living.

Chapter 12

Discussion of FairMormon questions and answers on professional clergy, paid ministry, and tithing

The Paid Ministry Issue

The FairMormon site asserts many bold answers to the question concerning a paid ministry. Unfortunately, essentially none of their answers are in conformance with the Scriptures or with any kind of theological logic. They begin with the very questionable assumption that every religion needs to be run exactly the same way as a modern Fortune 500 company. Only in that frame of reference do any of their arguments make the slightest ounce of sense, and there is no basis whatsoever to make that assumption in the case of the restored church of Christ. Here are the questions and answers they publish, all of which need to be carefully answered and mostly refuted:

Mormonism and church finances/No paid ministry

https://www.fairmormon.org/answers/Mormonism_and_church_finances/No_paid_ministry

< Mormonism and church finances_(Redirected from Mormonism and Church finances/No paid ministry)

FairMormon Answers Wiki Table of Contents

No paid Latter-day Saint ("Mormon") ministry

Summary: It is claimed that Mormonism prides itself in having unpaid clergy as one proof of the Church's truthfulness. They then point to the fact that some General Authorities, mission presidents, and others do, in fact, receive a living stipend while serving the Church, and point to this as evidence of the "hypocrisy" of the Church.

Subtopics:

Question: What do the scriptures teach about paid ministry in the Church of Jesus Christ?
Question: Does the Church of Jesus Christ of Latter-day Saints employ a professional clergy?
Question: Is the fact that some General Authorities, mission presidents, and others receive a living stipend while serving the Church evidence of the "hypocrisy" of the Church?
Question: Why do General Authorities receive living stipends?
Question: Do General Authorities receive a large sum of money when they are called in order to "keep them quiet"?
Question: Do General Authorities sign a non-disclosure agreement promising to never divulge what they are paid?

Question: Who is the highest-paid Church employee in the Church of Jesus Christ of Latter-day Saints?

Question: What do the scriptures teach about paid ministry in the Church of Jesus Christ?

HAVING A PAID CLERGY IS NOT IN AND OF ITSELF A TERRIBLE THING. PROBLEMS ARISE WHEN THE ISSUE OF MONEY BECOMES A GREATER MOTIVATOR THAN THE THINGS OF GOD

The scriptures mention circumstances in which a paid ministry is appropriate, and also provide several cautions about the practice.

Having a paid clergy is not in and of itself a terrible thing. Problems arise when the issue of money becomes a greater motivator than the things of God (and this can happen to any member). So the members support those who are engaged full time in the work of the Church if necessary, but we also do not have a system where one can simply choose to become one of these full-time workers (for example, by getting a degree and looking for a job as a clergyman). This lack of a professional clergy acts as one of the checks on helping to make sure that it is not the financial reward that drives those who serve in the church.

NEW TESTAMENT: "WHO FEEDETH A FLOCK, AND EATETH NOT OF THE MILK OF THE FLOCK?"

In general, the most explicit statement about it comes from 1 Corinthians 9:7-12:

> *7 Who goeth a warfare any time at his own charges? who planteth a vineyard, and eateth not of the fruit thereof? or who feedeth a flock, and eateth not of the milk of the flock?*
> *8 Say I these things as a man? or saith not the law the same also?*
> *9 For it is written in the law of Moses, Thou shalt not muzzle the mouth of the ox that treadeth out the corn. Doth God take care for oxen?*
> *10 Or saith he it altogether for our sakes? For our sakes, no doubt, this is written: that he that ploweth should plow in hope; and that he that thresheth in hope should be partaker of his hope.*
> *11 If we have sown unto you spiritual things, is it a great thing if we shall reap your carnal things?*
> *12 If others be partakers of this power over you, are not we rather? Nevertheless we have not used this power; but suffer all things, lest we should hinder the gospel of Christ.*
> *13 Do ye not know that they which minister about holy things live of the things of the temple? and they which wait at the altar are partakers with the altar?*
> *14 Even so hath the Lord ordained that they which preach the gospel should live of the gospel.*

The King James language can be a bit archaic; the NIV translation of the last two verses (13 and 14) may be more clear:

> *13 Don't you know that those who serve in the temple get their food from the temple, and that those who serve at the altar share in what is offered on the altar? 14 In the same way, the Lord has commanded that those who preach the gospel should receive their living from the gospel.*

MOST OF THE EARLY MEMBERS HAD A REAL DISTRUST OF PAID CLERGY

Within the church, we often tend to forget that the context for the "unpaid" aspect of the church goes back to general distrust of paid clergy at the time the church was formed (in 1830), which stemmed largely from a Protestant view of Catholicism—so most of the early members had a real distrust of paid clergy.

Within the lifetime of Joseph Smith it became apparent that you cannot have a religious organization with individuals who are devoted to the work of that organization (full time) without finding a way to provide for their material needs (and there were swings of opinion as to the extent that the church could or should support individuals even in the first couple of decades). The New Testament verse that they used to justify helping support some leaders in the early LDS Church was Luke 10:7, whose language was reflected in D&C 70:12 –

> Luke 10:7: "And in the same house remain, eating and drinking such things as they give: for the labourer is worthy of his hire. Go not from house to house."
>
> D&C 70:12: "He who is appointed to administer spiritual things, the same is worthy of his hire, even as those who are appointed to a stewardship to administer in temporal things;"

The Doctrine and Covenants Student manual notes:

> *In addition to his many responsibilities in the Church, Joseph Smith had a family, and he could not neglect them, although his responsibility was chiefly a spiritual one. Although not completely relieved from responsibility for his temporal needs at that time, the Prophet was told by the Lord to look to the Church for temporal support. Elder Bruce R. McConkie commented about those who are asked to give full-time service to the Church:*
>
> > *"All our service in God's kingdom is predicated on his eternal law which states: 'The laborer in Zion shall labor for Zion; for if they labor for money they shall perish.' (2 Nephi 26:31.)*
> >
> > *"We know full well that the laborer is worthy of his hire, and that those who devote all their time to the building up of the kingdom must be provided with food, clothing, shelter, and the necessaries of life. We must employ teachers in our schools, architects to design our temples, contractors to build our synagogues, and managers to run our businesses. But those so employed, along with the whole membership of the Church, participate also on a freewill and voluntary basis in otherwise furthering the Lord's work. Bank presidents work on welfare projects. Architects leave their drafting boards to go on missions. Contractors lay down their tools to serve as home teachers or bishops. Lawyers put aside Corpus Juris and the Civil Code to act as guides on Temple Square. Teachers leave the classroom to visit the fatherless and widows in their afflictions. Musicians who make their livelihood from their artistry willingly direct church choirs and perform in church gatherings. Artists who paint for a living are pleased to volunteer their services freely."*[1]
>
> *Temporal support from the members is probably only part of what is implied in these verses, however. The members were encouraged to support and sustain the Prophet in every possible way.*[2]

CHURCH MEMBERS HAVE A PARTICULAR SENSITIVITY TO ISSUES SURROUNDING PAID MINISTRIES PARTICULARLY DUE TO ADMONITIONS IN THE BOOK OF MORMON RELATIVE TO A PRACTICES KNOWN AS PRIESTCRAFT

Perhaps the most explicit scriptural statement about this issue from a negative perspective comes from 2 Nephi 26:31 (cited above).

Church members have a particular sensitivity to issues surrounding paid ministries particularly due to admonitions in the Book of Mormon relative to a practices known as *priestcraft*, which is "that men preach and set themselves up for a light unto the world, that they may get gain and praise of the world; but they seek not the welfare of Zion" (see 2 Nephi 26:29). It is warned against and decried repeatedly (see Alma 1:12,16, 3 Ne 16:10, 3 Ne 21:19, 3 Ne 30:2, D&C 33:4). For this reason, the idea of compensation for service seems contradictory to strongly held values of the Latter-day Saint community. However, it should be noted that priestcraft as it has been defined is a condemnation of intent (to get gain and praise, and not for the welfare of Zion), and not about an individual receiving support. Living stipends are not compensations for service, but recognition of a practical reality that individuals who dedicate their full time to Church service are sometimes unable to simultaneously provide for their own modest living needs.

The example of King Benjamin adds to the LDS value of self sufficiency of leaders in particular. Benjamin, while king, still labored for his own support (see Mosiah 2:14). This is a very admirable demonstration of humility on the part of the king. However, this example was being used in the context of his political position as king, and would be comparable to a President refusing to accept his salary for his service. It should not be used to condemn the practice of helping provide for the modest living needs of full time leaders who are unable to dedicate time to earning a living.

MANY PEOPLE OF OTHER FAITHS ADMIRABLY DESIRE TO SERVE AS CLERGY IN THEIR RESPECTIVE CHURCHES, AND GO THROUGH EXTENSIVE TRAINING TO DO SO

Many people of other faiths admirably desire to serve as clergy in their respective churches, and go through extensive training to do so. Most clergy live on subsistence level wages. Principles of priestcrafts apply equally to these people as to our own leadership. The scriptures denounce preaching the gospel *solely* from a desire to make money and get rich, or to defraud people (see 1 Peter 5:2). The Book of Mormon likewise defines "priestcraft" as teaching *for the sake of getting gain* while not seeking "the welfare of Zion" (see 2 Nephi 26:29. Likewise, many members of other faiths devote time to their churches without any monetary compensation. Certainly they follow the teachings of Jesus by so doing, and accomplish much good thereby.

Question: Does the Church of Jesus Christ of Latter-day Saints employ a professional clergy?

THERE CAN BE NO DOUBT THAT THE CHURCH *DOES* HAVE AN UNPAID MINISTRY. MORE PRECISELY, IT DOES NOT HAVE A *PROFESSIONAL* CLERGY

Some claim that because some of the General Authorities and mission presidents receive a living stipend, the Church's claim to have no paid ministry is false.
There can be no doubt that the Church *does* have an unpaid ministry. More precisely, it does not have a *professional* clergy.

Consider:

- the Church does not graduate individuals with degrees in theology for the purpose of being used in an employed position as an ecclesiastical leader.
- the vast majority of leadership positions in the Church are filled by those who receive absolutely no financial assistance and who have no formal training in theology or Church administration. This includes bishops, stake presidents, Area Authority Seventies, Relief Society presidents, priests, teachers, deacons, and elders, etc.
- Missionaries or their families typically pay for the costs of their missions.

the Church has no professional ministry — one does not "go into" the priesthood in Mormonism as a form of employment. The Church believes that "a man must be called of God, by prophecy, and by the laying on of hands by those who are in authority, to preach the Gospel and administer in the ordinances thereof."[3] No one can enter Church ecclesiastical government or administration as a career.

- •those few Church leaders who receive a living allowance, have already served for many years in unpaid volunteer positions of Church leadership, from which they derived no financial gain, and from which they could have had little expectation of making their livelihood by being elevated to high positions in Church administration.
- •the Book of Mormon makes provision for Church leaders to be supported by donations *if* they are in a position of financial need: "all their priests and teachers should labor with their own hands for their support, in all cases save it were in sickness, or in much want; and doing these things, they did abound in the grace of God."[4]
- •the Doctrine and Covenants makes provisions for Church leaders to be supported by donations (see DC 42:71-73).
- •General Authorities previously sat on the boards of Church-owned businesses. This practice was discontinued in 1996.[5]

LOCAL LEADERSHIP

Much of the day-to-day "ministering" that goes on in the Church takes place at the local, i.e., ward and/or stake level. Leaders at the local level -- that is, bishops, stake presidents, relief society presidents, elders quorum presidents, and other leaders or auxiliary workers -- do not receive any kind of pay for the temporary, volunteer service they render. They likewise do not receive any kind of scholastic training to prepare them for their service. A bishop usually serves for a period of 5 years, for example, but he remains in his normal occupation (accountant, welder, business owner, etc.) while he serves as a bishop. Early morning or release-time seminary teachers are an exception, but they are considered employees of CES (Church Education System).

MISSION LEADERSHIP

Mission presidents usually serve for a period of 3 years, and may sometimes receive a living allowance during their period of service, if it is required. Many mission presidents are financially able to take time out of work to support themselves during their service (and return to their vocations when their service is complete), and do not require a living allowance.

CRITICS MAY BE IMPOSSIBLE TO SATISFY

If provision did not exist for allowing those who are not "independently wealthy" to provide full-time Church service, critics might well then complain that the Church "favors the rich" because it would not allow those of lesser means to serve. Without some mechanism for providing for the needs of those giving full-time service, only the worldly elite would be able to serve. This factor becomes increasingly important as the Church expands out of North America, especially into nations in the Southern Hemisphere who are less materially well-off than the industrialized west.

Question: Is the fact that some General Authorities, mission presidents, and others receive a living stipend while serving the Church evidence of the "hypocrisy" of the Church?

THE CHURCH DOES NOT TRAIN OR EMPLOY A PROFESSIONAL CLERGY

It is claimed that Mormonism prides itself in having unpaid clergy as one proof of the Church's truthfulness. They then point to the fact that some General Authorities, mission presidents, and others do, in fact, receive a living stipend while serving the Church, and point to this as evidence of the "hypocrisy" of the Church. [6]

- Church leaders are "called" by leaders in greater authority to occupy positions such as Bishop, Stake President, or Area Authority 70. One does not campaign for nor apply for such positions, and such an effort would undoubtedly be considered grounds for disqualifications to serve in such a significant role. Article of Faith 5 states: "We believe that a man must be called of God, by prophecy, and by the laying on of hands by those who are in authority, to preach the Gospel and administer in the ordinances thereof." (A+of+F 1:5) What is more, those who fill these positions are not compensated.
- No tithing funds provide for General Authorities' living stipends; such funds are drawn from business income earned by Church investments.
- The Latter-day Saint practice of not paying our ecclesiastical leaders is not evidence of the truthfulness of the Church. As with other issues, the real question regarding the "truthfulness" of the Church hinges on the endowment of priesthood keys and authority on those who lead the Church. Temporal matters and how they are handled are governed by spiritual principles. Leaders who serve faithfully should be sustained regardless of their personal finances or needs for modest financial assistance.

There can be no doubt that the Church *does* have an unpaid ministry. More precisely, it does not have a *professional* clergy. Much of the day-to-day "ministering" that goes on in the Church takes place at the local, i.e., ward and/or stake level. Leaders at the local level -- that is, bishops, stake presidents, relief society presidents, elders quorum presidents, and other leaders or auxiliary workers -- do not receive any kind of pay for the temporary, volunteer service they render. They likewise do not receive any kind of scholastic training to prepare them for their service.

SOME GENERAL AUTHORITIES RECEIVE A MODEST LIVING STIPEND

Some members of the Church are unaware that at least some General Authorities do receive a modest living stipend. While it is true that some Church leaders receive a living allowance while they serve in a given position, it cannot be said that the Church has a *professional* ministry in the traditional sense.

RECEIVING A LIVING STIPEND DOES NOT QUALIFY AS PRIESTCRAFT

Church members have a particular sensitivity to issues surrounding paid ministries particularly due to admonitions in the Book of Mormon relative to a practices known as *priestcraft*, which is "that men preach and set themselves up for a light unto the world, that they may get gain and praise of the world; but they seek not the welfare of Zion" (see 2 Nephi 26:29). However, it should be noted that priestcraft as it has been defined is a condemnation of intent (to get gain and praise, and not for the welfare of Zion), and not about an individual receiving support.

CHURCH EMPLOYEES ARE NOT COMPENSATED FOR ECCLESIASTICAL SERVICE

While a small number of Church members seek full-time teaching positions within the Church Education System as instructors, they are not compensated for ecclesiastical leadership or service. No tithing funds are used to pay Church employees. Their salaries come from church investments in companies that deal with real estate like Deseret Management Corporation and Deseret Ranches, communications (TV, radio, Internet) like Bonneville Communications and Deseret News, and property management and services like Zion's Securities Corporation and Temple Square Hospitality.

Question: Why do General Authorities receive living stipends?

GORDON B. HINCKLEY: "THE LIVING ALLOWANCES GIVEN THE GENERAL AUTHORITIES, WHICH ARE VERY MODEST IN COMPARISON WITH EXECUTIVE COMPENSATION IN INDUSTRY AND THE PROFESSIONS, COME FROM THIS BUSINESS INCOME AND NOT FROM THE TITHING OF THE PEOPLE

Some members of the Church are unaware that some General Authorities receive a modest stipend as a living allowance. Nevertheless, it cannot be said that the Church has a *professional* ministry in the traditional sense.

Calls to serve in the Quorum of the Twelve Apostles or the First Quorum of the Seventy are calls to "for-life" positions, members of the Twelve serving full-time until they die and members of the First Quorum of Seventy serving full-time until retirement to emeritus status at age seventy. At the present time, calls to other Quorums of the Seventy do not require the same full-time commitment, so those who serve in these positions do not receive the living allowances.

The fact that this stipend exists has not been hidden. As President Hinckley noted in General Conference:

> *Merchandising interests are an outgrowth of the cooperative movement which existed among our people in pioneer times. The Church has maintained certain real estate holdings, particularly those contiguous to Temple Square, to help preserve the beauty and the integrity of the core of the city. All of these commercial properties are tax-paying entities.*
>
> *I repeat, the combined income from all of these business interests is relatively small and would not keep the work going for longer than a very brief period.*
>
> *I should like to add, parenthetically for your information, that the living allowances given the General Authorities, which are very modest in comparison with executive compensation in industry and the professions, come from this business income and not from the tithing of the people.*[7]

THE STIPEND HAS ALSO BEEN DISCUSSED MANY OTHER TIMES IN THE PAST

Conference reports published during 1940s and 1950s and 1960s always included financial reports; part of this was a "Church Disbursements," of which the first item read:

> *Office of the Corporation of the President: Including salaries of 49 employees: expenses of office; equipment; maintenance of the Administration Building; and the living allowances and traveling expenses of the General Authorities, all of which are covered by non-tithing income.*[8]

In 1979 it was common knowledge for a non-member to wonder about why a successful banker would settle for the modest "living allowance":

> *In Honolulu a few months ago I boarded a plane, sat in my seat, and was strapping myself in when a man sat by my side. I introduced myself to him and extended my hand in a greeting of good fellowship. He was of Japanese extraction, spoke impeccable English, and explained that he was on his way to Boise, Idaho, to attend a bank directors' meeting. Immediately I was curious.*
>
> *"Which bank?" I queried.*
>
> *"Citizens National," he replied.*
>
> *"Then you must be acquainted with Martin Zachreson, who is mission president in Southern California for the Mormon Church."*

"Yes," he said. "I wondered why he would leave the position of chairman of the board of a successful bank to serve as a mission president for a mere living allowance."

As you can imagine, that opened a door that I was anxious to walk through. So I asked, "May I explain to you?"[9]

We have seen above President Hinckley's discussion in the mid-1980s.

In the early 1990s, the *Encyclopedia of Mormonism* (prepared in conjunction with the Church) noted:

Unlike local leaders, who maintain their normal vocations while serving in Church assignments, General Authorities set aside their careers to devote their full time to the ministry of their office. The living allowance given General Authorities rarely if ever equals the earnings they sacrifice to serve full-time in the Church.[10]

In 2011, the Church's official magazine noted:

Serving as a mission president is both a challenging and a spiritually exhilarating three-year assignment. In dedicating themselves to this call, many couples essentially put their old lives on hold, including their jobs and families.

The interruption to professional employment can in some cases mean financial loss. While the Church provides mission presidents with a minimal living allowance, the couples usually have the financial means to supplement that allowance with their own funds.[11]

In a 2013 manual for Church teens, the text indicates:

In our day, General Authorities of the Church give up their livelihoods to serve full-time, so they receive a modest living allowance—enough for them to support themselves and their families.

Why is it appropriate for Church leaders who are called to full-time service to receive compensation for their needs?[12]

IF THERE WERE NO STIPENDS, ONLY THE WEALTHY COULD SERVE

If the Church did not provide living allowances, then only those who were independently wealthy would qualify for Church service. Some critics would doubtless be troubled by this scenario, and would probably then claim that the Church exalted wealth and personal prosperity, and would not allow any without it to serve.

MANY CHURCH GENERAL AUTHORITIES COME FROM RESPECTED PROFESSIONS FROM WHICH THEY MAKE A SUBSTANTIAL LIVING

Dedicating themselves full time at the sacrifice of substantial careers, these leaders live modestly, work tirelessly, keep grueling travel schedules, and continue doing so well past an age when others retire. They are also demonstrably men of education and accomplishment; one can hardly claim that they were unsuited for work in the world given their accomplishments prior to being called to full-time Church service.

Michael Otterson, formerly head of Church Public Affairs, observed:

I can hardly believe it when I hear people question the motives of the Brethren for the work they do, or when they imply there is somehow some monetary reward or motive.

Let me share the reality. Not all the Brethren have been businessmen, but most have had extraordinarily successful careers by the time they are called to be an apostle. As President Spencer W. Kimball once pointed out, the ability to lead people and an organization is a more-than-helpful attribute in a Church of millions of people, especially when combined with spiritual depth and a rich understanding of the gospel. Because several have been highly successful in business careers, when they become apostles their stipend and allowances may literally be less than a tithe on what they previously earned.

Some of the Brethren have been educators. Elder Scott was a nuclear physicist, Elder Nelson a heart surgeon. Several were highly successful lawyers. Right now we have three former university presidents in the Twelve. President Boyd K. Packer was also an educator by profession, although in his spare time and in his earlier days he loved to carve beautiful things out of wood. That sounds curiously related to another scripturally honored profession — that of a carpenter.

Can you imagine what it would be like to be called to the Twelve? In most cases you have already had a successful career. You know you will continue to serve the Church in some volunteer capacity, but you have begun to think of your future retirement. The First Presidency and the Twelve, of course, do not retire. Neither are they released. With their call comes the sure knowledge that they will work every day for the rest of their lives, even if they live into their 90s, until they literally drop and their minds and bodies give out. Their workday begins early and does not end at 5:00 p.m. The Twelve get Mondays off, and those Mondays are frequently spent preparing for the rest of the week. If they have a weekend assignment, they will often travel on a Friday afternoon. Periodically, even though in their 80s, they face the grueling schedule of international speaking conferences and leadership responsibilities.

What about when they are home? I have the cell phone numbers of most of the Brethren because I sometimes have to call them in the evening, on weekends or when they are out and about. I'm not naïve enough to think that I am the only Church officer to do so. So even their downtime is peppered with interruptions. I invariably begin those calls by apologizing for interrupting them at home. I have never once been rebuked for calling. They are invariably kind and reassuring, even early in the morning or late at night.

Their primary time off each year is from the end of the mission presidents' seminar at the very end of June through the end of July. And while this time is meant as a break, most of the Brethren use this time to turn their thoughts, among other things, to October general conference and preparation of their remarks. During Christmas break they do the same for April conference. Every one of them takes extraordinary care and time in deciding on a topic and crafting their messages. The process weighs on them for months as they refine draft after draft.

This is not a schedule you would wish on anyone. Yet they bear it with grace and find joy for some overwhelmingly important reasons — their testimony and commitment to be a witness of the Savior of the world and their desire to strengthen His children everywhere. They would be the very first to acknowledge their own faults or failings, just as we can readily point to the apostles of the New Testament and see imperfect people.[13]

IN 1996, THE STIPEND WAS IN THE NEIGHBORHOOD OF $50,000 PER YEAR. IN 2014 IT WAS INCREASED FROM $116,400 TO $120,000

In 1996,[14] the church altered some of the responsibilities given to General Authorities. Prior to this point in time, they also served on corporate boards of church-owned companies and for these positions they received a stipend. At that point in time, some of the financial information was disclosed, indicating that the stipend was in the neighborhood of $50,000.00 a year.

To give a sense of proper comparison, US Department of Labor statistics list the 1996 average salary of a civil engineer at $52,750, that of a computer programmer at $50,490, and that of the average junior college teacher at $49,200. Therefore, the living allowance, which provides for most of the normal day-to-day expenses of a full-time authority and his family (including house payments, personal transportation, food, clothing, entertainment, etc.), is in line with that of a professional employee. It is far lower than the large management salaries that might be expected for someone with the skills that these General Authorities must have and the responsibilities that they must shoulder.

Question: Do General Authorities receive a large sum of money when they are called in order to "keep them quiet"?

CLAIMS THAT GENERAL AUTHORITIES RECEIVE LARGE "HUSH MONEY" PAYMENTS ARE PURE SPECULATION WITH LITTLE DATA

This type of criticism seems intended to imply that General Authorities perform their duties out of greed, rather than sincere belief. This seems implausible, given that most are at or beyond retirement age when called, and many have been highly successful outside of Church service. Furthermore:

- Non-disclosure agreements are standard practice with regard to salary and compensation.
- The numbers suggested have consistently escalated over time, despite an absence of hard data.
- Those who provide such accounts attempt to make normal practices seem nefarious or hidden.
- The Church has not hidden the fact that general authorities receive a stipend, and there is scriptural warrant for the practice.

THESE KINDS OF SPECULATIONS AS TO MONEY RECEIVED ALMOST ALWAYS COMES FROM DISAFFECTED AND FORMER MEMBERS, AND INVOLVES LARGE ROUND NUMBERS SUCH AS $300,000, $500,000 OR $1,000,000

They all claim (in true conspiracy theory fashion) to have an inside source. They always make claims with no evidence - and use nice big eye-catching round numbers such as $300,000, $500,000, $1,000,000, and so on. Should the church provide some data, it would almost certainly be dismissed as a cover up of the truth (protected of course by those NDAs, right?). There may be a lot of reasons why people become General Authorities, but it seems doubtful that getting wealthy is one of them. You would think, with hundreds of General Authorities, all supposedly getting excessive payments from the church (as the allegations go) for the last century, there might have been some sort of financial scandal that the critics could pin their speculations to. But it doesn't seem like it, does it?

Question: Do General Authorities sign a non-disclosure agreement promising to never divulge what they are paid?

IT IS HIGHLY LIKELY THAT GENERAL AUTHORITIES SIGN A NON-DISCLOSURE AGREEMENT

Not only do many of the employees of BYU sign such non-disclosure agreements, but, those who have access to this information are also required to sign such agreements. Generally speaking, these agreements allow organizations to sue for damages when a breach of confidentiality occurs. The major point here, though, is that if general authorities are given a stipend (for living expenses), it is quite possible that the stipend comes with a non-disclosure agreement (an NDA). This would be the "contract promising never to divulge to anyone what they are paid". Of course, it is presented in a way that makes all sorts of insinuations. But probably if such a thing exists and happens, it follows the standard boiler plate legal language used elsewhere by the Church's legal team to handle the same issue. That contract wouldn't actually list the compensation, and so while this person may have seen the NDA, we can be certain that they have no personal knowledge of what the compensation actually is. The $300,000.00 figure is just being tossed out with no real evidence behind it, save anonymous hearsay.

Now, what is the point of this sort of agreement? Mentioning the NDA in this kind of discussion is intended by the critic to demonstrate that something nefarious is going on. That is, we are meant to conclude that the Church is covering a big secret of some sort with the use of NDAs.

A NON-DISCLOSURE AGREEMENT DOES NOT GUARANTEE SECRECY

This, however, doesn't make much sense. One problem with an NDA is that in order to get relief the injured party must sue. And in suing, the contract itself would become part of the court case, and potentially available for public scrutiny. If the objective is complete secrecy, then the concept of an NDA utterly defeats the purpose in this case. Not only would it open up hidden information for public consumption, it would also tend to confirm whatever had been said by the general authority who offered information. This would only be some sort of problem if the church was trying to hide something. And so if the church is trying to hide payments to general authorities, then the whole process of having a NDA creates far more problems than it would solve.

Question: Who is the highest-paid Church employee in the Church of Jesus Christ of Latter-day Saints?

THE HEAD FOOTBALL COACH AT BRIGHAM YOUNG UNIVERSITY IS LIKELY THE HIGHEST PAID EMPLOYEE

Who is the highest paid church employee? As of 2014, it is probably Bronco Mendenhall (the head football coach at BYU). His base salary is estimated to be at least $900,000 a year. With incentives and bonuses, it could be as high as $2,000,000.00 per year. Even at 2 million a year, he would only rank 59th (of 126) college football coaches (a lot to us individuals, not excessive by the narrow standard of his peers).[15]

Of course, nobody is really quite sure how much he makes because, like most employees of BYU, Bronco Mendenhall has signed a non-disclosure agreement (NDA) about his salary. And being that he works for a private university, you cannot simply request this information. This is, by the way, standard practice for private universities in particular, but it's also true of most private entities. Organizations where salary information is widely available are usually managed by group contracts and are often unionized. The Church does not fit that particular mold. The business side of the Church (and its corporate employees) follow business practices that recommend these kinds of NDAs.

Notes

1. Bruce R. McConkie, *Conference Report* (Apr. 1975), 77.; or "Obedience, Consecration, and Sacrifice," *Ensign* (May 1975), 52.

2. https://www.lds.org/manual/print/doctrine-and-covenants-student-manual/sections-21-29/section-24-declare-my-gospel-as-with-the-voice-of-a-trump?lang=eng
3. Articles of Faith 1:5
4. Mosiah 27:5
5. Lynn Arave, "LDS programs evolve over the years," *Deseret Morning News* (30 September 2006).
6. Bill McKeever, "Mormonism's Paid Ministry," (accessed April 28, 2008); Sandra Tanner, "Do Mormon Leaders Receive Financial Support?" (accessed April 28, 2008).
7. Gordon B. Hinckley, "Questions and Answers," *Ensign* (November 1985), 49.
8. This example is from *Conference Report* (6-8 April 1945), 18.
9. Royden G. Derrick, "The True Value System," BYU address (15 May 1979).
10. Marvin K. Gardner, "General Authorities," in *Encyclopedia of Mormonism*, 4 vols., edited by Daniel H. Ludlow, (New York, Macmillan Publishing, 1992).
11. Heather Whittle Wrigley, "New Mission Presidents Blessed for Exercise of Faith," *Liahona* (December 2011). See also an on-line "Church News" feature which reproduces this material from 1 July 2011.
12. Unit 15: Day 4, D&C 69-71," *Doctrine and Covenants and Church History Study Guide for Home-Study Seminary Students* (Salt Lake City, UT: Intellectual Reserve, 2013).
13. "FULL TRANSCRIPT: Michael Otterson addresses FairMormon Conference," *lds.org* (7 August 2015).
14. Lynn Arave, "LDS programs evolve over the years," *Deseret Morning News* (30 September 2006).
15. http://www.coacheshotseat.com/SalariesContracts.htm (accessed 28 March 2014)

https://www.fairmormon.org/answers/Mormonism_and_church_finances/No_paid_ministry

Comments -- first reactions to paid ministry justification argument
As long as we are dealing in metaphors concerning flocks, as mentioned above, I would prefer to use the image of fleecing the flock, something that con men do for a living.

As the proponents of a paid ministry point out here, perhaps unintentionally, the shepherd metaphor is not really the completely correct metaphor for what should be going on in the church, although it is in fact the correct metaphor for what is actually going on in the church today. Church leaders are not supposed to be sacrificing church "lambs" for their own needs, although that is in fact what shepherds do with portions of their flock. That metaphor is correct only so far, and falls apart if you exceed its rational application.

In their bringing up the topic of warfare as part of their argument, they have inadvertently given away a secret – the church leaders are empire builders at heart, not religionists. Religion is just an excuse, like Islam -- for building an empire with an army, like Islam, making the LDS church just another "warlord religion."

Some are certainly better than others, but there is no such thing as a completely righteous paid ministry, where "paid ministry" includes the ideological feature that people are required to pay money for salvation, delivered through a self-appointed bureaucracy – a moneymaking "salvation bureaucracy."

People may indeed be given priesthood power, but the instructions for the use of that priesthood is that it was "freely have ye received, freely give." The instant that that priesthood power is used for money -- to generate personal income -- we are back with Simon the Sorcerer before he came to understand the true gospel.

Even short-term missionary work has its problems. As soon as the church puts missionaries on its payroll, then they are employees, not free-will missionaries. If a missionary can pay for his own mission, one way or another, or perhaps his parents or friends can do so, then the necessary freedom of choice and charitable attitude is maintained. But the second that a missionary becomes a church employee, and becomes part of an army, things start to deteriorate. The church can then start to treat that missionary like an employee and make them part of their command-and-control system, which gives the church organization too much power.

At one point, Joseph Smith was first voted a salary and then was voted to have no salary. That was the status for the rest of his life, as far as I know. If this answer implies that Joseph Smith had such an official salary, then it is a complete lie. Or, if not a lie, then this is what we might call sophistry, playing games with the truth so that people believe a lie, even if, technically, there were no lies told. This might involve the skillful parsing of words, or playing language shell games, to trick the listener.

Most of the problem here comes from one little logical and ideological trick. It is true that people who love the gospel and wish it to succeed should be willing to support those who are actively engaged in moving the church forward. That is the essence of spontaneous, free-will charity. The difference between the original church of Christ and today's church is that today's church has taken this logic the next step and said that a person cannot be a good member of the church and be assured of salvation unless they pay a mandatory tax to support the church and purchase their salvation. It is that step of turning charity into a mandatory tax that is the essence of today's priestcraft. The church then functions like a typical government where it takes a tax without making any commitments about exactly where that money will be spent, and then treating it like a standard government appropriation process where the member/taxpayer had no say about the money going into the system or how the money is spent once it's in the system. In a true charity system, the people decide exactly what they're willing to spend their money on, and they are perfectly welcome to administer it themselves, if that is more efficient, which it normally is, or whether they wish to give some or all their money to an organization which promises to the more efficient than an individual could be. If that promise of greater efficiency or more effectiveness is not upheld, then the giver is perfectly justified moving his funds elsewhere. That particular form of religious freedom is exactly what the current church has removed from its members, or at least teaches and claims that it has that the vast power over members' time and resources and the property. That is a clear case of unrighteous dominion, and it ought to be clearly labeled as such.

Does a person's having the highest of high priesthoods entitle him to control everyone and all their property? Like some kind of divine right of Kings? That was Satan's argument, but the truth, according to God the father, is exactly the opposite. The one who has the most priesthood power must be the servant of all. That was the essence of the temptation of Christ, and he passed it with flying colors, although a very large number of his followers, given similar choices and opportunities, have failed that test.

Those apologists who present the arguments here should get points for clever sophistry, but they do not get points for complete truth and accuracy. There are so many things wrong with these assertions, that it could easily take several books to straighten it all out. I have only one short article I am planning to write, so I can't cover everything, but hopefully the reader can get the basics here.

How is tithing calculated

Mormonism and church finances/Tithing/How is tithing calculated

https://www.fairmormon.org/answers/Mormonism_and_church_finances/Tithing/How_is_tithing_calculated

< Mormonism and church finances | Tithing
Table of Contents

Calculation of tithing

Summary: I've been told that the Church expects or teaches its members to tithe on gross income. What can you tell me about how tithing it taught in the Church?

SUBTOPICS:
Question: Can one pay tithing on only net or surplus income and still be a temple worthy and faithful Latter-day Saint?
Robert D. Hales: "The First Presidency has written what the law of tithing is for us today"

Question: Can one pay tithing on only net or surplus income and still be a temple worthy and faithful Latter-day Saint?

First Presidency statement: "The simplest statement we know of is the statement of the Lord himself, namely, that the members of the Church should pay 'one-tenth of all their interest annually,' which is understood to mean income"

Members of the Church covenant to pay tithing—the word comes from "tithe," meaning "a tenth."

This has naturally led to the question, "A tenth of what? Gross income? Net income? Pre-tax? Post-tax?"

Quite simply, the method is left up to the individual. The First Presidency issued the following statement in 1970, which is repeated the current (2006) Church Handbook of Instructions:

> *The simplest statement we know of is the statement of the Lord himself, namely, that the members of the Church should pay 'one-tenth of all their interest annually,' which is understood to mean income. No one is justified in making any other statement than this.* [1]

No member is ever to be told how to calculate their tithing

Each member is to prayerfully decide how to interpret this statement. No member is ever to be told how to calculate their tithing. No member is authorized to tell another how to pay tithing.

Each year, members of the Church meet with their bishop and declare their tithing status—they either indicate that they are full tithe payers, or not. No questions are asked about the means whereby this is determined—such matters are between the member and the Lord.

Anyone who claims otherwise bears the burden of proof, and should be required to produce a statement which differs from the First Presidency's statement of 1970, to which leaders have repeatedly appealed since. This includes the most recent Church handbook.[2]

Robert D. Hales: "The First Presidency has written what the law of tithing is for us today"

Elder Robert D. Hales:

The First Presidency has written what the law of tithing is for us today: "The simplest statement we know of is the statement of the Lord himself, namely, that the members of the Church should pay 'one tenth of all their interest annually,' which is understood to mean income. No one is justified in making any other statement than this." (First Presidency letter, 19 March 1970.) [3]

Notes

1. First Presidency letter, 19 March 1970. This letter has been quoted in numerous talks by general authorities and Church lesson manuals. A convenient examples is Robert D. Hales, "The Divine Law of Tithing," *Ensign* (December 1986), 14. off-site
2. *Handbook 1:Stake Presidents and Bishops* (2010), 14.4.1. In accordance with Church policy, FairMormon will not reproduce the contents of the first volume of the handbook here. Members who wish to consult this volume can do so, however, by asking to see their bishop or branch president's copy.

3.Robert D. Hales, "The Divine Law of Tithing," *Ensign*, March 1970
https://www.fairmormon.org/answers/Mormonism_and_church_finances/Tithing/How_is_tithing_calculated#cite_ref-1

Comments
This 10%, supposedly solely calculated by the members, is not really a free will gift to the church. The required amount to achieve salvation should be zero. Obviously, any version of 10% is a great deal more than zero. And it is not completely spontaneous. People are repeatedly told not to rob God of the tithes and offerings, and they're also told that it is fire insurance which they need. They are also told to contribute a generous fast offering, usually in the same phrase, so that "generous" is the controlling word. In other words, it would be going much too far to say that it is left completely up to the membership to decide without constant encouragement from church leaders to give more. So there are many different kinds of "full-tithes," and you'll probably never hear someone tell you to give a minimal tithe.

Responding more formally to the current FAIRMormon answer

I would like to challenge most of the answers to the main question concerning a paid ministry, and offer an alternate explanation. In order to appreciate the practical importance of this issue, an understanding of the strategic situation is very helpful. However, I have put the 4-page strategic overview at the end of this document to make it clearly optional reading.

Contents

I will first point out the difficulties I see in the logic FairMormon has provided,[1] and then go on to lay out what I believe is the correct scripture-based answer.

Your answer begins by saying that "Having a paid clergy is not in and of itself a terrible thing." As I intend to point out later, I believe that Christ, and all the prophets who have written about the question in the scriptures, or made policy decisions concerning it, including the first three prophets in our dispensation, would completely disagree, and for very good reasons. A paid ministry is, and has always been, the main vehicle by which the gospel is gradually distorted and transformed until it is almost unrecognizable and becomes completely ineffective as we have seen with the gradual formation and behavior of the Catholic Church over many centuries.

We should be grateful that human nature never changes, but we would also be foolish to give mortal men the unlimited power, along with ample incentives, to change the gospel and its administration for their own advantage. Only if mortal men have no chance whatsoever to benefit financially from the gospel, and are in fact most likely to have to sacrifice great things for the gospel, are they likely to stay honest and true. If they "own" a church position and salary they will inevitably abuse it, even if they are not fully conscious of their actions. The careerists who might naturally be drawn to the church as a source of income will go elsewhere to make their fortune, leaving only the truly committed members to work on behalf of the gospel at their own expense or dependent on charity. Some may be driven mostly by seeking financial awards, but others are driven by the opportunity to exercise power over others, administer large budgets, establish a religious empire, etc. That might be the most dangerous reason of all, as explained by D&C 121, and that has nothing to do with whether they have some appropriate college degree or not.

I'm sorry to say that it seems like a very weak and time-specific argument to say that a paid ministry/priestcraft situation can only come about by someone seeking a religion degree and then looking for a job as a clergyman. We can safely guess that Nehor and Korihor in the Book of Mormon did not have prestigious seminary degrees, nor have thousands of other preachers who felt the call to the ministry, for whatever reason.

We certainly have situations such as our seminary and Institute program where someone can indeed "simply choose to become one of these full-time workers." The system we have might be even more pernicious than the "professional clergy" argument given. We might actually be better off if those who take over the top leadership positions had been fully trained in a rigorous (currently nonexistent) LDS theological seminary before they took those positions.

As it is, we seem to count vast ignorance of Christian theology and church history as a net positive in being appointed to church leadership positions. Top church leaders typically are not theologians or religious historians or religion management experts, and are usually poorly prepared to make worldwide gospel policy decisions at the beginning of their calling. It appears that they are more apt to simply learn the ropes as an apprentice might do, absorbing all the bad and good biases and prejudices of those they work with. This might ensure that the leaders have a truly homogenous, not to say monotonous, view of what a church leader should do, which would tend to minimize the range of issues that might be considered in new situations.

Rather than having an objective view of exactly what the gospel includes and does not include, and why, the enormous amount of relativism which is introduced by this amateur apprenticeship program is a great deal more likely to cause trouble than to be a benefit. In the process of creating a peer-reviewed "gold-standard" or "constitutional" curriculum for a formal course in Mormon doctrine for potential leaders, hopefully many people would notice any significant differences between what the scriptures teach and what the church has taught and implemented.

Currently, it is not very difficult for nepotism and attempts at dynasties to be part of the church organization, since almost anyone can be considered qualified by a modicum of experience to accept important management positions. A rigorous meritocracy would be far superior and more desirable. It appears that many staff positions are filled by people with no particular qualifications as a religion content manager. But these people might actually have more effect on day-to-day policy then even the top church leaders.

I assume there are many different channels through which people can indicate their interest in becoming a paid worker at church headquarters. These paths are probably just a little less obvious than the Protestant or Catholic route of seeking a seminary degree and then seeking a job. Strangely enough, similar seminary study is the path the church requires for many of its college level religion teachers, who would otherwise be unqualified to teach many technical religion topics. Presumably, those who gain experience as a bishop, stake president, area authority, etc., are part of the feeder system that results in one receiving a calling at the top levels. This is like going from the minor leagues to the major leagues, and certainly includes a selection process and perhaps a competition process. The fact that the process may take longer than a four-year seminary degree, does not really change the nature of the selection process. In any event, it becomes as much of a political process as any other.

These days, most of the men chosen as leaders have served a large portion of their lives as volunteer church administrators such as bishops and stake presidents and area authorities. Most of them are indeed good administrators, and almost without exception will have provided for their own retirement, with private pensions, Social Security, other personal resources, etc., so that it would be no great burden for them to serve as central church leaders without a salary. It is hard to see why they would need a church salary. Some reasons for supplying a salary might include the church organization's desire to make it look like a business by paying everyone a salary. That would help justify the staff getting generous salaries. If only one or two needed financial assistance, someone might propose paying everyone a salary just so those one or two would not feel different. But, of course, a salary provides the church with a control mechanism to maximize cooperation and minimize dissent. It is very questionable whether that typical bureaucratic control mechanism should have a place in a church organization.

I think there is still great value in making those top positions require continual sacrifice on the part of those doing the job, simply to keep out those who would naturally tend to seek money and power (which is almost everyone), and to keep them humble and unbiased in the decisions they make concerning the use of church resources, avoiding any kind of appearance of self-dealing or self-interest or conflict of interest.

A broader view

Looking at the world on a broader scale, it is my opinion that anyone who would suggest that a paid ministry is not a bad thing must be completely ignorant of most of the world's history, and is intentionally focusing on the microdot-sized bit of history which might justify that person getting a church salary. No matter where or when we look at the world and its organizations, the existence of a paid ministry is always evidence of vast corruption, and always involves some kind of religious corruption, although it may not be perfectly evident in all cases. Whether we look at the paid ministries of the Egyptian pharaohs and their priestly class, the priests of Baal or of Moloch, the priests directing the worship of Nebuchadnezzar at the time of Daniel, the pagan priests of Rome, the law of Moses, the Hindus, the Buddhists, the Muslims, the Marxists, the fascists, the medieval kings and their courts, etc., ad infinitum, we see the same pattern over and over again. These bureaucracies are set up for the exact purpose of gaining political and economic power through deception, fear, and force – whatever it takes. Usually that involves inventing a religion or value system which strives to convince people that they are not entitled to freedom and that their personal resources belong to the religious or political or religious/political governing body.

Worst of all, when the "true religion" finally and inevitably adopts these corrupt and exploitative practices, it gives license to every other political con artist to earn a very generous free lunch through rhetoric, propaganda, deception, and force. 4 Ne. 1:26. Apparently, historically, it is always the church which first forms classes based on paid ministry concepts, even while it teaches that classes are bad thing, indicating the standard hypocrisy involved in all of this. The extreme cases are in Marxism and Communism where the rhetoric of avoiding classes is used to create the most rigid set of classes imaginable. Apparently, people never get any smarter, and they always fall for this total nonsense every time it is used. Inquisitions are one of the standard tools of maintaining this corrupt power structure. The LDS church has not yet gone as far as many of these organizations in killing dissenters, although "inquisitions" might still be an appropriate title for some of the "disciplinary councils" that are directed from church headquarters while deceptively pretending that it is totally a spontaneous local phenomenon.

Does a person's having the highest of high priesthoods entitle him to control everyone and all their property, like some kind of divine right of Kings? That was Satan's argument, but the truth, according to God the father, is exactly the opposite. The one who has the most priesthood power must be the servant of all. That was the essence of the several temptations of Christ, and he passed it with flying colors, although a very large number of his followers, given similar choices and opportunities, have failed that test. That applies to every one of the tens of thousands of people who are currently part of the LDS paid ministry.

Are there really any New Testament Scriptures that *defend* a paid ministry?

The scriptures cited by the FAIR Mormon answers seem like very weak support, if not actually antagonistic to the paid ministry issue.

1 Corinthians 9:7-14 is a rather strange scripture as a beginning quote on this issue. It mostly seems irrelevant to this paid ministry issue. The chapter headnotes for 1 Corinthians 9 include the phrase "He preaches the gospel to all without charge," indicating that the people who added the headnotes saw no basis for any paid ministry, or that Paul made any actual claims for payment.

Verse 7 begins with "Who goeth a warfare any time at his own charges?" We might wonder how warfare has anything at all to do with a paid ministry question. It may be that those engaged in warfare only go out at the behest and at the expense of someone else such as a warlord or government leader. But does that have anything to do with doing missionary work? It is hard to see how. The disciples and apostles went out individually, on their own, not under the control of some warlord. They had received special experiences with the Savior's life and works or other miracles, and it was based on their personal experience and personal desires to spread the gospel that they were out teaching. That truly has nothing to do with any kind of warfare thinking or related military bureaucracy and salary payments. If they were soldiers they would usually expect to be paid for their labors, but that, again, has nothing to do with spreading the gospel. This can be nothing more than a bad and inapplicable analogy.

Worst of all, a soldier is not expected to have anything to do with setting policy, but only to do his assigned job. How would it work out if every soldier saw himself as a general? What interesting policies might they invent to make their lives easier? The apostles were setting church policy at every moment of their lives, and if they were hoping to become part of some grand empire, then they were most definitely in the wrong line of activity. Under Roman rule, they were most likely to be killed for their efforts, as many of them were, rather than be paid for their efforts.

Considering the rest of the quotation, it is true that the gospel constantly supports freedom and fairness, which includes ownership of property and freedom of action, so it makes perfect sense for someone to expect to be paid or repaid for the work they do in the normal flow of commercial life or in farming. Slavery is epitomized by forcing someone to do work and then not paying them a fair wage for that work. But what has that got to do with purely charitable gospel activity? Paul does make a strange claim to be repaid by the people whom he has taught "If we have sown unto you spiritual things, is it a great thing if we shall reap your carnal things?", but then completely refuses to use that power or claim over them. "Nevertheless we have not used this power; but suffer all things, lest we should hinder the gospel of Christ."

(As Alcuin notices, making people pay huge amounts of money to learn and live the gospel would have been an enormous restraint on the spreading of the gospel. That was the exact problem which kept the law of Moses from going any further than among the Jews. If you want a good message to spread widely, and change the way the world operates, it must clearly be a net benefit, not a net cost to the proselyte.) (See Alcuin's comment mentioned in the book on tithing by Rev. Clark?)

If Paul brings up this potential claim against the goods of his converts (perhaps just playing the super lawyer for the fun of it, perhaps merely to bring up the point that those who received the gospel had a duty to repay that gift somehow, just as he felt driven to teach the word), and then specifically refuses to follow through with any such claim, what is the policy we are to follow today? Should we not make the exact same choices Paul did, for the exact same reasons, or do we use his throwaway logic to actually enforce claims over church members? If we are going to follow Paul's actual policy, then we take nothing, and we refuse any paid ministry situation. even while we find other productive ways to "give back" to the larger cause.

Concerning verses 13 and 14, under the Law of Moses which governed nearly all the practical affairs of the Israelites, yes, it is true that under the arrangements specified for Levites and non-Levites, the Levites were provided their living and were paid for their work under the Law of Moses, especially during their once-a-year visit to the temple, but how far does that go as a metaphor or analogy in today's world? The Law of Moses was done away after the death and resurrection of Christ, including ending the Levite tithing arrangements, which put almost everything up in the air as unsettled, so exactly what are the rules for today that you are espousing? Are you saying that we are and should be living the Law of Moses today? If not, then you have to give a great deal more background than just cite this one seemingly irrelevant scripture. Rather than having appointed lifetime priests as under the rigid and cumbersome Law of Moses, as with the Levites, every man today is his own priest and no one should expect to be paid for being his own priest. Is every man going to go through the meaningless ritual of paying himself for his church service?

The next topic is entitled "History of the concern within LDS thought," but this paragraph doesn't mention a single thing about why "the early members had a real distrust of paid clergy." Was this a purely baseless bias, or did they have good reasons that ought to apply to themselves then and to us now? I don't know of any automatic mechanism that protects church members from oppressive church leaders.

We might mention that other churches reached the exact same conclusion as the early Mormons. One incident involved the Baptists in Connecticut writing to Pres. Thomas Jefferson about the state level persecution of Baptists by churches incorporated under state law and given political powers. The Baptists refused to be incorporated, lest they become just as secularized and oppressive as these other more favored Protestant churches. Whether it was intentional or not, the Mormons started out agreeing completely with the Baptists on organizational matters, and only later adopted the potentially repressive statist Protestant views and procedures and also those of the Catholic Church. Obviously, the power-seeking of Catholic Church clergy was evidenced by their constant goals to accumulate property and money, and build a religious empire. Also obviously, the Catholic Church changed gospel doctrine and policy as a means to support their vigorous self-aggrandizement and empire building. It has been amply shown that even the first step down that path is corrupting, no matter a person's good intentions. The option to change church doctrine and policy for one's own benefit, especially monetary benefit, will always be exercised if there is any opportunity whatsoever.

The next citations are Luke 10:7 and D&C 70:12. Notice that Luke 10:4 says "Carry neither purse, nor scrip, nor shoes: and salute no man by the way." These Seventy who were sent out were clearly missionaries, who were dependent on the goodwill of their contacts to take care of them. Ideally, their contacts would be hospitable enough and grateful enough to supply their needs as they passed by, but there was never the slightest hint that these local people were required by any law to recompense these missionaries. This is purely activity in the Good Samaritan kind of charity.

The quoting of Luke 10:7 as support for a paid ministry seems completely irrelevant and inappropriate.
"And in the same house remain, eating and drinking such things as they give: for the labourer is worthy of his hire. ..." This has absolutely nothing to do with a commercial contract for labor. The Seventies could not possibly have a legal claim for payment. This is pure, direct, individual charity. The teaching by the missionaries is charity, and the providing of food by their guests and contacts is charity. There is simply no support whatsoever here for a paid ministry, unless that "paid ministry" amounts to something as innocuous as the missionaries having dinner appointments every night with different members.

As a small sidenote, the phrase "Go not from house to house" sounds like bad news for our missionary program today. This seems to end tracting and perhaps refers to some kind of a referral process.

The D&C 70:12 reference is the only one that has any real possible significance, and that seems to relate only to a short-term historical situation which doesn't apply at all today. From about 1831 to 1833 Bishop Partridge was assigned to handle church real estate matters and welfare distribution matters related to gathering the Saints to Jackson County, Missouri. That was a critical administrative function, but it mostly came to an end when the Saints were driven out of Missouri. With a little less chaos and a little better church organization, most of those functions could be done by volunteers, as is done today at the ward and stake level.

The story that appears in Acts 18:3 seems relevant even though it is not cited in the FAIRMormon answer. We find Paul living in Corinth, practicing his tentmaker trade along with members there who worked in the same trade. Presumably, Paul worked to earn money to supply his own wants and needs. If he felt he had broad claim on everyone else's goods, why would he bother to work himself? Verse 4 tells us "And he reasoned in the synagogue every sabbath, and persuaded the Jews and Greeks." Does this pattern of working and preaching sound like someone who has an independent living as a paid preacher? I believe we can say that Paul taught in the synagogues without pay. Acts 18:4.

The FAIRMormon answer includes the sentence "Although not completely relieved from responsibility for his temporal needs at that time, the Prophet was told by the Lord to look to the church for temporal support." But that statement leaves out a lot of relevant factors.

> D&C 24:3 Magnify thine office; and after thou hast sowed thy fields and secured them, go speedily unto the church which is in Colesville, Fayette, and

> Manchester, and they shall support thee; and I will bless them both spiritually and temporally;
> 4 But if they receive thee not, I will send upon them a cursing instead of a blessing.

Joseph Smith was not let off the hook for doing all that he reasonably could to support himself and his family, and the support he was to receive in Colesville and elsewhere was to be short-term and in the nature of friend-to-friend charity, with nothing like a legal claim or a commercial transaction. Those people were to be much blessed for doing good and would be cursed for not doing good. That keeps it completely in God's charitable realm, like the widow who fed Elijah from an unending barrel of flour and jar of oil, with no connection whatsoever with normal business operations. It was all to be completely informal. There is no talk of paying tithing, no council on the disposition of the tithe dispensing monies, etc.

It is also a little bit strange that 2 Nephi 26:31 is cited as a proof text for supporting a paid ministry. Together with verse 30, the two verses actually argue against the paid ministry conclusion.

> 2 Nephi 26:30 Behold, the Lord hath forbidden this thing; wherefore, the Lord God hath given a commandment that all men should have charity, which charity is love. And except they should have charity they were nothing. Wherefore, if they should have charity they would not suffer the laborer in Zion to perish.
> 31 But the laborer in Zion shall labor for Zion: for if they labor for money they shall perish.

This actually has two possible interpretations, neither one which support the paid ministry arguments. I believe verse 31 tells us that all people who labor in Zion should indeed labor idealistically and altruistically for Zion. If they labor for money, perhaps as a careerist might do, they shall perish. That seems like an explicit argument against even the slightest whiff of a paid ministry.

Looking at it a different way, those who labor for Zion, which might include missionaries, should receive charity from other people in Zion, although the missionaries are not ENTITLED to demand it (as a matter of enforceable religious law). All the Saints should be willing to help other Saints engaged in a good cause, but none of this is contractual or mandatory. If the missionaries are not receiving support for their labors, they would be well advised to go somewhere else where they were made more welcome and WOULD receive support for their labors.

I believe we can say that a "paid ministry" situation is not merely a matter of the attitude of the people who are receiving the payments. The instant that they believe they have the power to change doctrine or policy or practice for their own convenience, they have already started down the paid ministry/priestcraft route. No human can resist this force, unless he engages in extreme determination and preparation. Christ himself might have resisted it, but he made sure that he was never in a situation where he might have to compromise the smallest iota. I don't know why we imagine that we can be more constant and righteous than he, with no external constraints on us.

The FAIRMormon answer also includes a quotation from Elder McConkie arguing that "those who devote all their time to the building up of the kingdom must be provided with food, clothing, shelter, and the necessaries of life." The question he does not touch on is "Who gets to decide whether central church payments are needed and for what?" Do the people who are going to receive those payments get to decide what those payments are? That sounds like an obvious conflict of interest. We might look to Christ and the Apostle Paul who both performed many astonishing works, and they never sought or claimed anything, and only took what was charitably and freely and spontaneously offered them.

I think we have an amazing example of the restraint of Christ on these points. At one point He was starving to death and could have turned stones into bread to relieve his hunger, but he didn't do it, because that would be a misuse of his sacred powers for his own selfish needs. Humans might have trouble being as precise as he was, but we ought to keep that standard before us, and attempt to be as full of integrity as he was. Freely and enthusiastically embracing the concept of self-interest is the complete opposite of trying to meet his standard.

If people who never receive anything from the church, and are considered doctrinally unable to receive anything from the church, directly or indirectly, make the decision that others should receive something from the church funds, that might at least lower the risk of corruption. It would be better if no one gets anything from the church organization so that the temptation can never arise. That was the process that went on for hundreds of years (after the life of Christ and for the first 80 years in our own time) and was very successful, so it has real merit as the ideal situation. In that situation, EVERYTHING is spontaneous charity so there is no way to do any corrupting empire-building and bureaucracy-building.

Who decides HOW MUCH needs to be paid out? The normal rules of fairness and constitutional behavior indicate that those who pay in should be the ones who decide how much is paid out and for what. Before 1923, the members had a legal way to put a damper on inappropriate spending or typical bureaucratic empire building. Unfortunately, after the 1923 secular incorporation of the church, we now have a "taxation without representation" situation where all important decisions are totally uncontrolled. We have no constitutional division of powers, etc. This absolutely guarantees eventual corruption. No matter how good the men are, they are still men and need constant constraints.

In the section entitled "Priestcraft," the FAIRMormon answer tries to limit the question in this way: "However, it should be noted that priestcraft as it has been defined is a condemnation of intent (to get gain and praise, and not for the welfare of Zion), and not about that individual receiving support." I beg to differ. I believe all the scriptural evidence is that an individual's original good intent has nothing to do with it. If people have the option to claim money from the church and its members, that alone is a corrupting influence, and the bad intent will always creep in, no matter what. And if that claim is long-term and general, as opposed to some specific transaction such as buying building materials to build a specific chapel, and if there is the slightest opportunity to affect church doctrine and policy in any way for one's convenience, then corruption is guaranteed.

I believe it is easy to show that the church today has changed several critical aspects of the gospel and its administration, about six in number, and they are all a result of first embracing the corrosive effects of a paid ministry.

Strangely enough, doing church administration the right way seems to be many times more effective than doing it the empire-building way. That alone ought to be enough to end the arguments for a paid ministry. In Christ's frame of reference, building a world church is not something to be carefully and closely managed in typical profit-making corporate administrative fashion. It is actually impossible to manage and control it, and even the attempt is very damaging.

The Correct Answer

I am challenging the conventional LDS answer concerning the issue of a paid ministry. To do a thorough job of it, my answer and alternative will have to be rather lengthy, but hopefully it will be worth the trouble concerning this important issue. It should be useful to briefly explore the concept of a paid ministry during three historical periods: in the Book of Mormon before Christ, during Christ's ministry in Jerusalem, and today. The doctrines said to be in effect are the same in the first two periods but are radically different in the third.

Considering the life of Christ and the writings of the apostles and prophets in any detail, I don't see how an argument for a paid ministry could possibly be correct. Unfortunately, that also means that the church today, which has a very big paid ministry program, is very much out of order when compared to the scriptures. It may usually be admirable to be defending current church policy, but in this case, when the central church has deviated on a grand scale from all scriptural instruction, the honest thing to do is to acknowledge the problem and try to fix it. I guess the FAIR Mormon organization has to decide if they are apologists for the basic and eternal GOSPEL, or are they apologists for current church leadership and staff. Unfortunately, those are two very different things today.

I consider myself a stalwart defender of the gospel, but I think part of that includes noting all the many places where the current church has wandered off the path. In the year 2020, the gospel will have been on the earth for 200 years in our era (with a formal church organization in place for 190 years), and in every other situation when the church has reached the 200-year mark, it has been in the process of falling apart. A serious theologian and historian would take that into account as an inescapable gospel law and look for the deviations that almost inevitably must have happened at this stage. It should be no surprise that after 200 years of enduring strong secularizing pressures, NO organization can remain on course without a very vigorous self-examination process, and we have no such process. A vigorous self-review of the church by people who care about such things, as is likely to be found among the FAIRMormon apologists, might be a way to establish a grassroots process that keeps the main church on track. One of the things which needs to be reconsidered is the nature and tasks of living prophets. Granting them unlimited and unexamined powers to change things has not turned out very well.

I believe this needs to be a grassroots amateur volunteer effort, simply because anyone who might be considered a professional is probably already tied in with the paid ministry scheme of things as part of his career and career options, and is going to defend a paid ministry theory out of self-interest, even if his logic and scriptural reasoning makes no sense at all.

Our nation is currently engaged in a great ideological battle concerning our federal government's Supreme Court. We now have at least four members of the Supreme Court who see no reason whatsoever to honor the originalist interpretations of the words of the Constitution. They feel fully justified in saying that their personal ideologies, which are firmly Marxist, and which consider the original Constitution nothing more than an unimportant piece of ancient parchment, ought to override whatever those dead founders may have had in mind. (I consider Marxism just another term for Satanism).

Unfortunately, the church today has the exact same problem about understanding and applying the originalist positions of the scriptures, and like the four leftist members of the Supreme Court, the current church leaders have decided that their personal preferences about interpreting the scriptures, usually for their own convenience, with no checks on their behavior by outside members or theologians, should easily override the original intent of the scriptures. Do the current prophets get to rewrite the scriptures any day of the week on a whim, or are they tightly bound by those ancient teachings? With no one to check up on them, they apparently feel they can do whatever they wish.

At this late stage of the game, as we near the typical 200-year implosion, I consider it highly unlikely that the current church leaders' positions on the paid ministry issue, and on several other issues of about the same importance, can be corrected so that we somehow avoid the almost inevitable 200-year gospel meltdown. Nonetheless, it seems worth making a heroic effort to avoid the crash. We see plenty of symptoms that this crash is in the process of occurring, but somehow many of us plug our ears and cover our eyes rather than recognize the obvious.

I am guessing that all the current hubbub about church members "learning things they never knew before" about the church, and complaints about lack of "transparency," leading them to doubt or leave the church, is part of this "winding up scene" in our own time. Suddenly, for reasons which they often cannot articulate, the church doesn't make much sense anymore. Most of their lives they were just going through the motions out of habit without any in-depth understanding of the gospel before, and all of a sudden, the whole thing seems like an illusion. Any small pebble thrown by the church's enemies results in an enormous hole in their glass house. The few answers which the church does offer seem like too little, too late, to explain why we are where we are. Those few timid and incomplete answers may actually give rise to a great many more new questions than they answer.

I believe the gospel can be fully defended, at any philosophical, doctrinal, or historical depth level that is desired by serious questioners, but, at this point, there is no place that those questioners can go to get the fully integrated truth. The central church organization itself seems as bewildered as anyone else. Like the members, they have been going on autopilot for 100 years now, and there is no one alive at church headquarters who has the slightest clue as to how to understand and interpret exactly what happened during the first 100 years of the church's existence (or for the second 100 years either, for that matter). We either need to find some 200-year old church member/leader historians and theologians who can just tell us what we need to know, or we need to improve our game by a factor of 20 or 100 times in the areas of studying church history and theology. Our continued laziness and broad ignorance will simply make it absolutely certain that the church will soon fall apart, as it always has before. One might hope that a fully literate population would remember important things much longer than a purely verbal society, and avoid distortions, but apparently the practical difference is not that great.

Christ the exemplar

It seems like the best place to start would be with the life of Christ himself. He has been our source of instruction at every phase of the world's existence, especially during his actual life on earth. He may not have always presented his teachings in giant black headlines in our current language and idiom so that we could not possibly make a mistake of interpretation, like "NEVER ALLOW A PAID MINISTRY OF ANY KIND," but all the important teachings are there if we will but look for them. For example, he did not spend a whole chapter of the Gospels telling us what an evil and destructive thing a paid ministry would be, but he did pattern his own life and instruct everyone around him to take great pains to avoid even the slightest semblance of a paid ministry situation. It should not be too hard to understand his teachings on that point if we simply are asking the right questions as we read the New Testament.

In reviewing his instructions to us, it seems very important to start with the Matt. 10:8 "freely ye have received, freely give" theme before we get into this discussion any further.

It is a little bit strange to pay people full-time to dispense charity on behalf of other generous, charitable persons, which is what the tens of thousands of church employees today are paid to do to a large extent. Obviously, paying people to dispense charity usually gobbles up a very large chunk of the charity and can quickly mostly neutralize the effect of the original charitable giving. It would be far better if the charity delivery system was itself charitably donated. This is especially true when what is being donated and passed along is priesthood power to do good. Here are a few more of the instructions:

> Matt. 10:
> 7 And as ye go, preach, saying, The kingdom of heaven is at hand.
> 8 Heal the sick, cleanse the lepers, raise the dead, cast out devils: <u>freely ye have received, freely give</u>.
> 9 Provide neither gold, nor silver, nor brass in your purses,
> 10 Nor scrip for your journey, neither two coats, neither shoes, nor yet staves: for the workman is worthy of his meat.

The most critical instructions here are in verse 8. Without requesting any remuneration, they were to do many charitable works among the people. "Freely have you received, freely give." They would be giving away everything, from the benefits of their priesthood power to earthly goods, if they had that option. In many ways, the church today has ceased to be a charitable organization, and has become a profit-making organization, working to charge for all the good it does, as through centrally-required tithing.

Matt. 10:10 says "for the workman is worthy of his meat." That may be true, but the big question is who gets the bill? God accepts that bill, and does not pass it along to men in any coercive way.

If the apostles are giving away free teaching and free miracles, is that just a set-up, a teaser, a loss-leader, so that they can then charge people for the ordinances they get later? We might notice that baptism and the Gift of the Holy Ghost were given away freely, by John the Baptist and by Christ himself and his apostles Peter and John, so is that, again, just a teaser to get people into the system so that they can be charged for the higher ordinances of endowment and eternal marriage which they will be taught to desire?

Doesn't it seem a little bit strange that if the apostles are doing such unusual things as raising the dead and casting out devils, they would do that for free, but would want to get paid for officiating at more ordinary events such as temple weddings? If one were marketing these many services, one might expect that raising the dead would bring a much higher price than simply officiating at a wedding.

It should be useful here to mention the case of Simon, sometimes known as a sorcerer, as described in Acts 8, who later repented of his errors when he learned the full truth. Simon saw the powerful effects of people receiving the Gift of the Holy Ghost and wished to be given that same power to bestow the Gift of the Holy Ghost, and was willing to pay for that power. It was made very clear to him that priesthood power was not for sale, just as the priesthood ordinances are not for sale, but are to be freely bestowed where appropriate.

We hear people arguing that church members are not required to pay for the temple ordinances they receive today, but that just demonstrates the cleverness and subtleness of the current system. Today, those higher ordinances are not provided in some inexpensive endowment house but only in the very expensive temples. And no one gets into those temples without a temple recommend, and no one gets a temple recommend without paying a full tithing to the central church. There is no other pathway. There is nothing so blatant as having a computer records check of payments before one can get into the temple door, or some kind of cash register operation, but the same operational effect is achieved by the more dispersed and low-key temple recommend system.

It seems logical that a truly charitable organization would give priesthood ordinances based on people's desires and needs, not their ability to pay. The focus should logically be on the needs of the one, not the needs of the central organization. As soon as the needs of the central organization become primary, we have someone who is trying to build an empire based on dispensing religious favors and services.

It is always suspicious to have clergy charging for religious ordinances, regardless of how that "charging" is done. The question keeps coming back to "are we a charitable organization or not?" Or are we explicitly a business, carrying on this activity for profit-making purposes, perhaps trying to build an empire?

There is a bit of irony operating here when temple ordinances warn against being able to buy anything in this world for money, but then require the indirect payment of money for those very ordinances.

Some tithing and temple recommend history

Without access to detailed church historical records, it is difficult to give more than a high-level overview as to how tithing policy has changed radically over time, but it is still possible to indicate a likely beginning point, middle point, and endpoint. As a beginning point, there was no mention of the need for a temple recommend until 1856, and tithing was then mentioned as one of the criteria to be considered. Before that, concerning the Kirtland and Nauvoo temples, there is no mention of any need for a recommend, and presumably no specific requirement for tithing payment. As to a middle point, the 1899 series of presentations by President Lorenzo Snow on the topic of tithing were considered quite a departure from the normal policies on the question of tithing. It can be shown that Pres. Snow was pleased by the increase in the central collection of tithing as a result of his messages, but that new level in the payment of central tithing only came to about one dollar per church member per year, probably a great deal less than a "full tithing" for all. Concerning an endpoint, it was not until 1964 that a temple recommend question asks whether applicants "are" full tithe payers. Before that, lesser standards such as "undertake to become" a full tithe payer were often acceptable.[2]

It appears that in the late 1800s, arguments were occasionally made that Church members ought to be required to pay a full tithing to the central church before they could receive a temple recommend. It appears that there was some justification for that desire to collect more money centrally, since the Salt Lake Temple had not been completed, and was not completed until 1893. However, the desire to get more money flowing into Salt Lake City apparently went far beyond just desiring to get a temple finished, and really was the beginning of a desire and agitation to build up a more elaborate and expensive central bureaucracy.

It appears that those early arguments for keeping members out of temples unless they had paid a full central tithe had little effect, quite possibly because at that point the church members were considered to be the real owners of the church and its property, even though the church members appointed a trustee to act on their behalf, usually, but not always, whoever held the office of the church president. In other words, there was no church officer who had complete control of the temples as against any claims of the members. The trustee would need the permission of the church members in order to take such radical and separate control of the temples, and it was unlikely that the members would be willing to agree to that.

This issue of needing to pay a full central tithing to receive a recommend was probably further advanced in 1923 when the church leaders (quietly, even secretly, I presume) executed what I will call a lawyers coup and rejected the church organization which had been in effect for nearly 100 years in which the church members acted as an unincorporated religious association which periodically appointed a trustee to manage their affairs, and instead incorporated the church headquarters as an arm of the new Utah state government, partially merging church and state. Where before the church had been a creature of the membership, it now became a creature of the political state and got a good start on its gradual and inevitable secularization.

It was a coup in another sense, simply because there was no such thing as a "purchase" or an "investment" by the church leaders. They just took control of it through some imagined "right of conquest" kind of thinking. This self-perpetuating headquarters autonomy continues today as leaders are invited from the normal commercial activities of the world to become church apostles and managers today without investing a dime of their own money, while they are given unconstrained control of many billions of dollars in income and assets.

We should note that the original scriptural pattern was that the members would assist in choosing the candidates for leadership, thus avoiding a completely isolated leadership monoculture at the apostle level. Acts 1.

Apparently this 1923 action meant that the church leaders were able to take central control of all church properties, especially including temples, however illegitimate that new control was, and now, as the exclusive owners of the temples, they could set the rules for attending the temples and exclude anyone they wished. Obviously, at the top of the list, was a requirement that people pay in a full tithing to the central church organization before they could have access to the temples. For nearly 100 years before that, people had paid tithing locally, and managed it themselves mostly, with only some of it being directed to central church headquarters, presumably based on the members' perception of centralized needs. I believe we can say that that 1923 event was the beginning of a very serious and determined paid ministry regime in which access to the temples was limited to those who paid their tithing to the central church in exactly the way specified by the new "owners" of the temples.

Having supplied all the resources and labor, I believe the members legally did own the temples, and the church trustee did not. He was only an agent of the members. That is why this was corrupt, since the leaders took control of something that was never theirs, and never should be theirs. If the members felt they owned the temples at least as much as leaders, they had good reason to think that, based on logic and history. The temples are a charitable effort to be shared by the church members, church leaders, and all the world who are willing to accept the gospel. Anything else is certainly priestcraft, trying to extract money out of people based on religious arguments and trickery, including guilt trips.

As I will explain in more detail later, I believe this lawyers' coup was a great curtailment of LDS personal responsibility and their religious freedom to manage their own religious resources, and was an example of an exercise of unrighteous dominion under the terms of D&C 121. That was the beginning of the end for the church in our time. Nearly all other deviations from the scriptures stem from this one, since defending their coup, their winnings, and the promise of its eternal flow of income became the prime directive. Everything that might interfere with that flow of money or the personal ease and convenience of the leaders would naturally be curtailed, especially including any potentially expensive and troublesome commitments to make any positive changes to the society around them, in accordance with their actual scriptural charges.

Historically, one of the main goals of operating a religion business was to find a way to sell that which many people desire the most -- salvation, and a sure place in heaven. The Catholic practice of indulgences is an interesting example, where people were told they could buy forgiveness of their sins before or after the fact, with the church pretending to act as the Savior himself in issuing "forgivenesses" or pardons.

Even though the scriptures tell us that priesthood power is freely received and should be freely given, the first impulse of any one who desires to be part of a paid ministry is to get control of that pathway to heaven and start charging tolls. The LDS headquarters has managed to do that through charging for access to its temples, and that has apparently turned out to be a very profitable "tollbooth." With these policies in effect, those "tollbooths" are naturally concentrated where people have the most money and have the most anxiety about assuring their place in heaven, including places for their families and ancestors and friends. It also helps that we have a very glorious description of heaven, and people's possible experiences there, which increases the desire to qualify. If people had a much more modest view of what heaven entails for them (or the possible horrors of hell), they might be much less driven to make extreme sacrifices here to try to add certainty to their own religious future.

To further bind down the members and make sure that the income was dependable, for many years those recommends had to be renewed every year, where now it is reduced to only every two years. That would help get rid of the possibility of people only seeking a recommend (and paying a centralized tithing) when they actually needed it. This way, people would feel that they were not in good standing in the church if they did not have a current recommend, even though they were in fact doing everything that the gospel requires them to do, including distributing tithing to the poor and to other good purposes. Put another way, a person without a centrally-sanctioned recommend (from paying central tithing) is considered to be partially disfellowshipped, out-of-favor with the church. Their salvation insurance policy has lapsed. This is a useful fear factor in controlling the masses and their money.

The real truth is that most people only need to go through the temple once for their own purposes, but that doesn't make the temples work very well as highly productive and dependable tollbooths. To overcome that problem, you need to put a huge effort into promoting genealogy research, family history work, and temple work. People need to be made to worry anxiously and continuously about the fate of their ancestors once they have taken care of themselves. This is very much like lighting the candles in the Catholic or Russian Orthodox churches to give prayers for the dead to help their eternal progress. That should seem like a strange process to us since we know that lighting candles is a very ineffective way to do proxy work for the dead. But the proxy work we do for the dead is only slightly more effective and it is enormously more expensive. (As I present in detail elsewhere, the cost for each new unique name which is processed through the temple system is about $2000, instead of the $2 that it could be with a better procedure.)[3]

But, again, the truth there is that the best evidence we have is that those on the other side will be taken care of just fine, with or without our help. Going to the temple multiple times is mostly for our personal benefit, not for the benefit of the dead. Under current conditions, we can never do the temple work for more than a microscopic fraction of the 70 billion people who probably have lived on this earth, all of whom are our ancestors, and still only the tiniest fraction of even the 7 billion people for whom there might be records remaining.

Obviously, for fairness purposes, we should expect there are heavenly contingency plans for all these people that have nothing to do with our responsibilities and abilities during our lifetimes. We have reason to believe that there have already been millions of people resurrected in the First Resurrection which started with the resurrection of Christ. How does such a person get judged, resurrected, and exalted without any of the basic ordinances? Presumably someone already has a plan to take care of that little administrative problem. Perhaps there are processes going on right now on this very earth that we know nothing about that deal with this little detail.

We have the interesting case of Joseph Smith's brother Alvin who had gone on to his celestial glory long before there even was any system available to do any temple work for him. D&C 137. (It doesn't specifically say whether he had been resurrected or not, but it seems hard to imagine that he would not have been resurrected if he was already in the celestial kingdom.) Perhaps the righteous people among those 70 billion people will all simply revisit the Earth during the millennium and take care of their own ordinance work for themselves without any help from us.

The important thing from the church paid ministry viewpoint as that people have to have a reason to be constantly going to the temple which means they will constantly pay their tithing so that the generous income to the central church will be guaranteed. This conclusion is a great deal more than just speculation on my part. From my very extensive research on genealogy computer systems, it is easy to demonstrate that with the current level of resources being put into genealogy work and temple work, we could finish the United States in less than a year, and the entire world in about 10 years. But notice that we have been carrying on this process for more than 100 years and for the last 18 years have been spending enormous amounts of time and money on the new Family Search system. We have spent about $36 billion so far on that system, far more than enough to finish the United States and the entire world, if the process were done as efficiently as it has been easy to do since about 2003 with newer technology.

But notice that the central church has not the slightest interest in adopting any of these new highly efficient procedures, presumably because that would greatly damage their paid ministry arguments and arrangements. To support that paid ministry argument, and all the money that flows to the central church because of it, the central church will continue to use their current procedures which require an essentially infinite amount of time and energy and cost to finish even the United States, let alone the world. (Actually it would cost about $960 trillion to finish the United States using current methods.) Their unstated but controlling fear is apparently that if we finished this project as quickly as we could -- this project in which the church has been assigned to prepare all available records for temple work -- their current generous flow of income might dry up, and that cannot be allowed to happen. What might it mean about their job security, pensions, etc.? I consider this a serious and ongoing example of unrighteous dominion on the part of church headquarters.

Paid ministry in the Book of Mormon, before the life of Christ
We have many examples from the Book of Mormon which severely condemn the concept of a paid ministry, or priestcraft, its darker cousin, which may be barely distinguishable in theory. We have King Benjamin and King Mosiah and Alma the Chief Judge who would take no money from the populace to support themselves, in either their political roles or in their religious roles. And then in the starkest possible contrast, we have Nehor and Korihor who apparently both instituted paid ministries among the Nephites, while, at the same time, showing all the worst forms of corruption that can come through that process, even including murder, a murder that came about apparently because of the unlimited ambition fostered by the hope of great riches and power to be acquired through the mechanism of a paid ministry, a kind of religious labor union exploiting a potentially monopolistic source of income -- religious control over the pathway to heaven. (Marxist government arguments for centralization, regulation, and bureaucracy are simply an atheist version of the same religious or ideology-based impulse. Marxism simply promises its heaven will be on earth.)

The scriptures tell us that that pathway to heaven should be free, but the goal of all professional priests is to extract some serious income from their claimed control of that pathway. Good intentions are not good enough. People will do the wrong thing no matter what, if they are allowed to. The profit and power logic is overwhelming, and humans will always be bent towards it.

Here is part of the scriptural story:

> Alma 1
> 2 And it came to pass that in the first year of the reign of Alma in the judgment-seat, there was a man [Nehor] brought before him to be judged, a man who was large, and was noted for his much strength.
> 3 And he had gone about among the people, preaching to them that which he termed to be the word of God, bearing down against the church; declaring unto the people that every priest and teacher ought to become popular; and they ought not to labor with their hands, but that they ought to be supported by the people.
> 4 And he also testified unto the people that all mankind should be saved at the last day, and that they need not fear nor tremble, but that they might lift up their heads and rejoice; for the Lord had created all men, and had also redeemed all men; and, in the end, all men should have eternal life.

5 And it came to pass that he did teach these things so much that many did believe on his words, even so many that they began to support him and give him money.
6 And he began to be lifted up in the pride of his heart, and to wear very costly apparel, yea, and even began to establish a church after the manner of his preaching.
...
12 But Alma said unto him: Behold, this is the first time that priestcraft has been introduced among this people. And behold, thou art not only guilty of priestcraft, but hast endeavored to enforce it by the sword; and were priestcraft to be enforced among this people it would prove their entire destruction.
...
16 Nevertheless, this did not put an end to the spreading of priestcraft through the land; for there were many who loved the vain things of the world, and they went forth preaching false doctrines; and this they did for the sake of riches and honor.
17 Nevertheless, they durst not lie, if it were known, for fear of the law, for liars were punished; therefore they pretended to preach according to their belief; and now the law could have no power on any man for his belief.
...
26 And when the priests left their labor to impart the word of God unto the people, the people also left their labors to hear the word of God. And when the priest had imparted unto them the word of God they all returned again diligently unto their labors; and the priest, not esteeming himself above his hearers, for the preacher was no better than the hearer, neither was the teacher any better than the learner; and thus they were all equal, and they did all labor, every man according to his strength.
27 And they did impart of their substance, every man according to that which he had, to the poor, and the needy, and the sick, and the afflicted; and they did not wear costly apparel, yet they were neat and comely.
28 And thus they did establish the affairs of the church; and thus they began to have continual peace again, notwithstanding all their persecutions.

Alma 30
12 and this Anti-christ, whose name was Korihor, (and the law could have no hold upon him) began to preach unto the people that there should be no Christ.
...

In this Alma 1 situation, there appears to have been no church-required centralization of contributions of any kind, indeed no central bureaucracy at all, and the decentralized administration of aid to the poor was perfectly effective.

One might raise the sensitive question as to whether a church's policy of centralized collection of nearly all contributions, on pain of being partially disfellowshipped, as in denial of temple attendance, could be considered an enforcing of priestcraft. It is perfectly obvious that most contributions are, in the end, spent locally among the members, or ought to be spent locally, and having them be required to pass through a central site employing a paid ministry makes those funds subject to the standard fraud, waste, abuse, and mismanagement found in every centralized government.

We also might wonder how we should analyze and process the situation today where church leaders' expressed beliefs and actions do not match the scriptures on several important points. There may be no obvious legal case against them, no way to enforce their adherence to and compliance with the scriptures, since it may be a matter of their belief, but should they nonetheless continue to have untrammeled management authority over nearly all member resources?

The paid ministry issue at the time of Christ

We might naturally wonder whether Christ himself taught us any lessons on this topic or not, and it seems that he did. One of his early temptations from Satan was that with his enormous innate powers he could own the earth and rule the earth. Actually, as our god before coming to earth, he had "owned", and always would "own" the earth in one sense already, and could rule it to the extent he chose. But notice that, as part of his teachings to us, he wanted absolutely nothing to do with having any of that direct ownership and control when he was actually a mortal. Apparently, Christ was incorruptible, but even he had to prove it, at least to himself and to Satan and to God, if not to anyone else. And if he still took every possible step to avoid being corrupted himself, in spite of all the tests he had passed already, why would we imagine that mere mortals could toy with, and even embrace, all the most corrupting powers which he avoided, and have those mortals still come off perfectly clean and blameless and correct in all their policies?

Considering Christ's prayer: "Oh my Father, if it be possible, let this cup pass from me: nevertheless not as I will, but as thou wilt," Matt. 26:39, perhaps he would have been even more tempted to skip his atonement assignment if he were living a really pleasant and luxurious earthly life. That is the problem with too much prosperity, potentially supplied by a paid ministry system.

Christ had this overwhelming job to do, and that was to give up his life, and any potential control over anyone or anything, when he could have had control over everyone and everything, exactly as Satan had wanted to do himself. But he stayed away from that impulse and opportunity completely, apparently so that he could carry out his critical mission. Other people had obviously been tempted, and had quickly and eagerly failed that test, as we see in the case of the Scribes and the Pharisees and the Sadducees who DID have complete control of the earth as far as the Jews were concerned, and would have liked to increase their physical control of the earth and its peoples.

Today's Sanhedrin?
It is hard to imagine that, after all the bad things Christ said about the scribes and the Pharisees, the members of the Sanhedrin, that Christ would do even the tiniest thing that looked like the behavior of the members of the Sanhedrin. And yet today the church central headquarters looks and operates very much like the old Jewish Sanhedrin, complete with hundreds of lawyers, as it attempts to centralize control over every aspect of the church worldwide, and keep and defend its power base from any internal or external threats.

With perhaps a $12 billion annual resource budget, the church is a larger governmental agency than any one of about 69 countries in the world today. That makes them quite a bit larger religious government than the original local Sanhedrin, I assume. The LDS church probably does not have the income of the Catholic Church, which is estimated to be about $170 billion from its United States operations, probably the largest single source of its income, but the LDS church seems to take the Catholic Church as its model in empire building. One difference is that the Catholic Church spends enormous amounts of money on schools and hospitals, something which the LDS church doesn't do, leaving the LDS church with a much larger percentage of uncommitted "disposable income" from its income sources. We might guess that the total worldwide Catholic church income is about $240 billion, making it about 20 times the size of the LDS church, making the LDS church budget actually relatively larger than one might guess from its being only 2% or 1/50 the size of the United States, or 0.2% of the size of the world.

Instead of getting involved in even an ounce of this ego-feeding earthly control of everything, Christ made sure that he did not have the slightest amount of earthly bureaucratic powers, and not even the appearance of any such powers. He told Pilate that his kingdom was not of this Earth, and Pilate believed him, and would have released him from any charges of being a power-seeking political competitor. And we can be sure that Pilate was extremely sensitive to such questions. That would be the first thing he would worry about at all times, perhaps especially because he would surely know that the Jews were looking for a Messiah to come and save them from what they considered to be bondage under the Romans. (Are we just like the Jews in wanting a Messiah to come and solve all our problems for us? If so, that simply means we have no idea who the Messiah is, or will be, in spite of all his teachings.)

So apparently Christ's actions and statements were quite convincing, at least to Pilate. And perhaps we could also say that his actions and words were quite convincing to the Jews in a different way, in that he sought no earthly powers of any kind. He did not even collect and keep enough income to pay his taxes, and relied on miracles or good fortune to provide even his tax payments, as with the coin found in a fish's mouth. Matt. 17:27. They convicted him of blasphemy and wished to kill him for that crime they had defined. They were looking for a Messiah, someone who would come and use his great powers to free them from the Romans and make the Jews a great power on the earth. Anyone who claimed to be the Messiah and then did NOT destroy their enemies and set them up with earthly powers would be a great disappointment, apparently worthy of death for even tantalizing them with that possibility of that greater power for themselves.

We might notice that he made not the slightest effort to build up an earthly bureaucracy with paid armies and thousands of paid minions to do his will -- all the accoutrements of a secular power structure. Not only did he not do any of this himself, but he constantly warned any potential followers that there was absolutely no chance, at least as long as he was around, that there would be any paid ministry situations which then might become personally lucrative and also therefore personally corrupting.

Christ was the epitome of idealism and altruism, as he surely had to be to carry out his assigned mission concerning the atonement. He told everyone who followed him that they could not expect to have the slightest bit of earthly goods or power over anyone as a result of their position. ("The Son of man hath not where to lay his head," the lilies of the field and the ravens are taken care of by God, etc.)

> Matthew 8
> 19 And a certain scribe came, and said unto him, Master, I will follow thee whithersoever thou goest.
> 20 And Jesus saith unto him, The foxes have holes, and the birds of the air have nests; but <u>the Son of man hath not where to lay his head.</u>
>
> Luke 12
> 22 ¶And he said unto his disciples, Therefore I say unto you, Take no thought for your life, what ye shall eat; neither for the body, what ye shall put on.
> 23 The life is more than meat, and the body is more than raiment.
> 24 <u>Consider the ravens</u>: for they neither sow nor reap; which neither have storehouse nor barn; and God feedeth them: how much more are ye better than the fowls?
> 25 And which of you with taking thought can add to his stature one cubit?
> 26 If ye then be not able to do that thing which is least, why take ye thought for the rest?
> 27 <u>Consider the lilies how they grow: they toil not, they spin not; and yet I say unto you, that Solomon in all his glory was not arrayed like one of these</u>.
> 28 If then God so clothe the grass, which is to day in the field, and tomorrow is cast into the oven; how much more will he clothe you, O ye of little faith?
> 29 And seek not ye what ye shall eat, or what ye shall drink, neither be ye of doubtful mind.
> 30 <u>For all these things do the nations of the world seek after:</u> and your Father knoweth that ye have need of these things.

One rich young man who wanted to follow Christ was told to sell all his goods and give the money to the poor and come and follow Christ, indicating that it would COST this young man a great deal to have the honor of being a disciple or an apostle, perhaps just the opposite of what this ambitious young man had in mind. Matt. 19:16-22. Latter-day attempts to downplay the "vow of poverty" implications are not very convincing. Perhaps some of the Catholic monastic orders had it partly right after all. We might wonder whether these religious orders were a reaction to the excesses of the main Catholic Church.

We might notice that Christ and his group did collect some money which was then distributed to the poor, but even that was not something he considered to be his job, apparently, or the job of his main group of disciples. When that process of transferring money to the poor became burdensome, he transferred that function to a completely separate organization and apparently had nothing more to do with it.

Not only would his time have been largely wasted in welfare administration, but perhaps he specifically did not want any temptations to arise, for him or his followers, from having that amount of money concentrated among his followers who were charged with teaching the Gospel and setting church policy.

We might notice that Judas was the treasurer, the one who carried the purse for their group, and he was also the one who some think wanted to force Christ to take on the role of the Messiah, if that was possible, presumably with Judas and other followers thereby gaining great power by being near the all-powerful Christ. Judas was also the one who allowed himself to be corrupted by the blood money of 30 pieces of silver. This seems to indicate that money handling for the church has a way of corrupting those who handle the money (or attracting those who are easily corruptible) to the point where they think only of themselves and are willing to commit a kind of treason by selling the members into slavery, so to speak.

Removing the vast financial and physical power of today's top church leaders would go a long way to remove any distrust or sense of unease about ANYONE having such completely unbridled power, whether religious or not. Christ made sure he had no such power, so why should it be counted as righteousness for men to seek or accept that kind of church-related power today? Just as a curiosity, we might notice that a resource budget of $12 billion makes the LDS church a larger operation than about 69 different countries in the world. That certainly seems like a large enough government to have proper constitutional principles apply[4] (although some of today's church leaders might argue that the gospel overrides and cancels out the U.S. Constitution in some situations).

We might recall the parable of the servant who expected to be released from his position so he quickly sold many of his master's goods to other masters at fire-sale prices. Luke 16:1-12. That meant that he would be well received by other masters when he left the employ of the first master. Our current system might discourage some of this behavior because the lifetime assignments of leaders would tend to remove some of the future value from this kind of disloyal behavior. However, in contrast, there is also the much worse possibility that servants might change gospel policy or misuse or give away valuable assets to make their lives easier, especially because they could expect to always maintain their office and never be challenged by anyone.

This corresponds to the usually very lucrative "president for life" leaders we see in so many Third World countries. In those cases, the chief lawgiver can also be the worst lawbreaker with impunity, because he totally controls the application of the law. As part of the church's teaching mission to the world, one might expect the church leaders to carefully apply internally the principles of fairness contained in the U.S. Constitution, but I don't see that happening. The church headquarters may not necessarily behave like an unrestrained dictatorship, but if it is formally set up to operate that way, as it is today, that appears to teach a very bad lesson about the church approving and modeling the concentration of absolute power in one or a few men. As in times past, apostles should be able to operate perfectly well without a large and complex church attached, although the church might have difficulty operating without such leaders.

Finally, we might ask ourselves if we have accepted some of the Jews' logic today about expecting a mighty Messiah or, something similar, a church organization that concentrates great temporal power in the name of the gospel. We can be reasonably sure that accumulating direct power is always a bad idea, based on Christ's example, although a vigorous program of correct teachings could bring great wisdom and wealth to the general populace. The trick is to avoid any direct control but only offer all needed teachings and advice. "Building up Zion" cannot include the church gaining great temporal power, since that would inevitably mean a new Catholic Church would be born. I don't believe man's basic impulses ever change, so the organizational safeguards can never change. This is the basic wisdom of the U.S. Constitution and the scriptures on the "paid ministry" issue.

Did Christ change any of his patterns in the new world when he visited the Nephites? Apparently not. I think it is interesting that the church leaders, the normal apostles, and other special cases such as the Three Nephites, behaved in a completely different way than one might see today. In several cases, when the Nephites were not listening and were not worthy of having the disciples among them, the disciples simply left. Mormon 1:13; Mormon

3:1; Moroni 8:10-11. If we think a moment, we might realize that they would not want to do that when the right time came if they were feeling very prosperous in a paid ministry situation. The very fact that they had succumbed to that temptation to receive a nice salary would probably mean that they had already made the choice that they would stay with the church members no matter what the level of righteousness of the church members might be, because they would have become accustomed to living in a high style. And even if they were very humble about everything, they would probably still have entangled themselves in endless bureaucratic administrations so that it would be very disruptive, to themselves and to the people they ruled, for them just to disappear whenever they felt that the Nephites were unworthy of such ministrations.

Christ as Jehovah dislikes kings and their bureaucracies
In the Old Testament, Christ, as Jehovah, discouraged Israelites from having kings and encouraged them to elect judges to govern themselves. All of this was to encourage them to live as free men so they could better live the gospel.

> 1 Samuel 8
> 6 But the thing displeased Samuel, when they said, Give us a king to judge us. And Samuel prayed unto the Lord.
> 7 And the Lord said unto Samuel, Hearken unto the voice of the people in all that they say unto thee: for they have not rejected thee, but <u>they have rejected me, that I should not reign over them.</u>
> 8 According to all the works which they have done since the day that I brought them up out of Egypt even unto this day, wherewith they have forsaken me, and served other gods, so do they also unto thee.
> 9 Now therefore hearken unto their voice: howbeit yet protest solemnly unto them, and <u>shew them the manner of the king that shall reign over them.</u>
> 10 And Samuel told all the words of the Lord unto the people that asked of him a king.
> 11 And he said, This will be the manner of the king that shall reign over you: He will take your sons, and appoint them for himself, for his chariots, and to be his horsemen; and some shall run before his chariots.
> 12 And he will appoint him captains over thousands, and captains over fifties; and will set them to ear his ground, and to reap his harvest, and to make his instruments of war, and instruments of his chariots.
> 13 And he will take your daughters to be confectionaries, and to be cooks, and to be bakers.
> 14 And he will take your fields, and your vineyards, and your oliveyards, even the best of them, and give them to his servants.
> 15 And he will take the tenth of your seed, and of your vineyards, and give to his officers, and to his servants.
> 16 And he will take your menservants, and your maidservants, and your goodliest young men, and your asses, and put them to his work.
> 17 He will take the tenth of your sheep: and ye shall be his servants.

18 And ye shall cry out in that day because of your king which ye shall have chosen you; and the Lord will not hear you in that day.
19 Nevertheless the people refused to obey the voice of Samuel; and they said, Nay; but we will have a king over us;
20 That we also may be like all the nations; and that our king may judge us, and go out before us, and fight our battles.
21 And Samuel heard all the words of the people, and he rehearsed them in the ears of the Lord.
22 And the Lord said to Samuel, Hearken unto their voice, and make them a king. And Samuel said unto the men of Israel, Go ye every man unto his city.

If wanting a king means they have rejected Jehovah, why would Jehovah then want to become their king? He would be false to himself and false to them. Christ considers himself as reigning over the Israelites when they hearken to his word which includes having representative government.

Even when the people disregarded the Lord's and prophet's counsel and wanted a king, they were allowed to make that choice. They were given freedom to reject freedom.

In the Book of Mormon we have King Mosiah who, as a result of inspiration, wished to end the pattern of king's and replace them with elected judges. Mosiah 29.

These new scriptures from our own time praise the Constitution of the United States as inspired, and essentially incorporates its provisions of representative government by reference. D&C 134:5; 98:4-10.

Based on this long-term pattern of discouraging kings and dictators and promoting representative government ("teach them correct principles and let them govern themselves"), why would we think that Christ would want to come and actually fill the role of a traditional king in the future? Unless his position of "king" was purely ceremonial, as an outlet for our feelings of worship, he would be proving himself a hypocrite, and would be destroying the lessons he had taught to humans for 6000 years. Worse than that, he would cease to be teaching us correct principles and allowing us to govern ourselves. He told Pilate that his kingdom was not of this world, and I think he meant it for the entire time of earth's existence. It does seem a little bit silly for him to be the God of this earth, which would allow him to do anything he wanted to, theoretically, and then be inconsistent in his application of those teachings. He has no need whatsoever of any human adulation as king and direct lawgiver, and I don't know why he would seek it now.

It is really quite hard to imagine Christ as a typically functioning king, with crowds of courtiers and palace intrigue and lobbying, etc., all the mundane aspects of a typical kingly government, complete with guards and soldiers and generals and royal ranks and ceremonies and decrees and regulations and taxes, all focused on creating and maintaining a class society, where the king is served by the masses, rather than the king serving the masses.

Christ would be the sort of King who was never in the palace because he was out serving the people. So why would he even need a palace and all the accoutrements, something he completely avoided during his life? Having some grand architecture in Salt Lake City, besides the temple, may give many people a sense of pride, but the more that Salt Lake City begins to look like the Vatican or like the palace complex of some king, the more worried I get that we have absorbed a touch of paganism.

The very problem in the past is that the people wanted a king, apparently as a way to show that they could have great public works and pageantry and battles and celebrations like all the pagan cultures. And, of course, that very behavior caused them to become and stay pagan to some extent, making temporal appearances become everything. The concept of individual freedom and maximum individual development and responsibility was the very thing they were trying to avoid with their pagan leanings. After all this time and experience, does it really make sense for Christ, at the end, to adopt some of the techniques of Satan in gathering to himself glory and power just because he can? He might not be as cruel and ruthless a ruler as Satan might be, but he would certainly be passing up the "and let the glory be thine" attitude of an earlier time.

If his church on the Earth were set up like an earthly kingdom, as it is now, complete with a grand bureaucracy or king's court, how likely would it be for him to approve of it?

Anti-paid ministry instructions from the first two prophets in our own era

Joseph Smith and Brigham Young both spoke often and emphatically against the ideologies of Marxism, communalism, collectivism, socialism, statism, etc., which promote the exact same arguments as are used to promote a paid ministry, because they all have the same goals, and introduce the same costs and dangers to a religion and a society. Those arguments are always with us, they are always anti-freedom, and they are always wrong. Like the constant and ubiquitous force of gravity, this ideological force is always present, and is always strong, and is Satan's constant thumb on the scale to try to make things go his way.

If someone wishes to follow this topic further, the detailed history of the statements of the first two prophets and related circumstances have been published in two books.[5] Although the two prophets' messages were clear and identical, it may be that at times, Brigham Young spoke most forcefully on this point. Here is one good example from 1856 (emphasis added):

> In the days of the Apostles, the *brethren sold their possessions* and laid them at the Apostles' feet. And where did many of those brethren go to? To naught, to *confusion and destruction.* Could those Apostles keep the Church together, on those principles? No. *Could they build up the kingdom on those principles?* No, they never could. Many of those persons were good men, but they were filled with enthusiasm, insomuch that if they owned a little possession they would place it at the feet of the Apostles.
>
> Will such a course sustain the kingdom? No. Did it, in the days of the Apostles? No. Such a policy would be the ruin of this people, and scatter them to the four winds. We are to be guided by superior knowledge, by a higher influence and power. JD 4:29 BY Aug. 17, 1856 SLC. Quoted at BYUO p. 128-9.

I quote this specifically because his prophecy has come true. The church has been completely neutralized in our time, at least as compared to its prophetic mission, very largely because of its adoption of a paid ministry and related concepts. Luckily, we have not been scattered to the four winds, but our effect on the society around us is very minimal, producing the same result. The church and its leaders have accepted the spurious charges of its enemies concerning communalism being a required doctrine as though those charges were the truth. For some reason which I have yet to understand, almost every church historian (and almost every other kind of historian) has accepted some or all of the many possible Marxist ideologies and have worked very hard to impose them on their societies, including the church organization itself. Any long-term organization must take specific action to counteract that constant negative force, or suffer the consequences, as we have.

Joseph Smith and Brigham Young both went to great lengths to combat the idea that church doctrine dictated some kind of required socialism or communalism and its inevitable centralized paid bureaucracy. In spite of their strenuous efforts to end this myth, one would probably find the majority of today's church leaders and members firmly believing that some form of socialism or communalism is, or will be, a church requirement, at least sometime in the future. This indicates that the church's enemies and detractors have won their ideological argument for church-sponsored socialism, literally over the dead bodies of Joseph Smith and Brigham Young. As noted above, Brigham Young believed that this false teaching could destroy the church, and he may yet be proved correct. It certainly has helped neutralize the church.

It seems clear that this kind of theological wandering around and deviation has given the church's detractors plenty of material to work with today to try to show that the Gospel is inconsistent throughout various time periods and often makes no sense to us today, and that the church leaders within the last

200 years, and at other times in the recorded history of the world, have been all over the map on their interpretations of certain aspects of the Gospel and its administration.

It seems to be high time that we did the hard work of exploring and clarifying this mass of confusion, this Gordian knot of Mormon theology. If this current confusion prompts us to straighten out this series of questions and clarify the Lord's word and intent on every topic of importance, then the church's detractors now and for the last 200 years will have performed a service, to goad us to clear up what should be cleared up. No church planting or restoration has previously lasted more than 200 years, and it appears that ours will not exceed that limit either, if this large accumulation of errors and deviations is not recognized and corrected, and the proper interpretation modeled for all to see.

This paid ministry issue is one of the most major and obvious deviations of today's church from scriptural teachings, and presumably this issue has had to be carefully centrally managed to reach this point without there being a membership uprising concerning the excesses. One might wonder if some version of this heretofore-delayed potential member uprising has anything to do with the sense of a crisis of belief touched on by Elder Holland in a fireside talk addressed to young single adults in Arizona in the spring of 2016.[6]

One might also reasonably wonder whether what is going on in the Western world these days has some relationship to what is going on within the church today. We have Britain which recently voted to leave the European Union. We have some of the citizens in Germany voting against the almost uncontrolled immigration promoted by that country's leaders as part of more a general European Union policy. We have Donald Trump apparently leading a movement in the United States to overthrow the entrenched political establishments of both main political parties. Perhaps the voters and members are saying that what they are seeing is a relentless concentration and centralization of money and power and control into certain organizations. And large numbers of them, perhaps a majority, have decided this has all gone much too far, and something has to change. Perhaps all of these groups of citizens are no longer willing to support these overgrown organizations which, apparently, commonly use manipulative tactics to continue their relentless growth in power to the detriment of the normal citizen or member.

Priestcraft does seem to always contain some necessary propaganda about the desirability of centralizing all power in one place, which benefits religious leaders trying to consolidate their power and income, and that ideology quickly and easily and naturally supports the generally statist/Marxist teachings of Satan as he tries to set up his centers of earthly power and control which also usually degenerate into some form of slavery or near-slavery. There is thus an inevitable connection and cooperation between church and state to control people. Following that path leads to the horrors of the Catholic Church as seen during the Dark Ages. This relentless pressure toward an anti-freedom position in organizations is described in the O'Sullivan's Law concept: "O'Sullivan's Law states that any organization or enterprise that is not expressly right wing will become left wing over time."[7] The LDS church appears to be a long way down that leftist political slippery slope already.

Paid ministry today

As one might have sensed already, this general topic seems to deserve at least one book length treatment, if not several such treatments. Perhaps the main question to be posed about the church organization today is this: The critical startup and wide expansion of the church at the time of Christ in Jerusalem, and thereafter, all happened without any central organization and no money flows. In other words, we could say that the cash cost per convert was about zero. It could not have cost anything because no one had any money to put into the process. All they had was their individual commitment and efforts. The exact same thing happened in the time of Joseph Smith and Brigham Young.

If we look at the church today it is not too difficult to notice that we have a huge bureaucracy which absorbs most of the money contributions of the members with little output to show for it. This means that in total resource terms, it costs about $400,000 for each new long-term member which is added to the church. That is about $200,000 in cash and perhaps $200,000 in volunteer member labor. The church was exploding at about an 8% rate, and had great social effect, when it was not centrally coordinated and had no money. Now that we have a huge bureaucracy, lots of money, and very extensive central coordination, the growth of the church is barely measurable, at about 0.2%. I am guessing that if the members doubled their contributions and their volunteer labors, that would simply mean that the cost for a new long-term member would then be $800,000, as the central bureaucracy quickly absorbed all that extra money and effort like a black hole. This situation makes it seem that any flair of enthusiasm like the "Hasten the Work" initiative is doomed to fail before it even begins because many other changes have to be made in preparation for that burst of enthusiasm to make any difference.

> Convert cost calculation: Although the church typically reports about 300,000 new converts each year, if we look at the number of new organizations and new meeting spaces that are provided to the members, it appears that only about 30,000 people become long-term members each year, requiring new branch or

> ward organizations and appropriate new meeting spaces. Since we don't have access to accurate data on these points, we might guess that the LDS church has a cash budget of about $6 billion a year, plus about $6 billion in volunteer member labor. If we divide that $12 billion by the 30,000 new members, we get an overall resource cost of $400,000 for each such new member.

Can those known as prophets today say that their kingdom is not of this world, in the same sense as Christ made that claim? With a $6-$12 billion resource budget, and with other tens of billions in property and asset holdings of many kinds, I don't believe they can make that same claim. Their lives have only the slightest similarity to the life of Christ, and to all the prophets in the history of the world. I know of none of those ancient prophets who had vast financial holdings and controlled huge bureaucracies. Anywhere but in the United States, such a separate religious effort to gain political and financial power and to control people would have been crushed out long ago. Dictators do not like any kind of competitors for the hearts and minds of the citizens. But building a church empire was not necessary for great religious success in the Roman world, for example.

Would someone like to explain to me how we got here, and why, if it was not caused by adopting the paid ministry concepts forbidden in the Book of Mormon? On the surface, it appears that when the church has a large and expensive central bureaucracy, it becomes almost completely ineffective in carrying out its main mission of spreading the gospel on the earth. Is it just possible that Christ, and such men as Joseph Smith and Brigham Young, actually understood something about church administration that has been completely lost? This deserves a great deal more treatment, but perhaps I have sufficiently raised the question. It would be interesting to see a central church response explaining why all past eras of church administration were wrong and the new way is the right way.

Today's advances in communications technology should mean that the church, like every other practical organization on the earth, could operate very effectively with a high degree of decentralization and dispersion to minimize costs to members and maximize overall church effectiveness. This makes it seem like the church is determined to maintain maximum centralization for policy reasons which do not include minimizing costs and maximizing effectiveness.

The proven path to gospel success

The path which has apparently not been tried in the past century is to remove all public indicators of pride and corporate power and allow the gospel to spread in the way that Christ handled it, and required all his disciples to do likewise, which is to positively reject all indicators of earthly power while still spreading Gospel teachings through the membership. For example, during his life, news of Christ's latest teachings and miracles spread like wildfire in spite of his occasional counsel to keep silent. Perhaps that is the kind of "viral" message that a newly decentralized church organization would generate, especially in this age of social media.

Satan offered Jesus, the man, power over all the earth. Christ not only utterly rejected that, but he insisted that none of his disciples would have a place to lay their head or know where their next meal might come from. That should make maintaining constant humility a little bit easier. Christ most certainly had no paid bureaucracy and received no titles or power of any kind from the institutions of men. By necessity, Joseph Smith and Brigham Young used similar methods with similar success, but things changed after their time. Brigham Young worried that prosperity would be a problem for the church,[8] and we seem to have proved his fears to be correct, although perhaps in a slightly different way than he expected. Jesus was quick to squelch any flattery of himself as a leader, but that is not the normal practice today.[9] This all seems to be another application of the great Pogo observation: "We have met the enemy and he is us."[10]

In the New World, when the church members would not follow the teachings of the disciples, the disciples simply left them to their own devices.[11] Can anyone imagine the disciples today leaving all of their indicators of earthly power and privilege, equal to that of many earthly governments, if the saints were not living the Gospel correctly? As professional managers and politicians, their expected secular impulse would likely be to find out which way the crowd was moving and try to stay ahead of it, thus keeping themselves administratively relevant.

Christ insisted that his kingdom was not of this world, and Pilate believed him. Would a naturally suspicious political leader today be willing to believe that the LDS Church was not seeking earthly power and would not accept it if offered? I don't think so. This kind of self-limiting discipline would represent a different kind of pacifism, where we disarm ourselves bureaucratically to win ideologically. This might mean that members would use their own resources very effectively to spread the gospel as they best saw fit, and with that creativity, in contrast to the top-down command and message control structure of today's church, should be expected to do many remarkable things.

Dismantling our extensive and expensive central bureaucracy would certainly be painful and upsetting to those involved, but if that is the action which stands between us and the church's long-term success, then it would be well worth the disruption. Hopefully that would allow us to reenact on a grand scale the spreading of the Gospel throughout the known world[12] in ways similar to its earlier growth in the Mediterranean area, in Book of Mormon lands, and in gathering the saints from Europe to Utah.

As an extra benefit, if there were no massive concentration of resources and power in Salt Lake City, the LDS Vatican, there would be no tempting target for greed-based lawsuits and hostile governments, greatly reducing the vulnerability of the entire church. Not incidentally, it would unloose and embolden member action, where, in contrast, today's central staff naturally tends to be very timid as a way to make their lives easier, and they would naturally direct others to act similarly.

If the Twelve left the Salt Lake bureaucracy behind, that alone would mandate its dissolution, since the staff would then plainly be leaderless and disavowed. Can you imagine the extreme resistance the staff would put up to that kind of a change? We sometimes hear about the inability of the US president to get control of the massive federal bureaucracy, and that, in fact, the bureaucracy controls the president. Why wouldn't we expect the same would be true at church headquarters?

A Strategic Overview -- plus conclusions and consequences

So what is at stake here?
When we are talking about such things as a paid ministry, we are potentially talking about the most basic organizational principles and goals of the church. In order to connect all the pieces together, it seems necessary to consider all the major possible options and how we got where we are.

1. The original situation

As I will show in more detail below, the original, and definitely most effective way exhibited so far to spread the gospel is to have no effective central administrative headquarters at all, but let each individual member administer all important aspects of the church and its growth, including using the priesthood, doing their own missionary work, spending their own tithing, and executing charity as they see fit. That is the situation that existed for about 200 years after the life of Christ and for about the first 80 years after the gospel was restored to Joseph Smith in 1820. Obviously, if there is no central church worldwide command-and-control system, there would naturally also be no central church cost for adding new members, no central constraints to tell people what they cannot do to spread the gospel, and the members would be free to use their creativity in spontaneously uniting their resources and accomplishing great things.

2. A theoretical alternate policy

Another possible strategy might be to collect nearly all the church's resources into one central place and then use the latest technology and management techniques to cause the gospel to be spread at a furious pace. But that would require a fearless and aggressive management group at church headquarters, something we definitely don't have, and, because of social forces, human nature, and the nature of large bureaucracies, there appears to be no possibility it could ever happen in the future.

3. Today's situation -- very bad

What we have today is the worst of all possible worlds. We have the central church collecting up all the tithing money of all the members, and then basically doing nothing very useful with it or even wasting it. We are spending about $400,000 in church resources on our central bureaucracy or on ourselves for every new long-term member we add. Only a tiny amount of those resources get to the "end of the furrow" to help bring in new members. That should tell us that our goals and our priorities are very confused for a church with the mission to spread the gospel worldwide.

This "centralize and waste" strategy means that members are paralyzed to act on their own and actually get the desired results, unless they wish to provide a second tithing which they administer themselves or direct it to some other member-governed entity which then might actually get something done that they desire.

This is further complicated by the fact that the various levels of political governments, through taxes, also collect "tithing," sometimes up to the level of three or four or even seven times a religious tithe. These various governments all promise to do the charitable work that a church ought to be doing, that is, take care of the poor, provide for education, etc., even though they also mostly waste that money, and very little of it gets to those who actually need it. This leaves us with the situation that members would have to pay somewhere between three and six times a religious tithe if they wanted to actually accomplish the simple basic social purposes of a single tithe. Obviously, that is not ever going to happen. If the church were engaged in teaching correct principles of government and working to reduce the share of the nation's resources taken from its citizens and misused by the political governments, then perhaps the church leaders could help arrange for a single tithe to be sufficient to meet a society's needs, as has been true before. (It might have been true during King Benjamin's time, and King Mosiah's time, and after Christ came to the New World, and perhaps at other times of minimal central government.)

Our church managers have found a way to collect up the most money and spend the most money with the smallest possible effects on the world. It is almost as though they had done some extensive scientific studies to find out how to get the smallest possible effect from money spent for religious purposes.

As one practical illustration, my daughter fulfilled a mission in Bolivia, and she tells me that during a very short time there, the church built 80 chapels throughout that nation, even before they had anyone to use them. Perhaps their idea was that "if we build them, they will come." At the time she left her mission, many of those chapels were empty and unused. This sounds like a good way to spend $100 million with only the vaguest idea of who might eventually benefit from it. Doesn't that seem to get the cart before the horse? Might not that church display of overconfidence and hubris actually offend some locals before the proselyting process even begins? Shouldn't the church possibly have something like an aggressive advertising or public teaching program which could help to build up a membership, and when the membership locations have been determined, then actually build some chapels?

In calculations that appear elsewhere in this paper, I demonstrate that the cost in church resources, cash and volunteer labor, for a single new long-term church member today is about $400,000. I hope that is a shocking number which perhaps will cause a few people to study the problem a little bit more. How can our church managers be so depressingly inefficient? What in the world are they doing with the church's money? In contrast, the central cost of a new church member was zero for the 200 years after Christ and for the first 80 years after the gospel was introduced to Joseph Smith. (Church membership was about 500,000 in 100 A.D., about 70 years after Christ's death, and about 250,000 in the year 1900 A.D., about 70 years after the church was organized.)

As one simple illustration of the current deplorable level of inefficiency and outrageous costs, a family of five joining our church would mean that the church spent $2 million in resources for that family. That would be enough to buy them a new home and allow the parents to retire for life, regardless of their age. It should be obvious that we could greatly speed up the amount of successful missionary work we accomplish if we simply offered that $2 million as an incentive upfront to families rather than filtering it through the oversized and grossly inefficient church bureaucracy.

With the level of bureaucratic insensitivity we see today to current levels of church inefficiency in spreading the gospel, if the members were to double their contributions in money and time to the church cause, the most likely outcome is that the cost for a new long-term member would jump to

$800,000, the equivalent of $4 million per convert family of five. The Salt Lake City headquarters black-hole would most likely absorb all the additional resources provided.

A policy of timidity

Although young missionaries are often encouraged to be bold, unfortunately the central church appears to be managed very timidly. If Joseph Smith were in charge of the church today, we could expect that he would be creative and aggressive. For example, Joseph Smith sent out a proclamation to all the leaders of the world that the church had been restored, and asked for their help in building up the restored church. It is inconceivable that our church today would attempt any such radical thing. (Actually, it was the 12 apostles who sent out the proclamation, acting on Joseph Smith's instructions and on his behalf after his death.). See D&C 124:2–3 and the very bold and audacious Proclamation full text.[13]

One might wonder whether the advanced age of most of the church's leaders today might have something to do with this policy of timidity, but there seems to be little connection with age. That basic timidity seems to come from a standard human trait. I believe this extreme timidity is based on the natural desire of leaders to be loved by everyone, and to avoid all conflict of any kind, therefore making their lives as calm, peaceful, and uneventful as possible. But avoiding all conflict worldwide means that the church is completely useless in changing the society of the nation and the world for the better. Such a force for change should culminate in a gospel-based civilization as has always been intended.

This official policy of timidity has been made into a strategic plan, even though I believe it is a very defective one. The idea seems to be that if the church can be as invisible and bland and innocuous and stealthy as is possible, then the dictators of the world will allow it to operate in their countries without objection. But that also means that the church must be absolutely inert and even negative on the issue of freedom, a very important aspect of the theology and practice of the gospel, and must never try through any public media effort to fully explain what we really believe -- what the scriptures actually teach us to believe and to do. The gospel in its fullness is actually quite disruptive to much of today's corrupt world, so it must be kept hidden to the extent possible under the current policy.

This policy of extreme ideological timidity might be a good worldwide strategy to avoid political difficulties if we were McDonald's and we were only selling hamburgers, but we are not McDonald's and we are not supposed to be only selling hamburgers. Our assignment is to change the national and world society to achieve a gospel-based civilization, and we are doing essentially nothing about that, while spending more than enough money to actually accomplish our assignment.

It appears to me that the church today has a near-zero advertising budget, where it ought to be in the $billions. The only thing it seems to be doing is to run an occasional ad to demonstrate that Mormons are not weird -- they're just like everyone else. But otherwise, those occasional ads are almost content-free concerning our religion itself.

And even when the church gets free advertising as the result of a TV news interview, we pretend we don't know what we believe on important points, and then spend what little airtime we have telling the world that we are not weird, whatever that means. We don't seem to be able to get past the "magic underwear" level of discourse.

The basic problem seems to stem from the simple fact of concentrating all church resources and most management and public relations responsibility in a few hands. If all the blowback from missionary work and gospel ideological arguments is to come back on a few men, those men are naturally going to quickly become very timid and will tend to use most of the resources collected together to protect themselves from any conflicts that arise. This turns the whole centralized process into a big self-justifying but ineffective and paralyzing waste, a pointless "self-licking ice cream cone" as the astute military people would call such an arrangement. This is like a big computer that spends all its compute cycles setting itself up so that it never actually gets around to doing any real work.

If the resources and the individual responsibility were widely dispersed, the pressures on any particular person would be infinitely less than on today's church top leadership corps. The mere fact that billions of dollars in resources are collected in one spot opens up that single spot to a wide array of political pressures and greed-based lawsuits, none of which would happen if there were no such centrally concentrated target or prize. That was the genius of the church expansion within the Roman Empire, and the process could work exactly the same way today. If the church's enemies have to go door-to-door to seek their victims, they are probably not going to do it, but if all our resources and media outlets and potential "victims" are in a single place, that makes them easy to find and attack. Where the central church has billions of dollars in its treasuries, offering a great temptation to the wicked, individual members typically have too little money to make it worth the trouble to sue those individual members or otherwise harass them.

Minimal mindshare

During the Proposition 8 political activities in 2008 in California concerning same-sex marriage, some surveys were done which, as I recall, seemed to indicate that about 90% of the people knew absolutely nothing about the Mormon church, and that for the 10% who had some information, most of that information was completely wrong or even backwards. That sounds like a really pitiful information situation to be in for a religious organization that has been in existence for almost 200 years and now has a budget of at least $6 billion to devote each year to spreading its message.

The LDS church should be able to compete very effectively in the marketplace of ideas with Hollywood (industry size $11 billion for North America) and with TV broadcasting ($51 billion in the United States) to affect the nation's understanding of the church and its doctrines, especially if it is expressing a freedom-based and nationalist message as we should be, based on our own scriptures. This is where the extreme timidity issue comes in. Strangely enough, our public relations goal seems to be to minimize what anyone in the world understands about our scriptural doctrinal positions, certainly nothing about us or our teachings that would challenge their dictatorial systems, even though that has been the main mission of Christianity for hundreds of years, and is the only reason the church was able to be restored in our time.

Information-spreading calculations

In the advertising community, especially as it relates to business startups, there are discussions about the cost to acquire new customers as it relates to the Lifetime Value (LTV) of a customer. As one example, Domino's Pizza can afford to spend $800 to acquire a new long-term customer since the lifetime value of a Domino's Pizza fan is about $4000.[14]

The lifetime value of a new LDS church member in the United States could easily be in the range of $200,000, assuming that person will pay $5000 in tithing each year for 40 years. Using the 1-to-5 relationship of the Domino's pizza example, that should mean that it should be worth up to $40,000 to acquire a new long-term church member. That does not compare very favorably with the zero central cost during the 200 years after the life of Christ or during the 80 years after Joseph Smith's first vision. But that seemingly exorbitant $40,000 sounds cheap compared to our current cost of $400,000. Based on these calculations, perhaps we should offer a full four-year college degree for free, at a cost to the church of about $40,000, if a person joined our church, where that person could learn the gospel well and gain an occupation.

Another interesting calculation has to do with our direct missionary costs. If we say that a missionary works 2000 hours a year and we allocate a cost of $10 an hour to that work, that means missionary effort is worth about $20,000 a year. A two-year mission then becomes a $40,000 cost. Currently, it takes more than two years of missionary work to add a single long-term convert to our church, making the direct missionary cost for a new long-term convert about $50,000. One might reasonably ask if there is not a better way to do missionary work.

If Domino's Pizza can afford to pay up to $800 in advertising to acquire a new customer, I don't know why the LDS church could not do just as well, resulting in a system which is about 50 times more effective than our current direct missionary system ($50,000), and about 500 times more effective than our current overall costs for operating the church to spread the gospel ($400,000).

But all these kinds of calculations are completely pointless, since the church in its current form, with its current policies, can probably never be reformed to become a sensible participant in modern information spreading techniques. Based on just our experience, if we started over with a new bureaucracy, we would probably quickly get back to the same failed situation we are in, for all the same reasons.

Other very expensive problems with centralization

The current extreme church emphasis and focus on its headquarters and its leadership has several other bad effects. For one thing, in this "hothouse" situation, the leaders apparently forget completely about viewing the Mormons as a people, even though the term "peculiar people" continues to be used occasionally. For example, the failure to think of the Mormons as a unique people and to consider what is best for their welfare has cost those members at least $10 trillion so far in lost pension funds over the last 80 years. This vast amount of extra money could have been made available by taking advantage of an alternate Social Security system as many other citizens have done.[15] To illustrate the scale of this oversight, that $10 trillion is the equivalent of about 2000 years of today's current church budget. If individual members simply had that money to use to help in promoting the gospel in their senior years, they could have accomplished almost incomprehensible amounts of good beyond what has been done under central church leadership for the last 80 years. Improving other social insurance administrative options could probably have saved the church members another $10 trillion or more. There are many other possibilities as well, but what central church leader has ever taken the time to think about such useful things to be done for a "people?"

We should notice that these special programs, which could easily be adopted in concept by other groups in the United States, for the benefit of everyone, would be offering a slight amount of resistance and some reasonable alternatives to the Marxist-inclined central government. But even the tiniest possibility of any ideological conflict with the federal government and other governments appears to be more than the church leaders can bear, regardless of the consequences for the members.

4. A return to option one?
If we wish to make any serious progress as church members who wish to implement the teachings of the scriptures, it may be that the only option we have is to gradually work our way back to one of the "after Christ" versions where the central headquarters almost disappears and is shrunk down to a few handfuls of people.

Since it is extremely unlikely that we can ever disassemble the current bureaucracy in a straightforward way, so that members are expected to keep their tithing money and administer it much more effectively, and can probably never increase the tolerance for ideological conflict in the mindset of our leaders, it appears that the only effective strategy left is to simply stop paying money to the central church and strike out on our own, using our resources many times more effectively than the current central church does. This shifting of resources would gradually shrink back the central church to a much more reasonable size and effectiveness level. Naturally, there could be questions as to whether the new activist group would have the proper authority to do what it wants to do, but, on the other hand, once the new methods were shown to be effective, the central headquarters may choose to follow along. Surely at the beginning they would try to resist any change, but, later, they might finally come to accept Christ's suggested way of doing things.

Notes

1. "Mormonism and church finances/No paid ministry/Scriptural teachings" http://en.fairmormon.org/Mormonism_and_church_finances/No_paid_ministry/Scriptural_teachings, accessed 2010?

https://www.fairmormon.org/answers/Mormonism_and_church_finances/No_paid_ministry, accessed 12/14/2019

2. Edward L. Kimball, "The History of LDS Temple Admission Standards," *Journal of Mormon History* Vol. 24, No. 1, 1998, pp135-176, p.163. http://digitalcommons.usu.edu/cgi/viewcontent.cgi?article=1030&context=mormonhistory

It is interesting that apostle Moses Thatcher disagreed with the idea that the Twelve could spend tithing money on their own personal matters, although all others, including Lorenzo Snow, did agree with that more liberal policy. This seems to be a major reason why Moses Thatcher was removed from his position as an apostle in 1896. This seems to help identify the "beginning of the end" on using all centrally-collected tithing money for any and every headquarters purpose, a requirement for a robust "paid ministry." I believe that is the precise definition of a "paid ministry:" where the paid ministers use the contributed money for their own personal needs.

See Kenneth W. Godfrey, "Moses Thatcher In The Dock: His Trials, The Aftermath, And His Last Days,"
Journal of Mormon History Vol. 24, No. 1, 1998, pp54-88, p.67.
http://digitalcommons.usu.edu/cgi/viewcontent.cgi?article=1030&context=mormonhistory

3. Family History and Temple work costs:
It appears that the genealogy/family history project is the largest single church project, even larger than its budgeted missionary program. It appears to also be plagued with phenomenal inefficiencies. From the limited data which the church makes available, it appears that the resource cost for each unique new name that ends up in the temple system is about $2000. There are new concepts and methods available which could bring that cost down to near $2 per name, potentially speeding up the process by 1000 times with no increase in cost to the church or its members.

> Calculation: The church probably spends about $0.5 billion a year in cash outlays for the genealogy/family history program, to which is added a volunteer labor cost of about $1.5 billion, giving a total resource cost of $2 billion. There are no published figures on the number of new unique names added each year to the temple system, but it seems reasonable to estimate that the number could be as low as 1 million because of the vast levels of unnecessary duplication that occur in today's systems. ($2 billion in total resources / 1 million new unique names = $2000 each.)

4. https://en.wikipedia.org/wiki/List_of_countries_by_GDP_(nominal)

5. Kent W. Huff, *Joseph Smith's United Order: a non-communalistic interpretation* (Springville, Utah: Cedar Fort, 1988); Kent W. Huff, *Brigham Young's United Order: a contextual interpretation* (Spanish Fork: Theological ThinkTank, 1998)

6. Elder Holland Arizona April 2016
https://www.youtube.com/watch?v=K4_LcENySzQ starting at 31:20.

7. https://en.wikipedia.org/wiki/John_O'Sullivan_(columnist)

8. Brigham Young on church prosperity:

> The worst fear I have about this people is that they will get rich in this country, forget God and His people, wax fat, and kick themselves out of the Church and go to hell. This people will stand mobbing, robbing, poverty, and all manner of persecution, and be true. But my greater fear … is that they cannot stand wealth. (James S. Brown, *Life of a Pioneer*, Salt Lake City: Geo. Q. Cannon and Sons Co., 1900, pp. 122–23.)
> https://www.lds.org/ensign/1991/05/beware-lest-thou-forget-the-lord?lang=eng

Brigham Young speaks more briefly on a similar theme in the Journal of Discourses:

> JD 7:44, Brigham Young, March 28, 1858
> The Lord cannot save us in riches, because we do not yet know what to do with them. And when we are
> blessed and favoured, like the children of Israel in olden times, we wax fat and kick.

9. Luke 18:18-19.

10. The famous quotation appeared in a 1971 Pogo daily strip presenting an anti-pollution theme for Earth Day. https://en.wikipedia.org/wiki/Pogo_(comic_strip)

11. Mormon 1:13; Mormon 3:1; Moroni 8:10-11.

12. Mark 16:15.

13. A small sampling of the Proclamation:

> TO ALL THE KINGS OF THE WORLD, TO THE PRESIDENT OF THE UNITED STATES OF AMERICA; TO THE GOVERNORS OF THE SEVERAL STATES, AND TO THE RULERS AND PEOPLE OF ALL NATIONS. Greeting. Know ye that the kingdom of God has come, as has been predicted by ancient prophets, and prayed for in all ages; even that kingdom which shall fill the whole earth, and shall stand for ever....
>
> Therefore we send unto you, with authority from on high, and command you all to repent and humble yourselves as little children before the majesty of the Holy One; and come unto Jesus with a broken heart and a contrite spirit, and be baptized in his name for the remission of sins (that is, be buried in the water, in the likeness of his burial, and rise again to newness of life in the likeness of his resurrection), and you shall receive the gift of the Holy Spirit, through the laying on of the hands of the apostles and elders, of this great and last dispensation of mercy to man.
> ...
> Again, we say, by the word of the Lord, to the people as well as to the rulers, your aid and your assistance is required in this great work; and you are hereby invited, in the name of Jesus, to take an active part in it from this day forward.

http://eom.byu.edu/index.php/Proclamations_of_the_First_Presidency_and_the_Quorum_of_the_Twelve_Apostles
https://www.lds.org/manual/doctrine-and-covenants-student-manual/sections-122-131/section-124-a-solemn-proclamation-the-priesthood-order-is-established?lang=eng

14. https://thrivehive.com/how-much-should-you-spend-on-advertising-to-get-a-new-customer

15. A further explanation of the alternative Social Security option:

In the 1930s, federal legislation was introduced to begin a state-sponsored pension system on a national scale, naturally using socialist principles and the government force of taxation which are nearly always provably inferior to free private action. It was called Social Security.

In potential contrast, if the church had supported principles of freedom and traditional morality, including personal responsibility, the church might have proposed that members provide for their own pension fund needs by using an alternate route provided for within the legislation itself, thus avoiding the damaging consequences of the federal program. That would have been a very wise practical choice.

Those organizations who took advantage of that alternate route have fared very well. The pensions they receive are approximately 5 times as large as the pensions received by those who accepted the misguided federal system, as demonstrated by three counties in Texas. Those private pension plans allow for growth of contributions at a 5% compound rate while the federal plan provides for no growth whatsoever, not even allowing adequate adjustments for inflation.

In such a private plan, a person (or his heirs) who paid into it all his life should be entitled to receive about $2.5 million in total benefits beginning at the time of his retirement. A person in the federal system can expect to receive $0.5 million during his retirement, assuming he or she lives a normal lifespan. If they die early for any reason, the pension payout ends, so that a person who worked all their lives and died at age 62 may get no payouts whatsoever. And even in the best case, those payouts will probably be less than the actual number of dollars paid in, with no adjustment for (always-government-caused) inflation. In other words, the government takes 80% of any potential pension benefits from someone in its program for its own purposes, while a person in a private program keeps 100%. That choice between the two programs seems like a no-brainer, as they say, but it would have required some personal initiative to take timely advantage of that very large opportunity.

What this means is that under a private church-encouraged system, a working person could expect to receive an extra $2 million beyond what the federal system might allow for. This system would encourage people to have larger families because it makes very clear the obvious point that the people who must normally pay your pension costs are your own children. This most basic bit of economics is indeed obvious in the rest of the world, but a government-intermediated pension system as in the US gives the false impression that you will magically receive a pension whether you have any children or not. Supposedly, someone else's children will pay your pension costs. But if everyone else also decides not to have any children because they are too much trouble, as has been true in our country since Social Security was invented, then the whole system collapses and implodes, as we can see today

That family economic principle writ large means that the general economy would be more successful by staying out of the hands of the always-covetous collectivists. Instead of tax-supported pensioners being focused on extracting ever-larger taxes from a shrinking group of younger people, the oldsters would naturally be focused on seeing that their investments and their families all prospered.

If there were 5 million church members who participated in this program, as a group they would have received about $10 trillion in extra benefits by now. They might choose to use those funds to directly benefit their family, which would help meet the Church's goals, or they might use those funds to help sponsor more general church activity by members such as funding missions. It is useful to note that $10 trillion is about the equivalent of 2000 years of a church budget of $6 billion.

One can do a serious amount of improving of society using $10 trillion, mostly through teaching and training the populace and giving them experiences they lack, whether they are in or out of the church.

Chapter 13

The uncertain basis for today's LDS tithing policies

Some general observations:
There is an uncertain basis for today's tithing policies. At no point in our voluminous scriptures or history is there a totally complete and unequivocal statement that fully supports the extreme claims made by the church today that every member must pay 10% of his income annually to the central church in order to attend the temple and otherwise constantly and continuously be considered a member in good standing. This also means keeping his salvation up-to-date and continuously effective in case he dies. This is our version of the Protestant idea of being "saved," although theirs is a better "once and for all" situation. This repetitive subscription model of salvation is a very clever way to extract money from people, playing upon their fears of not knowing if they are continuously approved of God. This puts the LDS church at least 60 years ahead of software subscription services such as Adobe who came relatively late to adopting this subscription technique for establishing a continuous revenue stream.

And, after receiving those payments, the central church then has accepted no responsibility whatsoever to report back what that money was spent for or to be responsible for achieving good results with that money or to even report how things turned out. Almost every other charitable organization is expected to report its receipt and application of monies, but the LDS church tells no one, not even its members. That seems to explain why the church is unrated by charity auditing organizations.

I have invented my own church charity rating system, and by that measure, the LDS church only effectively applies about 2% of the money it receives to its main scriptural mission of spreading the gospel. Certainly, the extreme upper limit of what it might be credited with spending effectively is not more than 10%, and I consider the whole situation almost a complete failure, based on original expectations

Overall, the church now spends about $400,000 in resources for every long-term member it adds to the rolls. It seems likely that in a better system, spending $4,000 would be much more than enough to give people the information and experiences that would bring them into the church, and it should really be much less than that. Using the $4,000 measure, that would indicate that the LDS church has a 99% overhead rate on administering the gospel, making it among the worst-performing charities.

The church headquarters unit has the good fortune of having a captive audience -- its members, perhaps mesmerized -- which apparently stopped paying attention to what the central church was actually doing nearly 100 years ago. No one seems to care anymore about any general church missions or accomplishments in the broader world as long as each individual member has his personal needs mostly met. This general self-centeredness is a major problem, as I see it. It is a gospel content problem as well as an administrative problem.

If a person does NOT pay his tithing, in today's church policy structure that is the equivalent of committing a serious sin, a crime, because that person becomes a person not in good standing and cannot attend the temple. That person is thus effectively partially disfellowshipped, regardless of any other factors that might be operating in his favor. The LDS concept of an afterlife does not include a Hell for people to burn in, but its leaders get the same rhetorical effect of consigning the members to a burning if they don't pay their tithing.

When defining a crime, it is common legislative practice (and presumably should be religious practice for sins as well, for the same reasons) to define all the elements of that crime so that there can be no misunderstanding, since the consequences of failing to abide by those rules can be very serious, possibly including fines and incarceration -- the loss of freedom. Justice cannot be seen to be done if a crime is not first carefully defined long before anyone can legally commit that crime. The principle is demonstrated in our nation's Constitution where it is forbidden to make something a crime after the fact – any so-called ex post facto legislation.

Reverting to some of the worst aspects of the old Law of Moses, times 10

Tithing

As a very general issue to be brought up before going on too far, it should be mentioned that the Law of Moses was very specifically ended with the restitution of the full gospel by Christ himself. That alone should make us very leery of reinventing even a single "Law-of-Moses style" rule within the church, especially if it is for the convenience of church leaders. The old Law of Moses rule of tithing was perhaps the most intrusive rule of all of the 613 constraints on Jewish behavior. It required the Israelites to send 1/10th of the foodstuffs they produced to the cities occupied by the tribe of Levi. The Levites in turn sent 1/10th of that 1/10th to the capital city of Jerusalem for supporting the Temple and priestly activities there. So, to begin with, under the law of Moses, the law of tithing was quite a bit less burdensome than the current rules, and, we might carefully note, only 1% of the foodstuffs made it to the central offices in Jerusalem for religious functions there. In other words, we start out with multiplying the Law of Moses at least times 10 in our own era by demanding that all contributions go to Salt Lake City. That ought to require an extremely strenuous explanation of why this "Law of Moses times 10" rule ought to be observed in our own time.

Supposedly, we have no more professional priests today, since under today's rules, every man is his own priest, and it would be foolishness for a priest to pay himself 10% for conducting his priestly duties. Nonetheless, at this point, we have a self-perpetuating "tribe" of extremely well-paid "Levites" carrying out their professional priestly duties in Salt Lake City, apparently in complete contradiction to the intent of Christ in doing away with the Law of Moses and most of its enforced social rules including tribalism and the Sanhedrin/central bureaucracy.

We should certainly notice that the Word of Wisdom -- something which sounds very much like an old Law of Moses law, and yet is a great deal less intrusive and demanding than the relatively recently imposed policy on tithing -- was not given to us in the form of an exact Law of Moses rule, but rather as "not by commandment or constraint, but by revelation and the word of wisdom." It certainly has some cleanliness and health factors to commend it, and we make quite a production out of letting people know that we don't drink or smoke or use illegal drugs. Logically, since tithing is perhaps 100 times more important to most people than the Word of Wisdom, we ought to make the biggest possible production out of telling everyone that we all must pay all of our tithing directly and only to church headquarters before we can be considered serious members of the church. If living the simple Word of Wisdom makes us seem like devout religionists, we ought to wear a big tithing receipt on our clothing at all times, or around our necks, like the old Jewish phylacteries, to signal our far more extreme level of exacting Mosaic virtue.

Recommends

Even making the 13+ questions of the recommend interview a critical part of living the gospel, including swearing fealty to a particular earthly organization, sounds strangely like bringing back the old Law of Moses lists of precise behavior to conform to before members can be certified as good members and considered pure and not unclean. Such a list, administered by a new form of Sanhedrin, was quite evidently NOT part of Christ's gospel. It seems like some kind of line has been crossed when the church moves from "teaching correct principles," and providing good examples, to enforcing certain quality control rules so that the central church can claim they have created a specific standardized product out of their members.

https://www.reddit.com/r/mormon/comments/3dqj2m/here_are_the_13_questions_lds_bishops_will_ask/

Christ not only said that he came to end the law of Moses, but he spoke with scorn about its tithing aspects. "Ye pay tithe of mint and anise and cummin, and have omitted the weightier matters of the law." Matt. 23:23. It appears that the precise tithing aspects are objectionable for the very reason that they are so precise and thus can give the illusion of having completely fulfilled one's responsibilities. The concept of an exact tithing is advocated in our own time by saying that by fulfilling that law precisely, one can then claim they are perfect in at least one thing. But it is that very precision that might be sought for and claimed in religious matters that is indeed an illusion and a diversion from the more imprecise but more valuable feelings of empathy for the needs of other people.

As has occurred in our own time, members can justifiably claim that they have fulfilled all of their charitable duties by sending their 10% to Salt Lake City, and then they can forget about any other needs around them, whether obvious or not. This actually creates an insensitive and insular state of mind which does not have much to recommend it.

One might expect that if Christ were going to change his mind on something he had treated with such disdain during his life, that he would "repent" if he had earlier made a mistake on this point, and then would explain in excruciating detail exactly how one was supposed to live this law in the times that were prophesied to contain the gospel in its most perfect and complete form.

There is no sign in the New Testament that the early Saints had any such program, although they did have a great reputation about taking care of their own members in times of hardship, along with taking care of their neighbors, in commendable Good Samaritan fashion. It seems they were indeed being better Christians than we are today when we have allowed power-seeking central organizations to take very large amounts of our money and then spend it in unchristian and wasteful ways, seriously interfering with our ability to act spontaneously as good Christians as the early Saints obviously did.

Our own more recent Scriptures do use the word "tithing," but even those scriptures make it clear that the term "tithing" just refers to any and all member contributions. Even when the modern-day Scriptures seem to set 1/10th as an expected minimal level of contributions, it never explicitly says that those funds may not be administered by the members themselves without any precise Law of Moses payment to some central organization, if such a central organization even exists.

Getting into some details
Maybe the time has now come to analyze and account for every use of the word or concept of tithing in the doctrine and covenants and other scriptures. The point is, I believe that nowhere in the doctrine and covenants -- today's important revelation and policy document -- is the complete tithing policy today justified by any clear statement. There are fragments of statements dealing with the issue of tithing, but they never add up to today's policy.

Rather, they support the exact historical behavior of the Saints, as being the correct behavior, at least until 1896 when the church leaders attempted to change this rational and very effective tithing policy to something else which was tailored to the personal desires and empire-building ambitions of church leaders. The reported 1899 statements of Lorenzo Snow, at least on their face, were simply a restatement of what had always been the gospel policy on tithing after the ending of the Law of Moses. It appears that only by implication and unofficial and off-the-record administrative statements and policy changes was that restatement gradually and secretly rewritten to reach where we are today.

Here are all the D&C verses that appear to deal with the definition of tithing:

> **64**:23 Behold, now it is called today until the coming of the Son of Man, and verily it is a day of sacrifice, and a day for the tithing of my people; for he that is tithed shall not be burned that his coming.
> ...
> **85**:3 It is contrary to the will and commandment of God that those who receive not their inheritance by consecration, agreeable to his law, which he has given, that he may tithe his people, to prepare them against the day of vengeance and burning, should have their names enrolled with the people of God.
> ...
> **97**:10 Verily I say unto you, that it is my will that the house should be built unto me in the land of Zion [Jackson County, Missouri], like unto the pattern which I have given you.
> 11 Yea, let it be built speedily, by the tithing of my people.
> 12 Behold, this is the tithing and the sacrifice which I, the Lord, require at their hands, that there may be a house built unto me for the salvation of Zion –
>
> Section **119**
> *Revelation given through Joseph Smith the Prophet, at Far West, Missouri, July 8, 1838, in answer to his supplication: "O Lord! Show unto thy servants how much thou requirest of the properties of thy people for a tithing." The law of tithing, as understood today, had not been given to the Church previous to this revelation. The term tithing in the prayer just quoted and in previous revelations (64:23; 85:3; 97:11) had meant not just one-tenth, but <u>all free-will offerings, or contributions</u>, to the Church funds. The Lord had previously given to the Church the law of consecration and stewardship of property* [a very questionable interpretation of church history], *which members (chiefly the leading elders)*

entered into by a covenant that was to be everlasting. Because of failure on the part of many to abide by this covenant, the Lord withdrew it for a time and gave instead the law of tithing to the whole Church [more questionable historical interpretation]. *The Prophet asked the Lord how much of their property He required for sacred purposes. The answer was this revelation.*

1–5, The Saints are to pay their surplus property and then give, as tithing, one-tenth of their interest annually; 6–7, Such a course will sanctify the land of Zion.

119:1 Verily, thus saith the Lord, I require all their surplus property to be put into the hands of the bishop of my church in Zion,
2 For the building of mine house, and for the laying of the foundation of Zion and for the priesthood, and for the debts of the Presidency of my Church.
3 And this shall be the beginning of the tithing of my people.
4 And after that, those who have thus been tithed shall pay one-tenth of all their interest annually; and this shall be a standing law unto them forever, for my holy priesthood, saith the Lord.
5 Verily I say unto you, it shall come to pass that all those who gather unto the land of Zion shall be tithed of their surplus properties, and shall observe this law, or they shall not be found worthy to abide among you.
6 And I say unto you, if my people observe not this law, to keep it holy, and by this law sanctify the land of Zion unto me, that my statutes and my judgments may be kept thereon, that it may be most holy, behold, verily I say unto you, it shall not be a land of Zion unto you.
7 And this shall be an ensample unto all the stakes of Zion. Even so. Amen.

Section **120**
Revelation given through Joseph Smith the Prophet, at Far West, Missouri, July 8, 1838, making known the disposition of the properties tithed as named in the preceding revelation, section 119.

1 Verily, thus saith the Lord, the time is now come, that it shall be disposed of by a council, composed of the First Presidency of my Church, and of the bishop and his council, and by my high council; and by mine own voice unto them, saith the Lord. Even so. Amen.

First of all, if the central church is going to claim to have the drastic right to receive 10% of everyone's income in order for them to be a church member in good standing and receive the higher ordinances, then they ought to have the highest possible proof of that assertion, not some pieced-together jumble. In this case I believe the concept of tithing is a great deal less mandatory and a great deal less detailed in its definition than is the Word of Wisdom, which started out as counsel and not commandment. The Word of Wisdom was counsel to everyone, and it did not become a commandment until many decades later. The concept of tithing as an absolute rule and a commandment did not become an absolute and binding commandment until about 1960, nearly a century after the word of wisdom was accepted as a commandment.

There are some difficult and confusing events that the Saints suffered through in their first few years, and it would make no practical sense to take any ambiguity or confusion which comes out of those early decades as an absolute law to be adopted much later. The leaders of today interpret these tithing statements as absolute and binding commands, but it is very important to notice that the church members of the times did not, nor did the leaders. By today's interpretation of the terms of tithing, nearly every church member up until 1960 would have been ineligible to be a church member in good standing, and attend the temple and receive its ordinances, and they were supposedly all subject to being burned at His coming, since it was not required that they say any more than that they thought tithing was a good idea, whether they actually lived it or not. This should tell us that there is something fundamentally wrong with our current interpretation of the words in the Doctrine and Covenants.

Sections 64 and 83 tell us that we need to be tithed to not burn at His coming, but it does not define tithing to only be considered correct and complete if every last penny of it is paid to the central church headquarters. Joseph Smith and Oliver Cowdery administered their own tithing before the church was organized, and that was the rule, in general, up until at least 1899. I don't believe anyone would say that all the church members up until 1899 would have deserved being burned at His coming because of the supposedly faulty way in which they handled their tithing. They did enormous amounts of good with that tithing, not the least of which was getting the Saints established safely in the West.

Section 97 is a little more specific, in that it tells the Saints that they should plan to focus their future contributions (referred to as tithing) on building a temple in Jackson County, Missouri, much like they had done earlier in Kirtland. But, apparently, that was not to be, and the next focus was on the temple in Nauvoo.

Section 119 sounds very specific on first reading, but in fact it does not completely define and support today's tithing policy. On the "excess" issue, from what I can see of church history, there was hardly a single person who made it to Jackson County who had anything that would be considered "surplus property." Most of them had only the barest amount of property that would sustain them and allow them to get to Missouri. The idea of putting that property into a central pool for others to use made no practical sense at all. In most cases, an inventory was kept, just to go through the motions, but very little made it into the common fund.

My assumption is that the members continued to do what they always did, which is to help each other as needed, and even this suggested, limited, one-time, level of church government tax-and-spend administration was pointless and ineffective.

There probably were a few wise, careful, and industrious souls who made it to Jackson County with some excess cash which could be put into the pool to pay off the very large real estate loan negotiated by Joseph Smith.

But, as the leaders more than once complained, too many people just pulled up stakes and left behind whatever valuable property they might have had, taking little of that value with them in their haste. Their responsiveness and eagerness is commendable, but it was still impractical to conduct a large-scale migration with no resources, simply because no one took the time to preserve and transfer those resources to the new location. Quite sensibly, later arrangements were made to sell land left behind, or to swap it for Missouri land.

With the short-term need to pay off those real estate loans, contracted for the direct benefit of the members, not the leaders, it made sense for the members to pay for the land they occupied, if they could. But this does not suggest that the church leaders had the permission of the members to spend money willy-nilly on their behalf or for any random purpose without any consultation. The leaders were taking great financial risks on behalf of the members, rather than the other way around, as we typically see today.

It was important for Joseph Smith and other administrators to be able to pay off the real estate loans they had taken out on the land where the Saints were settled. That would make it important to apply every dollar that was available and to avoid any kind of waste. Certainly, it would be wasteful to have land or goods that went unused when there were people who needed them and could put them to good use. The Saints were all in this together, and this was an extraordinary tribal kind of situation where all of them working together was barely enough to allow them to survive.

Those extraordinary measures were indeed unusual and it would be unreasonable to continue them after the critical need was past. Ordinary self-reliance, perhaps along with various individualized insurance programs should normally be adequate. It would be like the pioneers who participated in essentially an army operation as they crossed the plains, as a matter of necessity. But it would be foolishness to then decide that was the ideal state for all of life and to continue those military-style living arrangements for the rest of their lives for some arbitrary religion-based reason.

There seems to still be great confusion about the supposed "law of consecration." As vaguely suggested in the headnotes, the United Order (or United Firm) was really nothing more than a silent business partnership, requiring no specific government authorization to operate, which was organized among a few of the leaders to help take care of church business. It never applied to anyone else, and it was never intended to.

Incidentally, an entry in Joseph Smith's History of the Church indicates that the Kirtland Temple was owned by the group of men who contributed to it and helped to build it, indicating that there did not even exist a church formal business unit to hold title, or that if there were, it would not be appropriate to put the title there.

It is one thing for church members to be expected to contribute 10% of their increase to gospel purposes. It is quite a different thing to expect that all of that 10% would go to church headquarters for the use of the leaders, especially when anyone associated with church headquarters was not in a position to do anything much more with it than simply help pay off the general costs of lands that had been occupied by church members. Again, the most convincing evidence of the correct interpretation is the behavior of the members and leaders for the next 40+ years as each man used his own good sense about where 10% of his income might be best allocated. In the alternative, is anyone willing to charge all the early saints with apostasy? Since we are now nearly 200 years from the restoration, it is more likely that they were right than that we are, after a long period of doctrinal drift.

Those early Saints were right on many things where we have it wrong. For example, the Mountain Meadow Massacre incident appears to be a case where the early Saints had the better sense and better morals, and it appears that we malign them today simply because we are trying to defend our policies today, many of which are indefensible, while the early saints had it right, such as on the tithing issue. Our trying to make them seem foolish and evil perhaps is done to try to make us today look more wise and righteous, but, by so doing, we are being unfair, and we simply verify that we are indeed the more foolish and unethical ones.

A portion of Section 119:

> 4 And after that, those who have thus been tithed shall pay one-tenth [to where or to whom?] of all their interest annually; and this shall be a standing law unto them forever, for my holy priesthood, saith the Lord.

I think we should more closely consider the phrase that "this shall be a standing law... for my holy priesthood." By that I believe is meant every man who holds the priesthood, not just those who have special assignments such as the apostles or the first presidency. I think there is a tendency to read it as though it said "TO my holy priesthood [meaning only the top church leaders]," or that the tithing is "FOR my holy priesthood," meaning that the leaders should get all the tithing, but I don't believe either reading is what is said or is meant in the situation.

Obviously, it would be much better for the church today if there *were* an unequivocally clear statement about how much was to be paid, exactly where it was supposed to go, perhaps some more regulations on exactly how it was supposed to be used, etc. But since we don't have that sort of thing, a Law of Moses level of detail, in today's "law" itself, it is useful to go to the "legislative and administrative history," or, in other words, how it was interpreted by the members and leaders at the time. And I believe it is perfectly clear that no one interpreted these words that way at that time.

Section 120 designates a management group to decide what the central church should do with whatever tithing (member contributions in general) the church might receive, given at member discretion, as required by basic religious freedom, but it does not go beyond that to aggressively define tithing and turn it into a precise religious law of a binding nature such as aspects of the old and disavowed Law of Moses.

We might note as a practical matter, that there really WAS no functioning church headquarters which could do much more than print a few books and vaguely discuss and plan a movement West, for most of the time up till 1896. In many cases it would have been the height of foolishness to try to send one's tithing to the central church headquarters, especially when that headquarters was about to be dissolved and all its assets taken by the federal government. That was perhaps the most striking situation, but there were many of those kinds of situations over the 76-year period from 1820 up to 1896.

Certainly at the beginning, and perhaps at all times, "tithing," that is, potential member contributions, was better kept "on the hoof" (something like the concept of a walking blood bank), that is, in member possession, up until the time of actual need, rather than attempting to centrally gather great stores of wealth in any one place, creating a great temptation to leaders and outsiders, and creating a great risk that attempts would be made to rob it or take it by crime or by legalized force.

It appears that this "on the hoof" policy would be a good practice for all time. If the church leaders actually had faith in the wisdom of the members, and truly sought to be servants and not masters, they would not see any need to stockpile resources for any such purposes as creating pensions for church leaders or employees, or setting aside "rainy day" funds to keep the church operating at full budget in difficult times, completely independent of what might be happening to the members.

There are two great risks associated with a political government -- a standing army, and government access to a large amount of "standing" money. The federal government-sponsored central bank, known as the Federal Reserve, constantly debases our money for its own profit while giving the government borrowing and budgetary powers it ought not to have without specific legislation. We also have a large standing army and the associated military-industrial complex which spends our money excessively and irresponsibly and constantly encourages war.

With the church, we see the problem today from the centralizing of assets so that the church headquarters is under constant political, legal, and criminal attack, and it must maintain a huge army of very expensive lawyers and other staff to stave off the barbarians attacking from every direction. If there were no centralized assets, but only specific requests at specific times for specific, clearly justified needs, most or all of those very expensive central preparations and bureaucratic fortifications would be completely unnecessary, and the leaders would not need to constantly feel such crippling fear of actually pushing the gospel message out into the world, and possibly getting some unpleasant reactions, which they alone had to deal with.

The first century A.D. Saints had no problem finding the best places for their "tithing" or contributions or charity to be allocated, and they were extremely successful in spreading the gospel. If we could do as well today, using the same methods, then perhaps we ought to be using their methods.

We should remember that the federal government attacked the church viciously in Brigham Young's day, confiscating property where possible, including the church's money and even the temple. Political attitudes and risks may have improved slightly since those days, but it is hard to say whether things are really better or worse, simply because the church is now so much wealthier. The LDS Church, which is widely known to have many billions of dollars in property holdings and income concentrated in one place, might reasonably be targeted by those who wish to get money from the church's deep pockets or to hurt its progress, or both.

The persecutors of Joseph Smith imagined that if they killed him, the entire movement would fall apart. A little bit later the federal government hoped that if they dissolved the church corporation and took all of its assets, it would also cease to exist. The same impulse to supposedly cut off the head of the church and therefore destroy it completely seems to keep recurring, but the essence of the church is NOT found in one or a few men at the top, but no one seems to understand that, including the leaders themselves, as they keep making themselves more important and indispensable, continuously presenting a tempting target to the world. Many millions of dollars are spent each year to defend the church leaders and the church itself from actual and potential outside attacks, when most of that very expensive defensive structure would be completely unnecessary if church headquarters collapsed back to a tiny shadow of its form today. In other words, the very fact of having a large and wealthy central headquarters sets up a feedback loop which causes further enormous unnecessary expense, which accomplishes nothing except to keep presenting a target which needs an expensive defense. This is the perfect world for bureaucrats, who "earn" and justify their salaries merely by their superfluous existence. This is bureaucracy self-created ex nihilo, like god creating himself.

We might recall that there was an attempt to declare a salary for the church leaders, just Joseph Smith and Oliver Cowdery, I believe, which proposal was first passed and then specifically defeated. That ought to clear up the question of what the church leaders and members thought about that matter in the early days. That policy probably had not changed until Wilford Woodruff decided that he was extremely committed to making that policy change, even willing to basically excommunicate an apostle for apostasy for not agreeing with him on the controversial and contentious issue of using tithing for the personal support of church leaders -- basically giving them an official salary for the first time. Not incidentally, such a salary would likely serve as a means of controlling and disciplining leaders who ought to be able to use their untrammeled judgement in all important matters pertaining to the gospel. But now as employees, they would tend to be very subservient to the church president who controlled their salary and other perquisites of office. The pretense that apostles should be independent "prophets" would be greatly weakened.

More details and side issues

•Church historians and leaders have done the church a great disservice by continually trying to keep alive an attempt to insert socialism into the church teachings and organization where it was always completely foreign to gospel freedom concepts. These continuing attempts to insert political power doctrines into an ideology which explicitly condemns the seeking of power over others are completely misguided and self-serving.

•The higher ordinances were at times administered in such places as the rooms of Joseph Smith's store in Nauvoo, or in the endowment house in Salt Lake City. Although it is apparently preferred that these ordinances be administered in a more formally specialized and designated temple, especially while doing work for the dead, those ordinances have been nonetheless perfectly valid when administered in other ways. A suggestion was recently made by a junior general authority (obviously speaking out of turn) that similar "endowment house" methods might be used even today, when the Saints in a particular area might have great difficulty in building a proper Temple because of lack of resources or perhaps because of political resistance, but there is no obvious reason why they should be denied access to the higher ordinances because of these local difficulties. The 33 A.D. saints seem to have found easy solutions to this problem.

•In locations where civil marriages are very difficult or expensive, bishops or missionaries should be able to marry people for free (even at the risk of some conflict with the political government), and sealings should also take place in local facilities. The central church's stern insistence on being sealed only in temples which might be far away, and could cause a family great difficulty to reach, appears to be just a disguised, dishonest, and altogether unnecessary plea to extract more money from members through a semi-extortionist process, part of which is telling sob stories of families selling all they had to travel to a temple, presumably damaging their livelihoods and their futures as a result, all supposedly as a trial of their faith.

•The church does sometimes claim that the contributions which go towards humanitarian assistance throughout the world are delivered without any deduction for administration costs. That is commendable, and should encourage more such contributions, but it should also be remembered that is probably just a case of robbing Peter to pay Paul, since whatever administration costs there might be are simply borne by other kinds of contributions to the church. It seems likely that the reason the church can claim to deliver humanitarian assistance money without deducting for administrative costs is simply because the bulk of that money is simply transferred to some other humanitarian assistance organization which WILL then spend a significant amount of that money on its administrative overhead. In other words, there is a more than a little bit of imprecision and obfuscation in presenting church policies and their practical consequences.

Analysis of D&C sections for establishing today's church tithing policy							
Today's tithing policy elements, in increments	Source: D&C sections/Admin. Policy (unwritten)						Comments
	64: 23	85: 3	97: 10	119	120	Poli cy.	
It is a religious duty to make useful religious charitable contributions to someone or for some good purpose	X	X	X				An unremarkable view of common religious charity. Not unique to LDS.
It is a religious duty to make charitable contributions to someone or for some good purpose or **be burned** at his coming	X	X					This is not an argument to pay all religious charitable contributions to the central church. God will make this determination, not the central church.
It is a religious duty to pay 10% of income as charitable contributions to someone or for some good purpose. (This sets only the level, but not the disposition.)			X	X			There is some contextual implication that all tithing (10%) goes to the central church, but it was never done in practice until it gradually and very slowly began in 1899 and ended in about 1960, indicating that was not the original accepted meaning.
It is a religious duty to pay all religious charitable contributions to the central church						X	Never commanded, and very contrary to Christ's actual practices
The central church is empowered to spend all the money received through charitable contributions at their unrestrained and unreported discretion					X		But this was never done legally or in practice until it began in 1923 and became complete in about 1960, indicating that no one thought that was the intended policy in the 1838 revelation, now D&C section 120.
It is a religious duty to make useful charitable religious contributions to someone or for some good purpose or be partially disfellowshipped, as in losing temple attendance privileges.						X	Not enforced consistently until about 1960, indicating that no one thought that was the policy commanded in any of the Joseph Smith-era revelations. And we have no written and approved and canonized revelations to that effect yet.
Explanation: The main point here is that none of the D&C sections covers all the elements of today's church policy on tithing in one place so that the meanings and interrelationships of all the elements are clear. In fact, none of the D&C sections include more than two of the elements of unique church policy. And all of the sections together, even if overlaying them and making them cumulative were legitimate (which it probably is not), that still does not clearly provide all of the elements of today's tithing policy. Only by adding very significant extra-scriptural administrative decisions can today's church tithing policy be pieced together. On such a critical point as "tithing" mere habit and tradition should not be acceptable as complete and binding. In my view, the ancient law of Moses should not be reinstituted today unless Christ came himself and very forcefully issued very clear instructions on that seeming act of serious sabotage to the new gospel he instituted.							

Chapter 14

The use of "increase" vs. "interest" in tithing scriptures and history

There are a host of issues potentially raised in the following quotes, which relate to contributions and "tithing," which ought to be fully explored for the lessons that are in them about church administration, but
what caught my eye and began this analysis is simply the unexpected appearance of the word "interest" where one might expect to see the word "increase."

There is a strange and unexplained disconnect between the latter-day printed revelations on the topic of tithing, and the historical practices and rhetoric associated with that topic of tithing. It has to do with the inconsistent use of the terms "increase" and "interest." Since the inconsistent use of these terms is unintelligible, and unresolvable based on the information that is available, I am going to take this opportunity to supply meanings which I consider more consistent with the long-term history of the gospel of Christ.

The following three extracts from the history of the church are presented in order of their appearance in the history of the church. The sequence begins with the July 8, 1838 revelation on tithing now published as section 119 in the Doctrine and Covenants. The term "interest" is used for apparently the only time in the history of scriptures on the topic of tithing. The revelation is followed by an epistle by the Twelve Apostles dated December 13, 1841 on the topic of baptism for the dead, where the term "increase" is used, and then by an October, 1844 address by John Taylor on the same topic as the earlier epistle, where the term "increase" is also used. (We might wonder if John Taylor was actually the person who wrote the earlier 1841 epistle.)

One point to be made here is that even though several years elapsed between the date of the revelation and the following two important entries in the history, it is as though the text of the revelation had very little effect on how church leaders spoke concerning this policy. In both cases, the leadership language follows the overwhelmingly predominant theme in the Scriptures concerning the (Old Testament) definition of tithing (undefined and unused in the New Testament version of the gospel since tithing had no meaning in that religious system), which is that one is to pay tithing on one-tenth of a person's "increase." The supposedly new and thus potentially important term "interest" is simply never used in any later public discourse. Perhaps either the language they read in the revelation was different from what we read today, or the words of the revelation were so imprecise and confusing that they simply ignored them and used the standard Old Testament formulation.

D&C 119
History of the Church p.525 of 3032

The three revelations which I received January 12, 1838, the day I left Kirtland, were read in the public congregation at Far West; and the same day I inquired of the Lord, "O Lord! Show unto thy servant how much thou requirest of the properties of thy people for a tithing," and received the following answer, which was also read in public:

[Obviously here "tithing" clearly doesn't mean exactly one-tenth, as the word itself implies, or why would there even be a question to be asked here? To make logical sense, the term "contributions" or "financial responsibility" probably should be used to replace the term "tithing." As the headnote below suggests, any free-will offerings or contributions were often referred to as "tithing."]

Revelation, Given at Far West, July 8, 1838.

[Headnotes added later: *Revelation given through Joseph Smith the Prophet, at Far West, Missouri, July 8, 1838, in answer to his supplication: "O Lord! Show unto thy servants how much thou requirest of the properties of thy people for a tithing." The law of tithing, as understood today, had not been given to the Church previous to this revelation. The term tithing in the prayer just quoted and in previous revelations (64:23; 85:3; 97:11) had meant not just one-tenth, but <u>all free-will offerings, or contributions</u>, to the Church funds. The Lord had previously given to the Church the law of consecration and stewardship of property* [a very questionable interpretation of church history], *which members (chiefly the leading elders) entered into by a covenant that was to be everlasting. Because of failure on the part of many to abide by this covenant, the Lord withdrew it for a time and gave instead the law of tithing to the whole Church* [more questionable historical interpretation]. *The Prophet asked the Lord how much of their property He required for sacred purposes. The answer was this revelation.*

1–5, The Saints are to pay their surplus property and then give, as tithing, one-tenth of their interest annually; 6–7, Such a course will sanctify the land of Zion.]

Comments on headnotes: There are at least two interpretation errors or unjustified assertions concerning D&C 119 as presented in the headnotes. They seem to want us to accept 10% as a baseline and then add other church contributions on top of that. But that is not at all what I read in the revelations or in the history. That seems to be nothing more than current leadership wishful thinking. The current church leadership wants to assert that the law of consecration and stewardship was a marvelous invention that gave church leaders massive control over the economics of the Saints. But it was nothing of the sort. It was nothing more than a version of the corporation of the president for that time period which was really just a standard silent business partnership put together for a short time to handle certain specific aspects of central church administration. I wrote two books on that and related topics. This narrative about withdrawing the supposedly comprehensive law of consecration and stewardship and replacing it with the more "limited" tithing is a complete fabrication. It has nothing to do with the gospel of Christ or with actual church history from any known time period.

1. Verily, thus saith the Lord, I require all their surplus property to be put into the hands of the Bishop of my Church of Zion,

["Surplus property" is a very vague definition – obviously to be determined by the property owner. Who else can wisely determine what is "surplus" in each of the cases of thousands of busy members without arbitrarily causing economic damage and loss of religious freedom?]

2. For the building of mine house, and for the laying of the foundation of Zion and for the Priesthood, and for the debts of the Presidency of my Church;
3. And this shall be the beginning of the tithing of my people;

[To be paid to whom? It is not clear – free will charity is the gospel answer, and property owners make that determination, not central bureaucracies.]

4. And after that, those who have thus been tithed, shall pay <u>one-tenth of all their interest</u> annually; and this shall be a standing law unto them forever, for my holy Priesthood, saith the Lord.
5. Verily I say unto you, it shall come to pass, that all those who gather unto the Land of Zion shall be tithed of [be asked to make contributions from] their surplus properties, and shall observe this law, or they shall not be found worthy to abide among you.

[Were any thrown out from among them? None that I know of.]

6. And I say unto you, if my people observe not this law, to keep it holy, and <u>by this law sanctify the land of Zion unto me</u>, that my statutes and my judgments may be kept thereon, that it may be most holy, behold, verily I say unto you, <u>it shall not be a land of Zion unto you</u>;
7. And this shall be an ensample unto all the stakes of Zion. Even so. Amen.

The use of the word "interest" here is somewhat obscure or nonsensical, so I shall attempt to define it in a way that could make some practical sense. I am going to slightly rewrite verse 6: "by this law (of member individually administered contributions made to improve society) sanctify the land of Zion unto me, that my statutes and my judgments may be kept thereon, that it may be most holy, [and] behold, verily I say unto you, it shall ... be a land of Zion unto you;"

The key thought is that members should maintain an "interest" in performing charitable deeds and an "interest" in improving society and establishing Zion by using their own resources, their own charity, and acting accordingly.

I argue that it is only idealistic Christian charity that can make a degenerate worldly society into a Zion. We can be certain with any kind of bureaucracy, civil or religious, will not do it -- they are the problem, not the solution. Solving that problem is the assignment of individual church members. As we have proven over the past 120 years, it is quite pointless to expect church leaders to take all of those necessary steps on their own. They will just spend the money on themselves and essentially waste it. We see that although "tithing" is nearly perfectly enforced today according to Old Testament ways of thinking, there has been no measurable improvement to our society through its use, especially since the leaders have been holding all the money for their own use and have applied not a dime of it to major improvements to our society. In other words, since the centrally-collected tithing is essentially all wasted or hoarded, the payment of a formal 10% actually leads to far less improvement to the society than if the members had kept that money and used it as they saw fit.

Following another line of logic, I consider it plausible (but fairly unimportant) that the normal business use of the term "interest" could make sense here. In our current tax code "interest" is considered unearned income. Perhaps one member's version of "paying tithing" could be to pay 1/10 of whatever he receives as a passive return on investment which would be called "interest" under today's accounting rules. As I see it, under the rules which Christ set out, no one is legally bound to pay a single penny in mandatory "tithing" to be eligible for salvation here or to maintain good standing in the church. So, paying 1/10 of a person's unearned income is just as good a measure as any other. Perhaps the flexibility in today's individualized tithing calculation (gross versus net, etc.) exists because of the lack of precision in the scriptural computation methods plus the lack of confidence in the whole concept of making salvation contingent on paying tithing.

Nauvoo temple and baptism for the dead

I hate to be critical of the Nauvoo Saints and all their efforts and the many exhortations they received from their leaders to do even more, but I believe there may be another way to look at this whole situation. A review of all aspects of church history at this point would be helpful to reach a balanced view, but it appears to me that the strategic thinking of the Saints was very lacking here and it caused them many difficulties. If these people had followed Joseph Smith and his suggestion that they go West as soon as possible, they could have saved that onerous and largely wasted effort devoted to the Nauvoo Temple and used it to build a temple after they reached a safer place such as Salt Lake City (if a temple is needed at all).

It strikes me that here we have the Twelve trying to whip the saints into building a temple to save their dead, which is an all-too-familiar bit of rhetoric and excuse and guilt trip to get more out of the saints than they may otherwise be prepared to give (and to have church administrators advance themselves to become administrators of members' resources, which is normally none of their business.) It is only in crisis "wagon train" mode that it makes sense to have church leaders be temporal administrators. We left the wagon train phase long ago, but we have kept the redundant and destructive temporal administration aspects.).

Perhaps this is essentially a partial return to law of Moses concepts, involving rules and physical structures and ritual sacrifices, since the Saints refuse to understand and live the actual gospel concepts. Maybe, in our case, we had to repeat an old cycle, we had to go back to the law of Moses and then break away again from that mechanical thinking when we can finally comprehend what the gospel actually teaches. Perhaps as a result of our ignorance, we can only move forward if we see Christ crucified again, so to speak, or have our current leader, in this case Joseph Smith, die, before we can finally make the mental leap to the true higher law. As it turned out, we almost made it and then we fell back again and have not recovered.

To summarize, in my opinion, we would need much more voluminous and explicit and authoritative instruction than this one ambiguous and incoherent revelation containing a critical word which is unintelligible on its own to prompt us to switch to a full-blown law of Moses religious society, complete with the mandatory paid ministry and mandatory tithing to pay for it. Even if this revelation represented proper wisdom for that moment in time, it has now simply been stretched beyond what it can bear.

The ears perk up of every would-be professional priest looking for a free lunch when the subject of a potential increase of contributed money arises. That appears to include the Twelve themselves in the next two quotations:

> History of the Church p.1564 of 3032
> BAPTISM FOR THE DEAD.
> An Epistle of the Twelve Apostles to the Saints of the Last Days.
>
> The building of the Temple of the Lord in the city of Nauvoo, is occupying the first place in the exertions and prayers of many of the Saints at the present time, knowing, as they do, that if this building is not completed speedily, "we shall be rejected as a Church with our dead;" for the Lord our God hath spoken it.
>
> But while many are thus engaged in laboring and watching and praying for this all important object, there are many, very many more, who do not thus come up to their privilege and their duty in this thing, and in many instances we are confident that their neglect arises from a want of proper understanding of the principles upon which this building is founded, and by which it must be completed. [Under the law of Moses?]

The children of Israel were commanded to build a house in the land of promise [under the law of Moses, not Christ's gospel]; and so are the Saints of the last days, as you will see in the Revelation given to Joseph the Seer, January 19, 1841, wherein those ordinances may be revealed which have been hid for ages, even their anointings and washings, and baptisms for the dead; wherein they may meet in solemn assemblies for their memorials, sacrifices, and oracles in their most holy places; and wherein they may receive conversations and statutes, and judgments, for the beginning of the revelations and foundations of Zion, and the glory and honor and adornment of all her municipals through the medium which God has ordained. [Temples are not required. God needs no place of stone to lay his head.]

In the same revelation the command is to "all the Saints from afar " as well as those already gathered to this place' to arise with one consent and build the Temple; to prepare a place where the Most High may manifest Himself to His people. No one is excepted who hath aught in his possession, for what have ye that ye have not received? And I will require mine own with usury, saith the Lord; so that those who live thousands of miles from this place, come under the same law, and are entitled to the same blessings and privileges as those who have already gathered. But some may say, how can this be, I am not there, therefore I cannot meet in the Temple, cannot be baptized in the font? The command of heaven is to you, to all, gather; and when you arrive here, if it is found that you have previously sent of your gold, or your silver, or your substance, the tithing and consecrations which are required of you for this building, you will find your names, tithings and consecrations written in the Book of the Law of the Lord, to be kept in the Temple, as a witness in your favor, showing that you are a proprietor in that building, and are entitled to your share of the privileges thereunto belonging.

One of those privileges which is particularly attracting the notice of the Saints at the present moment, is baptism for the dead, in the font which is so far completed as to be dedicated, and several have already attended to this ordinance by which the sick have been made whole, and the prisoner set free; but while we have been called to administer this ordinance, we have been led to inquire into the propriety of baptizing those who have not been obedient, and assisted to build the place for baptism; and it seems to us unreasonable to expect that the Great Jehovah will approbate such administration; for if the Church must be brought under condemnation, and rejected with her dead, if she fail to build the house and its appurtenances, why should not individuals of the Church, who thus neglect, come under the same condemnation? For if they are to be rejected, they may as well be rejected without baptism as with it; for their baptism can be of no avail before God, and the time to baptize them may be appropriated to building the walls of the house, and this is according to the understanding which we have received from him who is our spokesman.

[Perhaps the real purpose of building the Nauvoo Temple was to encourage more gathering -- something which was certainly needed. Recall that 90,000 members from England and Europe were needed to bolster the Saints in Utah enough to survive there.]

Let it not be supposed that the sick and the destitute are to be denied the blessings of the Lord's house; God forbid; His eye is ever over them for good. He that hath not, and cannot obtain, but saith in his heart, if I had, I would give freely, is accepted as freely as he that gives of his abundance. The Temple is to be built by tithing and consecration, and every one is at liberty to consecrate all they find in their hearts so to do; but the tithings required, is one-tenth of all anyone possessed at the commencement of the building, and one-tenth part of all his increase from that time until the completion of the same, whether it be money, or whatever he may be blessed with.

Many in this place are laboring every tenth day for the house, and this is the tithing of their income, for they have nothing else; others would labor the same, but they are sick, therefore excusable; when they get well, let them begin; while there are others who appear to think their own business of more importance than the Lord's. Of such we would ask, who gave you your time, health, strength, and put you into business? And will you not begin quickly to return with usury that which you have received? Our God will not wait always. [More guilt trips.]

We would remind some two or three hundred Elders, who offered to go on missions, some six months, others one year, and some two years, and had their missions assigned them at the general conference to labor on the Temple, that most of their names are still with us, and we wish them to call and take their names away, and give them up to the building committee.

Brethren, you have as great an interest at stake in this thing as we have, but as our Master, even the Master-builder of the Temple, whose throne is on high, has seen fit to constitute us stewards in some parts of His household; we feel it important for us to see to it that our Master is not defrauded, and especially by those who have pledged their word, their time, their talents, to His services; and we hope this gentle hint will suffice, that we may not be compelled to publish the names of those referred to. [More guilt trips.]

Probably some may think they could have gone on a mission, but cannot labor, as they have no means of boarding themselves, but let such remember that several score of brethren and sisters in this city, offered at the general conference, to board one or more laborers on the Temple till the same should be completed, and but few of those as yet have had the opportunity of boarding any one. To all such we would say, you are not forgotten, we have your names also, and we expect soon to send someone to your table, therefore put your houses in order and never be ready to refuse the first offer of a guest.

Large stores of provisions will be required to complete the work, and now is the time for securing it, while meat is plenty and can be had for one half the value that it can at other seasons of the year, and the weather is cool and suitable for packing. Let the brethren for two hundred miles around drive their fat cattle and hogs to this place, where they may be preserved, and there will be a supply till another favorable season rolls around, or till the end of the labor. [This image of hundreds of food animals being collected at the Temple to keep processes underway at the Temple sounds more than a little bit like what went on at the

Temple of Herod in Jerusalem with its constant stream of sacrificial animals. That makes this whole process sound very much like a law of Moses operation.]

Now is the time to secure food, now is the time that the trustee is ready to receive your droves. Not the maimed, the lean, the halt, and the blind, and such that you cannot use; it is for the Lord, and He wants no such offering; but if you want His blessing, give Him the best, give Him as good as He has given you. Beds and bedding, socks, mittens, shoes, clothing of every description, and store goods are needed for the comfort of the laborers this winter; journeymen, stone cutters, quarrymen, teams and teamsters for drawing stone and all kinds of provision for men and beast, are needed in abundance.

There are individuals who have given nothing as yet, either as tithing or consecration, thinking that they shall be able to do a great deal some time hence if they continue their present income to their own use, but this is a mistaken idea. Suppose that all should act upon this principle, no one would do ought at present, consequently the building must cease, and this generation remain without a house, and the Church be rejected; then suppose the next generation labor upon the same principle, and the same in all succeeding generations, the Son of God would never have a place on the earth to lay His head. [He doesn't need one.]

Let every individual remember that their tithings and consecrations are required from what they have, and not what they expect to have some time hence, and are wanted for immediate use. All money and other property designed for tithing and consecrations to the building of the Temple must hereafter be presented to the Trustee in Trust, President Joseph Smith, and entered at the recorder's office, in the book before referred to; and all receipts now holden by individuals, which they have received of the building committee for property delivered to them, must also be forwarded to the recorder's office for entry, to secure the appropriation of said property according to the original design.

The Elders everywhere will instruct the brethren both in public and in private, in the principles and doctrines set forth in this Epistle, so that every individual in the Church may have a perfect understanding of his duty and privileges.
BRIGHAM YOUNG, HEBER C. KIMBALL, ORSON PRATT, WILLIAM SMITH, LYMAN WIGHT, WILFORD WOODRUFF, JOHN TAYLOR, GEO. A. SMITH, WILLARD RICHARDS. Nauvoo, Illinois, December 13, 1841.

In this epistle the Twelve seem already were pressing to reach a semi-law-of-Moses condition. Perhaps this epistle is the genesis of the LDS priestcraft movement which started small, with nothing more than some typical human inclinations and frustrations, but has now blossomed into the desired full-blown law of Moses operation.

Paying a huge amount of money to save your dead is a familiar religious theme which apparently started in 1841 and has now gone about as far as it can go. One might wonder how those early Christians in the Mediterranean area managed to fulfill their duty to the dead inexpensively with no temples and no computers and presumably few records. Why can't we do the same today?

At a conference in 1844, John Taylor once again advocates for doing work for the dead and completing a temple for that purpose:

> History of the Church p.1863 of 3032
> CHAPTER XXIII.
> MINUTES OF THE IMPORTANT CONFERENCE OF OCTOBER 6TH TO 8TH, 1844----THE CHURCH SET IN ORDER ----DUTIES OF THE PRIESTHOOD EXPOUNDED----ECONOMICS CONSIDERED
> ...
> 1867/3032
> He [Elder Taylor] exhorted the saints to be virtuous, humble and faithful, and concluded by blessing the saints.
>
> He said further, in relation to the baptisms for the dead, that it would be better for the saints to go on and build the Temple before we urge our baptisms too much. [Is Elder Taylor implying that the Temple is optional for doing work for the dead?] There are cases which require being attended to, and there are provisions made for them; but as a general thing he would advise them not to be in too great a hurry [Is he perhaps saying that our duty to the dead is real, but that our duty to the living is more real?]. He said one of the clerks had asked whether any should be baptized who had not paid their tithing; it is our duty to pay our tithing, one-tenth of all we possess, <u>and then one-tenth of our increase</u>, <u>*and a man who has not paid his tithing is unfit to be baptized for his dead*</u>. It is as easy for a man who has ten thousand dollars to pay one thousand, as it is for a man who has but a little to pay one-tenth. It is our duty to pay our tithing. If a man has not faith enough to attend to these little things, he has not faith enough to save himself and his friends. It is a man's duty to attend to these things. The poor are not going to be deprived of these blessings because they are poor; no, God never reaps where he has not sown. This command is harder for the rich than the poor; a man who has one million dollars, if he should give one hundred thousand, he would think he was beggared forever. The Savior said, how hardly do they that have riches enter the kingdom of heaven.

The irony here is that the (confused) underlying theological logic seems to be that a person has to be fully in conformance with the old law of Moses, including the mandatory payment of tithing which was to be used to support a mandatory paid ministry, the Levites (the Twelve seem to be informally nominating themselves for that role), before that person can actually do any work for the dead, a New Testament concept. But we should notice that the law of Moses had no power to do anything about work for the dead since no one had the proper priesthood powers to do that work, and had no procedures in place for any such ordinances (and Christ had yet done the preparatory work in the spirit world so that work for the dead could proceed). Something does not compute, as they say.

Word use statistics
There is some subjectivity involved in making some of these word-use counts, but I don't think that affects the outcome in any way. On the scriptural use of the word "increase," in the LDS Topical Guide we find 27 instances, with 7 of them obviously relating to issues relating to tithing. Concerning the word "interest" as found in the LDS Topical Guide, we find 0 instances, since the topical guide does not even have an entry for the word "interest."

In the Index to the Triple Combination, we find 8 entries for the word "increase," with none of them clearly having anything to do with tithing topics. For the word "interest" we have 4 entries, with only one of them obviously relating to tithing issues, D&C 119.

The use of a complete concordance gives us some larger numbers, with 173 entries found in the LDS Scriptures for "increase", and 15 entries found in LDS Scriptures for "interest." As far as I can tell, this extended list of words in each case has no effect on the final conclusion, which is that the use of the word "interest" only occurs once when discussing topics related to tithing, in D&C 119, and indeed appears to be an anomaly in that single case.

Other detailed comments
The use of the word "interest" seems to be an anomaly here, perhaps a typographical error made at the time it was first printed. It appears to be the only place in the entire body of Scripture where this thought is expressed using that word. In every other case I can find, the term "increase" is used, and that implies a very different meaning and answer.

The use of this word is such an anomaly, that it is even possible that it was an intentional change made much later by the advocates of a paid ministry. The word "interest" is very confusing, but the word "increase" is not confusing. I'm going to guess that the Lord originally gave the least confusing answer to the question, not inserting something which is basically incomprehensible.

Chapter 15

The terrible church performance statistics a paid ministry creates

It was the question of church performance statistics that got me started on this entire line of research which resulted in this book about a forbidden paid ministry supported by forbidden tithing, both items condemned by the scriptures, which items are also the cause of all current church problems, including extremely slow church growth. As I saw the church reporting very bad statistics year after year, with the trend going downward, instead of upward as one might hope, I was alarmed that this could be going on without my understanding the process in any way. Certainly, the church leaders were not openly giving us any data and related commentary on this important general question. I was told on one occasion by a very senior church leader that it was none of my business to worry about such things -- they were the only ones who needed to know about such things. Nonetheless, I couldn't see why every member on the planet would not want to know about how well or how badly the church was doing and what the factors might be that were involved.

During the 1980s I was researching two interrelated books concerning *Joseph Smith's United Order* and *Brigham Young's United Order* mostly to explore the unusual doctrinal issues that arose during that early time period. Both of those books on history had much to do with the growth and progress of the church in the 1800s, so I naturally became curious also about more current church growth, and began to locate and collate statistics on that topic.

The Church Almanac was a book that was published each year for many years which gave all the statistical data available about the church and its growth around the world, beginning in 1830. It also included other news items such as information about the temples which were added, etc. Unfortunately, that publication is now out of print, possibly because that series of books documented what has gradually become mostly bad news.

I got copies of the Church Almanac as they came out each year, and selected and compiled and graphed that data as a major portion of my third book entitled *Creating the Millennium: Social Forces and Church Growth in the 21st Century*. I consider this, my third book, to be full of interesting information, but I still had not come to understand what the basic problems were that were keeping the church from being as successful and as influential as I thought it should be. It was only later that I finally "got to the bottom of it," at least as I see it, which is why I am finally writing this current book. In my *Creating the Millennium* book I suggested ways that social forces could be harnessed to increase church growth rates. Unfortunately, the most powerful social force of all was something I completely missed. Everyone wants to have the "benefits" of being part of a comprehensive social insurance system. That is the description of the original charity-based social insurance system which the early members of the church invented and experienced at the time of Christ and at the time of Joseph Smith.

As I mentioned, I spent years researching the growth levels of the church to see why we were growing so slowly, with that growth rate continually going down, and wrote a book about it. In the process, I noticed a downward inflection point in the time range of about 1960 and could find no obvious reason for that change in direction. Growth rates had generally been going up before that, and then turned downward until we have reached a zero-growth rate today.

It took me many years to discover the reason, but I believe I have it now. It was about 1960 when the church began to refuse to issue temple recommends unless a person had paid a full tithe to the central church. Before that, paying a full tithe, in one of many possible ways, was seen as aspirational, something everyone should be striving to do. Members could still do a great deal of good around them with their personal resources, and not be penalized by the central church for doing so, which is the essence of the current requirement of sending all church contributions -- "tithing" -- to the central offices, where it is largely wasted on unnecessary and prideful things instead of being put to good charitable uses to benefit the members and the world.

After those original church performance studies, I then began another course of study on what I thought was a totally unrelated matter, the systems for doing genealogy research. At the time, I was a computer professional, specializing in computer information system design, and also had an interest in genealogy research. It was in about 1989 that I decided to do some genealogy research for my family, and, in the process, found that the old library/paper-based systems were far too random and disorganized and subject to massive duplication of research effort by the millions of people involved. I decided to design a system to be much more efficient, up to 1000 times more efficient if the practitioners of the art were willing to accept some new concepts and greater cooperation and discipline.

I found that the mathematics of efficiency were so overwhelming if cooperation could be fostered, that I thought no one who understood the concepts could resist the possible gains. I even went so far as to obtain a federal patent for the process. When I triumphantly but naïvely presented these ideas to the fledgling Ancestry.com company and later to the church itself, in about 1998 and 2004 respectively, expecting to be well-received, I was stunned to learn that there was no interest whatsoever in implementing these new cooperation concepts even though they promised an easy 30 times improvement in efficiency. Gains of 200 times were only a little bit harder, and gains of up to 1000 times were perfectly possible but naturally were harder to reach.

I discovered that neither Ancestry.com nor the Church had an interest in efficiently and quickly finishing this huge data processing project, but instead had the seemingly mostly cynical goal of stretching a very large revenue stream out forever. To put this into better context, the church was spending about $2 billion a year, with about $0.5 billion a year in cash and about $1.5 billion a year in volunteer labor, and hoped to maintain that activity level forever.

The various commercial genealogy companies altogether were bringing in about $3 billion a year and also hoped to keep that revenue stream flowing forever. Only by maintaining the maximum levels of inefficiency and research duplication could they keep up these revenue levels forever.

My general project computations were that $1 billion would be more than enough to complete all the genealogy research for the entire United States, and it would require about $20 billion to complete the entire world, to the extent it could be completed, based on the availability of records.

If we only consider the genealogy research done since about 1998 using the Family Search Church-sponsored computer system, the Church alone has spent about $40 billion in church resources, enough to do the United States about 40 times over, or to have completed the entire world at least twice. If we add in the resources absorbed by all the other commercial genealogy systems, totaling about $3 billion a year, amounting to about $60 billion in all since 1998, you can see that the entire world could have been completed about 5 times over. The rates of spending on this activity have not decreased at all, and no major blocks of research have been completed, such as the United States, meaning that the next major logical question to be understood and answered is why the Church would tolerate such massive inefficiency, faced with a supposedly critical need to provide salvation for all our known ancestors.

The cynical answer is that this is all part of a system that keeps the church central bureaucracy supplied with perhaps $15 billion a year, and possibly up to three times that much, forever. As things stand, one must pay tithing to do temple work, thus keeping this process going on forever as a way to ensure the church's income does not diminish. The last thing the church wants to do is to complete all research and temple work for the dead. The only goal is to bring in large amounts of money and keep people perpetually very busy and distracted on a giant makework project, a kind of socialist government-style project reminiscent of the Great Depression projects – like the old WPA or Works Progress Administration projects -- where building up a force of political activist supporters was a large part of the project goals, far more important than any valuable projects actually completed.

The work of the 300,000 LDS genealogy volunteers (and perhaps 2 million other US genealogy hobbyists), is almost completely unnecessary, but it does seem to make some people happy to do church work without ever having to interact very much with the rest of the world as would be required in proselytizing the living. It makes it appear that "saving" a soul who is dead is much easier and cheaper than helping or saving any living person (especially since current costs for saving the living are unnecessarily astronomical), even though the value to the receiving person is infinitely higher for those who are living than for those who are dead. Living people often have extreme and critical time constraints, but the dead have almost no time constraints at all.

The church has essentially monetized the sale of ordinances for both the living and the dead. If the church's and the nation's genealogists were ever to finish the basic genealogy for the entire United States, that would be viewed as a catastrophe for all the involved religious and commercial bureaucracies. Obviously, these many bureaucracies must work together to maintain the same inefficient goals and practices, lest one of them accidentally solve the general problem of genealogy research for a tiny fraction of the current costs and thereby completely undermine and make obsolete all the others.

Of course, the church is also spending a few billion dollars a year on building temples, but that is also a benefit to the church, not a cost, since all that money must first come in as tithing which can then be spent very liberally on supporting a massive construction bureaucracy made up of naturally very loyal supporters of the church which pays their generous salaries and expenses and provides prideful results. The building of temples and chapels and the research work for the dead are all basically unnecessary, nothing more than cover stories to justify members supporting a lavish bureaucracy. Our concern for the dead is probably no more effective than that of the Russian Orthodox Church where people simply buy and burn a few candles to get people out of purgatory, but our solution is certainly a great deal more elaborate and expensive, which is the point of it all.

Luckily for a greedy and deceptive church (who may themselves be deceived in some cases), most members are still unacquainted with today's astounding information technology possibilities, and so are willing and even happy to assume that "doing genealogy" is an infinitely large task that can never be finished, even though it can be easily demonstrated that six months work at any time in the last 20 years could have finished the entire United States, and every new 6-12 month period could finish the genealogy for another mass of humanity as large as the United States – about 300 million people and all their documented ancestors. The United States is about 1/20 of the world, so finishing the world within 10-20 years is easily possible. In other words, the church leaders and their technical assistants must maintain a huge fraud indefinitely on many levels to keep the money pouring in, spending it all on themselves with almost nothing going to actual real-world charity.

Twenty years from now we will have spent $80 billion by the church and $120 billion by all other groups, and no measurable progress will have been made (by conscious design) on genealogical research and temple work. We will simply have another generation of people who will have devoted that much more to the effort, most of it wasted.

In the process, the church has created its own multilevel feudal social class system, including a "Kings Court" of tens of thousands of loyal paid retainers who would naturally resist any threat to their paychecks. As pointed out in detail elsewhere, there is actually no doctrinal need for either temples or chapels, but the construction of these buildings is a very generous source of income to the church and its associated bureaucracy. This all sounds very medieval, like the masons who spent their lives building massive cathedrals for the corrupt Catholic popes.

In summary, almost none of the central church spending is necessary for successful church operation, and in fact is the exact reason it is now so unsuccessful. If nearly all of that money were devoted to the charitable needs of its members or other needy aspects of society, as it should be, instead of wasting it on prideful and unnecessary and often extravagant buildings, then the church would be meeting all the needs both spiritual and temporal of its members and potential members, and so would be growing at an explosive rate as it did when it was new and focused on charity as the ruling principle as it was at the time of Christ and at the time of Joseph Smith.

Today the church is in the exact situation that the Roman Catholic Church found itself in that prompted the criticism of Martin Luther in his "95 Theses" which inadvertently started the Protestant Reformation. It was all about ignoring the needs of the poor and taking that money to provide a sumptuous globe-circling living to the current paid ministry and to construct expensive and prideful buildings for their control and use.

In other words, what we have today is a giant scam in long-term operation by the Central church. The existence of that officially supported scam, and the naïveté and corruption it engenders, may partly explain why so many people in Utah have been scammed out of their savings by unscrupulous salesmen, often having positions of religious authority over people at Utah, such as local bishops.

Only a tiny fraction of the money that goes to Salt Lake City through the tithing system actually is justified, and even that small legitimate amount should not be subject to any "religious extortion" where one must pay money to a central bureaucracy to receive some sense of feedback or confirmation that one's salvation is secure. The money that goes to Salt Lake City as tithing is nearly all wasted on frivolous matters, supporting a self-appointed class of "new Levites" who believe they should receive their living from ordinary members

"Freely have ye received, freely give" is the correct rule for holders of the priesthood. The priesthood is to be a joyful burden, not a means of earning a living at member expense.

To bring in a few more numbers on the genealogy topic, we are spending perhaps $2000 for each new unduplicated name that enters the temple, where that cost could be as low as $2 if done correctly.

The amount spent on the proselytizing of the living is also outrageously out of bounds. We should note that there was an approximately zero cost for new members at the time of Christ and at the time of Joseph Smith, and sometimes there was a net positive gain to the group as it expanded.

Since the church has recently essentially ceased to grow, with zero new members, and the church is taking in at least $15 billion in tithing revenue, we can say that we are paying a nearly infinite price for each new long-term person added to the church's total size. A few years ago, when there were actually up to 30,000 new long-term members being added to the church each year, we could at least calculate that each new long-term member cost about ($15 billion/30,000=) or about $500,000 each. A family of five would thus cost about $2.5 million. That number could be up to three times that large if the church income were shown to be $45-50 billion dollars as some have estimated. These numbers do not compare well with the zero costs of earlier times. We could probably increase our growth rates today to any number we wanted by simply offering every family of five $2.5 million. They could all buy a new house and retire for the rest of their lives.

These are the absurd levels of expenses found in today's church, and the church members would be fully justified in ending their support for this extremely wasteful system and demanding a return to prior practices.

There are several other ways to make interesting calculations concerning the cost of new members. The church typically reports about 300,000 new converts each year. The Church does not report the number of deaths of members each year, but we can estimate those deaths to be about 225,000 on a base of 15 million members who have a life expectancy of age 75. That means that just to keep from shrinking in size, the church must add at least 225,000 each year. If another 75,000 leave the church each year for other reasons, that would account for our having zero net growth in active members with 300,000 converts each year. The recent reports of up to 185,000 people resigning from the church each year, based on their alarm at reading on the Internet about alleged errors in church history, means that there is probably a huge net loss in active members each year.

With 60,000 missionaries finding 300,000 converts a year, that means about five people are added for each missionary each year. But all of that is simply to keep the church from shrinking, and adds nothing to its operational size.

Each of those replacement members is costing church members about $15 billion/300,000 = $50,000. Since it costs about $5,000 a year to sustain a missionary who produces about five replacement members at $1000 each, one could say that we are paying 50 times as much for each new member as is necessary.

The church members do not even begin to have enough children to solve the growth problem of the church. The highest number imaginable is about 60,000 new children who are baptized each year, only about 1/5 of the number necessary to keep us from shrinking, let alone supplying any actual growth. That was the issue that the old polygamy program was supposed to solve, and certainly did to some extent.

In contrast, if the Church were anxiously engaged in doing effective charity work with all the money it had itself from its own sources plus what it might get from some other outside sources, the church would be growing at a furious pace as it has in times past when charity was the essence of the church.

So we find that our maximum sustainable missionary program may just barely keep us from shrinking in numbers. This does not sound like what was intended to be happening to today's church.

These calculations have been made based on the number of new church units -- wards and branches -- that are added each year. In 2018, a total of

30 wards and branches were added (the number of each type is not separately reported). If we assume an average of 100 people for each new ward or branch unit, that would give us a growth of 3000 people in 2018. For a church the size of ours -- about 16 million are reported -- that is close enough to zero to call it zero. And the trend is downward, not upward, so we will be lucky to even do as well in 2019, unless something remarkable happens.

Naturally, some missions do well and many do poorly, so it is uncertain how much success any particular missionary can expect to have. That may explain the high levels of anxiety and depression found among many groups of missionaries.

Perhaps if LDS missionaries sense that they are doing nothing more than keeping the church from shrinking, they are not going to be too sure that the gospel is actually as true and exciting as they are constantly told it is. They are not indeed changing the world or really gathering Zion, since they are just working hard to avoid shrinkage. We are running as hard as we can just to stay in place. Most missionaries would probably like to feel that their extreme effort and sacrifice ought to achieve much more than that. They might reasonably wonder whether the "product" they are "selling" is really as wonderful as the scriptures and church leaders tell us it is.

Notes

An interesting historical example of other makework projects which had questionable unstated political purposes:

> United States History
> Written By: The Editors of Encyclopaedia Britannica
>
> Works Progress Administration
> Alternative Titles: WPA, Work Projects Administration
>
> Works Progress Administration (WPA), also called (1939–43) Work Projects Administration, work program for the unemployed that was created in 1935 under U.S. President Franklin D. Roosevelt's New Deal. Although critics called the WPA an extension of the dole or a device for creating a huge patronage army loyal to the Democratic Party, the stated purpose of the program was to provide useful work for millions of victims of the Great Depression and thus to preserve their skills and self-respect. The economy would in turn be stimulated by the increased purchasing power of the newly employed, whose wages under the program ranged from $15 to $90 per month.

Terrible performance statistics

See Article History
https://www.britannica.com/topic/Works-Progress-Administration

Chapter 16

The LDS Church is finally being called to account

In an earlier chapter we mentioned some of the vast inefficiencies of how the church is currently operated. Obviously, the church leaders feel that they have an adequate income to support their preferred lifestyle, and there is no reason to disturb their peaceful lives by trying to extend the ideology and church operations any further. They have become extremely timid since they see no personal advantage to pushing back against any of the worldly pressures that they would have to counteract in order to expand the influence of the gospel. One might reasonably wonder whether the church leaders are total captives of the current secular society or not. Perhaps it is inconceivable that they could change their ways.

Recent developments and Mormon-leaks-style revelations have shaken things up a little bit and may become a major source of embarrassment for the church leaders. Their extreme self-interest and self-centeredness and timidness over many decades can be quantified by noticing that the church has about $124 billion in reserves which have never been used for any church purpose and most likely never will be used for any legitimate gospel purpose. This is a measurement of the unwillingness of the church leaders to find valid and valuable places to invest the charitable monies it receives from its church members, even when they have more money laid at their feet, "laid at the feet of the apostles," than they can reasonably spend in their current state of mind. It would be ridiculous to say that the world is perfect and has no need for any charitable Christian interventions, but obviously the church leaders haven't the slightest intention of defining what those charitable needs might be and then fulfilling them, beyond the approximately 0.5%, or less, of the money they receive in tithing which they then pass on to actual humanitarian purposes.

It should be clear by now that the LDS church is 100% a business, not a church. Or, rather, it is a business which promotes a religious-seeming franchise using borrowed concepts which have gradually been mixed together to accomplish the maximum income stream, and it attempts to maximize its income through every means available. An oft-repeated observation is that

> [B]usiness has no conscience... Capital is a coward.[1]

As we occasionally hear from those who comment on economic and market events, "when things can't go on, they don't." That seems to be the lesson of this formal discovery that the LDS church has about $124 billion in reserves which it has refused for many years to spend on appropriate charitable projects.

The following *Washington Post* newspaper article is presented in full as an introduction to this problem of the church's vast reserves brought about by its absolute unwillingness to find social problems and fix them. There is much more detailed information available in the 74-page complaint made to the IRS by the whistleblower, but this will present the basic situation.

Mormon Church has misled members on $100 billion tax-exempt investment fund, whistleblower alleges

December 17, 2019 Washington Post

by Jon Swaine, Douglas MacMillan, and Michelle Boorstein

A former investment manager alleges in a whistleblower complaint to the Internal Revenue Service that the Church of Jesus Christ of Latter-day Saints has amassed about $100 billion in accounts intended for charitable purposes, according to a copy of the complaint obtained by The Washington Post.

The confidential document, received by the IRS on Nov. 21, accuses church leaders of misleading members — and possibly breaching federal tax rules — by stockpiling their surplus donations instead of using them for charitable works. It also accuses church leaders of using the tax-exempt donations to prop up a pair of businesses.

The church did not respond to detailed questions from The Post about the complaint and said in a statement Monday that it does not discuss specific financial transactions. On Tuesday, after the first version of this story was published, the church said it takes seriously its responsibility to care for members' donations.

"Claims being currently circulated are based on a narrow perspective and limited information," said a statement attributed to the church's First Presidency, its top governing body. "The Church complies with all applicable law governing our donations, investments, taxes, and reserves."

The complaint provides a window into the closely held finances of one of the nation's most visible religious organizations, based in Salt Lake City. It details a church fortune far exceeding past estimates and encompassing stocks, bonds and cash.

The complaint was filed by David A. Nielsen, a 41-year-old Mormon who worked until September as a senior portfolio manager at the church's investment division, a company named Ensign Peak Advisors that is based near the church's headquarters.

Nonprofit organizations, including religious groups, are exempted in the United States from paying taxes on their income. Ensign is registered with authorities as a supporting organization and integrated auxiliary of the Mormon

Church. This permits it to operate as a nonprofit and to make money largely free from U.S. taxes.

The exemption requires that Ensign operate exclusively for religious, educational or other charitable purposes, a condition that Nielsen says the firm has not met.

In a declaration signed under penalty of perjury, Nielsen urges the IRS to strip the nonprofit of its tax-exempt status and alleges that Ensign could owe billions in taxes. He is seeking a reward from the IRS, which offers whistleblowers a cut of unpaid taxes that it recovers.

Nielsen did not respond to repeated phone calls and emails seeking comment.

His twin brother, Lars P. Nielsen, provided a copy of the complaint to The Post, along with dozens of supporting documents. Lars Nielsen, a health-care consultant in Minnesota, said he prepared the complaint with his brother and helped him submit it to the IRS.

Lars Nielsen said in a statement to The Post that his brother asked him to write an exposé on his former employer.

"Having seen tens of billions in contributions and scores more in investment returns come in, and having seen nothing except two unlawful distributions to for-profit concerns go out, he was dejected beyond words, and so was I," Lars Nielsen wrote.

He said he was coming forward without his brother's approval because he believed the information was too important to remain confidential. "I know that sometimes newspapers use anonymous sources," he said. "But that is usually not best for a story."

In remarks last year, a high-ranking cleric in the church, Bishop Gérald Caussé, said it "pays taxes on any income it derives from revenue-producing activities that are regularly carried on and are not substantially related to its tax-exempt purposes."

The church typically collects about $7 billion each year in contributions from members, according to the complaint. Mormons, like members of some other faith groups, are asked to contribute 10 percent of their income to the church, a practice known as tithing.

While about $6 billion of that income is used to cover annual operating costs, the remaining $1 billion or so is transferred to Ensign, which plows some into an investment portfolio to generate returns, according to the complaint.

Based on internal accounting documents from February 2018, the complaint estimates the portfolio has grown in value from $12 billion in 1997, when Ensign was formed, to about $100 billion today.

The church also owns real estate worth billions of dollars, according to the complaint, which focuses on surplus tithing money and says that the church may have additional holdings not managed by Ensign.

While accumulating this wealth, Ensign has not directly funded any religious, educational or charitable activities in 22 years, the complaint said. No documents are provided to support this claim, which is attributed to information David Nielsen gleaned from working at the company.

Philip Hackney, a former IRS official who teaches tax law at the University of Pittsburgh, said the complaint raised a "legitimate concern" about whether the church's investment arm deserved its tax-exempt status.

Bridgewater Associates assets under management (Largest hedge fund)	$160 billion
Microsoft cash and short-term investments (Largest corporate cash reserves)	$136.6 billion
Bill Gates net worth (Richest person)	$111.5 billion
The Church of Jesus Christ Of Latter-Day Saints investment fund	**$100 Billion**
Bill and Melinda Gates Foundation endowment assets (Largest philanthropic fund)	$46.8 billion
Harvard University endowment (Largest university endowment)	$40.9 billion

Sources: Bridgewater Associates, internal church documents, Microsoft, Bloomberg, Harvard annual report, Bill and Melinda Gates Foundation

THE WASHINGTON POST

"If you have a charity that simply amasses a war chest year after year and does not spend any money for charity purposes, that does not meet the requirements of tax law," Hackney said in an interview. Hackney, who served in the IRS chief counsel's office, has been retained by The Post to analyze the whistleblower documents.

IRS rules dictate that a nonprofit organization must carry out charitable activity that is "commensurate in scope with its financial resources" to maintain its tax-exempt status. No threshold for this test is specified, and the agency instead considers examples case by case.

In its statement Tuesday, the church said the "vast majority" of the funds it receives from donations are "used immediately to meet the needs of the growing Church," including temples, education and missionary work.

"Over many years, a portion is methodically safeguarded through wise financial management and the building of a prudent reserve for the future," the statement said. "This is a sound doctrinal and financial principle taught by the Savior in the Parable of the Talents and lived by the Church and its members. All Church funds exist for no other reason than to support the Church's divinely appointed mission."

Details of the church's expenditures on charitable work are not publicly available, but in a lecture at the University of Oxford in 2016, a senior elder said the church had spent about $40 million a year over the past 30 years on welfare, humanitarian aid and other international projects. He did not mention Ensign. The church said in a report last year that its charitable arm had spent $2.2 billion in assistance since 1985, but did not provide a breakdown on spending.

While declining to discuss the extent of their holdings, church leaders have sought to explain the practice of continuing to collect tithes while accumulating financial reserves.

In a speech in March 2018, Caussé linked the church's financial strategy to the "prophecies about the last days." Just as the church maintains grain silos and emergency warehouses, Caussé said, so it "also methodically follows the practice of setting aside a portion of its revenues each year to prepare for any possible future needs."

According to the complaint, Ensign's president, Roger Clarke, has told others that the amassed funds would be used in the event of the second coming of Christ. Clarke did not respond to an email seeking comment.

Nielsen's complaint is sharply critical of church leaders for continuing to ask for tithes, even from members who are struggling financially, while the church sits on a fortune. "Would you pay tithing instead of water, electricity, or feeding your family if you knew that it would sit around by the billions until the Second Coming of Christ?" he wrote in a 74-page narrative that accompanied his complaint.

He suggests church leaders favor continuing to collect tithes to avoid "losing control over their members' behavior" by releasing them from their financial obligations. In June, the church raised the monthly charge paid by most families to cover the cost of their children serving as missionaries from $400 to $500 per month.

Leaders have consistently tried to downplay speculation about the extent of the church's wealth. Quoting a former church president during the speech last year, Caussé, said: "When all is said and done, the only real wealth of the church is in the faith of its people."

When interviewed by a German reporter in 2002 about suggestions that the church had amassed billions, then-President Gordon B. Hinckley said: "Yes, if you count all of our assets, yes, we are well-off. But those assets, you have to know this, are not money-producing. Those assets are money-consuming."

Unlike other nonprofits, religious organizations are not required to publicly report their income or assets.

Nielsen's estimate of Ensign's assets places the Mormon investment organization among some of the country's wealthiest companies and charities. Microsoft, Alphabet and Apple each hold between $100 billion and $136 billion in cash, according to the most recent company filings, while Harvard University has the country's largest academic endowment at $40.9 billion. The Bill and Melinda Gates Foundation is the largest private philanthropic foundation in the world at $47.8 billion.

In addition to criticizing the scale of wealth accumulated by the church, Nielsen's complaint accuses church leaders of acting improperly on the rare occasions that funds have been paid out from the investment division.

According to Nielsen, $2 billion from Ensign has been used over the past decade to bail out a church-run insurance company and a shopping mall in Salt Lake City that was a joint venture between the church and a major real estate company.

Citing an internal presentation that he includes as an exhibit, Nielsen alleges that in 2009, Ensign spent funds on rescuing the insurance firm, Beneficial Life, which was suffering from its exposure to mortgage-backed securities amid the financial crisis.

At the time, a church-owned newspaper reported that a different commercial church company, Deseret Management, had injected $594 million into Beneficial Life to make up its deficit. Mark Willes, Deseret Management's president and chief executive, was reported to have said that no tithing money was used in the transaction.

Yet the internal presentation supplied to the IRS by Nielsen refers to a $600 million "withdrawal" from Ensign to Beneficial Life in 2009, citing a page from an Ensign slide presentation entitled "Framework and Exposures" and dated March 2013. Nielsen said the funds were taken specifically from the Ensign account that receives surplus tithing. Nielsen said the transfer was not treated as a loan and was not recorded as an investment on Ensign's balance sheet.

Despite the bailout, Beneficial Life announced it would terminate 150 of its 214 Utah workers and stop writing new insurance policies.

Neither Willes nor an official from Beneficial Life responded to messages seeking comment.

Nielsen's complaint further alleges that between 2009 and 2014, Ensign pumped $1.4 billion in several installments into the City Creek Center, a shopping mall in downtown Salt Lake City featuring a retractable roof. The mall, partly owned by the church, had also been hit by the financial crisis.

Amid complaints from members about the church venturing into retail, church leaders have repeatedly made assurances over several years that no money from tithes would be spent on developing the mall, a joint venture with the Taubman real estate group.

"I wish to give the entire church the assurance that tithing funds have not and will not be used to acquire this property. Nor will they be used in developing it for commercial purposes," Hinckley said when plans for the mall were unveiled in 2003.

On Monday, the church told The Post that through its involvement in the City Creek mall, it had "increased local economic activity during a financial downturn and attracted visitors and residents to Salt Lake City's historic downtown."

A Taubman spokeswoman declined to comment.

Hackney, the University of Pittsburgh tax law expert, said the payments would raise red flags if they were indeed made to for-profit entities that were separate from Ensign and not recorded as investments.

While the church may argue Ensign contributes to a broader religious and charitable mission, as a separate corporate entity, it must show that "it furthers a charitable purpose exclusively on its own," Hackney said.

"Once that money comes in, it's gotta go back out," he said. "They have to come up with a justification based on the entity alone. Looking at the other organizations shouldn't be a means of justifying hoarding."

IRS rules state that nonprofits "must not provide a substantial benefit to private interests" and that the earnings of registered religious organizations must not benefit "any private individual or shareholder" to avoid jeopardizing tax-exempt status.

The Mormon Church's wealth and investment acumen has been widely reported. A Time magazine cover story, "Mormons, Inc.," published in 1997, estimated the church's total assets at $30 billion or more. A 2012 Reuters article reported that the church owned "about $35 billion worth of temples and meeting houses around the world, and controls farms, ranches, shopping malls and other commercial ventures worth many billions more."

Nielsen's complaint comes as many Mormons across the United States are engaged in discussions with their bishops, traditionally held in December, to "settle" their dues to the church. His estimate of $7 billion in annual revenue points to a relatively high rate of contributions from the 15 million members. By comparison, the Catholic church in the United States was reported in 2005 to receive $8 billion in annual tithes. There were 75 million Catholics in the U.S. in 2010, according to Pew Research Center.

The complaint filed by Nielsen comprised a signed Form 211, the formal piece of IRS paperwork for reporting tax avoidance, a notarized cover letter to officials, plus the 74-page narrative document co-written with his brother in which he detailed his allegations at length.

These documents were sent to the IRS whistleblower office in Ogden, Utah, together with a thumb drive containing digital versions of documents and emails that Nielsen collected during his time at Ensign, the complaint says. He also provided information on Ensign's bank accounts and a list of employees whom officials should contact.

Nielsen told Ensign in a resignation letter dated Aug. 29 that his employment had become unworkable after his wife and children left the Mormon Church and asked him to follow them, according to a copy of the letter provided by Lars Nielsen. David Nielsen offered to continue working until Oct. 4.

Ensign's human resources director told him in a reply that managers had decided it would be best to terminate his employment Sept. 3.

"We appreciate your years of service and the contributions you have made for the church," the letter concluded.

The complaint describes an aggressive guarding of information by leaders at Ensign. Ensign employees "are trained to be especially sensitive" about data flowing outside the corporation, the complaint states. "Of course, all corporations need to guard their information, but the lengths that [Ensign] goes to borders on paranoia."

Only four senior Ensign executives are permitted to see the company's full financial statements, according to the complaint, and investment staff members may access information only on the Ensign assets relating to their own area of work.

Little has been publicly disclosed by Ensign, whose website address redirects readers to the church's homepage.

The company files abbreviated annual tax returns that report the taxes it paid on the small fraction of its investment activity that is taxable. The returns, which are publicly available, show that in some recent years, the company has reported losses of millions of dollars — a period in which, according to the complaint, a fuller accounting of its operations would have shown billions of dollars in profits.

This limited type of tax return requires Ensign to disclose the total value of its holdings, which the complaint asserts, has for years run to tens of billions of dollars. On those returns, Ensign has sometimes stated that it held $1 million, other times "more than $1,000,000," and it once left this section of the paperwork unfilled.

During his 2002 interview with a German reporter, Hinckley was told that several major denominations in Germany published records of their finances. Why not the Mormons?

"We simply think that information belongs to those who made the contribution, and not to the world," said Hinckley, who died in 2008.[2]

This recent *Washington Post* story shows some of the extreme effects of misinterpreting practical aspects of scriptural teachings. Here a church employee has declared himself a whistle blower, claiming that the LDS church has collected and is hoarding about $124 billion in tithing funds which it has not used for the charitable purposes for which it was contributed, most likely constituting a breach of fiduciary duty.

The excuse that the church was holding this massive amount in reserve to be used for contingencies at the Second Coming of Christ seems like an extremely weak and even laughable excuse for withholding that enormous amount of money from current member-intended charitable works. This excuse is especially weak since there is no way for us to know when that Second Coming might occur or whether our current society and its paper investment and ownership records and the underlying properties and processes would even survive such a potential uproar and calamity. It is more likely that all of those centrally collected paper resources would be lost. It would be much better to have those resources in the hands of the members, or to have used them for good purposes to prepare our society for something like the Second Coming.

The article itself quotes a church leader saying that the only real assets the church has is the faith of its members -- "When all is said and done, the only real wealth of the church is in the faith of its people" -- which seems to be an accurate statement, but the leaders have obviously not had the "faith" to put that philosophy into practice. The church members might indeed be considered a "walking charity bank" in the sense that these millions of individuals are the ones who ought to have these resources, since they actually have the power to preserve them through a crisis, who could then send some of those resources to the central church or to other places or projects based on the actual known needs.

A response

A lengthy bit of apologetics logic was quickly produced by a BYU professor. We might notice that as a direct or indirect employee of Brigham Young University, his professional position depends on the church being in existence and providing the money for his position. That puts him in the position of a more than slight conflict of interest. He does seem to know something useful about charitable organizations, but we must assume a heavy bias and a bit of non-objective blindness based on his station in and viewpoint on the world. We might notice that the church has put into reserve approximately one million times his annual salary, and he is happy to defend that long-term choice that clearly favors his personal financial future.

> **The $100 Billion 'Mormon Church' story: A Contextual Analysis**
>
> December 20, 2019 by AARON MILLER
>
> In an age inundated with headlines, the American public has perhaps become accustomed to sighing and shaking their heads with reports of corruption. So, when the headlines pointed at the Church of Jesus Christ this week ("Mormon Church accused of stockpiling billions, avoiding paying taxes" or "Mormon Church has misled members on $100 billion tax-exempt investment fund, whistleblower alleges"), the takeaway for many readers was likely clear-cut.

But, the story beyond the headline merits a closer look. As you may have read, a whistleblower alleged this week that the Church of Jesus Christ of Latter-day Saints' investment arm, Ensign Peak Advisors, potentially violated tax law by building a $100 billion investment fund, with minimal or zero "charitable" distributions. The whistleblower's report also alleges that the fund made two "illegal" distributions.

This article is an analysis of the allegations, the facts as I understand them, and the pressing questions many are asking regarding these and other issues related to Church finances. In my estimation, despite the allegations, the facts and applicable law suggest that the Church has not evaded taxes or done anything illegal or improper.

Many, however, will still wonder whether the Church should distribute more of its reserves to charitable causes, publish more financial information, or if such a large endowment should be taxed. There are many reasonable perspectives on these issues. Below I discuss the potential trade-offs, benefits, and costs associated with such decisions.

Are the Church's reserve funds illegal or somehow evading taxes?

For tax purposes, as an integrated auxiliary, the investment arm of the Church, Ensign Peak Advisors, is under no obligation to make minimum distributions. The allegations appear to stem from the whistleblower's misunderstanding of tax law. For unknown reasons, the whistleblower apparently didn't hire an attorney or a tax expert to help write this report.

One can only assume this is why so many of the conclusions in the whistleblower report diverge from the law. Not only does the whistleblower report misconstrue the definition of "charitable," but it also applies something called the commensurate test (explained below) in a way never before applied by the IRS, and it fails to give enough evidence to demonstrate that two alleged investment disbursements were in fact improper.

For starters, the federal tax code does not have a minimum disbursement requirement for what are called "public charities," a category of 501(c)(3) tax-exempt organizations. Churches are public charities by default.

There is a requirement that all 501(c)(3) entities carry out charitable activities that are "commensurate in scope with their resources." This ostensibly means that a charity cannot merely accumulate assets and remain a charity. The law does not set a fixed threshold for this though, and the IRS instead takes it on a case-by-case basis, applying the commensurate test very rarely. But, even by the whistleblower's own admission, each year the Church is in fact spending $6 Billion a year on its tax-exempt activities.

There is an interesting wrinkle in this case, though, that the whistleblower's claim relies on. Ensign Peak Advisors, the legal entity where the LDS Church holds these investments, is exempt as a separate 501(c)(3) Supporting Organization. (Notably, the whistleblower also disputes this status, but without directly addressing how Ensign fails to meet the legal definition. He instead focuses on the "spirit" of the status.) As a Supporting Organization, Ensign is an independent nonprofit. The whistleblower claims that this requires Ensign to pass the commensurate test all on its own – and not as part of the larger whole of the Church.

But according to the IRS's own definition, Ensign is also an "integrated auxiliary" managed by the Church, a legal treatment that combines their activities in certain ways. This is a critical detail that the whistleblower report only briefly mentions and seems to misunderstand.

If the Church directly held these investments, it would likely pass any legal tests without concern. Does it make a legal difference if Ensign does the investing for the Church as an integrated auxiliary? This difference—a relatively narrow and technical one—has never been questioned by the IRS or a court, according to Sam Brunson, a Latter-day Saint and Loyola law professor who specializes in tax-exempt organizations.

After looking at the facts and allegations involved, Peter J. Reilly, a non-Latter-day Saint CPA and tax specialist, observed in Forbes that "Ensign is not a private foundation. It is an integrated auxiliary of a church. And there is nothing in the tax law that prevents churches from accumulating wealth." Reilly reached out to Paul Streckfus, another tax expert who runs a trusted publication focusing on tax-exempt organizations. He too concluded that the "matter does not merit IRS attention."

Is saving $1 Billion a year for a "rainy day" fund wrong or abnormal?
What the whistleblower appears to be concerned about is the fact that the Church is investing $1 billion a year in an endowment fund and not distributing it or the interest earned. But, is building a reserve endowment illegal or wrong?

Maintaining large financial reserves is actually a common and encouraged practice among nonprofits and governments. Two similarly large organizations show somewhat how the IRS might consider the case. Both The Bill and Melinda Gates Foundation and Harvard University operate with endowments of around $50 billion, roughly ten times their annual budget. The IRS has not considered either one to be in violation of the commensurate test.

If the whistleblower numbers are correct, The Church of Jesus Christ is maintaining an endowment equal to about 16 times their annual budget, a ratio that is within typical practices for endowed 501(c)(3)s. Many private foundations annually distribute the minimum 5% of their total assets, making endowments equal to 20 times an annual budget very common. So, this practice of keeping a sizeable financial reserve is not likely to violate the commensurate test.

Why would the Church have a rainy-day fund?

Even if Ensign Peak were required to make distributions by law—and as mentioned above it appears that it is not—when the report says that Ensign Peak Advisors should be distributing its wealth for charitable causes, it appears to misunderstand what the law considers charitable.

Under the federal tax code, any religious purpose is a charitable one by definition, including saving against the Second Coming of Jesus Christ. Though thinly sourced, this was a rationale the whistleblower claimed that Ensign Peak Advisors was using to justify the endowment. As noted by Forbes commenter Peter Reilly, the IRS likely wouldn't question the legitimacy of this religious purpose.

Of course, the Church likely has many other religious reasons to have an endowment fund and has publicly stated that it saves and makes prudent investments to uphold spiritual teachings. Such a fund might be built to prepare for heavy growth in third world countries (especially as membership is trending toward the global south and slowing in places like the United States). They might keep such a fund to help, as it often does, after natural disasters that could come with greater frequency due to climate change conditions. A source with first-hand knowledge says the Church thinks about such considerations.

Obviously, rainy day funds are also typically built to prepare for possible future economic downturns. Recently, some state governments have been building sizable "rainy day" funds that together now total more than $70 Billion. Some have wondered if such funds are adequate in the event of another downturn, climate conditions, or other circumstances.

There are even more reasons the Church may want to hold large reserves. Given that major party politicians, and others like the whistleblower, have stated with greater frequency that they would like to see the Church and other religions lose tax-exempt status, this is yet another reason why such institutions might want large reserves. The Church, having had its property confiscated in the 19th century in both Missouri and Utah, also has a historical rationale for building especially large reserves.

What about the two alleged distributions, those must be illegal, right?

The whistleblower alleges that Ensign Peak made large distributions to bail out a failing insurance company and to help fund City Creek Mall. First, there's some question of whether Ensign Peak made the kind of payment to Beneficial Life Insurance that the whistleblower alleges. It's more likely that they invested in Beneficial Life.

This is, in fact, the purpose of Ensign Peak, to make investments in various equity or other financial instruments which will, in turn, generate profit to support the Church's efforts and mission. It's not clear how such investments would be improper. As the Deseret News reported, the whistleblower alleges "that Ensign Peak delivered $600 million to Beneficial in 2009. Beneficial made full disclosure to the Utah Department of Insurance that Deseret Management Corp., its owner, provided $594 million to Beneficial during the 2008 financial crisis to strengthen its balance sheet. Those public filings are on file with the Utah Department of Insurance and the payment was reported in two articles published by the Deseret News at the time. Since 2009, Beneficial has paid dividends of almost a half-billion dollars back to Deseret Management Corp., according to public filings at the Utah Department of Insurance."

The reporting continues: "The second payment challenged by the Nielsens (the whistleblower and his brother) was made as part of the Church's City Creek development in Utah's capital city. The Nielsens alleged that Ensign Peak Advisors improperly sent $1.4 billion from 2010 to 2014 to the Church entity funding City Creek, Property Reserve Inc. The Church did invest in the housing and parking elements of City Creek. Taubman Centers, Inc., a nationally recognized shopping center developer, owns and operates the shopping center."

The whistleblower says the mall investment came from tithing funds, which contradicts what Church leaders said publicly, thus they claim the Church misled its members. However, even if initial tithing funds were used (and there's no strong evidence available to claim that they were) there are good reasons that non-invested tithing funds might have been used as an intermediary step until invested assets could be liquidated at a prudent time. This claim, in other words, doesn't engage in a very sophisticated analysis with regard to how reserve funds and returns might be managed in accordance with sound financial stewardship.

Because investing assets is legal, the remaining issue is that a charity can only invest its assets as long as it doesn't provide what the law calls an "excess benefit" to particular people in the process. There is no evidence available or provided by the whistleblower, that these investments did this.

Last, an audit over any of these legal issues seems very unlikely. Congress requires the IRS to have a stronger case for auditing a church than for other nonprofits. This case doesn't seem to satisfy that. The size of the endowment, relative to total activity involved, is common. The two "improper" disbursements can be easily justified as investment activities. Despite all 74 pages in the report, there's just not enough there.

Are there other public policy concerns?

The technical, legal issues are not entirely the root of the controversy, though, even if the accusation is coming from a whistleblower. Not even the whistleblower limits the issues to tax law. The online version of his report is addressed not only to the IRS, but also Church leadership, members, Congress, and the general public of the United States.

It is clearly intended to raise policy and ethical issues, not just legal ones. Other questions are:

1. Should a church hold $100 billion that could otherwise be spent on helping those in need?
2. Should a church have the freedom to avoid transparency into its finances?
3 Should a church, especially a wealthy one, pay taxes like the rest of us?.

Should a church hold $100 billion that could otherwise be spent on helping those in need?

To answer question one—and taking the whistleblower figures at face value—it's worth asking how the Church got that much money. Reportedly, it did so by saving and investing about 14% of the annual tithing payments of its members. Turning $12 billion in 1997, plus adding $1 billion per year, would only require a 7–8% annual return to get to $100 billion by 2019. It is not an unlikely scenario. This strategy simply reflects an approach charities use to build an endowment—or what anyone should do to build their savings.

And here's the paradox likely unknown to most people: giving money away effectively is generally much harder than earning it. The problem is that people assume that all giving is good giving when that is not remotely true.

A recent study by my colleagues Curtis Child and Eva Witesman showed that in prosocial initiatives, people are prone to assume only good outcomes and not anticipate bad ones. This is despite the reality that unintended negative consequences and waste are a constant risk of philanthropic giving. Cutting edge organizations like GiveWell and ImpactMatters are tackling this very issue.

Distributing a huge amount like $100 billion in a way that has a reliable, positive impact would be very, very hard to do, and would require a kind of effort far beyond what people realize. The Gates Foundation in 2018 spent about $1 billion on operations to give away $3.7 billion. They are widely regarded as effective stewards of their assets and are having a commendable impact.

This isn't to say that the Church shouldn't do more than it already does, but to do it well would probably require increasing expenses for its staff and operations by $1–2 billion per year, which by the whistleblower's numbers would be a 30% budget increase.

This is in spite of the already-existing Latter-Day Saint Charities arm that has spent $2 billion since 1984 on a wide range of projects including clean water, refugee assistance, and disaster relief. And, once again, by the whistleblower's own estimates the Church is spending $6 billion on its total charitable, educational, and ecclesiastical efforts annually.

Expanding its efforts and spending—humanitarian or otherwise—isn't a change that could happen immediately, but would take years of cultivating expertise and relationships. It appears that over the past several decades that's precisely what the Church has been steadily doing: increasing its capacity for non-denominational humanitarian giving (in addition to its own internal Church welfare and other philanthropic efforts).

What the Washington Post article really tells us is that having a very large endowment is a relatively new phenomenon for The Church of Jesus Christ after over a century of financial strain. It undoubtedly has new lessons to learn in managing this opportunity. But immediately expecting a historically large and effective grantmaking engine is probably unreasonable.

Should a church have the freedom to avoid transparency into its finances and should it avoid "opening its books"?

What about the Church providing more transparency into its finances? Criticisms over transparency have dogged the Church for decades, particularly over its fiscal resources. Keeping these figures private from the public is entirely legal, a privilege Congress offers to churches in the spirit of the First Amendment. Disclosing this information would be a voluntary step.

There are of course reasons for Congress affording this privilege. Religions want the primary public focus to be its message, rather than its money. If people want to focus on money, that's their prerogative, but churches, understandably, may like to keep the focus elsewhere. Of course, as human nature dictates, the more something is kept secret the more people and the press want to focus on it.

There are also legal considerations. Many organizations believe that, if you're known to have money, you might become subject to frivolous lawsuits or solicitations of bribes by bad foreign actors in order to operate overseas. There are even fears—not unfounded—that missionaries in foreign countries could be kidnapped for ransom if Church finances are detailed. Of course, now that this information has been leaked, many of these concerns can't be put back into the bag, since the numbers and the scope of holdings are now understood to be large. But that doesn't mean the Church would want to assist in publishing its holdings to exacerbate such risks or provide exact figures that could create a certain kind of exposure.

No matter these other considerations, it's also the case that some simply don't believe that it's right for so much financial power to be shielded from public accountability. And many feel that transparency, when appropriately applied, is important and comes with many benefits, like the aforementioned factors of reducing fraud and engendering public trust. There are many American churches that voluntarily disclose annual financial reports to their parishioners. For reasons the Church indirectly explains, it chooses to keep its finances confidential. This is surely a trade-off they have repeatedly considered and will continue to weigh.

Despite the lack of detail, there is other evidence over many years that the money is not being used nefariously or illegally, as alleged. Ask any Church employee or lay minister, and they can describe at length the culture of financial controls and of treating Church funds as sacred—only to be used with prudence and great care. It's also fair to argue, as has often been said, that there are just too many CPAs and lawyers, internal and external, to let things get too far out of compliance.

Related to this, and arguably the most revealing is the fact that those who control these assets are not getting wealthy from them. Part-time volunteer Church leaders are not paid. Full-time Church leaders are given an annual stipend that is frequently much less than what they were earning prior to their ministry. It's speculated that some or many of the wealthier full-time leaders simply donate much or all of their money back to the Church. The lack of transparency, whatever its motivation, doesn't appear to be driven by greed.

Is asking the poor to tithe morally wrong?

The whistleblower's brother, who co-wrote and publicized the report, says that maintaining such a large endowment especially deceives the poor people who give tithing at great personal cost—the widow's mite praised by Jesus Christ. Why should they give when their gift isn't needed by the Church?

First, the brother doesn't acknowledge in the Washington Post article that the Church has one of the largest private welfare programs in the world, benefiting people in this exact situation. It's very common that low-income people give what they can in tithing, but then receive through a local leader rent money or food assistance well in excess of the tithing paid.

Tithing is a religious principle viewed as an act of faith and sacrifice to God. This is a principle with ancient, biblical roots. But there are also pragmatic benefits to tithe, even for those with little means. In his book, *Who Really Cares*, Arthur Brooks shares research showing that charitable giving, including religious giving, increases the health and happiness of the giver. One of the ways it does this is by inducing gratitude in the giver—a state of being that psychologists praise for its emotional and physical benefits. Giving even appears to increase future income, by an average of $4.35 for every dollar given. Brooks notes that these are gains *resulting* from charitable giving, not just correlated with them. How the donation is used does not seem to affect these outcomes for the giver.

In truth, the whistleblower's claim—repeated in the Washington Post headline and by many others—that the Church misled its member donors is not well supported. While some Church members do wonder about the need to tithe, the vast majority of Latter-day Saints primarily tithe as a personal sacrifice to worship God and offer thanks for his blessings in their lives. It is unlikely that many of them feel misled because the primary purpose was fulfilled the moment they donated.

One might hope that tithe payers would demand more transparency from their religious leaders if only to assure against fraud or waste. But Church members constantly see the results of their tithing in the form of new temples and chapels being built, budgets allocated for local congregations around the world, and large-scale disaster relief efforts in which they personally participate. Additionally, the Church is audited on a regular basis both internally and through external auditing firms. As far as many Latter-day Saints are concerned, the lack of fiscal transparency is overwhelmed by the rest of the evidence around them.

While some have expressed distress over the whistleblower revelations, many Church members have reacted to the Washington Post article with positive responses. Church leaders regularly encourage their members to follow prudent financial practices, avoiding debt and saving for the future. They see this endowment as the Church doing what it preaches.

Should wealth escape taxation because it's owned by a church?

That's a question that takes us to the United States Constitution itself. The Free Exercise Clause of the First Amendment guarantees freedom of religion from undue government burdens. And taxation is as fundamental a government burden as it gets. So, the question is whether a tax is truly justified.

This is an argument we've had for decades—one that goes beyond the federal income tax because churches are also generally exempt from property and sales taxes in every state. Even aside from First Amendment issues, the idea of tax exemption is that exempt entities create more value for a community than what the government could do in their place. That seems to be true of churches, including the Church of Jesus Christ. Strong evidence by a wide range of scholars indicates that regularly attending church services (of any kind) leads to better health, a stronger community bond, and more donations of time and money, including to secular causes.

What about just taxing the excess wealth of a church? If the money is just sitting around, why not have the government put it to better use?

The money, of course, is not just sitting around. It's actually invested in lots of business and markets which in turn fuel the economy. Additionally, the idea that the money is 'just sitting there' challenges the very idea of an endowment (and personal savings for that matter), which is to have resources in reserve for growth or unexpected shortfalls.

If a government system could reliably cover every shortfall and fund every growth opportunity in exchange for taxing away a surplus, there might be room for arguing to forbid endowments. But, given the current realities, there's little suggestion that such a plan would work since the federal government is running a significant deficit, and it's unlikely the government would bail out a church.

Why not tax huge endowments, where the nonprofits have more than they could ever need?

The federal government is currently testing the idea by taxing large university endowments. While that tax does not apply to churches, public concern may lead to that outcome (First Amendment issues aside). How churches, including the Church of Jesus Christ, spend their money may be a factor in this discussion.

But the issue here also invites comparing the billions of dollars controlled by the Church with the billions of dollars controlled by individual billionaires or elite private schools. There are interesting arguments that no person or group should control such wealth. But, surely there's at least some difference between a large church—that's funded by and accountable to its 16 million members worldwide—

and Jeff Bezos or others. It's not unreasonable to trust a church—dedicated to explicit charitable and ecclesiastical missions—more than a single billionaire focused on building a business or simply personal wealth.

All of this said, just the idea of a $100 billion endowment held by a church will still offend some people. For some, it appears to contradict the humility and generosity that religion claims to foster. But considering all of the above, this may be a judgment made without full context. Moreover, such abundance is a relatively recent phenomenon for the Church, and time will tell how its leaders budget Church funds in the years ahead. They at least deserve the opportunity to prove themselves to be trustworthy stewards, as by many well-accepted measures they have been up to now. There are no scandals to date involving fraud or personal enrichment by Church leaders, just strong concerns about their frugality and transparency.

In the meantime, Latter-day Saints can appreciate the impressive arc of a church that was once on the cusp of financial ruin, and now, thanks to faithful tithing and prudent management, appears to have all it needs and more to carry out what they believe is a divinely-appointed mission.

AARON MILLER
Aaron Miller teaches nonprofit management and ethics in the Romney Institute at BYU. He helps direct the Ballard Center for Social Impact and is the co-author of The Business Ethics Field Guide.[3]

This professor may be an expert on business ethics, but that is of questionable value here. To begin with, we should not be using business ethics but gospel ethics, which it doesn't appear that he knows much about. Perhaps this commentator agrees with me that the LDS church is first and foremost a business operation, and only incidentally and indirectly a religious operation, an alias or alternative identity it uses only for its worldwide religious franchise operations.

My main point is that, whatever the relationship might be between the LDS church and the US government, the LDS church has contaminated the gospel in such a serious way that its decision to take tithing money from its members on pain of loss of salvation has caused approximately $124 trillion in total damage, making the $124 billion in ineffective and untouched reserves as small as a fly speck in comparison, 1/1000th the size of the damage done. Without this self-centered and highly damaging tithing requirement, to be paid always and only to the central offices, I believe the gospel would already have spread to hundreds of millions of people around the world, spreading even faster than did Christ's original church, and a huge amount of the vast damage done to societies by these greedy secular/atheist governments would have been avoided, and we would have moved a very noticeable distance towards a gospel society, otherwise known as Zion.

In other words, the LDS church has adopted nearly all the mechanisms of the secular governments, with all the problems that causes. Its "tithing" system is just another layer of taxes, hardly distinguishable from the church/secular taxes in Europe and other places. The church thus supports the basic proposition of the "divine right of kings" whereby any ruling body might claim the power to tax to an arbitrary agree anyone it claims to rule over, by "right of conquest," so to speak, meaning the citizens are really slaves to that extent. Where people around the world are always seeking the maximum amount of freedom, here we have the LDS church defending the right of self-appointed government bodies to extract as much as they dare from their populace, just as the LDS church is doing.

On the topic of the relationship between the LDS church and the US government, what we really have here is two organizations which are doing all in their power to exploit their overlapping constituency. They both use the same strategy and tactics to extract money from their constituents. That makes them both partners in crime and competitors. The LDS church has obviously done everything in its power to stay on the good side of the US government and of every other government in the world as a way to avoid conflict of any kind with those organizations. The church leaders realize that at the point where the church might attempt to advance the gospel in almost any way, however small, that will put it in direct competition with totalitarian-thinking secular governments everywhere. There may be room for businesses to operate alongside governments, but there is very little room for principled religions to operate alongside governments.

The competition for hearts and minds is ever-present. Even a greedy government will be kind to a religion which is totally submissive to that government. Even the most foolish governments realize that they cannot govern people who do not have good morals and ethics, even while the governments hate the religious organizations that might instill those good morals and good ethics in their citizens. If a church is willing to become part of the state religion, as the LDS church has done, then they can be more assured of kind treatment by the government, perhaps concerning its tax exemption as a charitable organization, even though that near-total submission to the government may mean that their gospel mission is all but obliterated.

The first principle of the gospel, in my view, is freedom, and all of these secular/atheist/humanist organizations are put in place for the very purpose of restricting the freedom of citizens to the largest extent possible. That means that there can be no reconciliation between the gospel and dictatorial governments. That leads to the situation in the United States where the church is given billions of dollars by its members, where those members hope that the church will take steps to further the gospel and freedom in the world, but the church refuses to do any of that, leaving it with large amounts of money it is fighting to avoid spending in any way that would improve the society of any nation, which would also cause these secular/atheist governments to push back against the LDS church and its leaders. The church leaders want to lead a perfectly pleasant and carefree life, which would end if they were to actually take up gospel causes. We ought to have some "Christian crusades" going on at many levels, but it would be difficult to find anything that meets that description today.

Explaining it all one more time

The current church has contaminated the gospel and made it a toxic poison to the rest of the world. We might compare this to a major E. coli contamination of hamburger meat. That toxin has very emphatically stopped the gospel from spreading. To understand the scale of that situation better, we need to consider the actions and budgets of the federal government.

The federal government uses about 70% of its budget for mandatory spending (Social Security, Medicare, Medicaid, and loan interest payments), with 30% going to discretionary spending which mostly goes for the actual government operations including the Defense Department. If we say that the mandatory spending (Social Security, Medicare, and Medicaid) is about $3 trillion a year, and this social arrangement has been going on for nearly 100 years, the federal government has taken about $300 trillion from the populace and used it for what would otherwise be charitable purposes, which I consider to be a nongovernmental religious function. That $300 trillion is the amount of money, that has been taken by the United States government and mostly wasted on pensions/medical care, etc., that should have been used for religious purposes instead of for Satan's anti-freedom purposes. Taking that money has contaminated the ideology and practices of the entire society. And that is the amount of damage the LDS church and its self-centered behavior has caused. If the $300 trillion measure seems too high, then it is certainly at least $124 trillion in value.

As part of this complex and corrupt arrangement, we have in Utah a corrupt "Sanhedrin" of Mormon high priests who are willing to act consistently in what they see as their strong self-interest of supporting the church as a powerful economic institution that benefits them, warping the civil and criminal law of Utah to constantly reinforce the power and influence of the corrupted economic church. This especially includes law firms, accounting firms, legislators, government employees, etc. This church-inspired and church-controlled mafia or "Sanhedrin" makes it very difficult to get objective justice in Utah.[4]

Follow the money

"Follow the money" is always good advice in untangling complex or secretive operations. This revelation about the church's obsession about keeping all the money it receives, without doing anything of a charitable nature that might seem to compete with any secular government, tells us an enormous amount about the way the church views gospel principles today. The church has in effect reinstituted the law of Moses which was a tribal-based system which rarely went beyond the "seed of Abraham." It was a nearly static religious body, with massive ties and duties to the central headquarters. The church which Christ set up on the Earth was a nontribal system, suitable for anyone to use anywhere, encouraging the maximum freedom and the maximum Christian responsibility and service. That is an extremely appealing concept and system, and what the church has adopted is just as unappealing as the old law of Moses. That explains why the church is going nowhere today, and never will, until it moves back to the operational concepts of Christ's original church.

The August 2019 fraud class action suit

Another major action which took place in 2019 is the filing of a major fraud class action suit against the LDS church entitled *Gaddy vs COP (LDS).* The plaintiff and her lawyer allege that the church has knowingly taught false information to children concerning the origin of the Book of Mormon, the life experiences of Joseph Smith, etc., much of which supposedly has now been shown to be historically incorrect. This fraud case will likely be harder to understand and harder to prove than the IRS complaint about the massive reserves of money which have been withheld from a church purpose. The church's claiming that this money is being held in reserve to be used at the second coming of Christ or that it is being held in reserve because of the fear that the church will come under new levels of persecution, similar to some of its experiences in the past, may seem semi-plausible at first. However, on further consideration, those seem like very thin and foolish excuses. At the second coming of Christ it is more likely that all of these paper assets will disappear overnight and the church will have nothing to show for it. I believe the church is in a "use it or lose it" situation where holding this money in reserve basically means throwing it away for fear of the consequences of trying to spend it properly. On the "future persecution" aspect, rather than being a defense, having all of that value in liquid assets concentrated in one place makes it a very tempting target, meaning that any serious persecution would likely mean that all of those assets would be taken by someone else. This is exactly what happened in Utah in the 1800s when the federal government took over all the church's assets. The only defense in that case was to have the assets so widely distributed in advance that there was very little to be confiscated at the central church level. Having the federal government take over the Salt Lake Temple was probably of little value except to provide a hostage. Except as a ransom, presumably there was very little value the federal government could extract from that immovable stonework.

An article, apparently written by someone who is quite familiar with the case, summarizes the current status of the case as of October 11, 2019. The article includes links to the original Complaint in the case, the Motion to Dismiss filed by the LDS church, and the plaintiff's attorney's Opposition to Motion to Dismiss. There is also a link to the results of a 2013 survey concerning LDS member faith crises. This material should provide a window into this case for those who want a better understanding. There are also many other related resources on the Internet concerning this case, many linked to the name of the plaintiff's lawyer, Kay Burningham.[5]

Notes

1. See that and other similar observations at https://www.barrypopik.com/index.php/new_york_city/entry/capital_is_a_coward

2. https://www.washingtonpost.com/investigations/mormon-church-has-misled-members-on-100-billion-tax-exempt-investment-fund-whistleblower-alleges/2019/12/16/e3619bd2-2004-11ea-86f3-3b5019d451db_story.html, accessed Dec. 18, 2019. https://hosted-washpost.submissionplatform.com/sub/hosted/5df933e0825bc6503a766434

3. Aaron Miller, "The $100 Billion 'Mormon Church' story: A Contextual Analysis," December 20, 2019 https://publicsquaremag.org/editorials/the-100-billion-mormon-church-story-a-contextual-analysis/

4. https://www.thebalance.com/current-u-s-federal-government-spending-3305763

5. Gaddy v COP (LDS Church) Opposition to LDS Motion to Dismiss https://www.xmoresources.org/Gaddy-Opposition-to-Motion-to-Dismiss-Lawsuit-for-Fraud-Against-LDS-Church/?q=kbase&sid=X1570815831

Chapter 17

Are all living prophets given unbounded powers to alter the gospel?

[A new text will eventually be prepared for this chapter and the next, but for the moment, a pair of articles from 2017 will have to serve for these two chapters.]

Living Prophets:

Evaluating, Interpreting, and Managing Them

The LDS Church claims that having living prophets is one of its great advantages, theoretically allowing it to answer new questions and adapt to new circumstances, perhaps including the ability of the church members to absorb and live more complex teachings, perhaps based on their greater levels of education. "Living prophets" sounds like a great resource to add to a religious tradition.

But what are the legitimate and inherent powers of a living prophet? Is any living prophet empowered to completely rewrite or reinterpret the words of all the living prophets since the world began, including the words and writings of Christ himself? Unfortunately, that is the interpretation of the meaning of "living prophets" adopted by today's living prophets of the LDS church.

At a minimum, a prophet is simply someone who speaks concerning the Word of God. That person may take great care to never say anything which is not in accordance with the existing written scriptures, and could still be properly considered a prophet. At the other extreme, where a prophet is claiming the maximum possible interpretive power, he might simply try to cancel out and replace everything that has been said before him by others who claimed they were prophets.

So, one might ask, are there any built-in constraints that can prevent or avoid any improper deviations from existing scriptures, or other evidences of the mind of the Lord? The truth is, today there are no such built-in constraints operating, apparently by design. There might have been a case where there were independent "dueling prophets" who were speaking as living prophets at the same time, but were operating individually and without any external organizational constraints. It seems possible that these dueling prophets might say things that were inconsistent with each other, giving one the opportunity to straighten out the words of the other.

One might imagine that that could happen today when the LDS Church claims to have 15 "prophets, seers, and revelators." However, if there is one who is greatest among them, according to organization, like the president of the church, then there would probably be little or no room allowed for any public discord or difference, so that they would all speak with one voice, even if there are internal disagreements.

In other words, that leaves the members of the church to decide for themselves whether their "living prophets" are always speaking by the power of God, or whether they are sometimes speaking on their own behalf as men or even as speakers for some other god or philosophical tradition than the one they profess to speak for.

It is easy to demonstrate that the "living prophets" today, that is, those who have been given the title of prophet since 1820, and more noticeably since 1896, have cumulatively adopted enormous changes from what the scriptures tell us, often leaving unexplained these great and important deviations.

Our federal government and its experience over the 251 years it has been in existence, slightly longer than the 197 years that the LDS church has been in existence, offers many enlightening insights about the difficulties of taking a constitution, defined by geniuses, and seeing what happens after it has been run by far lesser men for about 200 years.

One of the obvious logical difficulties with declaring that someone is a living prophet, unconstrained by any pre-existing principles or formulas, is that that is the basic definition for a philosopher-king, a dictator, or a tyrant. Such a person might begin with claiming authority over religious matters and organization, but there is no reason to think that his ambitions will be limited to that one area of life. Typically, dictators begin as warlords, and then add a suitable "warlord religion" and propaganda mill to help maintain their political power and to extend it, hoping to exercise some level of mind control. But it really doesn't matter whether a totalitarian leader began as a religious leader or as a warlord, if the process ends up in the same place.

So how do you tell whether a living prophet is being completely true to his assignment? We are told that God will not let our prophet lead us astray, but how is that to be enforced, or how are we to know? Will God strike him dead if he makes any significant mistake? There are supposedly some minor examples of that in the Scriptures (remember Ananias and Sapphira, King Herod, Acts 5:1; 12:22-23), but I know of none today. And, in the case of the original church's morphing into the Roman Catholic Church, the church obviously went completely off the deep end, and became anti-gospel, but I have never read of any popes or would-be popes being struck down by God for leading people astray.

A government analogy
The judicial branch, topped by the Supreme Court, which is one of the three branches of the federal government, is an interesting example of what has happened to an autonomous and somewhat self-defining governmental institution. Theoretically, the Supreme Court can be constrained by the Congress, but that seems never to have actually happened. Near the beginning of the Republic, the Supreme Court declared that it could nullify congressional acts based on claims of unconstitutionality, putting itself in the driver's seat, instead of the other way around, and no one has seriously challenged that early assertion of superior power. As a result, the Supreme Court has essentially declared itself a third legislative body which operates completely independently from the two legislative bodies that make up the Congress.

The political liberals in our country have discovered that by shopping for sympathetic judges at the entry level, the district level, and carefully considering the ideologies of the nine justices on the Supreme Court, they can get much "legislation" passed into law, even binding state law, which neither the federal Congress nor the state legislatures would ever be able to pass and enforce. This has made the US Supreme Court a law unto itself, dominating the federal government and the state governments on many important legal issues.

The most basic ideological issue is whether to interpret and enforce the Constitution based on its original intent, or to throw aside any attempt at divining original intent and just use the individual political attitudes of the current judges so that the Constitution becomes a "living document," meaning it has almost no binding significance. This is essentially ripping up the document that was the basis for our new Republic in the first place. That obviously strikes at the foundation of our political union and our original compact, but that rarely seems to be of concern to the Marxism sympathizers on the court.

Some mechanism of impeachment or some legislation passed by the federal Congress might be able to correct some of the worst excesses of the Supreme Court, but that seems never to have happened nor is it likely to happen in our society which is approximately equally divided between the liberal Marxists and the conservative constitutionalists.

The "LDS Supreme Court"
It seems useful to think of the LDS top leadership as the "court of the living prophets" who would be well advised to function very much like the US Supreme Court. That Supreme Court only exists because it was defined and implemented by a grand political covenant called the U.S. Constitution. Since its very existence is based on that critical founding document, the US Supreme Court ought to have the greatest respect for its content and intent, although it does not always do so.

Like the US Supreme Court, the "LDS Supreme Court" is set up to operate as a totally autonomous body. But in order to justify its position and its power, it ought to be completely respectful of and controlled by the gospel Constitution, the Scriptures and other church history, which defined and authorized it in the first place. But, as with the US Supreme Court, which can have faithless judges, the LDS Supreme Court can also have its faithless judges who think that their individual will and opinion and convenience should override all other prior events and opinions and considerations.

As a side excursion, it might be useful here to notice that the LDS top leadership have combined the executive, legislative, and judicial functions of a world government into one body. The dangers of a single body holding all those powers, with no separation of powers, was duly noted in the debates leading up to the U.S. Constitution, presented as a solution to this need for a separation of powers to avoid the tyranny which is essentially unavoidable over the long term when all powers are placed in the hands of one or a few men. Today's LDS Corporation sole gives all powers to a single individual without the need to even consult with anyone else, let alone seek permission.

In practice, it appears that the "legislative" functions of the 15 can be kept quite secret, and the "judicial" functions of the 15 can be kept quite secret, and only the smallest aspects of the "executive" functions of the top leaders need to be revealed to the public, as when a new building or a new program is announced. It is a strange situation indeed when the legislative, judicial, and executive functions of the federal government can be very open and accessible to the public, and where that transparency is aided by armies of investigative reporters operating as intended under the First Amendment, but the government of God is a sealed book, with dire penalties for anyone who tries to understand what is actually happening inside the Church Office Building. In the days of Paul the apostle, he declared that "this thing [the restoration of the gospel] was not done in a corner," but today EVERYTHING is done in a corner where that is at all possible. (Acts 26:26). The recent news of the Church keeping at least $100 billion in liquid assets comes to mind.

A religious "two state solution" to a long-standing problem?
How do the LDS members rein in an out-of-control set of living prophets? There is no obvious way for that to happen short of ceasing to support the physical empire they have built. Theoretically, that requires one to "risk their salvation" by being unable to hold a temple recommend for not paying tithing. However, the church has deviated so far from the scriptural norm that the burden ought to be placed on THEM to demonstrate that they even still hold the authority they claim to hold. The Roman Catholic Church lost their authority at some point, and, for all we know, that authority has been lost again in our own time, for the exact same reasons, after a similar 200-year period. As seen in at least two other cases, where Christ restored the gospel personally in Jerusalem and in the New World, the whole religious enterprise eventually disintegrated. In the case of the Jerusalem/Roman church, perhaps the members had no way to discipline and restrain their leaders/prophets, and perhaps that is a partial explanation for that church's demise. It appears we are on the cusp of that same thing happening again, apparently for all the same reasons.

It appears that unless the general membership of the church is willing to organize themselves separately from the current leadership and take action to greatly constrain and discipline the current leadership, the current church organization will soon expire itself, mostly being pulled apart by violently disagreeing factions within the current "big tent" church which tries to represent everyone, meaning that it actually represents no one, no one but the headquarters themselves.

An interesting article published May 29, 2017 essentially argues that when the church leadership goes along enthusiastically accepting all the progressive leftist policies of the current federal government, and someone states a more traditional and conservative opinion, that person can be accused of being a bad Mormon for not following their leaders. In other words, at least according to the writer of the article, the revealed message of the living prophets is that the church is to always stay in tune with political Babylon, and anyone who dissents must be considered an apostate. That seems like the perfect path to another Roman Catholic Church.[1]

Obviously, these kinds of differences of opinion cannot go on very long until the church will naturally divide itself into two or more factions, one which is fashionably politically liberal, and one or more subdivisions that accept traditional morality, including the best rules for political relationships, at least one of those groups specifically adopting the principles of the U.S. Constitution which have been incorporated by reference into our existing Scriptures.

All of this kind of thinking points to the need for a "constitutional convention" for the LDS Church itself, where leaders either agreed to return to the original principles of the scriptures, or the members divided themselves up into subgroups and separate churches according to their own opinions, something which is the essence of freedom of religion as described in the U.S. Constitution. In other words, it would be out of order for the current church leadership to try to claim any governmental or scriptural basis on which to forbid church members from choosing to associate with and cooperate with those who agree with them on basic ideologies and morals.

Notes

1. "Mormon blogger trumpets alt-right racial views, but is out of tune with her religion," May 29, 2017 http://www.sltrib.com/home/5116879-155/mormon-blogger-trumpets-alt-right-racial-views

When Is A Prophet A Prophet?:
Is It Real Revelation Or Subtle Administrative Overreach?

One of the commonly expressed ways that church members can know that their leaders are acting under God's direction is that they can receive their own testimony of the value and correctness of any change. But, for the last 120 years, many of the most critical changes to doctrine and policy have happened in secret, or at least without notification of the intended changes, without any explanation given to the public, and certainly without the membership being allowed to vote on it. Any legal or practical consequences of "common consent" behavior have been dead for about 100 years, at least as concerns church headquarters.

How can someone have a testimony of a doctrinal or policy change if they don't know about it or the consequences have not been explained to them?

It seems that the minimum of fairness requires that whoever is the current head of the church should explain carefully each change that is proposed and implemented. The living prophets should be expected to list all the issues which anyone looking at the situation might raise, and to deal with all those issues.

This is what the US Supreme Court does. It has no armies or clerks or police to back up its decisions. It must rely on the logical power of its decisions if it wishes to maintain respect and compliance among all the people for the decisions it makes.

In our case, the prophets have a lot of catching up to do. Hardly any important matter during the last 120 years has been dealt with openly in public – with members notified, fully informed, and given an opportunity to cast their vote, where appropriate.

It may be useful to expand the US Supreme Court analogy. The Supreme Court justices are a fairly close analog to religious prophets, as they are empowered to scan the universe for philosophical insights supposedly beyond the powers of ordinary men, and are given great powers to enforce their insights in the practical world.

We have the interesting case of the infamous *Roe v Wade* decision. We find out after the fact that the entire decision was a fraud perpetrated upon the court and on the nation, and yet the case still stands, in the face of a continuing series of challenges, a continuing lie maintained by the fanatical power-seeking behaviors of the very influential political left. The subject person, the plaintiff, was not seeking an abortion, so she could not be denied it, and so there was no issue to be adjudicated. That person did not have standing to sue for something she did not want and was not denied. This set of actions was all based on the gross misbehavior of the attorneys involved who were willing to lie to the courts and to the nation to accomplish their self-assigned highly controversial political mission.

Naturally, the Supreme Court did not bother to admit and explain clearly that they were taking over the legislative powers and administrative powers of all the states in making this declaration of this new "right." Apparently, in their virtual legal universe, if one can make something a "right," conceptually adding it to the original Bill of Rights, then that naturally trumps all state and federal law and no other clear explanation is needed. The levels of fraud willingly perpetrated by the plaintiff's attorneys and by the Supreme Court are truly breathtaking.

The Constitution reserves to the states all powers not specifically given to the federal government. This *Roe v Wade* decision was in direct contravention of that aspect of the Constitution. It was a naked power grab, forever delegitimizing the court itself in the eyes of at least half of the citizens of the United States. As evidenced by the many states who have since legislated very serious constraints on that sweeping decision, the issue was not settled, and by its very nature could never be settled, by a pronouncement of a few staunchly committed Marxists/statists on the Supreme Court.

Switching back to the religious realm, we might wonder whether if the prophets chose to make a naked power grab, and also conveniently invented some new theology to justify that power grab, would or could those actions serve to delegitimize the prophets in the minds of the members, and perhaps in the mind of God? Would that equal a loss of priesthood authority, including the power to perform all ordinances necessary for salvation? These are live questions in the situation where we seem to find ourselves today.

Because of the dangers of making long-term errors in the area of religion, one might expect that the living prophets would go to great lengths to make sure that they do not deviate from the proper course, including avoiding every possibility of even giving an appearance of evil. Events caused by inexperience or bad judgment would need to be quickly rectified, the church headquarters itself accepting repentance as a recurring activity, but none of that concern for crystal-clear accuracy seems to be part of the traditions at church headquarters. The leaders might personally take great care to not be seen alone with a woman who is not their wife, lest the members get the wrong impression. As with the wife of Caesar, they must always be beyond reproach in these practical situations. The question then becomes how they can wander into disreputable areas of theological thought without their personal alarm bells sounding. They would never go to a city's red-light district, but they seem perfectly comfortable letting a little Marxism or atheism affect their thought patterns.

Especially if there is money or political or economic power involved or affected by some decision-making process conducted by the living prophets, then the members would be completely justified in being suspicious and requesting a complete explanation. On the other hand, if there are no apparent options for some of the prophets to have any personal or general practical effects, then there may be little or no basis for member suspicions.

It always seems useful to remember that Christ went to extreme lengths to make sure that neither he nor any of his disciples had even the slightest economic or political power over men. The only way to be safe from the temptation of these worldly influences was to own and control nothing except the clothes on their back, and always remain subject to the charity of the people and the generosity of God.

Testimony versus blind faith

If one does not have enough information on which to base a solid testimony, then all one is left with is blind faith. Although blind faith can give the leaders some room to experiment, it can also be quite dangerous by allowing the leaders to veer very far off course without any obvious correcting mechanism. The blind faith of the last 120 years has gotten us very far off course, so far that it seems almost impossible that we could ever get completely back on track.

Blind faith, once betrayed, is almost impossible to reestablish

It seems perfectly plausible that many of those who are objecting to the church today are coming upon critical policy questions that they never heard of before, and they often make the point that much of church history is news to them. Perhaps what they are really saying is that they thought they were safe in having blind faith in their leaders who seemed to be so thoroughly supported and trusted by those around them, so that they need not spend any of their own time investigating the behavior of the living prophets, but could treat them as a reliable force of nature, such as gravity, which is perfectly predictable, and they could safely go on about their lives with only minimal attention to concern about the truths embedded in religious matters.

Suddenly these church members find out the frightening truth that the church headquarters is exactly like every other man-made organization on the Earth. It has its own agenda of manipulating and exploiting all other persons and organizations in society and has to be watched carefully for trickery and misbehavior. The one thing they thought was perfectly safe, all of a sudden is not so safe.

In the normal marketplace, the law tells us to "let the buyer beware." There is every imaginable kind of fraud or error or mistake which can occur in the marketplace of things or ideas, and in most situations, the buyer is well advised to be quite suspicious and careful and to only purchase or accept something they have thoroughly examined and evaluated first.

It is quite a shock to discover that a member would be wise to maintain an arms-length competitive relationship with church headquarters, carefully examining every product or bit of counsel they offer. The tendency among members is to assume that the church leaders only have the members' best interest at heart in everything they do. Our Scriptures tend to support the belief that church leaders will always act in good faith as leaders of a people, a modern Israelite tribe, even sacrificing their own interests upon occasion for the benefit of the members. But what if they are found to NOT be acting in good faith in such a role, but, like all other humans, are always looking to their own interests first?

How does one heal that enormous and legitimate loss of faith, once it happens? In our situation today, it would require a truly heroic effort.

The truth is that the leaders have operated in a stealth mode for about the last 120 years. They have played the empire-building religious entrepreneur (some might say robber baron) as they have showed the minimum of respect to all the prophets who went before, including that great prophet Christ himself, as they have excluded or rewritten whole sections of the Scriptures, including the Bible, the Book of Mormon, the Pearl of Great Price, and the Doctrine and Covenants. Each of these rewritings ought to be explained in great detail. It is not enough for someone to offer what appears to be their opinion in a church talk, even a General Conference talk, and then claim that that unsubstantiated opinion is binding Revelation on the entire church, subject to no objection or discussion. Without a public vote of the members, or an extremely clear statement by the leaders, how is a member supposed to know what is homily and what is Revelation?

Here is a road to hell, paved by good intentions, if there ever was one, and this deplorable situation is not likely to fix itself. Elder Holland has expressed anger at the members' lack of sufficient blind faith, but he seems to offer no path back to earlier times where the leaders were more comfortable and unchallenged.

Just as the Supreme Court has produced a medium-sized library full of decisions over its about 250 year history, with many of those entries being extremely lengthy and detailed, the church owes its members and the world the same kind of issue-specific discussions of changes made to church policy and practice and doctrine so that a member could seek his own knowledge and testimony on an issue if he so wished.

It is ridiculous that members and nonmembers can both say that the LDS church does not have a fixed theology, simply because the living prophets can change anything at any time. A more precise database and formulation of church beliefs would be the basis for a truly exhaustive treatise on LDS theology, something which is sorely lacking today. Honestly, how can the church declare itself to be the true church, when it cannot even fully explain its own beliefs?

As an example of an early stealth operation, when Wilford Woodruff decided that the Law of Moses tithing concept was going to be reintroduced and radically changed and enforced in a new way, eventually leading to the use of coercion and a unique kind of spiritual extortion to collect tithing at the central offices from the members, on pain of their losing the benefit of their temple covenants, those built-in tendencies should have been noted and fully explained. But, of course, no one can actually explain that with a straight face when the issues are clearly pointed out. That is why all these important things were done in secret without ever notifying the world as might be done in a government economic regulation proceeding, and certainly never taking comments and never offering a decision, a clear decision, as the Supreme Court might do after receiving briefs from all interested parties.

In other words, in the Supreme Court we have a perfect example of the procedure which the prophets should follow, but the prophets have not followed that. They have preferred to operate in secret, always a very questionable religious practice. "[T]his thing was not done in a corner" -- to quote Paul the apostle, speaking of the restoration of the gospel in his time, (Acts 26:26) -- but in our time changes to it HAVE been done in a corner.

The Joseph Smith papers versus the never-created papers
Joseph Smith went to extreme lengths to record his experiences with the heavenly world and with the practical world so that church members and leaders would be able to learn and understand the gospel as it was presented to Joseph Smith and through Joseph Smith. However, it appears that many of the prophets that followed him were a great deal less intent on recording and making public critical events that could affect the content and trajectory of the church.

The Journal of Discourses in 26 volumes proved to be a pretty good substitute for a continuation of a more formal church history, simply because almost every conceivable topic of interest to the church members was discussed in general conference during those years. Whether it was national politics that affected the saints or more individualized spiritual matters, almost everything was discussed in that forum. The various speakers, especially Brigham Young, would present their thoughts and feelings and plans, and explain the reasons. In order to survive, the Saints had to be successfully acting as a group on a wide variety of topics, and there was no better way to inform everyone and seek their allegiance and their cooperation than through these discourses.

Apparently, since we are now under no threats, and the leaders only need our money and not our physical defensive powers as actual soldiers, there is now no reason to keep us acting as a cohesive group to defend ourselves and our leaders. This is a little bit like Stalin changing his policy on the church in Russia, seeking to use religion and loyalty to the motherland to improve the defense of his beleaguered country then under German attack. In the earlier more peaceful times, Stalin was happy to be blowing up churches and generally subverting and destroying the influence of religion on the Russian citizenry. In other words, in our peaceful times, social cohesion appears to be of minimal value.

It seems likely that almost everything of importance that was discussed and decided and done by the church leaders has been recorded in some form or another and exists in church archives. However, the strong tendency has been over the past 120 years to keep all the important discussions and decisions and actions as secret as possible and only inform the members of those things that the church's hired public relations professionals think that the church members need to know. There has developed a two-class system, an us-versus-them attitude, where the concerns and the events of the church headquarters are one world and what the members are told is a completely different world. Once upon a time there was such a thing as a Mormon people, where the leaders and the members were all engaged in the same enterprise. But gradually church headquarters and the membership have gone their separate ways and the membership became just a group of clients or a vague constituency to the central headquarters managers.

At this point, allowing the members to be involved in any important decisions would just muddy the waters and constrain the freedom of the church leaders to do whatever they wish.

The church magazines have become a place for happy talk, not any serious administrative matters. A house organ could serve to let church members know about all the important affairs of the kingdom as they arise, as was true in the time of Joseph Smith and Brigham Young, or that house organ could also become just a carefully selected collection of fluff that becomes almost a sales brochure or a propaganda rag.

The conference talks have been largely reduced to homilies, or a social advice column, where serious church concerns and strategies have no place. Even the doctrines taught there are usually greatly watered down. For example, nothing is said these days about the current plague on our society of atheistic philosophies, including evolution, apparently lest those in control of the thought and opinion centers of our society be offended.

There are many people besides the 15 top leaders of our church who care a great deal about how the gospel can and should be managed in our time. That is one of the great untold stories of our time. The going forth of the gospel to fill the earth ought to be almost an obsession with the church leaders, including describing things which were tried which were either successful or failed. But this administrative history of the Church, and any related strategies and opportunities or threats, are kept as deep dark secrets. No errors can ever be admitted. If a church member, not of the top 15, is interested in the detailed affairs of the kingdom, it has been declared that it is simply none of their business.

This means that there are millions of able practical and spiritual managers who are kept in the dark and could not coordinate their personal activities with those of the church even if they wanted to. Like all bureaucracies, the church headquarters bureaucracy keeps many secrets, since keeping secrets is one of their main sources of power. If no one knows what they're doing, there are many things they could do that they could otherwise not get away with. At the federal government level, much of what is "classified" is kept secret for the very reason that it would be embarrassing to those involved. "National security" very often gets confused and mixed up with "job security" and personal power for those who are on the government payroll and are misusing their positions in various ways.

The church ought to be sensitive to that particular form of bad behavior, and take steps to make sure that it doesn't happen there, but it appears to happen there just as much as in our federal government, if not more. Our laws about First Amendment rights are actually much more effective in the political realm than they are in the religion realm. At least investigative reporters are not usually charged with heresy and apostasy (a good medieval Catholic technique – as in the Inquisition) if they seek out embarrassing and inconvenient secrets of government leaders.

Keeping lots of secrets is something that a private corporation would feel perfectly justified in doing as they plan their profit-making activities in a world of competition. But there should be very little secret-keeping in a public government or in the church of Christ. The very fact that all those secrets are kept by the Church today is a strong indication that it sees itself as a small closely held group of leaders, in constant potential conflict with its membership "political and economic" constituency and everyone else in the world. That is certainly not the way one builds a movement and a people, although it is a way of pursuing self-aggrandizing behavior, probably wrongfully imagining that one can build great personal power through that mechanism. But it is exactly that building of great personal power in the temporal world which is not part of the gospel. We certainly did not find Christ measuring his success by the size of the worldly bureaucracy he could build up.

Are the living prophets weaning us from the Scriptures?

Have we somehow found a way to become the first post-scriptural Christian church on the planet, easing toward something perhaps like the Unitarian Church which I am told believes in everything and nothing at the same time? I was once asked to prepare a lesson for priesthood meeting, and was somewhat shocked to see that the references listed at the end of the conference talk consisted of five citations to the talks of other general authorities. Not a single Scripture appeared there, although there were a few scriptural citations sprinkled throughout the talk itself.

This alerted me to the possibility that we might be drifting even further off the path than I had imagined. Are the church leaders and their clerical support staffs actually trying to create a separate bubble of religious wisdom, completely derived from and extracted from and separate from the Scriptures? That seems to be what they are doing as a result of the correlation program. If it is just too difficult to manage a church which has deviated to a large extent from the Scriptures we were originally given, and difficult questions keep arising about the doctrinal drift, one creative solution might be to simply declare all the Scriptures obsolete, and replace them with an online database which is infinitely malleable and completely subject to incremental correlation.

The Catholics achieved a similar result in a non-information age by making sure that no one had a Bible to read. If only the priests could read Bibles, then the priests could say anything they wanted without fear of contradiction. If people are continually noting the inconsistencies between the Scriptures and the correlated gospel as it is presented today, then why not simply break free from the ancient Scriptures and create an entirely new and internally consistent religious database or creed, something that would look a great deal more like a typical Protestant church might subscribe to today, with all the unusual and inconvenient doctrines blotted out?

In the case of the conference talk which only cited other conference talks, it might be difficult for a member to determine whether or not there were any new teachings or doctrines discussed in that conference address. The very fact that there was very little scriptural logic included in the talk might alert one to an attempt by a general authority to deviate from the Scriptures without making it too obvious. In this particular case, I did not notice any such thing, but then I was not focused on that possible issue either.

As a helpful study aid, every new conference address might be required to certify whether or not they intend to be introducing any new doctrines or practices. That would assist any serious student of the Scriptures in questioning any specific assertions and perhaps seek clarification if it appeared that some change of policy is claimed or implied.

Where does faith come from? How is it established?
In the times of Joseph Smith, when Joseph Smith had regular consultations with heavenly beings, and shared those consultations with numerous other people, sometimes hundreds or even thousands of other people, as in the case of the experiences at the Kirtland temple, it is obvious on its face that these things are approved by the heavens. When those kinds of widely known and spectacular heavenly influences are no longer commonplace, then at least the constitutional processes are honoring all the prior Scriptures and Prophets and Christ himself by explaining a change, at least in that situation a person can receive their own testimony that the proper actions were taken.

Otherwise, as we have seen, without this clear brake on the impulses of man to take actions for their own convenience, there is no reason for church members to have blind faith in their leadership. Blind faith is a very dangerous thing, and it is not part of the Gospel, at least as to new policy pronouncements and actions by our leaders.

The current leaders owe their respect to all prior prophets and Scriptures which have been compiled and retained at such great personal and financial cost.

The idea that a serious student of church history and theology can say that the concept of living prophets completely obliterates any concept of theology is simply outrageous. If that is true, as it seems to be, then it is beyond outrageous. It is itself a form of apostasy, or at least a matter of extreme carelessness.

I believe the very idea that Mormons have no theology, but only a history, is an enormous stain on the history of the Church. It is said that the Mormons cannot have a stable theology because of the continuous wildcard options of having "living prophets." But we should notice that having no fixed theology offers the opportunity for leaders to veer off the path for their own convenience, as has indeed happened.

In other instances, when the Twelve are defining apostasy to mean any deviation from their commands, as though they were firing rebellious employees, and then refuse to explain themselves, and even use the subterfuge of requiring local leaders to act in their stead "spontaneously," they only compound the illegitimacy of their decisions and their doings. These local officers are probably operating under the implied threat of themselves being subject to a church court because of their lack of obedience. That kind of fear and coercion has no place in the church.

The term is extortion for what the church is doing on the issue of tithing and temples. It is a clear crime against the Scriptures and there should be no great surprise that there is a great deal of dissent and discord among church members and those who have already left.

If they want to heal this ongoing schism, this rolling schism, then they need to start over at the beginning and explain themselves and make the corrections. Obviously, it is extremely unlikely that they are going to explain themselves and make those corrections because they have become accustomed to considering themselves unchallenged monarchs in this particular realm.

We have lawyers and even Supreme Court justices among the Twelve who are going along with this charade and who ought to know better, Elder Oaks being a specific one who ought to realize that what they are doing is not justified.

Every one of the deviations which I have identified elsewhere needs to be fully explained in Supreme Court form. Of course, it *cannot* be explained convincingly in that form, indicating that it is a fraud which has been perpetrated upon the members and the world. Unless the church leaders are willing to repent and repair this last 120 years of damage, the church will certainly remain as crippled as it is, if it does not in fact disintegrate because of all the built-in subterfuge and lies and bad policy.

To regain and maintain legitimacy for now and for the long haul, they will have to invent a new form of church history. Joseph Smith took as much care as he could to record the revelations and the situations and the reasons for them. That mostly ceased after his death. That intellectual history, that policy history of the Church, needs to be reinstituted and brought up to date and all errors corrected before we continue on. Obviously, that would make an enormous change to our current organization. A few staff from outside might be commissioned to write this very history and react to comments and offer decisions. But this payback is awful. Catching up for 120 years is an enormous effort, but the church cannot go on without doing it.

We should not have to be satisfied with a vague history and an incomplete

and undecided theology.
The church needs to make itself very clear on a whole host of issues so that its history and theology are kept perfectly in sync and in tune at all times because of the explanations which are provided and comments are taken and dealt with.

Perhaps this needs to be in a new blog form where church members can comment, and the brethren will be duty-bound to respond appropriately. Joseph Smith labored very hard on his history, but today's leaders apparently can't be bothered. That might be a sufficient discipline. It should be. This century of secrecy and implacability must end. We have a weeping God but we have an implacable leadership who has assumed the monarchical attitude of "never apologize, never explain." That is not a Gospel attitude or behavior.

The apostles are ordinary men
They may be unusually good men, but they are still just men. They do not become superhuman beings just because they are chosen and ordained as apostles. They entered the world like anyone else with no recollection of their life before this. All they can have in their head is what they have learned during this life. If they have gazed into heaven for 5 minutes, as Joseph Smith spoke about, then they would know more than anyone here on earth. But I don't know that any of the men today even claim that they have gazed into heaven for 5 minutes.

They are subject to all the same foibles as any other human. If they are given unusual opportunities to have physical or religious power or to change policies, they would be really unusual people if they did not bend to those forces. Most especially, over the last 120 years, there have been a large number of incremental changes, perhaps none large enough to destroy the church, but the accumulated effect has been very powerful.

Is God less tolerant of error today?
Apparently God WILL let the leaders lead us astray, simply because he obviously has. He has done it before. I don't know why he would change the basic rules in our day. I don't know of any mass deaths concerning the Roman Catholic Church being set up. Popes may have died through violence, but it was from the violence of their earthly competitors.

Apparently God is quite tolerant, to the point of there being no immediate personal consequences for serious deviation. If the opposite had been true, then Wilford Woodruff would have been struck dead when he first decided to take tithing for personal use.
It may sound nice that the Lord will never let us go astray, and it may sound nice that Daniel had a good prediction and prognosis for us, but that is not in

fact the way the Lord works.

In fact it may be a form of deception to quote these kinds of scriptures in support of building a religious empire which might otherwise obviously carry the risk of failure, as has happened before. Those scriptures should not be used to encourage people to support leaders no matter what they decide to do, even if they indulge in a kind of spiritual extortion.

Two Supreme Courts

Although the Supreme Court has adopted a fairly moderate level of self-discipline, this self-imposed practice of explaining the decisions they make, notice that the court has still gradually veered far off the constitutional path in many areas of the law, especially in their lack of respect for state's rights and in their overly aggressive agreement with the expansion of federal powers. The *Roe v Wade* and Affordable Care Act (ACA) cases are examples. As a practical matter, the only discipline or punishment the Supreme Court justices might experience for their misbehavior is simply the social opprobrium they would receive and deserve for moving so far away from the original intent of the Constitution. The Constitution was designed by geniuses, but it has been often interpreted by idiots, often by those who are living today who subscribe to the philosophies that the Constitution was specifically created to counteract, especially including the monarchist or dictatorial or totalitarian attitudes of King George the third.

In a similar fashion, the LDS living prophets have gradually veered very far off the gospel constitutional path, the path of the Scriptures, and more general philosophies consistent with the Scriptures, which we might call theology. Almost certainly they have moved much further than they probably would have gone if they had faced strong pressure from the members to explain their conclusions and reasoning at every step of the way for any changes they introduced. At the top of the list are issues concerning tithing, paid ministry, freedom, evolution, education, etc.

The existence of these major deviations should make it easy to understand why the church headquarters is so committed to maximum secrecy on every issue and at every level. They would have a potentially explosive situation on their hands, perhaps even a massive scandal, if church members ever realized how far off the path the church headquarters has wandered on a very long list of important issues.

I assume that observation summarizes the overwhelming bulk of members' objections to the current church leaders these days - that they explain very little and hide a great deal. They occasionally talk about transparency, but their compliance with that transparency concept seems very minimal and appears to only be done with great reluctance in an attempt to lessen outside pressures. Obviously, in this spring-loaded situation, real transparency could lead to too much general knowledge which could result in the kind of explosion and scandal I just mentioned. I'm sorry to say that it appears that a good scandal is exactly what the church needs right now to cleanse it and get it all the way back on the track it should have been following for the last hundred years.

To rub salt in the wound on this issue of transparency, the current church leaders often behave as though they consider themselves as having monarchical powers, the divine right of kings to rule over the members and claim their time and resources as a matter of right. The monarchist attitude of "never apologize, never explain" seems to be their style on all things administrative.

How can our theology not be stable?
If God and the eternal gospel are unchanging, how can our theology not be stable? Is it really only our understanding which is flawed and incomplete?

It seems to me that our theology should not be changing like the weather on a daily basis, or even with the seasons, on an annual basis, or even like climate change which might move around on the charts over the decades or the centuries. Without degenerating into a mass of detailed laws like the old Law of Moses, the essentials of our theology still ought to be set in stone, something like the 10 Commandments. We should not be waking up some morning in the middle of our lives and finding out that the gospel we learned when we were children has been gradually changed almost beyond recognition, changed by the society we live in and even by the church organization we belong to. The church headquarters ought to be more like the keepers of the eternal flame of gospel truth, not the main source of changes in concepts for the convenience of the current leaders.

It is true, that our theology can essentially only be derived from our history and our experience, but that should in no way give us reason to change the gospel continually, simply because we have some new history and some new experience. All those events should be things which are incorporated into our theology, not to change it in any way, but to enrich it and more carefully define it. In most cases, there really is only one gospel truth, and we should be approaching that gospel truth asymptotically as we gain more knowledge, not veering off in either direction, pulled away by the "next new thing."

A continuing formal process of establishing and verifying our theology should be going on. There should not be a continual process of "simplification" wherein the most basic underlying concepts such as freedom and personal responsibility are degraded to supposedly help us become better citizens of

Babylon.

Chapter 18

Are the historical Scriptures now treated as Secondary sources of religious truth?

In order to properly answer this seemingly somewhat obscure and slightly speculative question, we need to review where we are and what it means. As I have described elsewhere, at this point, the LDS church has taken many extreme steps to move itself away from a New Testament church towards being an Old Testament church, and making many other important changes along the way. This includes reinstituting the Old Testament concept of tithing, used to support a large paid ministry, which means essentially the end of charity which is intended to be the heart of a New Testament church. It has also decided to ignore the freedom-supporting concepts of the U.S. Constitution and to blend-in to the extent possible with the secular/atheist governments of the world. This is exactly the opposite of what a Zion-seeking church would be doing.

One might wonder how a church could make these massive changes, without a membership being alerted to this top-to-bottom overhaul of the gospel which Joseph Smith began and Brigham Young solidified in the West. One might expect that process of creating a rhetoric, which appears to honor the gospel while mostly ignoring it and even contravening and reversing it, would need to be just as far-reaching as have been the underlying doctrinal and practical changes. So, what are some of the patterns we might expect to see in developing this new replacement rhetoric, this new approved version of the scriptures?

Some of those patterns might be fairly simple and some might be more complex. The simple techniques would be to simply ignore certain doctrines, hoping that if the leaders never bring it up for discussion, no one else will either. The issue of freedom certainly falls in this category. While the church should be vigorously taking every action necessary to maintain the freedom of its members and the rest of society, the church has self-righteously declared itself to be nonpolitical, and presents that as being pure and good in and of itself. By becoming officially pacifist, somehow that allows the gospel to avoid all the nasty political concerns of Satan trying to take over the world through corrupt political actors. We read that Capt. Moroni was a great man in the Book of Mormon for spending his life defending the freedom of his people, but today he would probably be treated as an embarrassing criminal by the church for being so "extreme" and obnoxious about defending freedom, bordering on insurrection, they might say. Certainly, they would criticize him and want to disown him if he were still a church member.

As a rather aggressive and edgy technique, the church leaders have been quite successful at supporting their deviant programs by quoting scriptures that should not apply to our situation. The biggest example involves quoting tithing scriptures from the Old Testament, conveniently ignoring the rather striking fact that tithing was ended in the New Testament. This is a blatant misuse of scripture, but they have gotten away with it and claimed $1 trillion in member funds in the process, supposedly as a matter of right.

On the issue of charity, the church argues that it is exercising foresight to save in bank vaults hundreds of billions of dollars rather than invest them in real time in needful charitable projects which would benefit individuals and the society. Frugality becomes the measure instead of effective charity. It is okay to give a little personal service using just one's time but no one should actually spend any of their *money* on charitable activities since all of that needs to go to Salt Lake City. Paying for any those real-world charitable activities is what we have our corrupt governments for. We give them much of our money and they take care of everything for us, supposedly, although they do not intend to use gospel principles in their administration of that money.

Still, on many issues, the church leaders have to either completely avoid many of those issues or defend the indefensible in order to maintain their income and their power among the members. This requires that some kind of secret pact be formed and rigorously maintained and defended, lest someone speak out of turn and upset the entire applecart and introduce conflict and discord into the central message and lose the confidence of the members. Since they have abandoned the scriptures on so many issues, they have to have another standard and method that they can use to keep their message consistent. As we all know, to be a good liar, one has to maintain consistency with all his prior statements.

There are at least two patterns one would expect to see in the situation. Apparently, the church leaders who speak in public are just as likely, or even more likely, to quote their comrades in arms than they are to quote the Scriptures. This creates and perpetuates a kind of rigorously enforced groupthink which is necessary to maintain the appearance of a consistent message as a factor in maintaining mental control of the members.

The first time I became aware of this groupthink tendency was while reviewing the April 2016 talk by President Eyring on the topic of "Eternal Families." At the end of the talk were 5 footnote references, and all five of those references referred to other current or prior general authorities, either their conference talks or their published writings. There is obviously nothing particularly unusual about one presentation that quotes other presentations. That is one of the common processes of academic writing. However, subconsciously, I had expected to see authoritative references to critical Scriptures, interpreting and applying those Scriptures, rather than academic references to the writings of other general authorities. Perhaps my expectations were unreasonable, but that's how I felt. That is the basis for my skeptical reaction to this talk, which started a long chain of reflections on how the church is instructed and managed today.

In this case, the process is to speak of these other leaders as having "taught" certain principles. There is nothing particularly wrong with that either, except that in many cases we speak of certain ancient prophets having "taught" certain principles, and at that moment we are treating them as very literal prophets of God. It is not true of every case where the word "taught" is used, as when we speak of a member father having taught his children, but when the word "taught" is used in the same sense as we refer to the scriptural pronouncements of prior prophets, then we are, by inference, granting prophetic status to current or recent church leaders. One might say that the living prophets quote each other as prophets as a way to sustain the authoritative nature of each other in the minds of the church members. If somewhere in the chain of reference, the leaders are referring to solid scriptures, that may be acceptable, but if they are simply offering their own opinion, then the question arises as to whether they should be treated as prophets concerning that statement of opinion.

There is another tendency which has caught my eye which is worth mentioning here. It seems like today every comment on every topic, and especially every tiny change which is made administratively, is spoken of as being "revelatory." In my personal opinion, that term "revelatory" is being grossly overused.

I think I can relate this to the law of Moses, since today's church doctrines and policies contain so many of the major principles of the old law of Moses. Under the law of Moses there were perhaps 613 different specific rules which the church members were supposed to obey at the exact right time, and by living any one of them, supposedly those members became more pure and more holy, even though some of us might consider that meaningless minutia they were asked to obey. Certainly, it seems out of the spirit of the New Testament where general rules are considered sufficient for almost every situation, and men who are considered to be their own priests are to make the decisions about what is right and wrong rather than have a separate book of rules to keep. The patriarch Abraham is considered the ideal model of the informed church member who holds the priesthood and has great freedom to conduct and direct every aspect of his own life and of the lives of his family. He had no bureaucracy to contend with except one of his own making. That seems like the ideal heavenly state for exalted beings.

On a website for Orthodox Jews there is an article entitled "The 39 Categories of Sabbath Work Prohibited By Law."[1] The prohibitions there include tying or untying any permanent knot, with a few exceptions. Those restrictions do not appear to be part of the 613 commandments in the Old Testament law, but were added to that law.[2]

According to law of Moses thinking, presumably people are made more pure and holy by avoiding tying and untying knots on the Sabbath. It should be obvious that those kinds of Old Testament rules should have nothing to do with a New Testament church. I hope we can keep the term "revelatory" from ever applying to such common and mundane matters as tying ropes. Simply changing church schedules is often referred to as being "revelatory." That is an important piece of administrative work, although that seems too mundane to be made to appear to be exalted. Are changing church schedules really a "supernal" activity?

I think I have presented the case for why the church might be trying to indirectly proclaim that the old scriptures are obsolete and are gradually being replaced by a completely independent source of information which consists mostly of the ideas and opinions of current and recent general authorities. At least that gives speakers a fairly large body of internally consistent knowledge which has already gone through the vetting process of seeming to present useful gospel-related information while skipping all the difficult parts of actually having to conform with the scriptures as we have them.

Here are the references from the talk by Pres. Eyring which caught my eye years ago and made me wonder about what the internally approved church scriptural database might actually look like:

1. *Teachings of Presidents of the Church: Joseph Smith* (2007), 137.
2. Bruce R. McConkie, in Conference Report, Apr. 1970, 26.
3. N. Eldon Tanner, *Church News,* Apr. 19, 1969, 2.
4. Bruce R. McConkie, in Conference Report, Apr. 1970, 27.
5. Harold B. Lee, *Decisions for Successful Living* (1973), 248–49.[3]

Another talk uses the word "taught" more pointedly to try to emphasize that the current president of the church is fully as much a prophet as anyone found in the old scriptures. Elder Dallin H. Oaks in his 2019 October conference talk entitled "Two Great Commandments,"[4] which includes touching on the volatile LGBT issue, repeatedly follows the pattern of saying "President Nelson taught..." It is not my goal here to fully analyze these two example talks to see what else might be learned from them about current church leader rhetoric, although that would almost certainly be instructive. I want to limit my comments to merely pointing out these simple rhetorical patterns. I'm sure it would be well worth writing an entire book with this as the subject, but I will have to save that for another time.

Notes

1. The 39 Categories of Sabbath Work Prohibited By Law https://www.ou.org/holidays/shabbat/the_thirty_nine_categories_of_sabbath_work_prohibited_by_law/#28
2. All 613 Commandments in the Old Testament Law http://gods-word-first.org/bible-study/613commandments.html
3. https://www.churchofjesuschrist.org/study/general-conference/2016/04/eternal-families?lang=eng
4. https://www.churchofjesuschrist.org/study/general-conference/2019/10/35oaks?lang=eng

Chapter 19

The Church drops creation and adopts atheistic organic evolution at BYU, embracing the teachings of men

Introduction

This is the most upsetting topic of all to me, the heart of darkness, the worst case, of what the church has gradually done to the gospel. This is a complete surrender to the dark side, even including a celebration of that surrender. If some of the other retreats to pre-Christian theology and practices might be upsetting but bearable, this one is not bearable. For me, this is the last straw.

The ideologies of atheism have such a grip at every level on our nation and, apparently, our church today, that I have no way to know how many people still insist on believing that God is the creator of the Earth and all life upon it. But I would venture to guess that it is still a majority of the church members who believe that God is the creator, even if their church leaders and church school administrators do not.

I assume that BYU teachers and administrators still get complaints and expressions of irritation and worry from students and, especially, from their parents, on the way that BYU handles issues of creation and evolution. I assume that the school staff have steeled themselves to pay no attention to these people. But, on the other hand, if the church members actually had a say in how the premier church school was operated, they would change this doctrine and policy and practice concerning creation and evolution.

As it is, BYU is sealed off from any adult church members and alumni, twice removed from their influence. The members have no control whatsoever over the doings of church headquarters, having been officially excluded from any such influence in 1923, when the church reinvented itself as an aggressively independent corporation sole, and the members now have no effective way to influence the school, since the school is totally under the control of the church headquarters, and the church headquarters is under the control of no one but themselves, totally unencumbered by any effective legal duties or responsibilities.

For many schools with large endowments, voluntarily contributed by the alumni, those alumni at least indirectly have a say in how the school is administered. One of the bad influences of having a highly subsidized church school is that there is no place or way for the alumni to influence school behavior through their contributions or lack of them. If everyone had to pay full tuition, or rely on alumni contributions to supply scholarships, then the church would have to be responsive to those who are willing to directly pay the cost. As it is, the church headquarters and school administrators can essentially ignore what the parents may have to say.

The worst-case scenario

In most of this book I have been pointing out how the LDS church leaders have been directing and overseeing the deterioration of the church back to the pre-Christian gospel of the law of Moses, a semi-pagan precursor and schoolmaster that was intended to prepare a people to receive the true gospel. Apparently, we did receive the true gospel in our time, but then soon lost it again, slipping back to the law of Moses level. And we seem to be stuck there forever unless something cataclysmic happens.

Now I want to focus on the place and methods where the church has further directed and overseen the deterioration of the church even beyond the pre-Christian law of Moses, back to a pagan doctrine of many petty and competing gods, and then a further step back to pure atheism/materialism involving the ideological elimination of all spiritual influences in the universe.

Darwinism

I find it difficult to exactly classify Darwinism on this scale from the robust theism of Christ's gospel, through law of Moses rigidity, to its near-twin paganism, to total atheism/materialism. Darwinism is materialist in the sense that only non-spiritual materialist forces are allowed to be considered in its many speculations about how life came to be and how man came to be. But I also see Darwinism as pagan in that it worships the products of man's hands and brain, which have created a library full of speculations, the most important ones without scientific basis, that create an intellectual Tower of Babel, which is really a fragile house of cards. There is another pagan aspect in that the devotees of Darwinism seem to always be looking for ways to slip in aspects of intelligent design -- mini-gods or forest sprites -- who do magical things at critical points but cannot be explicitly recognized or named because their strictly materialist paradigm forbids it. There are a whole host of unknown and unrecognized gods in this pagan version of materialist Darwinism. Acts 17:23.

With Charles Darwin's publishing of *On the Origin of Species* in 1859, he initiated a 160-year multi-trillion-dollar seemingly loosely organized effort or industry to create that library full of materialist speculations which supposedly provide a way to explain all life on earth without there being an all-powerful creator involved. In effect, it has been very much like the building of the

Tower of Babel through the centralized administration of the political economy and related ideology to create a way and a structure that would make man independent from God, either being able to create his own heaven on earth, or to go to heaven on his own terms. One might suspect that this seemingly loosely organized effort has in fact been very tightly organized by the father of lies.

The Tower of Babel today

That general atheist/materialist ideology has progressed so far that we now have a godless "climate change" movement which argues similarly that man is in the process of quickly destroying his environment, this earth, and that the only plausible solution is that, Tower of Babel-like, some single political power center should take control of the entire earth and all its population and resources so that we can somehow save ourselves from certain doom. Besides imagining that we can get control of our entire earth to prevent this supposed catastrophe, some would go further and say that we need to get control of our entire solar system by finding a way to move our sun and all its associated planets a few million miles or light years to avoid a catastrophic collision with another galaxy a few million years from now. Obviously, these people have no faith that there is a God who controls the universe or that, if there is such a God, that he cares about what happens to us or has made any provisions for our future.

All the three steps of gospel deterioration, taking us from the gospel to the law of Moses to paganism and on to atheism/materialism, have only visibly happened at BYU, the church's premier teaching institution. Apparently, it is not considered wise or good public relations to teach atheism/materialism and Darwinism at the ward and stake level, but it is perfectly fine to go even further into paganism and atheism at the church's premier school.

Evolution at BYU

In about 1910 it was a big source of concern to find teachers at Brigham Young Academy teaching evolution, and teachers were fired for teaching that anti-Christian doctrine. Now, at the church's premier university, people who teach those exact same things, even more emphatically than was done in 1910, are celebrated as heroes. The on-campus Bean Museum accepts and proudly teaches the ape-to-man thesis of atheistic organic evolution and trumpets its acceptance to the world. The biology department at BYU considers it a major achievement to have every one of their graduates fully accept atheistic organic evolution by the time they leave Brigham Young University. Also, that same biology Department celebrates the fact that their continual teaching of atheistic organic evolution for a small part of the typical introductory biology class has gradually convinced more and more people, non-biology majors, that evolution is the right answer to how life came into being.

It seems incomprehensible that the leaders of the biology department, the leaders of the University, and the leaders of the church have not realized that teaching pure atheism and materialism does not mesh very well with teaching the theology of an all-powerful God creating the universe and everything in it, including all life forms. It does not take a great genius to figure out that there is no plausible way to reconcile the vigorous theism of a heavenly father with the cold materialism of atheism as embodied in all Darwinian speculations.

In other words, the church has shown its true colors, at least in this one sensitive doctrinal and educational place, by teaching and supporting pure atheism while simply avoiding this embarrassing topic and policy among the regular members who apparently are considered too ignorant to understand the beauty and power of pure atheism/materialism (and it's always-accompanying support for the central administration of everything human.)

Chapter 20

A major charitable activity suggestion concerning reducing abortions

This would be like conditions in Rome where saving discarded babies was a signature Christian activity

"Charity never faileth"

Except, in our case, it has already failed, or we have failed it.

The first principle of the practical Christian gospel is active charity. Unfortunately, today the first operating principle of the LDS Church is to require all members to pay all religious contributions to the central church where it is spent on everything BUT charity. The limited available reports indicate that less than 1% of the tithing money received centrally goes to charity. The central offices contain nearly ALL our welfare cases, so to speak. That kind of behavior will never convince anyone that we actually believe in and practice serious charity, raising the question as to whether we actually believe in the tenets of Christianity.

The text at 1 Corinthians 13 is probably the most forceful argument for the importance of charity, and it appears that this kind of charity was indeed practiced by the Saints who lived during the life of Christ and for at least 300 years afterwards.

> 1 Corinthians 13
> *Paul discusses the high status of charity—Charity, a pure love, excels and exceeds almost all else.*
> 1 Though I speak with the tongues of men and of angels, and have not charity, I am become as sounding brass, or a tinkling cymbal.
> 2 And though I have the gift of prophecy, and understand all mysteries, and all knowledge; and though I have all faith, so that I could remove mountains, and have not charity, I am nothing.
> 3 And though I bestow all my goods to feed the poor, and though I give my body to be burned, and have not charity, it profiteth me nothing.
> 4 Charity suffereth long, and is kind; charity envieth not; charity vaunteth not itself, is not puffed up,
> 5 Doth not behave itself unseemly, seeketh not her own, is not easily provoked, thinketh no evil;
> 6 Rejoiceth not in iniquity, but rejoiceth in the truth;

> 7 Beareth all things, believeth all things, hopeth all things, endureth all things.
> **8 Charity never faileth:** but whether there be prophecies, they shall fail; whether there be tongues, they shall cease; whether there be knowledge, it shall vanish away.
> 9 For we know in part, and we prophesy in part.
> 10 But when that which is perfect is come, then that which is in part shall be done away.
> 11 When I was a child, I spake as a child, I understood as a child, I thought as a child: but when I became a man, I put away childish things.
> 12 For now we see through a glass, darkly; but then face to face: now I know in part; but then shall I know even as also I am known.
> 13 And now abideth faith, hope, charity, these three; but the greatest of these is charity.

So, with this theoretical understanding of the importance of charity, what would an appropriate latter-day charitable works program look like? Perhaps it could begin with a basic, efficient, charity-based social insurance system that would gradually replace all the others in the world, at least for members of the church. It might then set the goal of going on to administer an annual budget of about $200 billion for active charity projects designed to improve many aspects of earth life.

Hopefully, we would be at least 10 times more efficient and effective than anyone else in administering charity. We could replace Catholic Relief Services and become many times larger and more influential than they ever were. It is not clear today why the LDS Church has any association with the Catholic Relief Services, since we should be perfectly able to do our own charitable works, if we so chose.

Project scale

To get some rough idea of how big an effective Christian charity-based project might need to be to completely change the direction of our nation, we might start with the observation that a US presidential campaign costs about $1 billion these days, or maybe up to $2 billion. That is one rough measure of how much influence on the world $1 billion of focused effort can accomplish. By various estimates, the LDS church receives between $15 billion and $50 billion a year and has about $100 billion in reserves, indicating that the church could execute the equivalent of up to 150 presidential campaigns if it chose to.

If we said that the colleges and universities of the United States absorbed about $500 billion each year, and the K-12 education systems absorbed another $500 billion, that would give us an idea of what it would take to counteract or replace the corrupt and pagan-philosophy-dominated school systems of our country. The mainstream media probably absorbs about $50 billion a year, and Hollywood might absorb something like $10 billion a year.

The Social Security system absorbs about $500 billion a year and the Medicare systems absorbs about $300 billion a year. Directly counteracting or replacing all of these currently powerful and even controlling secular influences on the people of the nation could require as much as $1.8 trillion every year. It is quite possible that it would not take anywhere near that amount to completely overturn all these negative influences, if we were clever in our strategy, but we may not know the answer to that question until we are well into some kind of a countercultural project.

The main point here is to think big and not settle for just a small amount of local influence, although that is a good place to start. The state of Utah ought to be a model society on every level, but it is currently far from that. For example, corruption of the court system seems both very deep and very blatant. Getting Utah straightened out would give us some good experience and show other people that it can be done.

It seems highly likely that we could assemble many allies in this process of fixing the degenerate culture of the United States, but someone needs to do the research and experimenting and lead out to help people move along new paths with confidence. That should be our first focus.

People today are generally so misinformed and confused on so many topics, that perhaps the first priority ought to be to improve the education process on every level. Education should be paramount. Everyone knows that it is better to teach a man to fish so that he can take care of himself for life, rather than just to hand him a fish that will feed him for one day. But the same education philosophy probably goes for many other aspects of life such as teaching a person how to understand politics well and how to vote wisely so that he can help repair a broken society, as opposed to trying to perform some vague "nation-building" projects without the full ideological support of the populace.

Administration costs

One way to improve the effectiveness of charities is to lower their administration costs so that more money gets to the desired goal instead of being eaten up by the process. It would be ideal if those who administer charity programs were not themselves receiving a salary, although they might indeed have their travel and communications expenses paid for. Keeping it all volunteer has a way of ensuring that only those who are doing the tasks for the right reasons will stay involved.

The participants would be doing their personal charity and "paying their tithing" by doing this work. We should end up with good, high-powered people working for free, or at least without salary. The church could pay all administrative costs so that 100% of contributions, even from outsiders, go to the intended purposes. For example, the church might expend $200 million, mostly on travel and communications costs, to administer $200 billion. That would give us the remarkable result of having only 0.1% in administrative costs. That nearly perfect administration system should encourage everyone with good intentions to contribute to these projects.

Ideally, we would develop plans and projects and test them, and then request large sums of money from like-minded people in and out of the church, based on the results of our pilot programs. This method of administration should bring in enormous amounts of outside money.

Macroeconomic effects

Another long-term goal of this project is to change the basic economics of an entire nation. Instead of continuing to support [allowing] the wasteful and constraining tax-and-spend government programs for retirement and medical care, which alone typically capture 15.2% of a person's income, all of those programs should be gradually replaced with a charity-based program which is easily 2 1/2 times more efficient and will probably be five times more efficient when operating correctly. That should have the effect of lowering taxes, since the biggest portion of government spending, perhaps 80%, is related to so-called "entitlement" spending for "charitable" purposes which has non-gospel effects on citizens, encouraging greed, fraud, waste, and abuse, which, together, double or triple the cost to deliver the desired services. This all has a "virtuous spiral" effect so that increasing charity decreases destructive taxes which then allows for more charity, or free will-based services. Getting rid of the vast inefficiencies of an atheist culture allows a gospel-based culture to shine and become "the city on the hill" which every instinctively good person wants to be part of.

When the Social Security program was first begun, there was an option to start an alternative system for pensions which could use free-market principles along with a few government contribution parameters. Numerous groups took advantage of that alternative system. The might most widely known cases are the three counties in Texas which is which adopted this alternate system. The participants in that program receive somewhere between 2.4 and five times greater pension benefits from that system. The participants actually own the money and can spend it themselves or give to the children, as opposed to the Social Security system where you only receive the money as long as you're alive. If you live until your 85, you do well. If you die at age 65, you get nothing. This problem disappears with the alternate systems used by these three Texas counties.

I think it is interesting that if the church had encouraged such systems in the 1930s, the people who have reaped church members who have retired since then, calculating as 5 million retirees over a 50 year period, would have received $10 trillion more than they did receive through the government pension program. One can do rather large amount of missionary work, or education work, or other good in the world with $10 trillion in extra money, with no extra fees involved. If the church had sponsored such a system when it was possible, the church members as a group would be receiving about $200 billion a year more than they are receiving now from government systems. That extra free money could easily fund most of the projects suggested here. With an administrative system which applies almost 100% of funds to the intended target audience, I believe many other people in the world will want to offer to support our programs.

The abortion avoidance/rescue/orphanage project

What follows are the segments of a brochure I put together to try to inform people about a much-needed charitable project and to seek their support.

Introduction

The basic problem we start out with is that there are about one million abortions each year in the United States, and nearly 60 million worldwide. These are staggering numbers which mean that a population the size of the United States is prevented from coming to earth every five years.

We should notice that the number of abortions worldwide is about three times as high per capita as we see today in the United States:

> Calculation:
> For the world: 60 million abortions/6 billion people = 1%.
> For the United States: 1 million abortions/300 million people = 0.3%.

Presumably that is because the United States is still the most Christian country in the world and still values life more than anyone else. Unfortunately, if the rapidly growing number of pathologically self-centered pagans in United States have their way, the number of abortions each year in the United States will gradually rise to about 3 million. That would put us on a par with the rest of the world. We should at least try to keep this one million number from rising any more in the United States, up to the 3 million level, even if we cannot set up a system to do something about the nearly 60 million potential beneficiaries of our program worldwide. In general, as we reach for a worldwide Zion, we should want to make the earth a more welcoming place for everyone, especially for new babies.

State-level antiabortion efforts

It is wonderful to see at least 17 of the 50 states working hard to minimize or end abortions in their states. But, unfortunately, it seems likely that, as a practical matter, most people seeking abortions do so because they do not want to raise that child for some reason, so if states are successful in limiting abortions, the number of unwanted children, potential foster children, could go up substantially.

Also, unfortunately, these same antiabortion states don't seem to be doing much to adapt for or prepare for the likely effects of having success with their antiabortion policies. Perhaps we can say that their Christianity goes far enough to want to avoid abortions, which is a good thing, but not far enough to try to solve all the problems that cause people to want to limit their offspring through abortions.

So, it appears that someone needs to provide a large and practical system that will do something about those impending consequences. If limiting abortions means we simply have more child neglect or abuse or even infanticide, those states will not have actually made much of a positive difference but may make worse the whole process of the birth and rearing of children. Hopefully, one element of a successful program will be to help mothers and fathers understand the value of life and be willing and able to raise these children themselves. If we cannot empower those parents, perhaps we can help in another way. We might start with providing a comfortable place where women can go to be cared for themselves until they give birth. If all else fails to get every child into a loving home, the child can be temporarily placed in our orphanage.

Some program limitations

One great difficulty is that, at the beginning, we will certainly not be able to care for all the nation's one million rejected babies, so we will have to engage in some kind of selection or triage process to choose the limited number of children we can assist and offer a nice life. Those outcomes may be determined for us in most cases, but there will surely come times when we have to choose.

Unfortunately, to create a viable and successful system we will probably have to focus on trying to save those children who are best equipped to live a successful and productive life. If we only choose the sick and disabled children at first, those very ones who might seem the most pitiful and needful at the beginning, we may not be able to give them the much higher and longer term help they need. We might find that those extreme resources, needed for one such child, could possibly be used to successfully raise 10 healthy children to maturity.

A large and successful general population can absorb and support a small percentage of seriously disabled children, but we would not start out with anything like a large "general population." But, hopefully, the long-term success of the program contemplated here, will include grown children giving back to the process, like alumni of any school, possibly including adopting some of these children themselves. That bootstrapping process should finally allow a large number of "institutionalized" or severely disabled children to be cared for within the system we create. Otherwise there is the risk that we might swamp and overwhelm the system with unbearable failure and sadness that never goes away.

We are not quite the same as Sparta, Athens, or the Eskimos. We don't have to decide to discard a child or keep it. We simply have to decide that since we cannot keep all the children, we simply keep the ones who are most likely to be successful, and we continue that way until we can find a way to accept all unwanted children.

Long-term considerations -- exponential growth?
There is another interesting issue here. The healthy and strong ones can grow up to have children of their own which they will probably value more than their parents valued them. This means that the number of "lives" that we are helping will grow exponentially, which seems like a good idea. If only the weak and sickly are saved, they are not likely to have any progeny of their own, or be able to take care of them if they did. So, if we are trying to optimize and maximize the number of spirits who can come to the earth and have a good experience, then we would want to start out focusing on those who can be successful.

Very long-term considerations -- genetic entropy
For purposes of the proposed project (and for the church more generally), we also have the very long-term problem that the human genome is continuing to deteriorate rapidly over time. After 300+ generations of humans on this earth, the mutation load is becoming critical. The number of chronic, genetics-related diseases goes up at a relatively fixed rate of about 0.7% a year, inexorably. This means that, by now, about 50% of all living people have at least one significant genetic disease. Diabetes and heart disease seem to be widespread current genetic diseases, but the rate of cancer is also going up, especially cancer among children. The occurrence of autism, which is apparently genetically related to childhood cancer, seems to be going up at a frightening rate.

At some point in the near future, perhaps in as little as 100 years or about five generations away, children may be born with such an overwhelming set of genetic problems, that they will not be able to survive after birth. This indicates that one of the very long-term goals of this project ought to be to do the medical research necessary to understand and deal with this long-term genetic entropy problem, to the extent that that is even possible. Our society is probably already devoting enough resources to medical research in general that they should be able to take on this research problem and devise the best available solutions. However, in general, the researchers appear to be so blinded by the false theories and speculations of atheistic organic evolution that they will never focus these available resources in the most fruitful places. Changing that pagan philosophy and refocusing those resources ought to be one eventual goal of this project.

Christ quickly drew many tens of thousands of people to his new religion, partly because he demonstrated the power to heal people of every imaginable disease, and even to raise them from the dead. At the present moment, it seems quite unrealistic for a modern-day church to offer anything like those levels of healing powers to people. However, if it turns out there IS any way for the church to offer healing powers on that scale, that would be an extremely powerful indication to the world that the church had the truth, and they would naturally flock to it. It might even provide a way to resolve the unpleasant practical and ethical difficulty of not being able to heal and help every child that comes into the world with an imperfect body.

The Leland Farms Project

A vigorous Christian response to the growing pagan practices of abortion and infanticide in our nation

Thanksgiving Point Curiosity Museum -- a sample of possible facilities to brighten children's lives.

Short Version

Leland Farms

Orphanage, farm, and schools

A 600-acre complex with orphanages, farms, schools, and colleges, plus appropriate housing for residents and visitors.

Education
The focus will be on education, and there will be facilities to promote education at every level.

Demographics:
For planning purposes, assume an eventual population of 16,000 orphans of all ages, although a much smaller size would still be beneficial and feasible

Funding:
There is a $0 funding option, a $1 million funding option, and a $3 billion funding option explored.
LDS families care about people and tend to be generous, so that it should be reasonable to expect a final investment or endowment of $3 billion, if the concept proves to be as valuable as it seems.

Volunteer staff:
Thousands of families in the Utah Valley area, especially those who are retired, spend large amounts of volunteer time on religion-related projects. Hopefully, these same groups of people would be willing to act as volunteer grandparents or Big Brothers/Big Sisters for the orphanage children.

History and philosophy
The early Christians were known for rescuing rejected children who had been "exposed" to the elements by other Roman citizens. Some of those children died anyway, and were given a Christian burial. In some cases, pagan people took these rejected children and turned them into slaves, but of course the Christians did not turn them into slaves, but kept them as their own children. This added to the ranks of the Christians in Rome, and presumably in other cities as well, since the exposing of unwanted children was a common practice in that society. We seem to be repeating all the practices and problems of Rome today.
https://earlychurchhistory.org/medicine/infanticide-in-the-ancient-world/

Expansion:
If another orphanage were to be created in St. George Utah, that could be something similar to what is planned for Utah Valley, with even better

weather. There would likewise probably be tens of thousands of honorary grandparents readily available to help out the project.

Instructive examples:
1. A Child's Hope Foundation. "Our Mission: Lifting Orphans from Surviving to Thriving"
www.achildshopefoundation.org/about/ -- Orem Utah headquarters, assists orphanages in Bulgaria, China, Mongolia, Ukraine, Peru, South Korea, Haiti, and Mexico, with more intense support for one orphanage in Haiti and three in Mexico.

2. Southern Virginia University is a private liberal arts college located in Buena Vista, Virginia. The school, though not officially affiliated with a particular faith, embraces the values of The Church of Jesus Christ of Latter-day Saints. www.svu.edu

Longer Version

Leland Farms

Orphanage, farm, and schools

A 600-acre complex with orphanages, farms, schools, and colleges, plus appropriate housing for residents and visitors.

I prefer the term "boarding school" to such terms as orphanage or group home, since the term "orphanage" has mostly gone out of style these days. The "boarding school" term tends to emphasize the learning part of this process. I fear that the term "orphanage" brings to mind the idea of rows of cribs which act as cages for children who are kept from exploring the world around them.

It would be ideal if we had the money immediately available to take a 600-acre block of land and turn it into a kind of planned "theme park," a "curiosity museum" even larger than the one at Thanksgiving point, with the entire Leland Farms project being designed for the maximum learning opportunities of children from age 0 through age 18. To imagine the broadest possible view, the project might begin on the east side with facilities to assist mothers who wish to give up their babies for adoption, with the "output" at the west end of the project, where young people have completed high school or even college work and are ready to take their place as adults in our society, having learned all the most important things about the world we live in, including the importance of religion..

The two major factors
1. I believe that Leland is a truly unique place which has been kept from being overrun by the normal population for a purpose which is quite different than just general economic progress. It is hard to imagine anywhere else in the world where you could easily name six or eight bishops or past bishops in the LDS church who own substantial amounts of property which are essentially contiguous. There are many other good people who are have not been LDS bishops but who subscribe to that same philosophy and might be willing to help this project in some way.

On the pure economics of the situation, I'm guessing that, except for the land right around the Benjamin exit, which will probably bring a major premium in land prices, the rest of the land in Leland is likely to be sold at about the same price whether it is sold to a standard commercial developer who is going to put in homes, or whether it is sold to a charitable organization for an extensive orphanage facility. The charitable organization might actually be able to pay the current land owners more, if they wish, and the payment of that money could take place in ways which might be more creative than might be typical for a standard commercial developer.

2. The battle of good and evil is accelerating every day in our nation, and one of the areas of greatest conflict concerns the bringing of new babies into the world. The atheistic political left considers that women should have the availability of abortion on demand, paid for by the government. About 1 million babies are aborted each year in the US, and, if the political left has its way, that number will soon rise to 3 million a year which would put the United States at the same rate as the rest of the world. Presumably the fact that Christianity still exists in the United States is what keeps the abortion rate much lower, but that may not continue for long. (Worldwide, there are about 56 million abortions a year as opposed to the United States' 1 million abortions. The US is about 1/20 of the world population, so, theoretically, there should be about 3 million abortions a year in the US. ~60/20=~3)

There is a very active political battle in progress. The godless left wants the *Roe V Wade* decision to be an eternal rule, while many of the states are putting all the restraints on abortion which they reasonably can, while undergoing constant scrutiny and litigation by the left. In at least one case, Georgia, the state hopes to be the means of overturning *Roe V Wade*. There is quite a patchwork of legislative results reached in the various states. There are currently 17 states that ban abortions beginning at 20 weeks. The latest move is for one of those states, Ohio, probably to be soon joined by Georgia, to ban abortions after six weeks when a baby's heartbeat can be detected. Technically, most babies have a heartbeat at five weeks, but apparently the legislatures have chosen six weeks as their target. Advances in medical science have made the *Roe V Wade* decision vulnerable to challenge, since that decision is based on the fact that there was no consensus then about when a child becomes a person. Georgia is declaring that a baby becomes a "natural person" at six weeks and is granted all the protection of the state, including the right to child support, the right to be claimed as a dependent, and the right to be included in George's population counts.

School curricula:
Montessori experiential schools and homeschooling are very popular in the state of Utah, and there are numerous excellent and well-tested curricula available. These methods also take full advantage of extensive online resources, many of them free. They offer a very frugal alternative to expensive public education with its enormous investment in centralized schools and the related busing systems. The assumption is that this entire operation, including the schools, will operate mostly independently of government and church funding and administration systems and the related

politics concerning warped values. The hope is that the farming activities could make the whole operation mostly self-sustaining, while also providing educational and productive work to the orphans and volunteers.

History and philosophy -- more

The early Christians were known for rescuing rejected children who had been "exposed" to the elements by other Roman citizens. Some of those children died anyway, and were given a Christian burial. In some cases, pagan people took those rejected children and turned them into slaves, but of course the Christians did not turn them into slaves, but kept them as their own children, in the process rejecting two immoral aspects of Roman society. This added to the ranks of the Christians in Rome, and presumably in other cities as well, since the exposing of unwanted children was a common practice in that society. We seem to be repeating all the practices and problems of Rome today. https://earlychurchhistory.org/medicine/infanticide-in-the-ancient-world/

I'm guessing that besides adding the children to the Christian ranks, other people who were sympathetic with the Christian value system were also drawn to that group of believers, offering a double sociological benefit to saving those children. We do know that the early Christians eventually grew to be the largest single religious group in the Roman Empire.

It would be useful to have more detailed statistics on the whole topic of children who might be well served by an orphanage, but it is instructive to learn that there are about 1 million abortions a year in the United States and a total of about 56 million abortions worldwide each year. Many other children are born alive but are not wanted, leading to abandoned children or infanticide, plus the classical orphans in cases where parents have passed away. I read of one case in Brazil where 200 children out of 1000 were killed or left to die by their parents. These are all staggering numbers, and it would take some heroic efforts to begin to do what the early Christians did in saving unwanted children, but on a worldwide scale. When you realize that every six years the entire population of the United States is lost to abortions worldwide, one might see this as an amazing opportunity to do good or as nothing more than a depressing statistic. One year's loss of life through intentional abortion or infanticide would replace the entire LDS church population three times. The 60 million children who have been aborted since 1973 in the United States would easily replace all those workers who are now being supplied in the form of desperate immigrants from South American and Central American countries.

Potential participating landowning families:

Larsen, Larson, Eaton, Christensen, Creer, Swenson, Nielsen, Westwood, Isaac, Baadsgaard, et al.

Some possible practical factors

1. County assistance to farmers

The county government for Utah County is considering a proposal to assist new farmers in being able to make a living on a farm. The County is proposing to give some kind of assistance to lower the beginning capital costs required to operate a farm profitably. This will be difficult, of course, because there is a constant upward pressure on the cost of land, making it very difficult to get a proper return on investment in land and the equipment required to work it.

2. Conservation covenants

In many places, land owners have the option to limit the future use of their land for themselves, their families, and others, by making a long-term commitment to keep the land close to its original form. That might apply in Leland if some of those who own land would wish to make that commitment. Perhaps that commitment would be easier to make if there was some remuneration for those landowners at the beginning. Using land for the charitable purposes suggested here may be far more valuable than using it for ordinary residential purposes. This needs to be explored quickly before the option passes of being able to do such a thing on a grand scale.

3. Dual-use construction

There is also the interesting possibility that if Leland were developed for purposes of supporting a large population of orphans and related people and facilities, that development might itself look very much like regular residential development. The main difference might be that the homes would be a little larger, with more bedrooms, so that they could be suitable for operating as group homes. It seems ideal if a new development can be created for the very purpose of orphanage-style operations. At least there would be no backlash later on as might happen if someone first developed the area as a standard residential area and then tried to move it piecemeal to becoming an orphanage-style operation. The typical Not in My Backyard (NIMBY) reaction would never have a reason to exist. If the project were not successful or if the concept or the location changed, those original houses might be repurposed to normal residential living much more easily than going the other way.

4. The current planning status

The surrounding cities of Spanish Fork, Salem, and Payson seem to be aggressively pursuing development of this area. It may seem like a sensible thing to do, but I don't know of any requirement for the cities to press for this kind of development. Presumably the cities are only driven by the opportunity to increase taxes on developed land and therefore grow the size of the city administration. However, the cities are theoretically supposed to be the servants of the people who live there, not their masters. If the people in the nearby areas where there is still raw land wish to restrict the growth of the cities and the growth of the city's power over those large parcels of raw land, that seems like something which should be possible. There is nothing inevitable about having to accept this kind of aggressive growth, for no other reason than for growth's sake. It is my opinion that many cities in Utah County have far too grand view of their own purposes and powers, and that attitude ought to be reset. Representative government is supposed to work at the local level, not just in Washington DC.

It may be that it would make a great deal more sense to leave Leland intact and to direct the typical developmental growth toward areas which are to the west of Leland, simply skipping over Leland. The commuter bedroom communities for offices along the Wasatch front easily extend down to Santaquin and beyond. There is no obvious reason why this particular tract of 1200 acres ought to be so avidly sought by city managers. Perhaps it would make more sense to start someplace like Benjamin or Lakeshore and upgrade the status of their cities and appoint THEM to be the ones who are annexing land for residential and business purposes. They would almost certainly be more democratic in how they planned for residential expansion.

I understand that Spanish Fork has zoned one area for 500 homes, and Salem has zoned another area for 1500 homes, and that Target stores has bought land near the Benjamin exit, and that Salem is planning to build a sewer facility in the area of Benjamin exit. But none of these things seem inevitable or even particularly necessary. It may be slightly cheaper to provide utilities for Leland from the existing cities, but it should only be a minor change in cost to leave Leland intact, jump the freeway going west and then continue development there. The general flow of water is obviously from the mountains to the lake, and there's no particular reason to stop at any particular point along that drainage slope to emphasize one area over another. "Doing what comes naturally" may not seem so natural if there are other important factors to be considered, such as the "boarding school" option.

I believe there are areas near Spanish Fork, Salem, and Payson that are rather low quality as far as farming possibilities are concerned. It seems obvious that those areas should be first moved into residential use before the higher-quality farmland is bothered. Perhaps that is what is already happening with the zoning of Spanish Fork and Salem, but I don't know the reasoning behind what they are doing.

A few interview results:

1. One local landowner had two reactions to the idea. One was that there are many people who want to adopt, and there are far too few babies for them to

adopt. On the other hand, the real difficulty, as he sees it, is in convincing pregnant mothers to go full term and give birth to their babies when there is abortion on demand where the government pays for the medical costs which make it free to the mother. Many adoptions can be very expensive, rising to as much as $50,000. There are still apparently more people who are willing to pay that amount than there are babies for them to adopt. That should give us a few clues about how the various programs might be set up.

He was not certain that it was necessary to build a big physical plant to make a big difference. That is a good point if we would like to get some kind of program going quickly. Obviously, if we delay as long as possible building any structures for an orphanage, we can do a lot of work at minimal cost in exploring who the children and families might be who would benefit from such facilities.

In contrast, I would observe that this may be a chicken and egg situation: if we have the facilities, then it's much easier to make it clear that we are prepared to take good care of any children that are entrusted to us. Perhaps beginning with building or renting a single group home, perhaps with 8-10 bedrooms, would be one way to kick off the project, get some office space, and get some experience with the whole process.

2. A Spanish Fork-based builder thought the general idea of a high-quality orphanage was a good one. He is very much aware of the state's efforts to build housing for people in need, but there is no state follow-up program to make sure these people get the individual help or encouragement they need.

The Basic Church Statistical Picture

Church growth statistics help explain what's happening to the church worldwide

.

Introduction

The last five years of church statistics show that almost everything is in decline as far as membership growth rates are concerned. There are fewer missionaries, fewer children of record added, fewer converts, fewer members added, fewer missions, and fewer districts. There is a small increase in the number of stakes, wards and branches, and church service missionaries. It is not clear why the numbers of stake organizations and wards or branches are going up, while almost everything else is going down, unless perhaps there was some decision made to increase the levels and concentration of local organizations in hopes of increasing local control and perhaps using that method to stimulate growth through more intensive administration. The increase in the number of church service missionaries, while the number of full-time missionaries keeps dropping, may be related numbers. That could easily happen if fewer people chose the more rigorous full-time mission option which usually involves more travel, and instead chose the more local and less rigorous service mission option.

Only an increase of 3,000 in new long-term members from 2017 to 2018? Or was it a net loss?

The statistics which the church supplies publicly are interesting, but they are far from thorough, leaving us to guess about what is happening in many situations. For dramatic effect I want to focus on the apparent gain of only 3,000 long-term active members during the year of 2018. But even a gain of 3,000 might be a stretch. It could easily be a net loss after all the factors are considered. I calculate that 3,000 by noticing that there was only an increase of 30 wards and branches worldwide. It would be much more helpful if we knew exactly how many branches and exactly how many wards were added, instead of seeing only a combined total. To get around that lack of more exact information, I'm going to assume that the average size of branches and wards is 100. Branches are smaller and wards are bigger, but 100 might be a reasonable average size. So, obviously, 30x100 equals 3,000. But notice that we have 30,536 wards and branches. If the church, on average, lost one person from each of those wards or branches, that would be a loss of 30,536 active members. That could mean that there was actually a net loss of about 27,536. The point is, that we are getting so close to zero growth, that we can't actually be sure which way it went. I will supply some other numbers later which will make it seem more like it was indeed a year in which the church had a net loss in active members.

Starting with some of the basics
I think it is useful to distinguish here between the basic maintenance level, baptizing enough people to replace those who have died or left the church, and actually going beyond that maintenance level to include raising the total number of active church members by bringing in new long-term members. I am more interested in seeing the church actually grow, not just avoid shrinking, so I would prefer to start with that growth viewpoint. But it is probably too confusing to start there, so I will start with the more basic maintenance level concerns.

Church statistics from 2018 show that there were 234,332 converts, and that the church grew by only
195,566 members. (We might wonder where those lost 38,766 went to? Was it because of an extra-large number of deaths or defections?) And supposedly, that increase of 195,566 includes baptized children of record. New children of record are reported to number 102,102, of which, historically, only about 60% actually get baptized, which would add about 61,261 for 2018.

But the church only grew by 30 wards and branches, which I would estimate to be 3000 people that were new long-term members. It is obviously hard to understand what is going on here without more and better data.

The church does not report deaths anymore, but an average life expectancy of 75 years implies that 1.33% of the population will die each year. For the current reported church population of 16,313,735 that would mean that the church should have about 216,973 deaths each year. With 234,332 converts reported, that would give us a net gain of only 17,359 of new members over deaths, without counting defections. But notice that last year the church only reported a gain of 195,566, which is 21,407 less than the claimed converts. Extra deaths or defections might be involved, but there is no way to know exactly what happened. Also remember that the church reported 102,102 new children of record, of which perhaps 60%, or 61,261, were probably baptized from prior years' blessings of children. So, the church might claim that converts, plus the baptisms of children of record from prior years, would be a total gain of 295,593, but they only report a gain of 195,566, an unexplained loss of 100,027. It's hard to guess what went on behind these numbers.

	A	B	C	D	E	F	G	H	I	J	K	L	M	N	O	P
1		**2,018**	DIF	%DIF	**2,017**	DIF	%DIF	**2,016**	DIF	%DIF	**2,015**	DIF	%DIF	**2,014**	DIF	%DIF
2	stakes	3,383	42	1.26	3,341	75	2.30	3,266	92	2.90	3,174	60	1.93	3,114	64	2.10
3	missions	407	-14	-3.33	421	0	0.00	421	3	0.72	418	12	2.96	406	1	0.25
4	Districts	547	-6	-1.08	553	-3	-0.54	556	-2	-0.36	558	-3	-0.53	561	-10	-1.75
5	ward and branches	30,536	30	0.10	30,506	202	0.67	30,304	288	0.96	30,016	395	1.33	29,621	368	1.26
6	members	16,313,735	195,566	1.21	16,118,169	235,752	1.48	15,882,417	248,218	1.59	15,634,199	261,862	1.70	15,372,337	290,309	1.92
7	increase in children of r	102,102	-4,669	-4.37	106,771	-2,475	-2.27	109,246	-5,304	-4.63	114,550	-1,859	-1.60	116,409	923	0.80
8	converts	234,332	603	0.26	233,729	-6,402	-2.67	240,131	-17,271	-6.71	257,402	-39,401	-13.28	296,803	13,858	4.90
9	missionaries	65,137	-1,912	-2.85	67,049	-3,897	-5.49	70,946	-3,133	-4.23	74,079	-11,068	-13.00	85,147	2,112	2.54
10	Church-Service Mission	37,963	1,791	4.95	36,172	2,477	7.35	33,695	1,916	6.03	31,779			30,404		
11	temples dedicated	2	-2	-50.00	4	-2	-33.33	6	1	20.00	5	2	66.67	3	2	200.00
12	temples rededicated	2	1	100.00	1	-1	-50.00	2	0	0.00	2	1	100.00	1	-1	-50.00
13	total temples in operatio	162	3	1.89	159	4	2.58	155	6	4.03	149	5	3.47	144	3	2.13
14	total temples announcec	209														

This chart presents the basic information reported by the church for the past five years. Each year shows the statistics reported for that year, with extra columns showing the difference between that year and the prior year, and the calculated percent difference between the two years.

2018 Church Statistics		Comments
Calculation 1		
Reported converts	234,332	
Estimated baptisms of children of record (60% of 102,102 reported children of record)	61,261	
Total expected growth	295,593	
Reported church net growth	195,566	
Unexplained loss	100,027	Extra deaths or defections?
Calculation 2		
Total expected growth	295,593	
Estimated deaths	216,973	
Estimated church net growth	78,620	
Reported church net growth	195,566	
Estimated church net growth	78,620	
Unexplained "gain"	116,946	Were many deaths unreported?
Reported missionaries	65,137	
Average converts per missionary per year	3.597	
Low estimate of church resources centrally assembled annually (could be 3 times that large)	$15 billion	
Cost for each of 234,332 converts -- $15 billion/ 234,332 =	$64,011	
Calculation 3		
For 2018		
Growth in number of wards and branches	30	
Estimated growth in new long-term active members, assuming 100 average for a ward or branch	3,000	
Low estimate of church resources centrally assembled annually (could be 3 times that large)	$15 billion	
Cost for each of 3,000 net new long-term converts	$5 million	
Cost for a family of five	$25 million	
For 2017		
Growth in number of wards and branches	202	
Estimated growth in new long-term active members, assuming 100 average for a ward or branch	20,200	
Low estimate of church resources centrally assembled annually (could be 3 times that large)	$15 billion	
Cost for each of 30,000 net new long-term converts	$742,574	
Cost for a family of five	$3,712,870	
For 2016		
Growth in number of wards and branches	288	
Estimated growth in new long-term active members, assuming 100 average for a ward or branch	28,800	
Low estimate of church resources centrally assembled annually (could be 3 times that large)	$15 billion	
Cost for each of 30,000 net new long-term converts	$520,833	
Cost for a family of five	$2,609,165	

Even if Mormons are extra healthy, we can still be fairly confident that there were somewhere around 200,000 members who died, plus an unknown number of those who left the church. After all that activity and all those changes, it leaves only about 3000 members who can be counted as actual growth. Of course, it is useful for the missionaries to replace the people who die and leave the church, but it is clear that the birthrate within the church is nowhere near enough to keep us from shrinking without the missionaries finding new people. That itself ought to be a cause for alarm, and evidence that the newer generations of church members don't value children very much – not enough to even replace those members who die. Here again, it seems like we ought to focus a great deal more on living people than on dead people who have already had their turn on Earth. They are much more able to take care of themselves than are these little ones.

If we said that the income of the central church was a mere $15 billion a year (some have estimated it to be three times that amount), bringing in about 200,000 converts to avoid the church shrinking from deaths would cost about $75,000 each (enough to keep out 25 missionaries for a year for each person baptized.). But, ideally, we would not be spending all of our money just to stay exactly where we are. We would be making some progress. The fact that we are not making any progress should tell us that there's something critically wrong with our current program.

In 2018, the Church added only about **3,000** people to the number of long-term active members. That is getting close enough to **zero** that the church leaders cannot really argue anymore that they have an effective program. The number of missionaries is shrinking as well, perhaps as people find out that they can go on their missions for 1.5 or 2 years, and, even though they may baptize on average about 4 people each year per missionary, many of them will not have a single convert that stays with the church long-term. On average, in recent years it has taken more than two missionary man-years to get one new long-term convert beyond the maintenance level, beyond keeping the church from shrinking, and now, as of last year, we see the church adding hardly any new long-term converts, meaning it takes about 20 missionary man-years for every new long-term convert which actually extends the size of the active members of the church.

The 3000 number represents the new long-term converts who added enough to the church activity rolls to justify adding a ward or branch somewhere in the world. Last year the church added 30 wards and branches. If we guess that there is an average of 100 people for each ward or branch, then 30x100 = 3000.

The church attitude towards missionaries seems to be that the people in Utah, their main constituency, their "breadbasket" so to speak, the source of so much of their money income and volunteers, really want their children to get out and go on missions and see the world, and so the church is supplying that experience for young people. However, at this point that whole system is so strikingly ineffective, almost counterproductive, with so many missionaries becoming depressed, that the time has come to end it or greatly reorganize it. Again, the whole thing was built up as a service to the money-paying people in Utah, and that whole program is falling apart. I could supply some statistics but that may not even be necessary. I think we are beyond statistics. People can plainly see that the whole thing is not working.

A few years ago, as in 2016, the church members were paying through tithing about $0.5 million for each new long-term member which would mean, overall, that we were paying about $2.5 million for a family of five. But that was when we were still bringing in about 30,000 new long-term people a year, as indicated by the number of new wards and branches that were formed each year. Today, the numbers concerning average cost have become astronomical. We are now spending about $5 million for each new long-term member, and about $25 million for every family of five.

Can you imagine how many children could be saved from abortion with that kind of money available to fund the program? Perhaps we should simply charge the church $1 million for each new long-term member we supply through the orphanage system. That would save them a great deal of money and get us off to a great financial start. This, of course, is another way to say that our whole system has collapsed, as well it should, because we are not following the simple program that Christ set out.

We have made up our own program which focuses on centralizing all the money which is possible, and then essentially intentionally wasting all that money at the central offices so that the members will not actually be able to use those resources to do something good in the world, since doing so would be so disruptive to the church's current business model of quietly enjoying a lavish income for doing almost nothing. That system is in a state of full collapse and we might as well recognize it and take some action to fix it. If church leaders are unwilling to face reality and "face the music," so to speak, then a few sturdy members are going to have to take action.

The truth is that my deepest reason for wanting to do this abortion/orphanage project is because of how confused the church has become after 200 years of operation – the point at which all previous restorations have collapsed. This orphanage program would be a serious project that does a lot of good, and is very necessary. It would start the process of people exercising their religious freedom to send their charity money where they think it will do the most good, and I hope that this abortion/orphanage project will seem like exactly the right thing for all these people to do. They can stop sending their money to the temple building/temple work charitable activity which keeps church members busy and off the streets but doesn't create any effect in the real world, or they can send their money to a project which is aggressively taking on Christian activities. There will be some members who would like to remain invisible and ineffective, but there are some who are a little more aggressive in their Christianity, and will want to send a message to the world that the Mormons support Christianity everywhere and are not shy about it.

This will probably terrify the current church leadership, and I don't know what they will do. They might even do something completely irrational. But it is time to find out, since we can officially declare that the old system has completely failed. It is no longer in doubt which way the right direction to go might be.

If the church does choose to help us, I would say Hallelujah, because that will mean that this hundred-year confusion about the mission of the church will finally be cleared up and we can get back on the right path. I'm not expecting that to happen, but that would be the ultimate measure of success for this project.

I believe there is a silver lining to this current bad situation or problem. We do indeed have many church members in other countries already, even though the cost of getting them has already been 100 times what it should have been. If we simply stopped trying to keep people from gathering, and let the gathering happen naturally in any way people wanted to do it, or could do it, we would suddenly have all these church members from all over the world flooding in to be living in the United States. And, using the examples from the 1800s, where 90,000 people came from England and Scandinavia to Utah within just a few years, constituting about 83% of ALL active members in about 1852, for every person who left a foreign land for Zion, there would be one or two people who would be getting ready to do the same thing. That process would never stop. Many arrived in Utah without ever officially joining the Church through baptism, presumably because of their eagerness to leave their bad situation in England.

That is the way it worked in England. People wanted freedom, and the church gathering process provided an organized way to escape the near-slavery the lower classes experienced in England. (We might remember that it was English ships who were bringing slaves to America, providing insight into the English viewpoint on slavery at that earlier time.) The opportunity to live in freedom is an enormous and constant electro-magnet (which we have intentionally turned off). If we would just get out of the way, we would only have to help a little here and there to have a constant flood of people joining us in the United States and greatly bulking up the number of pro-freedom people in the United States, hopefully enough to continually overwhelm the anti-freedom influences which keep growing in our nation.

When you have Zion all in one place, they will take care of themselves. You don't need a giant expensive bureaucracy to act as headquarters for 200 different scattered tribes or versions of the church living under 200 different versions of Babylon. You only need such a huge bureaucracy if you can insist on keeping everyone from gathering together. So, as a business model, you want to avoid the gathering because it hurts your tithing income going to your paid ministry labor union.

Here is a more precisely written version of that historical migration from Europe:

> In a chapter by Rodney Stark about LDS Church growth, he includes one subtopic entitled "The British to the Rescue."* The statistics he provides show that the British converts went from 23% of the 16,865 members in 1840 to 83.4% of the 52,640 members in 1852, then gradually down to 49% of the 188,263 members in 1889. This was a huge influx of members at a critical time for the Church. Of the 92,465 total British converts in the 1840 to 1890 period, 89,695 moved to the US, leaving 2,770 behind. The year 2000 membership figure for the United Kingdom is 165,100, so the emigration of that huge portion of early British converts does not appear to have caused any long-term problem for the Church in that country.
>
> *Rodney Stark, "The Basis of Mormon Success: A Theoretical Application" in James T. Duke, ed., Latter-day Saint Social Life: Social Research on the LDS Church and its Members (Provo, Utah: Religious Studies Center, Brigham Young University, 1998), pp. 29-67 (chapter 2).

Some further steps?

One of the very long-term goals of this project could be to establish an entire new social insurance system based on charity, which worked so well for the Saints during and after the life of Christ. That would mean replacing Social Security, Medicare, Medicaid, and perhaps 60 other patchwork tax-and-spend entitlement programs with a gospel-based/charity-based system. Such a system is easily twice as efficient as anything a government can do with its wasteful and corrupt methods, and these charity-based support systems can easily be five times as effective.

The church could have solved this general social insurance problem for all of us back in the 1930s when it was easy to do, bringing $10 Trillion in extra pension funds to church members up to the present. They didn't do a thing then, going along meekly with the New Deal then, so it is a little harder to do it now. But it is well worth the effort even if it takes several years to work out mechanisms that are suitable so that these tax-and-spend atheistic entitlement monstrosities can be replaced with something Christian and workable, without having to pay two or three times just for insuring that peoples' basic needs are taken care of when necessary.

The Leland Farms Project

A vigorous Christian response to the
growing pagan practices of
abortion and infanticide in our nation

An Administrative Addendum

Who should do this project?
Should it be a new, local, one-of-a-kind charitable organization which starts from scratch and gradually builds itself up, or should LDS Church headquarters have a role in this project? Or should there be some combination of the two?

Some possible topics for discussion:

1. If the Church was ever interested in making a statement that could change the course of the nation, this looks like this would be a good time to do it.

2. This would represent a new and seemingly unusual way to "gather Israel." Perhaps it could gradually be scaled up to compete on almost equal terms with the regular proselyting processes. The project should also have major ripple effects as it shows other Christian groups one good way to go about counteracting the pro-abortion influences on all levels.

3. If the Church wanted to increase its total number of proselyting missionaries and service missionaries, this might be a good way to do it, perhaps adding 20,000 to the young people and senior citizens involved. It seems likely that the senior citizens would be especially interested in this kind of service. Everyone loves children, and the social stresses and anxieties should be much less in assisting children than in cold-contacting unknown adults of the world.

4. Teaching children while they are a young, especially those who might feel some gratitude for having been rescued, is usually a better way to introduce the gospel than having to help people first "unlearn" what they have incorrectly learned in their lives.

5. The rate of church growth seems to be dropping in recent years. Setting up this Leland Farms project and system could help greatly improve church growth. I think this project could have many ripple effects which could raise

the church growth rate far beyond just the number of children who were helped directly by the project. Simply further emphasizing the LDS respect for life and respect for personal freedom would have a positive effect on people's view of the LDS church.

6. Although this may seem like a highly political move, in another sense it is not very political, even though it is a direct challenge to rampant paganism. The idea of killing babies simply because they are inconvenient to have around is not really popular anywhere. Almost everyone can agree that is a bad idea. Even the atheistic political left claims that they are really sad about there being so many abortions. They don't actually believe that, of course, but Christian thinking still has so much influence in our country that atheists would never publicly state that it is their goal to kill as many children as possible. The atheistic left would have to find a different argument against the project.

7. I have often thought it would be nice if, instead of sending humanitarian relief funds to Catholic organizations to be administered, a large amount of church funds could be sent to more specifically LDS projects such as this one, where the teaching of the gospel is an important part of the project.

8. We put a huge amount of effort into saving the dead, but maybe it is time to put some more effort into saving the living through this new channel of assisting children into this world and into gospel families.

9. Many states, at least 17, have tried very hard to constrain abortion to the extent they can at the state level, pushing back actively against the 1973 federal takeover a rightful state issue. This project could become a focal point for coordinating the activities of a large number of Christians in our nation who are taking aggressive action to limit the number of abortions, but who may not actually have a plan to follow through on some of the practical effects of the legal changes that are being proposed. The great efforts of these other Christians ought to be recognized and assisted where possible.

10. The church has been putting a lot of architectural effort into explicitly religious structures such as chapels and temples. Perhaps some of that architectural enthusiasm could be directed toward solving a social problem such as the new wave of abortions and infanticides. Housing and educating young people would become more important.

11. Once a project headquarters staff was assembled and trained, it is quite possible that the activities in Leland, the part that could be seen easily, would only be 1/10th of what was being administered worldwide.

12. There are many possible initiation and long-term management methods

that could be used. The LDS church might offer a loan or grant to this organization. Or the church might design and build it and then turn it over to someone else to operate, perhaps through some leasing arrangement. If the LDS church did not want to make its efforts too public because of potential public relations problems, there might even be a way for it to remain anonymous. It is conceivable that the original cost could be paid back over time.

13. It could be that a local management group would care little about what the world thought of them, since that local group might see themselves as having little to lose, and would not be subject to much social "blowback" from the project, while the centralized church might be more concerned about such matters.

14. The Church already has some undeveloped land in Leland. A fully developed project area might need multiple chapels.

15. I believe the LDS Church could easily do this project if it chose to. It could set up even the most ambitious version of the project within two or three years, perhaps by slightly delaying some of its many temple building projects. Even at the highly ambitious $3 billion level, that would probably not be much of a strain on the Church or change its other plans very much.

Current church strategy

(And why the Church leaders probably will not help us with the orphanage project, at least not at the beginning.)

The first three presidents of the church used the same basic program as Christ used himself. Christ made clear his extreme focus on charity, and imposed no other expenses on the members. We should be able to remember that Christ fulfilled and ended the law of Moses, especially including ending the law of tithing, for which he showed great scorn during his ministry.

Every separate group of church members had their own patriarch who held all the sealing powers, so they didn't need any central headquarters or any fancy or expensive buildings to be able to carry out every aspect of the complete Gospel. And with a built-in social safety net based on charity for anyone who joined the church, the church apparently attracted a lot of good people and grew at a rate of at least 10% a year for the next 300 years.

But starting with Wilford Woodruff, the church changed its strategy into something else, and it has been gradually going further and further in that new direction. It has finally reached the logical end of that path. It must change direction or face continual near-paralysis or perhaps even extinction. It certainly cannot continue to grow enough to matter to anyone.

There are a few simple, basic rules that seem to control nearly everything which the Church does at the strategic level:

Rule number one: the church is largely controlled by outsiders
Rule number one is that the nature of the Church today is mostly controlled by the corrupt governments of the world. This really means that we have about 200 versions of the church, one for each of the world's 200 countries, not just a single version of the church. One might guess that it takes a huge administrative bureaucracy to administer 200 versions of the church instead of just one version of the church, and that partially explains why we have such an enormous government-style overhead staff at the Salt Lake City headquarters which operates this diplomatic regime that directs all the activities of these 200 versions of the church.

In order for the church to go into other countries using its current corporate form and current policies, it must receive permission from those various governments which are more or less corrupt. That means that the church must do absolutely nothing to threaten any of these organizations. The church must be as bland as possible. It must make it clear somehow to these corrupt foreign leaders that the church will never promote freedom-seeking activities of any kind or do anything else which might seem even slightly disruptive to these various corrupt leaders or groups of leaders or their societies.

The way it affects us here in the United States is this: we are not allowed to do anything in the United States that would seem the least bit threatening to a government somewhere else. (Especially today, with all the many news organizations and the Internet constantly carrying masses of new information around the world, it means that anything new done in the United States by the LDS Church would soon, often almost immediately, be made known everywhere else.)

There are many things which could be helpful to the church which we could do in the United States because of the great freedom we have here that would cause it to grow and be successful and be a great blessing to many people. But all of those things must be tamped down or remain essentially invisible so that the leaders of these other countries will not feel threatened in the least by the church being present there as a formal organization with a major headquarters in Salt Lake City. The church budget is larger than at least 30 countries, and perhaps as many as 60 countries, so it is likely to be treated as a serious potential political threat, if it chose to be a threat.

This means that the nature of the church in the United States has to be the lowest common denominator of every other country in the world. If there is one country where we can't do something in the rest of the world, then we can't do it here, because otherwise word would get out that we are inconsistent and that we might be a threat to some other governmental organization somewhere in the world. For example, if we encouraged the gathering of members from around the world, we might be viewed as stealing their people or we might be viewed as being part of a brain-drain operation if we took their best people or allowed or encouraged them to move to the United States. Apparently, using this logic, the gathering has been officially canceled as of the 1970s, probably because that could be a source of irritation to these other governments.

(I should mention that some of the things I say here I am very confident are true, and other things I say are slightly speculative since I can't gather much data on some of these points. But I do believe that all the things I say are consistent, and if the church selects one policy then it must necessarily select another closely related policy to stay consistent.)

Rule number two: The lowest common denominator
So, the church in the United States having to be the lowest common denominator among all countries is the most basic rule of all. That really means that we can't do anything that normal Christians would do in the United States. We can't be actively promoting freedom as Christians have done for the past 2000 years, which process brought the United States into existence. The church has officially decided that it cannot continue that history of promoting freedom that brought us to where we are. That single factor causes me the largest amount of heartburn.

Again, we can't be promoting freedom here because that will, in the minds of the church leaders, lead to a suspicion by all the leaders of these other countries that we will inevitably start promoting freedom there in their countries, and of course those countries don't want that. A possible example is Venezuela today where there are quite a few church members in that country, and they probably would all like to be free, but the church presumably believes it cannot be involved in even the most bland way in helping them gain their freedom.

In other words, the church members abroad are expected to stay in the countries where they joined the church so that their leaving is not a threat. Many of those countries have such terrible economic and social situations that it makes it almost impossible for someone to live the gospel there because of all the conflicts that they will have with the mainline society and the government. At the same time, they can't take any steps to change that society to make it more bearable because that would be a threat to the ruling powers there. The local people, the old settlers, would say "This is our culture, not yours, and your changes are not welcome here." Remember Jackson County Missouri? Things did not go well for the members who wanted to actually live the gospel there.

Those conflicts with local societies argue very strongly for foreign members to leave their particular version of Babylon and come to the United States where the sheer numbers of church members would build up a huge pool of freedom-loving people who could keep the United States on an even keel and keep it from destroying itself through adopting worldly atheistic beliefs and practices. However, someone at church headquarters has made the choice that it is currently more beneficial to church headquarters to proceed using the current strategy. That means that individual church members out in these branches of Babylon are hurt very much by this church policy. They are asked to sacrifice needlessly on behalf of the church headquarters itself. Strangely enough, the very lack of privileges of members in those foreign countries gives excuses for the Salt Lake City bureaucrats to have additional privileges here as they travel to deal with some of the problems there. I see nothing fair or necessary about that at all. The church leaders in Salt Lake City can travel the world at will, and have a great time, but the members abroad are chained to their current locations.

Another layer deeper

So now it's time to go another layer deeper. So why would the church want to keep people living in these often very unpleasant Third World countries when they could come to the United States or perhaps some other First World country and enjoy the blessings of freedom and be able to live the Gospel exactly as they would like?

Apparently, through trial and error, the church headquarters has discovered that the people in Utah and in the United States will consistently pay the largest amount of tithing to church headquarters if there are certain conditions in effect. The church needs to keep members in these other countries, not for their own sake or for the sake of the other people there, but because they represent trophies which can be presented as reasons and proof that the church is being successful and why the church members should keep paying in their tithing money. Also, when the church is able to build chapels and temples in these other countries, that has multiple policy effects. It tells the tithe-paying people in the United States that the church must be achieving success because it has now been able to plant another symbol, another trophy, in one of these foreign countries, so that the people in Utah can feel like they are being successful even though they have no idea what's actually going on in the world.

Actually, I consider the building of a temple in one these foreign countries to be a major step backwards in many cases, the most egregious case being in East Germany during the Cold War. What that really means is that the church has finally given away enough of the freedom of their own members to make a deal with the usually corrupt powers-that-be there so that those people will allow us to build a temple there. We have dumbed down or simplified the Gospel to the extent that is required in that area so that we have satisfied the corrupt attitudes of the governing men or bodies of men so that we can build a temple there. I consider this, as I say, a step backwards. There might be many things that were possible for church members to do quietly before they became so visible through their temples, and perhaps to a less extent through their chapels, and now they can't do some of those things anymore because they have to behave in a certain prescribed way. They become hostages to that temple which has been built. That means, in most cases, their freedom and personal ability to live the Gospel in everyday life actually goes lower.

We then have a trade-off. Yes, those foreign members have the chance to go to a temple and perform some ordinances themselves and for the dead, but their own daily lives are worse than they were before or worse than they could be somewhere else. The temple actually keeps them peaceful -- it gives them an outlet for their energies which otherwise might be devoted to helping others and improving freedom. That makes the temple a kind of albatross around their necks, although I assume it is not obvious most of the time.

The church headquarters probably considers a temple to be a good thing because it will pacify those people and stop them from trying to leave or trying to disrupt the local corrupt society by trying to make it better. But it actually puts them in chains. They could easily go to some other country for their temple ordinances, especially if some element of the church helped them, and they would learn some interesting things in the process. Of course, it might also stimulate them to want to be more free to live the gospel, and that is what the church is trying to avoid. The church ends up having to manage member expectations.

Also, it should be mentioned here, that temples are not a necessary part of the gospel at all. The people after the time of Christ had no buildings at all for 300 years and they did very nicely. We somehow forget that rather important little historical fact. An endowment house served the people of Salt Lake City for 40 years before the temple there was finished. It seemed to be perfectly adequate.

The early Christians were always persecuted, at least in the sense that they could not build any buildings, whether chapels or temples. But that restriction turned out to be an unexpected blessing in disguise, because they could spend all of their resources on helping each other. We are requiring members in these other countries to live under all sorts of legal restrictions, somewhat the same way as the Saints had to live in Rome. None of that is necessary or desirable except that is the preferred business model of the Salt Lake City headquarters. I don't see any good gospel purpose for any of it.

I was told by a person who had once been a stake president, that the Church strives to keep a certain balance between those who live in the United States, who are paying for almost everything, and those in foreign countries who are spending a big part of that money in their countries. The church in these other countries cannot be allowed to get very large because the church cannot "support them in the style to which the church would like them to become accustomed," with buildings of specific kinds, unless they are getting enough money from the United States. It is nearly always a net loss overseas concerning contribution revenues. It is always a major expense (and sometimes a major embarrassment to the people receiving it) to support these foreign groups of people, at least if we insist on having lots of nice buildings for them. So it is good to have the church be large in the United States where the church gets all its money, but the churches in the rest of the world can't be allowed to get too large because we can't spend more money on them than is supplied by the people in Utah and elsewhere. That is the balancing act on the money scene.

Of course, those are all completely artificial barriers to growth in other countries, intentionally imposed by the church headquarters itself to maximize its control and its profits. After Christ, the church quickly spread through areas of Greece and elsewhere with no impediments because the only thing the new members had to do was take care of each other. There were no capital investment or start-up costs or taxes required to do that.

Almost inconceivable to today's church members, those early members did not have to send any tithing to anyone, so there was no need for banking operations, big buildings, etc. Those new members did not need to basically pay a franchise tax to some headquarters unit somewhere in the world to be allowed to move forward according to certain legalistic franchise rules enforced by a US religious corporate entity wrongly claiming exclusive copyright ownership of all the gospel texts and concepts.

If the church let these other areas of the world just do their own thing, as at the time of Christ, and pay no tithing/salvation franchise tax in order to operate successfully, the US members might suddenly get the idea in their heads that they didn't need to pay any franchise (or temple ordinance) tax themselves, and then the whole system would collapse (which is what needs to happen anyway). Priesthood ordinances are all supposed to be free, especially including temple ordinances.

The Salt Lake City people build buildings, but charge perhaps an outrageous overhead charge of perhaps 500% for doing so and allow no competition. They are a monopoly in this area and charge monopoly profits. Perhaps they internally sometimes justify their enormous overhead charges using that kind of government contract negotiation logic, although they would never use that logic on the members.)

The church has been engaged in a worldwide branding process which is unnecessary, but apparently makes the Salt Lake City people feel more important. They have greater control at the detail level in all these places, it seems to them. This apparently helps teach and reinforce the claimed need to pay a license or franchise tax for all church activities. And, there is apparently a lot of money to be made in constructing church buildings, which supports a whole construction bureaucracy of well-paid and therefore naturally very supportive members.

The temple building/temple work strategy

Again, through trial and error, church headquarters has discovered that, since the church tries to do almost nothing to change the society around it, and engages in hardly any measurable amount of charity, since doing serious charitable works can change societies, and that is to be avoided at all costs, one has to decide what happens to people's money and time in this headquarters-preferred situation. Building temples and doing temple work is actually a way of distracting church members, intentionally using up their money and their energies without allowing them to do anything that matters in the real world.

It is all very fine for members to do work for the dead. They can be reminded of how the plan of salvation works and they can feel like they're contributing, but, more importantly, they are being kept off the streets, so to speak. If people are convinced that the most important thing they can do is work for the dead, as opposed to work for the living, then that's going to keep them very tame. They send all their money to Salt Lake, they spend all their church time doing things which are invisible to everyone else, and there is no effect on the society, and the church can continue to seem completely bland and completely ineffective as far as any of the typical Christian activities would be. In other words, the temple building and temple work projects are giant make-work projects for church members to keep them from being active in the lives of living people, and instead encouraging them to spend all their time working on behalf of people who are not here and will not cause any trouble in society no matter what you do for them. They will not change their earthly attitudes or their votes, etc.

Spy vs. spy

Our little group needs to operate in a stealthy way, just like the church is operating in a stealthy way around the world. We think we are living in a Gospel society here in Utah, but we are not. We see the corruption of our local governments, and the church must take a lot of the blame for that. Since they will never support the Constitution anywhere else, why would they support it in Utah? That would be acting inconsistently. We are gradually importing all the wickedness of the world, and doing it intentionally, because the church leaders think we need to blend with the world, not be a peculiar people who stand out and who do important Christian things and who change societies.

So, the church itself is part of the corruption here in Utah because they have imported it because it seemed convenient. I think we have finally reached the end of that possibility. It should not be allowed to be stealthy anymore. The whole thing, the whole gospel project, is collapsing and going up in smoke because they have let it "grow wild" for so long, imagining that avoiding any active interference with the downward slide of society was actually in their business interest. So now a big charitable project will have to stay under the radar of the church for a while or they will try to squelch us and squeeze us out. We need to be aware of that, but simply not talk about it or make it much of an issue. We need to just go on our way and do what we can legally on our own in a free country which is barely just still free.

The church will start to feel like we are putting them in a bad light, making it seem like their old business model of total passivity won't work and they can't keep claiming and pretending that they are pushing the full gospel worldwide, when they are only promoting the thinnest shadow of the real gospel. They are just building up trophies to get money from United States people. It's quite possible that they have been doing this so long that nobody at church headquarters even knows what the basic strategy is -- they may just be mindlessly continuing the "traditions of the fathers" by rote But I'm sure there are some people who understand the strategy and enforce it, or it would have gone a different way already. We just need to be alert that we are playing a double game here, but feel confident that we are doing the right thing, nonetheless.

Likely church analysis and reaction

So perhaps we can discuss what the church will probably think about this Leland project. Abortion has become a major political issue, perhaps the biggest political issue of our times. If we agree with the good Christians who were active in Rome in rescuing and adopting discarded babies, we would want to do something about at least changing the effects of these pagan abortion rituals that are going on, this infanticide. But to do that, we obviously will have a political effect because we will be backing up the legislative work of the 17 Christian states who have decided to do what they can to minimize abortions that occur in their states. I am assuming they will not have a plan in effect to deal with the aftermath of the laws they pass. There will still be just as many unwanted children, even if they are allowed to go to full term and be born, but they will still be just as unwanted or perhaps more of them will be unwanted than the million a year who have been killed through abortions. So, someone needs to give those states the practical backup for their political crusade. So, we will obviously then be right in the middle of a highly emotional political issue.

We would be saying that we believe in the sanctity of life which includes the right to life, the right to be born, and that puts us squarely in conflict with the political left. We will be anything but bland. We will be sticking out like a sore thumb, as they say.

All of this potential political visibility is exactly what the church leaders will want to avoid because that will hamper their "non-political, business franchise 'McDonald's' operation" work, as they see it, in other countries. It's interesting to note that the abortion rate in the rest of the world, on a per capita basis, is about three times what it is in the United States. In other words, the Christian heritage of the United States has already kept the abortion rate quite low compared to the rest of the world. If the rest of the world sees LDS Church members here actively helping to lower the number of abortions, and to find homes for all of the children who are rescued, they are probably going to have numerous bad reactions to that. For example, they might say "Someone is stealing our children and using them against us by teaching them a different value system." Someone will fairly quickly figure that out and be upset. Just the idea of confronting and resisting the political left (a bland term for Satanism) is going to get us into deep trouble. The church will immediately want to stop this process because, as they will likely see it, it will be threatening their bureaucratic power and their stable income for all the reasons I mentioned above. (It may take some intricate reasoning to piece together the actual, possibly quite indirect, church reaction since leaders are not in the habit of speaking candidly about policy matters).

So, not only will the church probably decide not to help this project, it will likely engage in some active efforts to stop it. There is a tiny chance that if we war-game this out for them, and show that they have to support this project or become irrelevant themselves, then maybe they will support it. But that is extremely unlikely to begin with. The chances go up over time if the project is successful.

The central headquarters could decide to jump in and use all their assembled management expertise to give such projects a rocket boost, but that would require an enormous set of policy changes at church headquarters.

There is another aspect here which needs to be mentioned. It is likely that there are many church members who are quietly or even subconsciously a little bit uneasy about what the Church has been doing, in the last 50 years, of remaining completely passive on every important issue that relates to religion and politics. Religion and politics are always intertwined. There is no cure for that. Politics is the way we show our morality, and morality comes from religion, and there is no avoiding this conflict. In the long-term, you have to make a choice to go with Christianity or with Satanism, and unfortunately, the LDS Church has decided that their short-term benefit is to go with the political left on almost every issue, perhaps being just a few years behind them so that they don't seem to be either too eager or too resistant.

Church members can choose to continue to do more mostly invisible temple work, and pay for building more temples that do almost nothing to change society, and in this way the members can manage to do essentially no charity at all, or those members can take the gospel bull by the horns, so to speak, and take the scriptures seriously, and make charity our number one activity. If we devote billions of dollars to charitable activities that could be quite noticeable in the sense that we will be changing society for the better. In most cases that would be highly commended by other Christians in our country and would be condemned by the corrupt leaders and many of the people nationwide and worldwide. But the conflict would become very clear. If church members then decide to send their money to support these somewhat aggressive charitable activities like limiting abortion and promoting the gathering -- which are actually two unexpectedly interrelated aspects of the gathering, since they are just different paths to get all the good spirits together -- then that will potentially mean an immediate drop in the tithing income to the central church, assuming they will refuse to use the tithing money for any of these highly commendable charitable projects.

Incidentally, the church members should be eagerly involved in correct education instead of supporting corrupt state systems, that nearly all aggressively promote leftist ideologies, so that would be another project which would be a subproject of the Leland Project, providing the proper education for the children that are saved from the fires of Moloch, as they used to say about ritual infanticide.

So, we need to be ready to experience some pushback from the church and we might as well know why it's happening, so we will not get too confused or discouraged. Unfortunately, church leaders have been very clever in presenting to a politically unsophisticated church membership arguments for what they do which seem semi-convincing. Unfortunately, the truth is, that the church leadership have been skirting the truth and telling some outright lies in order to keep their control over the income flow of tithing from church members. It's rather an unpleasant shock to discover that LDS Church members have been manipulated so much for so long, but I think we have finally reached the point where the real story has to be told and people have to wake up.

The church should be at 200 million members
If the gospel were being taught and practiced properly, after 200 years of operation I think it would be at the 200 million level already, large enough to keep United States on an even political keel. However, the church today is only teaching and practicing about 25% of the gospel. We might find nearly all correct teachings somewhere buried in the literature, but we are not DOING any of those things -- we don't support freedom, we don't do charity on a grand scale, we don't resist abortion, etc., etc.

Last year, the church apparently added only 3000 new long-term people to its active membership. That is close enough to zero to call it zero. And it costs us at least $15 billion in total member costs every year just to keep from shrinking.

Our growth rate is so pitifully small, that it is hardly even worth discussing, but some of the numbers the church puts out may seem confusing, so only for that reason it might be worthwhile to present the various numbers and attempt to analyze and compare them.

There Must Be More to the Pro-Life Cause

May 16th, 2019
by Erick Erickson

I support legislation in Alabama, Georgia, and elsewhere to restrict killing children behind the euphemism of abortion.

I also think pro-lifers must do other things as well. Should we be successful, there will be women carrying children they do not want and there will be women who bear costs with no fathers around to help them. We must do more to provide social stability for these moms.

Pro-lifers must be willing to fight for adoption reform across the states. We should support making it more efficient to adopt by cutting bureaucratic red tape. We must work to end laws that allow mothers who give up their children to change their minds once an adoption has gone through. We must work to encourage more interracial adoptions.

We must also work to improve the social safety net to help women. Churches need to step up on this, not just taxpayers. This burden should be on the pro-life community, not just the state. We need to make it easier for mothers to get care they need. We need to make it easier for them to collect from deadbeat dads. Frankly, we also need to make it easier for deadbeat dads to find jobs to help pay for support. Sometimes a catch 22 develops where a father falls behind on payments to help his children and goes to jail, even though he is trying to earn money to help his child.

This cannot be a “ban abortion” approach because then the pro-life community will be accepting the abortion community’s critique that we only care about children in the womb.

Additionally, we need to understand the new fronts the left will open. Some activists will work to curtail adoption choices through targeting faith-based adoption agencies in the name of tolerance. They’ll shut off the avenues by which adoptions can happen in the name of tolerance, then complain that the adoption process is too burdensome and abortion is the answer.

Restricting abortion is a good thing. It is killing a human being. But restricting abortion without helping mothers and children is cruel. A healthy pro-life community will step up and move beyond restrictions on abortion towards greater social and community support for mothers with nowhere to turn.

https://theresurgent.com/2019/05/16/there-must-be-more-to-the-pro-life-caus

Ohio Just Became the Fifth State to Ban Abortion at 6 Weeks

Apr. 11, 2019 By Madeleine Aggeler

Ohio has become the fifth state to ban abortion at six weeks. A so-called "fetal heartbeat bill," which outlaws abortion before most women even realize they're pregnant, passed the state legislature on Wednesday morning; newly elected governor Mike DeWine signed it the next day.

Ohio joins four other states that have passed similar six-week abortion bans: Mississippi, Kentucky, Iowa, and North Dakota. In addition, Georgia passed a six-week abortion ban back in March, and openly anti-abortion Governor Brian Kemp, who has voiced his support for the bill, has until May 10 to sign it.

Heartbeat bills ban all or most abortions once a heartbeat can be detected — which is usually at the embryonic stage, around five or six weeks — severely restricting the usual, legal threshold at which states can ban abortion, which is considered to be when a fetus is viable outside the womb (around 24 weeks). Such bills, in effect, prohibit nearly all abortions, because they leave women with such a small window in which to confirm they are pregnant, and then have the procedure done.

While these laws have all been challenged in court, and blocked from taking effect because they run counter to *Roe v. Wade*, they are part of a larger effort to eventually overturn *Roe* at level of the Supreme Court, and a growing push against women's reproductive rights in the United States. Here is a closer look at what has happened with these bans in each state.

Ohio

Ohio's fetal heartbeat bill was shut down twice before, by former governor John Kasich. Ohio's current governor, however, Mike DeWine, signed it shortly after it passed the legislature. The ACLU has said it will challenge the measure as soon as it is signed.

Georgia (passed; not yet signed by the governor)

Passed in March, Georgia's HB481, or the Living Infants Fairness and Equality (LIFE) Act, would ban all abortions after six weeks, including in cases of rape or incest. It also redefines who is considered to be a "natural person," expanding the term to include "an unborn child." This new definition would **potentially make mothers** who receive abortions and doctors who administer them open to criminal prosecution.

https://www.thecut.com/2019/04/which-states-have-passed-six-week-abortion-bans.html

New York abortion law allows infanticide

Posted: Feb. 6, 2019 10:15 am
To The Herald-Whig:

Democrats hold many positions that I disagree with. But the one that has caused me the greatest pain is abortion.

I believe in the sanctity of life at any stage of development, but now the Democrats have crossed a line that no civilized person, regardless of their politics, should support.

The Democrats are now stepping beyond abortion to infanticide. If you're not familiar with that term, it is the killing of a baby after it is born, its heart pumping blood, its lungs pumping oxygen into that blood. The infant can cry and smile, and it can take in nourishment, either through its mother's breast or from a bottle.

New York lawmakers, with the support of Democratic governor Andrew Cuomo, have approved late-term abortions up to and including after birth. The New York law, in addition to approving abortion at any stage of pregnancy, also moves the state's abortion regulations from the criminal code to the health codes, prohibiting criminal prosecution for medical professionals who perform abortions. The Democratic governor of Virginia is pushing for a similar law.

Under the new law, in New York a medical professional is now defined as a licensed physician, nurse practitioner, physician assistant and licensed midwives. And under the new law, the decision to abort lies with the mother, regardless of the baby's physical condition.

Whether or not we choose to remain a civilized society will be decided in November 2020. If killing newborn babies doesn't bother you, vote Democratic. If you have one shred of respect for human life, you have to vote Republican.

If you believe abortion at any stage of development is OK, please go to YouTube and type in the search box "Dr. Levatino destroys abortion in two minutes." His description of a late-term abortion while testifying before a congressional committee sickened me. Today, he no longer performs abortions except to save the life of the mother.

William Mussetter, Quincy
https://www.whig.com/20190206/new-york-abortion-law-allows-infanticide#

March 2018
Fact Sheet

Induced Abortion Worldwide

GLOBAL INCIDENCE AND TRENDS

- During 2010–2014, an estimated 56 million induced abortions occurred each year worldwide. This number represents an increase from 50 million annually during 1990–1994, mainly because of population growth.
- As of 2010–2014, the global annual rate of abortion for all women of reproductive age (15–44) is estimated to be 35 per 1,000, which is a reduction from the 1990–1994 rate of 40 per 1,000.
- The estimated global abortion rate as of 2010–2014 is 35 per 1,000 for married women and 26 per 1,000 for unmarried women.1
- Women in developing regions have a higher likelihood of having an abortion than those in developed regions—36 vs. 27 per 1,000.
- Between 1990–1994 and 2010–2014, the abortion rate declined markedly in developed regions, from 46 to 27 per 1,000, but remained roughly the same in developing regions.
- The annual number of abortions during the period fell in developed regions, from about 12 million to seven million; in contrast, the number increased in developing regions, from 38 million to 49 million, although this change mainly reflects the growth of the reproductive-age population.
- The proportion of abortions worldwide that occur in developing regions rose from 76% to 88% between 1990–1994 and 2010–2014.
- Globally, 25% of all pregnancies ended in abortion in 2010–2014. Between 1990–1994 and 2010–2014, the proportion of pregnancies ending in abortion fell from 39% to 27% in developed countries, while it rose from 21% to 24% in developing countries.1

https://www.guttmacher.org/fact-sheet/induced-abortion-worldwide

Was Abortion the 'Leading Cause of Death' in 2018?

Leading causes of death worldwide and abortion estimates -- two different measures?

Bethania Palma, Published 3 January 2019 -- Snopes

On 31 December 2018, the Breitbart.com website reported under the headline "Abortion Leading Cause of Death in 2018 with 41 Million Killed" that "there have been some 41.9 million abortions performed in the course of the year," making abortion "the number one cause of death worldwide in 2018, with more than 41 million children killed before birth."

That article spawned a ripple of similar reports on various other sites, most of which referred back to the Breitbart piece, which itself rested on a figure gleaned from Worldometers, a real-time tool that "analyzes the available data, performs statistical analysis, and builds our algorithm [to feed our] real time estimates." Worldometers states that its abortion figures refer to induced abortions (as opposed to miscarriages), and that:

> The data on abortions displayed on the Worldometers' counter is based on the latest statistics on worldwide abortions published by the World Health Organization (WHO). According to WHO, every year in the world there are an estimated 40-50 million abortions. This corresponds to approximately 125,000 abortions per day.

However, the most recent figure on abortions from WHO we could locate dated from 2014 and was slightly higher than Worldometers' tally. WHO estimated that between 2010 and 2014, an average of 56 million induced abortions occurred worldwide each year.

If WHO's estimate of 56 million abortions annually held steady through 2016, when they released their survey on the top ten leading causes of death globally, it would be true that the number of abortions worldwide outnumbered overall deaths from heart disease and stroke, the top two causes of death that year. In 2016, ischemic heart disease and stroke killed a total of 15.2 million people worldwide, according to WHO, noting that "These diseases have remained the leading causes of death globally in the last 15 years":

Top 10 global causes of deaths, 2016

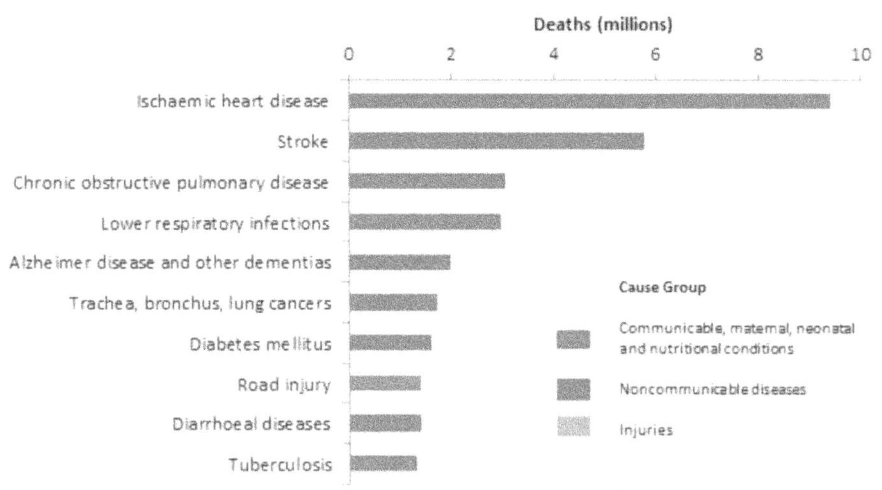

Source: Global Health Estimates 2016: Deaths by Cause, Age, Sex, by Country and by Region, 2000-2016. Geneva, World Health Organization; 2018.

We can infer from WHO statistics that the difference between the number of abortions worldwide versus the number of deaths from heart disease and stroke worldwide is not a new dynamic, although viral stories proclaiming that abortions "now" outnumber deaths from those other causes imply that fact is a recent development.

Stating that abortion is the "leading cause of death" worldwide (as opposed to a medical procedure) is a problematic pronouncement, because that stance takes a political position, one which is at odds with the scientific/medical world. The medical community does not confer personhood upon fetuses that are not viable outside the womb, so counting abortion as a "cause of death" does not align with the practices of health organizations such as WHO and the Centers for Disease Control and Prevention (CDC), as Heather Boonstra, director of public policy for the reproductive health research organization Guttmacher Institute, told us:

> Abortion is a legal, constitutionally protected medical procedure in the United States. It's not considered a cause of death by CDC, WHO and other leading authorities, and statistics on induced abortion are excluded in the CDC's national fetal-death statistics.

The legal, philosophical, religious, and scientific arenas provide no definitive answers as to when personhood begins. Medical advances continue to push the stage at which a fetus can be considered viable outside the womb, as *Wired* reported in 2015:

> When life begins is, of course, the central disagreement that fuels the controversy over abortion. Attacks on abortion rights are now more veiled and indirect — like secret videos pointing to Planned Parenthood's fetal tissue donations, or state legislation that makes operating abortion clinics so onerous they have to shut down. But make no mistake, the ultimate question is, when does a fetus become a person — at fertilization, at birth, or somewhere in between?
>
> Here, modern science offers no clarity. If anything, the past century of scientific advances have only made the answer more complicated. As scientists have peered into wombs with ultrasound and looked directly at sperm entering an egg, they've found that all the bright lines they thought existed dissolving.

Concluding an entry on the topic, RationalWiki quotes developmental biologist Scott Gilbert in saying that "The entity created by fertilization is indeed a human embryo, and it has the potential to be human adult. Whether these facts are enough to accord it personhood is a question influenced by opinion, philosophy and theology, rather than by science."

Although the U.S. Supreme Court ruling in the landmark 1973 *Roe. v. Wade* case held that unduly restrictive state regulation of abortion was unconstitutional, fetal personhood very much remains a legal issue and not merely an abstract philosophical one. As the *New York Times* reported, the enactment of fetal personhood statutes in some states has resulted in the prosecution of women over circumstances that ended or endangered their pregnancies:

> You might be surprised to learn that in the United States a woman coping with the heartbreak of losing her pregnancy might also find herself facing jail time. Say she got in a car accident in New York or gave birth to a stillborn in Indiana: In such cases, women have been charged with manslaughter.
>
> In fact, a fetus need not die for the state to charge a pregnant woman with a crime. Women who fell down the stairs, who ate a poppy seed bagel and failed a drug test or who took legal drugs during pregnancy — drugs prescribed by their doctors — all have been accused of endangering their children.
>
> So what motivates these prosecutions? The reality is that, in many cases, these women are collateral damage in the fight over abortion. As the legal debate over a woman's right to terminate her pregnancy has intensified, so too has the insistence of anti-abortion groups that fertilized eggs and fetuses be granted full rights and the protection of the law — an extreme legal argument with little precedent in American law before the 1970s.
>
> Frustrated by the Roe v. Wade decision that legalized abortion, many in the anti-abortion movement hope for a sweeping rollback under a conservative Supreme Court — one that would block access to abortion even in states that protect women's access to such health services.
> https://www.snopes.com/news/2019/01/03/abortion-leading-cause-of-death/

What the Alabama Abortion Law Means for Women Across the Country

By Macaela Mackenzie
November 7, 2018

The results of Tuesday's midterms marked a number of history-making elections for women: Alexandria Ocasio-Cortez of New York became the youngest person ever elected to Congress, Ilhan Omar of Minnesota and Rashida Tlaib of Michigan broke barriers as the first Muslim women elected, Sharice Davids of Kansas and Deb Haaland of New Mexico made major strides for Native American women with their wins, and Jahana Hayes of Connecticut and Ayanna Pressley of Massachusetts became the first black women to represent their states.

But the historic elections aren't just about who's repping the country. New abortion laws, which were voted on in three states—Alabama, West Virginia, and Oregon—have implications for women across the country. Two amendments passed last night are putting women's ability to access safe abortions in jeopardy.

ALABAMA
Alabama's abortion measure, which passed by a wide margin, is major. The amendment to the state's constitution is what's called a "personhood law," which grants the right to life from the moment of conception. Essentially, it means that in the state of Alabama, a fetus or embryo has the same rights as a full-fledged person.

"They've granted full rights to the unborn from the moment of conception—that means fertilized eggs—while they strip away all of the rights for pregnant women," says Yashica Robinson, M.D., a gynecologist in Alabama and a board member of Physicians for Reproductive Health.

> These laws are known as "trigger laws," which means if Roe v. Wade is overturned, they could trigger an outright ban on abortion, criminalizing the procedure for women in those states.

The threat to women's rights is bad enough, but abortion-rights supporters worry that the amendment might also jeopardize infertility treatments like IVF. "In any type of assisted reproductive technology treatment, most commonly in vitro fertilization, embryos are formed," Dr. Robinson explains. "Generally, you're going to form more embryos than you're going to use." What happens to those unused embryos is already a hotly debated issue, and Alabama's newly minted amendment could make the issue of disposing of unused embryos even murkier. "The way this amendment was written, it seems like it's just about abortion, but it clearly says that it protects the rights of the unborn—and that's from the moment of creation," Dr. Robinson says.

The approved amendment states that no provisions in Alabama's constitution provide a woman with the right to have an abortion—no exceptions for cases of rape, incest, or when the life of the mother is at risk.

For Dr. Robinson, that's not only "devastating"; it violates her duty as a physician. "As a physician I've taken an oath to do what's best for my patients. That means advocating for access to health care for them that values their privacy, their autonomy, and their dignity," she says. "My job, even when it's a hard decision to make, is to counsel the patient and help them to make health care decisions that are best for them. [The amendment will] harm patients and bind the hands of physicians."

WEST VIRGINIA
West Virginia also passed a ballot measure that will restrict women's access to abortion. Just as in Alabama, West Virginia's Amendment 1 paves the way

to criminalize abortion, stripping women of protections to their federal right to an abortion. The amendment also strips state funding for abortions through insurance programs like Medicaid.

"Being able to pay for an abortion is a key part of being able to access an abortion," says Yamani Hernandez, executive director of the National Network of Abortion Funds. "The reason why abortion funds exist is because abortion is out of reach for so many."

State laws that strip funding for abortion care, often disproportionately affect disadvantaged women, she says. "This is something that we consider to be discriminatory, something that targets people of color and people with lower incomes and discriminates against people based on the insurance coverage that people have."

> “We need legislators across the country to understand that abortion is health care, health care is a right, and a right is not a right if every patient can’t afford to access it.”

(Oregon voted on a similar ballot measure, which proposed ending state funding of abortion except when the procedure was medically necessary, but it was voted down by a wide margin.)

So what does this mean for women's rights to reproductive care across the U.S.? Alabama and West Virginia’s newly approved abortion amendments are important on a national level. Laws like the newly passed amendments in Alabama and West Virginia are known as “trigger laws,” which means if Roe v. Wade is overturned, they could trigger an outright ban on abortion, criminalizing the procedure for women in those states, The Washington Post reports. (In an NBC poll taken yesterday, two thirds of voters supported keeping the landmark ruling that grants the right to an abortion in place.)

This possibility is what worries abortion activists the most. "It makes our work dramatically more urgent and important, because if that starts to happen, it’s going to make travel to get abortions even harder," Hernandez says. "People are already traveling hundreds of miles to get an abortion. This makes the legal right to abortion completely out of reach for too many. "

In other areas of the country, voters elected officials with track records of fighting for reproductive health like Jacky Rosen and Tina Smith (who is a former Planned Parenthood employee). “In 2018 voters made their voices heard loud and clear: They want elected officials who champion reproductive health care and will stand up for women," Dawn Laguens, executive vice president of the Planned Parenthood Action Fund, said in a statement sent to Glamour.

Hernandez says those victories are cause to be optimistic about the future—she's not giving up on health care funding that includes abortion care. “We need legislators across the country to understand that abortion is health care," Willie Parker, M.D., board chair of Physicians for Reproductive Health, said in a statement sent to Glamour. "Health care is a right, and a right is not a right if every patient can’t afford to access it.”
https://www.glamour.com/story/what-alabama-abortion-law-means-for-women-across-the-country

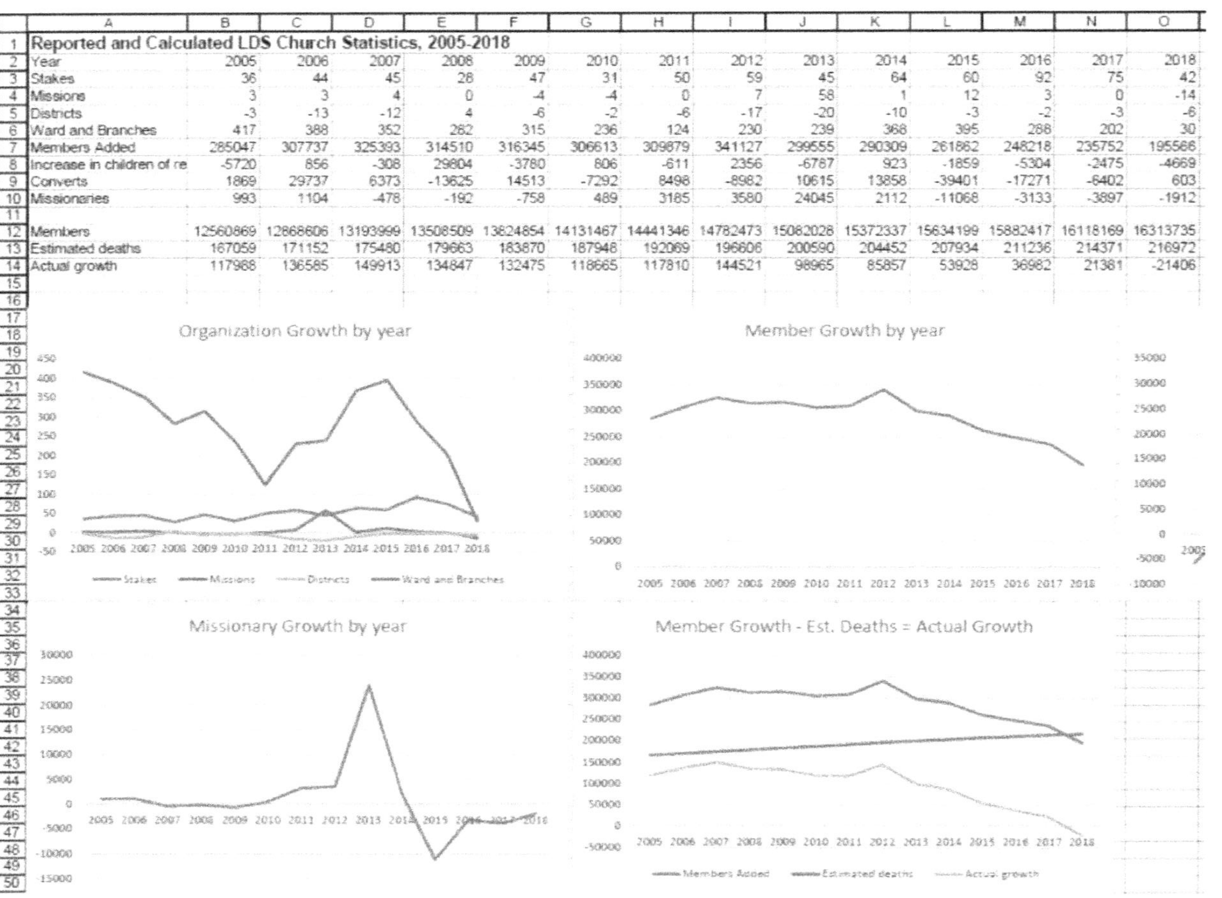

Reported and Calculated LDS Church Statistics, 2005-2018

Year	2005	2006	2007	2008	2009	2010	2011	2012	2013	2014	2015	2016	2017	2018
Stakes	36	44	45	28	47	31	50	59	45	64	60	92	75	42
Missions	3	3	4	0	-4	-4	0	7	58	1	12	3	0	-14
Districts	-3	-13	-12	4	-6	-2	-6	-17	-20	-10	-3	-2	-3	-6
Ward and Branches	417	388	352	282	315	236	124	230	239	368	395	288	202	30
Members Added	285047	307737	325393	314510	316345	306613	309879	341127	299555	290309	261862	248218	235752	195566
Increase in children of re	-5720	856	-308	29804	-3780	806	-611	2356	-6787	923	-1859	-5304	-2475	-4669
Converts	1869	29737	6373	-13625	14513	-7292	8498	-8982	10615	13858	-39401	-17271	-6402	603
Missionaries	993	1104	-478	-192	-758	489	3185	3580	24045	2112	-11068	-3133	-3897	-1912
Members	12560869	12868606	13193999	13508509	13824854	14131467	14441346	14782473	15082028	15372337	15634199	15882417	16118169	16313735
Estimated deaths	167059	171152	175480	179663	183870	187948	192069	196606	200590	204452	207934	211236	214371	216972
Actual growth	117988	136585	149913	134847	132475	118665	117810	144521	98965	85857	53928	36982	21381	-21406

Chapter 21

Women's duties and opportunities under a proper program of charity – a well-funded Relief Society

[A separate book should be written on this topic, but, as a practical matter, only a brief chapter can be part of this book.]

If the church can't get the correct balance between the roles and responsibilities of men and women, then I'm not sure who can, and, at the moment, the church seems to be seriously out of balance, with the male-dominated central headquarters claiming far too much power and importance at the expense of the women.

Even in these days of rampant gender confusion, it doesn't seem too outrageous to claim that men and women have traditional roles on earth and in heaven, where the men tend to be the warriors and the builders, and the women tend to be the nurturers. In most cases, both genders enter into the world well prepared for those roles.

Traditionally, the men are the bread winners, and the women spread the peanut butter on it and pass it to those in need. In today's world, it appears that the zeal of the church leaders to require every religious nickel to pass through their fingers, basically cutting women out from their traditional charity activities on charges of "duplication," has greatly skewed things as a practical matter. The money the church receives today should mostly go to charity, to be handled mostly by the women, but instead, the male impulse to create empires and build things has dominated where it shouldn't dominate, and most of that money is channeled into pointless and wasteful and prideful activities.

I believe in the religious realm, everything should be backwards from what it is in the normal economy. In the normal economy men get the resources and build facilities, and let the women fill those facilities up and teach and bring happiness to the people involved, as might be seen at a hospitals and schools where women typically predominate. When the religious leaders confuse religious activities with the normal economy, they get everything backwards. The men are supposed to run businesses in the real world, partly to get resources for religious purposes, not create a nearly pointless religious business to absorb resources and keep them from going to real charity, where that religious business becomes a very bad substitute for real charity.

The church leaders might very well help collect resources for the women to use in charity activities, and then get out of the way and let the women do the work they are best qualified to do. Women should be basically in charge of all charitable activities – education, health care, the needs of old age, both short-term and long-term needs, etc.

Women are the ones who can bring life into the world, and they ought to be given all the authority and resources they need to bring those young people into the world, and to educate and care for them as needed. If the women had the responsibility and the resources to take care of these things, they would see that they were done correctly, where the men would, as often as not, get confused about what to do, as they do today. For example, women who have been through the process of bearing children themselves would be able to devise effective systems where women could feel confident and even eager about bearing children when they are young, with continuing confidence that they will have a respected and productive place in society when they have moved beyond their childbearing years.

The women would certainly help each other having babies, and presumably they would do something to stop the needless abortions, likely making changes to our society to structurally end this abomination. Today's church leaders seem to care nothing about that issue anymore, but the women would probably not let it pass, and would take vigorous action if given the opportunity.

There is an ongoing agitation among some women for the church to "Ordain Women," which I assume is a reaction to the church leaders' demand that they have absolute control over everything church-related, including money, architecture, charity, women's activities, etc. Considering human nature, that is probably a bad thing simply because when anyone has absolute control of anything, they are going to do some foolish things, even including the dreaded "unrighteous dominion" mentioned in the scriptures. Simply dividing up the resources and responsibilities will make sure that there are multiple viewpoints to be considered. Church leaders counsel against husbands trying to dominate a family, arguing that husband and wife are equal, while at the same time the church leaders want absolute dominance over the women in all matters of church administration. There is philosophical incoherence here.

Every known totalitarian dictatorship always develops egregious policies simply because they believe they can. The U.S. Constitution is based on the concept that there ought to be a separation of powers in all governmental activities, if for no other reason than to keep people honest and restrained.

The church ought to be implementing those principles internally and spontaneously, since freedom is such a basic principle of the gospel. The church is supposed to be teaching correct principles, but it fails to do so when it argues for absolute and unquestioned centralization of everything. Any arguments that the church is exempt from the U.S. Constitution and other similar constraints on administrative power ought to be poorly received by the members.

I don't know the feelings of the women involved in the "Ordain Women" movement, but I am guessing that if they were given the full responsibility for all charitable activities, plus the resources to do it, they would feel quite satisfied and challenged with their assignments and their opportunities. I doubt that they really want to supplant the men in ward and stake administration when they could have a great deal more fun and satisfaction taking care of the needs of the young and the poor.

I assume that giving women all of these resources and powers would make them far more powerful missionaries than any we have now, especially if they were inviting people into a network of those supported by charitable giving, creating an entire social insurance system for those who are willing to abide by the rules of the gospel. It would be ideal if these well-informed and determined women could preside over a nearly complete replacement of the corrupt and wasteful tax-and-spend "charity" systems operated by secular governments, legislated for the very purpose of displacing religious charitable activity. These private charity systems are at least 2 to 5 times more efficient than anything any government can create, and their superiority in financial efficiency and in meeting individual needs would quickly make these awkward Marxist systems obsolete.

Some examples
I believe that the men in church leadership positions have indeed elbowed out the women, and the church is suffering some serious consequences as a result. I would personally like to see most of what Mormons now call tithing go to the various levels of relief societies to be spent on charitable activities of every sort. With a combined churchwide budget of perhaps $10 billion a year, the ladies could staff themselves and do their own work in their own organizations and leave the guys to try to keep up through other means. They could ask the guys to help them, if that was needed, but otherwise they would be on their own. That should give them a pretty serious and satisfying assignment to work on. Pointless competition between men and women would mostly be ended.

We often hear about the troubles and woes of single adult wards. Some seem to like being segregated and concentrated so that they can make friends and seek marriage partners. But at other times, people seem to feel isolated and separate from the mainstream family-oriented church.

Ending most of the tithing that goes to the central church and keeping it at the ward and stake level could have some interesting effects. I think that could put some real life into those single adult wards. Imagine that there was a single adult ward with 200 members, all of them working, and each of them making, on average, about $50,000, meaning that they could each be paying $5000 a year in tithing, totaling about $1 million in all. If instead of sending that money to Salt Lake City where it is simply put in the church's money vaults, the ward could work together to decide how to spend that money and then work to actually implement their plan. That should instantly cause a great feeling of community and would certainly give them something interesting and constructive to do. They could throw some grand parties, maybe "hunger parties," while still being a very noticeable good influence in their cities. They would not be in the situation of sending all their money to Salt Lake City, and then feeling patronized when church leaders buy them some chips and salsa for some kind of activity. They could operate quite independently and creatively, as long as they stayed within some general boundaries. Freedom is what the gospel is all about. These members would have the option to spend their church contribution money any way they saw fit, but I assume many of them would choose to put it into combined activities.

Things would probably be much the same in regular married wards. One of the differences might be that, assuming the guys are making more money than their wives, the guys would supply the money, and the women would get to spend it on charitable activities. That's probably not all that different than it is today in many families, it's just that the women would then have at least 10 times as much money to spend and could take on some serious projects with their million dollars per ward. That would give the local relief society some real economic muscle, as should have been the case all along. I think all of those "ordain women" people would feel a great deal better about things if it was expected that they received essentially all of the tithing money in the church to administer wisely and professionally. With a $10 billion budget each year, they could likely do some interesting things.

It might be assumed that the central church would continue to receive a little bit of money, perhaps something in the 1% range instead of the 10% range. The important thing would be to make sure that even the 1% was not received by claim of right, but only from spontaneous generosity, earned by being trusted and doing quality work. The central offices could come up with good things to do which people could freely support, and they could receive whatever money people thought would be wisely used. People doing charity work outside of church headquarters might actually get more money because they would not be in a position to claim any legal right to get money without any accountability, typically like the taxation powers of governments. That might mean that the central offices would have to do twice as well in their planned charitable activities as someone outside the church, simply to keep the church leaders from falling prey to the constant temptation to make paying 1% the new duty which one must fulfill in order to get into the temples, be saved, etc.

We might notice that with at least $124 billion in the bank, earning interest, as was recently revealed, the church could go on exactly as it is forever and not receive another dollar in tithing funds. That endowment should certainly take care of any long-term building maintenance problems, etc. I don't suppose that is what the church leaders had in mind while they were accumulating all that money, but it makes perfect sense from the membership level.

Chapter 22

Creating and demonstrating a charity-based welfare system for the world

Almost by definition, it is nearly impossible to set up a theoretical system to tell a group of people possessing religious, economic, and political freedom how they should define and set up a system to offer social insurance to their religious or other cohesive group. The very definition of freedom mostly precludes that. However, there should still be some basic items of general information and some basic principles and parameters which should be applicable and operating in almost every situation

Top-down

There should be some definable and quantifiable features of a particular nation or world society which helps describe what is going on currently, and what any glaring deficiencies might be. That original analysis will then let someone offer a suggestion as to where everything should be moving to make improvements. The ideological statists of the world have essentially taken over the entire globe, so that it is difficult to even find examples of how things might be done a different way. Perhaps some obscure tribes have a different system, but we don't know about it, and it may have its own objectionable aspects. There are numerous successful historical examples, but, naturally, everyone's memory is extremely short, so that no matter how appropriate or successful some system might have been in the past, it has been blown away by progressive/socialist ideology and activism until it has now mostly disappeared down the "memory hole."

It should be useful just to begin with where and how the nations of the world spend the resources they have as relates to classically charitable or welfare functions. Those functions which were previously taken care of privately or by religious organizations have now been aggressively taken over by the new atheist religion as a part of the progressive/socialist war against religion. That also furthers the progressive/socialist/communist goal of getting rid of all competing functions and loyalties so that one can gradually create an absolute dictatorship.

I will begin by using US data from 2019. "In FY 2019, total US government spending, federal, state, and local, is "guesstimated" to be 35.8% GDP."

That figure of 35.8% of the nation's GDP being spent by governments at some level is a staggering amount and surely could be improved upon. We read in the Book of Mormon that people felt extremely repressed when they had to pay 10% or 20% of their income to their conquerors and enslavers. Under the Israelite kings the tax burden probably reached about 50%. In all of these cases, the people felt extremely persecuted. On this scale, we see that we are not so bad off as some have been, but we still have allowed ourselves to become greatly persecuted and our personal freedom greatly restricted. In our technological age there may actually be some justification for centralizing a higher level of technical functions such as communication systems, road building, justice systems, and armies, but beyond that, there is really "nothing new under the sun."

We start out with a 2019 US Gross Domestic Product of $21.5 trillion. That is the largest national GDP on the globe, and it sounds very good by itself. However, we have to notice that we also have a total government debt, including all levels, of about $25.8 trillion, noticeably larger than our GDP, and growing by at least $1.09 trillion a year just at the federal level, indicating that whatever we are doing is seriously out of balance, with no obvious way to correct that imbalance.

It should be useful to get an idea of which levels of government spend how much money, as shown in the next table.

Fiscal Year	*Federal Spending*	*State Spending*	*Local Spending*	*Total Spending*
2019	$4.53 trillion	$1.89 trillion	$1.95 trillion	$7.63 trillion

The next table shows the expenditures by category for all government types. For our purposes here, we want to separate the classically charitable or welfare functions which have been handled by religious organizations in the past, from the strictly nondenominational secular governmental operations which were the real purpose for forming these governments in the first place. Governments at various levels, especially at the federal level, have been aggressively using tax-and-spend principles to take over the functions which were traditionally allocated to religious organizations. Of course, this is the atheist religion using force to restrict the scope of the Christian religions, so it is still a "religious" function at the state level, it is just that that religion is statism/humanism/atheism instead of Christianity. Obviously, the rules applied and the goals sought are immensely different under the two systems of ideology or religion.

I calculate the classical charitable/welfare functions which have been taken over by secular/atheist governments as representing 22% of GDP under current arrangements. These functions include the government takeover of portions of pensions, healthcare, and education, and some separate and smaller categories of "government welfare" that cover different government programs than are used for the major three of pensions, healthcare, and education.

2019 US GDP $21.5 trillion					
All gov now uses 35.8% of GDP					
	Category	%	$		
Pensions	Religious	7	1.51		
Health Care	Religious	8	1.72		
Education	Religious	5	1.08		
Defense	Gov't	4	0.86		
Welfare	Religious	2	0.43		
Interest	Gov't	3	0.65		
Other	Gov't	7	1.51		
		36	7.74		
Keep in government accounts			2.58		
Move outside government			*5.16		
				use to get same result	use for extra projects
Religious aspects of gov. now	Religious	22	*4.73	1.58	3.15
	*Some of these costs just disappear, as with ending the interest on the national debt which now becomes nonexistent because it has been mostly based on having to borrow extra money to deliver all the many entitlements unwisely promised. That drops costs at least from $5.16T to $4.73T.				

Based on the typical waste, fraud, and abuse patterns that go on in all government programs, I'm going to say that a properly administered charity-based social insurance system could operate for one third of that 22% which is now being spent at the various levels of government. The big categories of pensions, healthcare, education, and the smaller and strangely separately-named "government welfare" (since all the categories are government welfare) represent 22% out of the 35.8%. All of those categories could be moved into the much more efficient sphere of a charity-based social insurance system. That would move $4.73 trillion out of the government tax-and-spend system into the charity-based system. I believe that the same important services could be done for one third of that cost, or $1.57 trillion, and the rest of the money, $3.15 trillion, could simply be returned to the working populace as extra income to improve their lives, or that extra money could be spent to go far beyond the current levels of charitable services and social insurance to improve things. That would especially be useful in the area of education, so that the information and behavior of the populace could be much more wise and more Christian.

To mention some of the gross inefficiencies and other waste, fraud, and abuse, we have to realize that in order to operate these government money transfer systems, we have to have a huge and expensive bureaucracy which determines the taxation level and then collects the taxes. Then there is the group of people, another huge and expensive bureaucracy, who actually distribute that collected tax money. If this were all done voluntarily and spontaneously, then these current bureaucracies could be cut to just a few percent of the size of current government tax-and-spend systems.

And finally, we have a clientele who cling to "entitlements" and lobby for increases, whether they are needed or not. Each of these organizations has their own "labor union" or pressure group, which adds to the inefficiency and endless pressure to increase taxes and increase payouts, regardless of actual need. Very often, those who get the most money are the least worthy of it and will use it the least efficiently. All of these problems can be resolved using a proper charity-based system, where honesty and wisdom prevail, and it is easy to imagine the whole system being at least three times as efficient and effective as current systems. There may even be cases where a charity-based system could be five times as effective as current systems, as far as efficiently using the funds available.

A charity-based system would also avoid all of the extreme rigidities and bureaucracies that are built into these mammoth military-style tax-and-spend welfare systems. A charity-based system would never do anything that did not make sense in the moment, adjusting everything as conditions changed in the nation and at the individual or family level. No federal, state, or local program can have that kind of flexibility, with the largest problems naturally being at the most general federal level, and therefore must allow for everything, which means that there are enormous structural problems which grow to staggering levels without being corrected, most likely eventually bringing about the collapse of the whole system because of these rigidities.

Bottom-up

Continuing with the national statistics, we see that the Federal Poverty Level (FPL) has been set in 2019 at $12,490 for a single adult and $4420 for each additional family member, whether adult or child. This "poverty level" number is a key parameter and index in deciding which benefits or entitlements are available to whom. This is as close as the government gets to individualizing the delivery of welfare resources as opposed to the nearly completely personal level that is implied in a charity-based system.

For a family of five with an FPL amount of $30,170, that ($30,170 / 5 =) $6034 per person.
Presumably these are considered survival level parameters. On top of those figures come the costs of schooling and healthcare and pensions, which may all be paid for by the federal government without costs to poor people. So the societal cost for these family groups can be very large indeed if they are completely supported by the public treasury as opposed to being independent or nearly independent themselves. One of the great problems with these mechanical systems is that they invite manipulation and exploitation so that so-called "welfare queens" may end up with as high an income as any middleclass person without doing anything more than just manipulating the system, without actually doing their part to meet their own economic needs.

I assume that a charity-based system would very quickly both help and put some major pressures on these kinds of people so that the amount of irresponsibility and fraud would be greatly reduced. That alone might cut the cost in half of the current welfare benefits paid out.

Overall, for people living in normal families, the system-specified level of minimum income might make sense. But it's not hard to see how someone would immediately start to try to game the system even at this low level. For example, a single person gets $12,490, but each additional person counted as part of the family only gets $4,420 dollars. This presents an immediate incentive to try to break up the family into separate parts, since they could get nearly 3 times as much money that way than if they present themselves as a family. For poor people in a ghetto, this could present overwhelming incentives to never have any groups of people that could be appear to be functioning as a family group. It may be hard for a mother to present her children as not being hers, so that each could be qualified for their own $12,490, but it would be easy to keep husbands away so that they get their separate $12,490 instead of just the $4,420. One might hope that this kind of petty calculation would not be important, but I suspect that it happens all the time.

Counted separately, the family members are worth 5 x $12,490 = $62,450, while together as a visible and functioning family unit they are only worth $30,170. They would thus get an extra $32,280, more than doubling their income, if they can just scam the system a little bit by avoiding looking and acting like a family unit. That FPL rate translates into $34.21 a day for each person if they are all counted separately, or $12.11 a day if they are counted as children or spouses. I don't know the actual effect in practice, but it has to be perverse.

Tables (see sample) such as the FPL amounts would have almost no use in a charity-based system, since true individuality would usually prevail, although it is useful to know what the government legislators and administrators think makes sense. Their political and economic calculations might be interesting information.

The two systems would naturally be compared rather often, and someone would have to work out some simple metrics to aid in comparisons. Getting the education part of life right would probably have the greatest long-term effect, so that both self-reliance and concern for others would become much more common traits.

The government only cares about harvesting votes in general for the typical pro-Marxist government parties. That was nearly always the original reason for inventing these government systems, often with the goal of gaining political control of specific districts. Individual needs are specifically ignored if that policy will increase the number of votes through emphasizing victimhood, identity politics, and intergroup conflict, as seems to be the usual case.

The goal of the new project would be to at least cut in half the number of able-bodied people on welfare, if not almost completely eliminating them. This leaves open the possibility of cutting the welfare rolls and costs by 90% down to 10% of what they are now ("[an irreducible number of] the poor are always with you") and at the same time increase the size of the economy to improve everyone's life.

One of the other major goals would be to greatly lower taxes, since the government would no longer have any ideological excuse for collecting this huge amount of money. Keeping that extra money in people's pockets would improve the economy and also improve the desire and willingness and ability to take care of charity needs as they arise, or to prevent them from arising.

There are major ideological and political ramifications of these suggested economic changes, and the new programs of religious, economic, and political freedom and all their good effects need to be preached and sold and demonstrated vigorously. The Marxist, elitist, dictatorial crowd will have to be directly challenged and beaten back in a major propaganda war. But that is what is necessary to establish the church as a major proponent of freedom of every kind and to greatly weaken the modern day Gadiantons that now have nearly complete power worldwide.

2019 FPL Calculation Chart (Monthly Values)
Enclosure 1

Family Size	*Annual 100% FPL*	*Monthly 100% FPL*	*60%*	*100%*	*108%*	*109%*	*114%*	*120%*	*128%*	*133%*	*135%*	*138%*	*142%*
1	12490	1040.84	625	1041	1125	1135	1187	1249	1333	1385	1406	1437	1478
2	16910	1409.17	846	1410	1522	1536	1607	1691	1804	1875	1903	1945	2002
2 Adults	16910	1409.17	846	1410	1522	1536	1607	1691	1804	1875	1903	1945	2002
3	21330	1777.50	1067	1778	1920	1938	2027	2133	2276	2365	2400	2453	2525
4	25750	2145.84	1288	2146	2318	2339	2447	2575	2747	2854	2897	2962	3048
5	30170	2514.17	1509	2515	2716	2741	2867	3017	3219	3344	3395	3470	3571
6	34590	2882.50	1730	2883	3114	3142	3287	3459	3690	3834	3892	3978	4094
7	39010	3250.84	1951	3251	3511	3544	3706	3901	4162	4324	4389	4487	4617
8	43430	3619.17	2172	3620	3909	3945	4126	4343	4633	4814	4886	4995	5140
9	47850	3987.50	2393	3988	4307	4347	4546	4785	5104	5304	5384	5503	5663
10	52270	4355.84	2614	4356	4705	4748	4966	5227	5576	5794	5881	6012	6186
11	56690	4724.17	2835	4725	5103	5150	5386	5669	6047	6284	6378	6520	6709
12	61110	5092.50	3056	5093	5500	5551	5806	6111	6519	6774	6875	7028	7232
Ea Add'l	*4420*	*368.34*	*221*	*369*	*398*	*402*	*420*	*442*	*472*	*490*	*498*	*509*	*524*

Federal Poverty Monthly Income Level 2019 60% to 142%.

With far more money available for charity-based assistance, a much better job can be done in each individual case. In fact, the new concern might gradually become the risk of being too generous and creating a new class of parasites living off the fat of the land and hurting themselves and everyone else with their irresponsibility.

More Details

The interest on debt at the federal, state, and local levels might be removed from the list of costs of things that are done outside of the government tax-and-spend systems, and there would therefore be no need for any borrowing, especially if the costs are kept to a third of the current size.

It may prove useful to avoid any kind of tax-and-spend mechanisms, and also avoid any questions about investments that relate to minimum charitable pensions, if all of the basic functions of a social welfare of system are done on a strictly current basis. There would certainly be room for larger personal pension plans if people wish to manage that money themselves and place it into the economy, but all of that sort of thing would be done outside of the minimal safety net of a charity-based social welfare system.

I am guessing that there are many problems with organizations taking money from workers supposedly for pension purposes, and then simply using up that money or investing it poorly so that the promises made can never be kept. In most cases, people should have the ability to manage that money themselves, something like the 401(k) or IRA systems of today. That gets rid of that exploitative and irresponsible layer that puts itself between a worker and their pensions, which almost always causes things to turn out poorly for the worker.

It is difficult to figure out what would be the best way to handle general social principles at the lower levels. It is clear that individuals have a responsibility to care for themselves and their families, and if they are unable, then they naturally look to their families to help them. The next level up might be a religious organization such as a ward or a stake, and the next level up from that might be something even larger, although I cannot predict what that would be.

One of the main principles of the new systems would be to get the insurance companies out of the system, since it is their purpose to extract as much profit as possible from supplying these social insurance services. Essentially all of the functions of these insurance companies could be replaced by some charity-based system or set of charity-based systems. I won't even attempt to expand on what those organizations might be, but I'm sure that with a general change in attitude among the public, other far better systems could be devised.

One simple change would be to avoid building unnecessary office and meeting structures which may absorb enormous amounts of capital which could be used to deliver actual social services. This would be analogous to the early church members having no chapels and no temples for 300 years, making it possible for them to devote nearly all their extra resources to effective charity. We now have an amazing technical ability to cooperate without building huge office complexes and all traveling there repeatedly to meet together. Our "fingers can do the walking" so that there is much less need for masses of people to travel to meet together, and the world's work can still be done.

It would be valuable to get rid of these rigid, wasteful, government tax-and-spend "pseudo-religious welfare" systems simply because they are so inflexible. Once they have been started, they can't be stopped until they collapse. Our systems are indeed on the way to collapse, with promises they can't possibly keep. It would be very wise to find a way to phase out these systems before they collapse on their own, perhaps starting out new generations of workers using new systems.

Some private systems

As an example of private systems being more efficient than government systems, we have the famous case of the three Texas counties that took the option of an alternate Social Security system, back when it was easy to do so. In one simple case, that private system produced 2.4 times as much retirement revenue for the participants. But it is really worth much more than that because the participants actually own their retirement funds and receive them no matter how long that person lives. In contrast, the government system only pays a set amount as long as the participant lives. A private system pays it out no matter how long the person lives, so that his children can collect the money as heirs. In some cases, the person and his family may actually collect up to five times the government amount.

Cultural suicide

People don't seem to realize that adopting any of these centralized Marxist welfare schemes means adopting a culture of death. In every case observable today, the socialist countries of Europe and Eastern Europe, without fail, are gradually committing suicide as they shrink with every new generation, some of them dropping by half at each new generation, until that society implodes and is replaced by another society, usually hostile to the original society. This is happening in Europe in the form of the millions of Muslims being allowed into Europe. These people have been taught from birth to hate Christians and white people so that they delight in terrorizing and replacing the already dying ancient inhabitants.

There are numerous other important society-wide benefits from the new charity-based system that go beyond pure economics. A government system quietly and implicitly convinces people that since the government promises to take care of them forever, cradle to grave, then there is no need for them to have any children who can take care of them when they are old. Instead, the implicit argument is that one can plan on everyone else's children taking care of them when they are old. But, of course, all those other people also have no obvious economic incentives to have children of their own, so that the whole society is incentivized to collapse by having no children. This is demonstrated by all the European countries which are shrinking out of existence as, in the case of Italy, where each subsequent generation is only about half the size of the previous generation.

This gradually has meant that where there were 30 workers to support each retiree when the system started, now there are only two or three workers to support the retirees, meaning that the burden is simply too great and the whole system collapses under its own weight. To adapt, the government borrows money to fulfill its promises, but that only hastens the collapse, as debts accumulate which can never be repaid, so that the collapse of the system, the whole Ponzi scheme, is both guaranteed and accelerated.

The various social security systems were probably not originally sold as a suicide pact, but that is the inevitable result. All the European countries are on the same path to oblivion, just at slightly different rates for each.

Some of the countries have also chosen an even faster path to self-destruction by allowing in millions of young people from hostile and incompatible countries. Young Muslims who have been taught from birth to hate Christians and white people are invited into post-Christian Europe where they do not assimilate and instead stay separate while scorning their hosts and fomenting terrorism attacks on those hosts, which they explicitly hope to subdue and replace. This is literally a terrifying way to end these societies, as we are seeing it play out before our very eyes.

Apparently, without freedom, especially freedom from huge taxes and "entitlement" systems, societies simply commit suicide since they cease to have any reason to exist. Hedonism is apparently another way of describing a death wish for society. Having children becomes nothing more than an optional source of entertainment, a hobby, instead of a means to perpetuate a family, a tribe, and a nation.

There is also the partly historical attitude in the previously Communist countries of Eastern Europe that, ideally, no one should raise any children to feed and sustain the corrupt dictatorship, so that people choose a 0-child, 1-

child, or 2-child attitude, (where 2.1 children per woman are needed for replacement, which means that the whole society quickly shrinks, including a drop in the life expectancy along with the much lower birth rate. This is the effect of atheism and making corrupt, self-seeking human government the new god.

With its always implicit and often explicit atheism, the secular state has no way to convince people that there is any reason to live or reproduce, except to be good slaves available to their masters. The old traditional values of building families and tribes and societies simply because of commonly-held religious and social values are completely out of the reach of these strictly secular governments. These governments do not really hide very well their scorn for the masses they have conquered and their desire to control them and their children. It is certainly not irrational for active adults to want to deny the state the control of themselves and their children. There is also the more immediate trade-off and benefit of not having to sacrifice to raise a large number of children. People may choose to have one child just for the experience, but certainly more than two children is going to require some extra exertion which the self-centered person might want to avoid.

There is no sign of the idea that parents can bring in spirits from the other side as part of an extremely long-term plan of salvation. None of that thinking has any place in the self-centered mindset of the ruling elite. They are the only beings that matter in the eternities.

Through killing off "useless" old people and providing free abortions, public health services kill people in huge numbers and the whole society shrinks based on the new very negative incentives for life.
Life is low-quality and not worth living, so that making everything "free" means that it also makes life itself of no value.

On the issue of gun control, having no guns means no guarantee of freedom and thus less personal responsibility, which means the entire society shrinks many times more quickly than could ever happen from gun related homicides. In fact, society will grow, so that there is a net gain from having guns (and the resulting freedom).

On the issue of the "population bomb," one economist calculated that just the state of Rhode Island could feed the entire world if it resorted to the most intense forms of food growing possible today. This demonstrates that there is "enough and to spare" for many times more people than now exist on the planet, making it clear that any artificial limits have more to do with political parties and governments being more interested in controlling people than in helping them flourish. The typical dictatorial leftist attitude that "it is better rule in hell than serve in heaven" means the ultimate death of that society

Birth rates

In the United States there are about 10,800 births a day, or about 3,942,000 a year. That produces a rate of 1.87 children per woman. If women simply were willing to bear the replacement rate of 2.1 children per woman, a 12.3% increase, that would mean another 1328 births each day for a total of about 484,720 extra births a year, for a new total of 4,429,720.

There would be a list other benefits as well, because the mere fact that people began to value life more highly and were willing to make some sacrifices to bring more children into the world, it would likely mean that the death rate would go down rather than up, leaving far more people living.

The number of intentional homicides in the United States total about 17,284 for a rate of 5.30 per 100,000 population. We may conclude that a culture of life would mean an extra 484,720 extra births a year, as opposed to the losses from homicides of 17,284. The ratio of gains to losses is at least (484,720 / 17,284 =) 28 times. That may seem like a strange comparison to make, but the extra freedom that comes from gun ownership and other features of a free society means that there is a huge net gain in life which completely overwhelms any potential loss from deaths to homicides. And, as I say, the new emphasis on life would probably also serve to greatly lower the homicide rate so that one comes out ahead on every metric.

Simply seeing this world and its inhabitants as God sees them would make huge changes in how things are done. Inviting souls here for an interesting experience, aided by those determined to help them have a good experience, would be enough of an influence to create a true Zion.

Chapter 23

A gospel-based program for developing countries

The winner of the 1998 Nobel Prize in economic science, Amartya Sen, born in 1933 in India, wrote a book entitled *Development as Freedom* (1999) in which he points out the great power of individual freedom to overcome any obstacles to achieving subsistence and even prosperity for the people of a country. The LDS church should be a vigorous advocate of freedom and prosperity everywhere in the world, perhaps following his philosophy. We hear stories of entire nations changing their religious affiliation perhaps because a King was converted to a new religious viewpoint. That is not necessarily something we should set as a goal, but, as a practical matter, that could be the result if people are encouraged to understand the gospel and to understand freedom and to promote both of them to improve themselves and improve their nation.

Rather than very cautiously filtering a little bit of charitable money through an organization with a very different ideology, philosophy, and theology, such as the Catholic Relief Services, as in the past, in the future we ought to be administering very large amounts of money from various sources through an organization of our own design which promotes our own ideology, philosophy, and theology. That will assure us that the charitable money, from whatever source, will produce the "biggest bang for the buck."

Chapter 24

Government corruption in Utah: Our non-Zion could be transformed into Zion

We talk about gathering Israel and building Zion, but we seem to have not the slightest idea about how to do that in reality. We have been given the perfect pattern in the U.S. Constitution, and it has been incorporated by reference into our modern-day Scriptures, but we seem to ignore it completely. The perfect Zion is simply a place where the principles of the U.S. Constitution are in force and where, quite naturally, all of the good freedom-loving people of the world wish to gather together to assist each other in enjoying freedom and "being all they can be."

One might logically assume that in the state of Utah, where the LDS religion is predominant, one would find the closest thing to Zion which is possible. However, that assumption would be false. It is true that governments in Utah is not yet as corrupt as the governments in New York City, Chicago, and Los Angeles, but a claim that we are not yet quite as bad as those highly corrupt cities is not much evidence that we are actively seeking Zion here.

Unfortunately, the corrupt nature of Utah government is an excellent indication of how corrupt the church itself is, since, in Utah, the church organization and the Utah government organizations are simply two sides to the same coin, largely staffed by the same people or with people with similar working backgrounds and ideologies. If the LDS church were perfectly pure in its application of Christian principles in Utah, then, necessarily, the Utah state government would also be nearly as pure.

The thoroughly corrupt state of the Utah government and its many authorized and sponsored city governments as subunits became clear to me in a series of events that happened recently. This tale is perhaps all one needs to know to see what is wrong with Utah state and city governments, and how far we have to go to reach any semblance of "Zion."

I lived for 20 years in Spanish Fork, Utah, located on the south side of Utah Valley, with a population of about 30,000, where the typical human tendencies of the city government are just as corrupt as anywhere else in the state. The difference is that many of the old residents and families are still so steeped in the original gospel and in belief in the US Constitution that the city receives a great deal of resistance in its anti-freedom impulses. The City of Spanish Fork brags that it has the lowest total tax rates of any city in the state, and that is probably correct, but the City government is also doing everything in its power to raise those levels of taxes and make the City government more important and intrusive upon its residents.

In February 2017 my family moved to Orem, Utah, a medium-sized city of about 100,000 which is now almost completely urban and doesn't have the constant check on its behavior from a large body of active farmers and ranchers who instinctively resist corruption and anti-freedom tendencies of the typical city government. The City of Orem appears to have no respect whatsoever for the laws of the state of Utah or the U.S. Constitution or of any other aspect of the American legal tradition, including its own duly enacted ordinances. It seems to have no understanding at all about what it means to have a representative constitutional government. I call it a "constitution-free zone."

To be more specific, when we moved to Orem in 2017 we soon decided that it would be a good idea to add solar panels to our house which, with today's technology, promises to lower a person's electric bill by about $2000 a year and to provide a savings of about $100,000 in total housing costs over a 25 year period, even including the perhaps $20,000 cost of installing the panels. Many people are adding solar panels to their home, and state and federal governments greatly encourage such actions for the environmental benefits they bring of lowering fossil fuel use and lowering pollution. The state of Utah has a $2000 tax credit incentive to add solar panels and the federal government has an even larger tax credit incentive which would be about $10,000 on a $30,000 installation, subsidizing 30% of that installation.

We made all the arrangements for a company to do the installation and then we requested a building permit from the City of Orem to make that installation. That building permit is a necessary requirement for connecting the solar panels to the Rocky Mountain Power grid that serves our neighborhood. To our great surprise, the building permit was denied. It was claimed that the addition of a covered deck or pergola to our house made in 2002, about three years after the house was originally built, was not in compliance with the City zoning code.

The structure was completely in compliance with the City zoning code at the time it was built, but the City records do not show that a building permit was obtained in 2002. (It is highly questionable whether such minor and insignificant records would even be accurately available 15 years later, after paper records were converted to computer files and other clerical upheavals have occurred, but the City was adamant that its reasoning could not be contested.)

I should mention that another structure had been built earlier on the property, a detached garage or workshop, and it had received a proper permit. It seems likely that a permit was obtained for the covered deck addition as well, since it would have been easy and inexpensive to do it at the time, but there is apparently no way to prove that such a permit was applied for and granted.

In researching the situation very thoroughly, it was discovered that there are at least nine different important laws concerning permits and the general process for cities regulating land-use which apply to the City but which the City completely ignores. If any one of those legal requirements had been complied with by the City, I would have received my solar panel building permit.

One of those nine ignored laws requires that the city have a robust appeals system as a prerequisite for the city to do any land-use regulation. But, of course, the City of Orem has no such appeal system, even though they claim to have one. Apparently, there has been not a single appeal allowed or processed in the last eight years. In that time there have been about 9000 permits applied for to authorize about $1.3 billion in work to be done within the City, but not a single appeal has been allowed or processed. One might suspect that in a democratically operated local government a City employee could make at least one error in 9,000 permits that might require an appeal of some kind to clarify or revise some rules or proposals or decisions.

Another law has to do with the exact kind of covered deck or pergola which was added to the property. There was a City ordinance in effect at the time of construction which made it perfectly legal to add this pergola in its current location, but in later years that very specific City ordinance was dropped from the City's online code without being repealed by the City Council. It simply disappeared. It is not clear if this was done accidentally or with malice.

Other laws have to do with the state of Utah encouraging cities to allow the installation of solar panels, but they are all being ignored by the City of Orem. Apparently, the City loses about $500 in taxes each year when a homeowner converts to solar power, and the City's resistance to solar panels is probably based on that potential loss of revenue rather than on any actual concern about safety or aesthetics that might be a legitimate aspect of the City zoning code.

Several other normal aspects of the American legal tradition are ignored. Criminal laws, such as those relating to abiding by rules related to zoning permits, should not be adopted and enforced retroactively, as was done here, the ordinance apparently having been passed for the very purpose of denying solar panel permits based on previous events and circumstances.

There should be statutes of limitation for their application, especially concerning these real estate matters. Normally, any encumbrances on land-use must be recorded in public records so that any buyer will be aware of those competing claims or limitations. Otherwise, for most people, those claims become unenforceable, but the City of Orem ignores any such normal legal etiquette and makes no effort whatsoever to notify people in advance of its claims concerning zoning violations.

By state law, the state's cities are not allowed to enforce zoning code violations using anything more aggressive than an "infraction." An infraction has a limit of a $750 fine, with no allowance for jail time, and there must be ways that any such infraction can be paid off using community service. The City of Orem insists that it can enforce a "misdemeanor" in this situation, where the "misdemeanor" it defines can potentially impose larger fines and more jail time than most felonies, leaving out only the death penalty. Penalties of $1000 plus 6 months in jail for each day of violation are obviously outrageously out of proportion for these kinds of legal issues, making theoretically possible millions of dollars in fines and decades in jail for a small paperwork infraction.

I wrote up my findings on the nine ignored statutes and requested that I be able to appeal this to the City Council, as provided for in the City code. The City Manager refused to allow that. I then started a legal action against the City in the local state Fourth District Court located in Provo, Utah.

What happened next was quite amazing, and demonstrates the depth of the corruption of the state government, its cities, and its state courts. Although I didn't know this until five months after the initial filing, the City was somehow able to use its influence to tamper with the court complaint itself. I had prepared a 91-page document explaining the nine different serious legal requirements the state and other legal bodies had placed on the City, which the City was completely ignoring.

Normally when one files a case in a state court, the defendant, the City of Orem in this case, is required to answer that complaint. The City never did answer that complaint, presumably because there is no plausible excuse or reason for the City to be less than fully compliant with those nine different legal issues. In other words, the City could not answer the complaint honestly without admitting to its own guilt. Therefore, it didn't answer at all.

What had actually happened is that the City managed to have that 91-page complaint reduced to two pages of introductory material, and all the rest of the 91-page legal study was thrown away. That meant that the judge who might review that case would have no idea what the case was about. The case was actually denied because it supposedly did not "state a claim for which relief could be granted by a court." This seemed like an absurd result to me and so I appealed it to the Utah Court of Appeals, explaining exactly what had happened and how the original complete complaint and related legal study had been completely discarded.

The Court of Appeals simply confirmed the District Court's ruling that the complaint did not state a claim for which relief could be granted. At that point, theoretically I had the option to appeal to the Utah Supreme Court, which required a significant effort to prepare the appropriate brief, etc. A further appeal within such an obviously corrupt system seemed perfectly pointless.

The clear lesson here is that the court systems are corrupt to the core and are flagrant in their lack of concern about justice. They allow the cities to do whatever they want without any supervision from the state, at least in the areas that relate to regulating land-use, certainly, these days, a city's most extensive power.

I take this one specific case I experienced as more than adequate proof that the state and city governments of the state of Utah are completely corrupt. The courts and the City felt completely safe in taking outrageous steps to protect the City, part of the state government, from any outsider seeking justice. I conclude that this level of corruption can only exist if the church organization, a parallel administrative bureaucracy, it is just as corrupt. If the church organization were aggressively following and enforcing the law, my case could never have happened.

I conclude that it is probably almost impossible to fix the state government without first fixing the church government which underlies it. If we want to have a Zion government, we first must have a Zion Church, which we clearly do not have.

The legal concept of sovereign immunity has some value in protecting democratically elected governments from abuse by its own citizens and the citizens of other entities, including other governments. However, the state of Utah has run amok and has taken this concept of sovereign immunity to extreme and unreasonable lengths to the point where it refuses to accept responsibility for its own errors and misdeeds for which it ought to offer recompense.

We might also note that under current arrangements, the LDS church is a part of the state government in the sense that it is operating as an official state Corporation. The LDS church has obviously been seeking for a certain kind of "sovereign immunity" for itself, and has been quite successful, since its status as a "corporation sole" means that a single person can make decisions on every aspect of church property and business and doctrine without the need to consult with anyone, certainly not the ordinary members of the church. This was not true in the beginning when the church operated as an unincorporated association which periodically elected a legal trustee to do some of its business for it.

One might wonder whether part of this extreme application of the concept of sovereign immunity by the state government is simply derived from the church's desire to be completely immune from any opinions or actions of its members. Certainly, the two organizations seem to be pressing their "immunity" status to extreme lengths for their own unjust purposes.

Notes

The nine grounds from the proposed complaint are presented below in summary form:

Grounds for complaint -- summary

Over a period of about five years, about 1250 applications have been made to Orem city for building permits for solar panels. About 1000 were granted and about 250 were denied. Orem residents have been adversely affected by all the following consequences of City action:

1. Disregarding multiple explicit state and federal statutes encouraging solar panels (but not yet requiring solar panels as in California)
2. Informally and improperly adding extra restrictions to City ordinances
3. Improperly deleting critical City ordinances that actually authorized the homeowner's behavior complained of by the City.
4. Intentional retroactive application of statutes, especially criminal statutes
5. Failing to supply a statute of limitation on civil and criminal laws.
6. Failure of the City to give proper notice on public real estate records of claimed encumbrances on real estate
7. The City routinely threatens its citizens with outrageous penalties for minor and questionable zoning violations.
8. Orem City is actively resisting efforts by the state of Utah to use solar power to lower energy costs and pollution effects for state offices and for state residents, putting Orem City seriously out of step with other Utah cities. Orem seems to be the only Utah city that has such regressive solar panel policies.
9. Contrary to clear state statutory requirements needed to establish and justify city land-use and zoning powers, the City of Orem has no internal "appeals" system operating whatsoever, by its own choice.

Chapter 25

A breach of fiduciary duty by the LDS church?

This book has presented some of the many ways in which over the last 120 years the church headquarters unit has caused the LDS church to deviate greatly from the principles and policies of the original church of Christ established by himself during his life, and then reestablished through Joseph Smith. Those many deviations, done in almost every case to benefit church leaders financially and to encourage their prideful behavior, can nearly all be put under the category of "breach of fiduciary duty." It seems possible that the church leaders' consciences have been seared to the point where they have turned everything around completely. They would say that there IS no fiduciary duty on the part of the church leadership to the membership, and that only the opposite condition exists, with the members having many burdensome duties to the church leadership.

This whole process of deterioration has proceeded so far that it seems impossible that there is anything one could do to re-substitute actual Christian principles for the extreme levels of secularism and philosophies of men that have such a firm grip on the church organization today.

When we bring up the topic of breach of fiduciary duty, the first thing to be noted is that everything today is exactly backwards from what one would expect it to be, and as it once was in the original Christian Church.

Where once the church leaders were the servants of the members, now they see themselves as the masters of the members, as a matter of right, they would probably claim. The church leaders feel no discernible duty to the members. The only duties now are those enforced against the members by the leaders. The duty of a good member is to pay a full tithing and never say or do anything which would put any church leader in a bad light. Some people want to call the church a cult, and it is this top-down control and the church leaders' sense of ownership of the membership that perhaps gives some meaning to the term "cult." I am assuming that the idea of a "cult" involves some leadership interference with the freedom of the members.

At the beginning, the church was an unincorporated association, partly because it could not be anything else as it kept gathering in different places and moving to other places. Under that form of government, the church members could hold legally effective votes to choose a trustee to act on their behalf in legal and organizational and all other such practical matters. However, somewhere along the line, the church rearranged things and declared that church members had absolutely no legal powers to have any effect on how the church leaders managed the money they received or property they owned or any other aspect of church administration.

The process started in 1896 when Wilford Woodruff decided that church leaders could use church tithing funds to pay their personal expenses. It accelerated to the point in 1923 when the church declared itself to be operating under a new organizational method. It encouraged the Utah state government to make available the governmental corporation option called a "corporation sole," which the church adopted. That also makes the church a creature of the state government, which has only bad effects, as far as I can tell. This is the process of "secularization by incorporation," a process validly feared as a corrupting force by other church groups.

The secular attraction of the corporation sole is that it gives absolute control of everything to a single man who holds a specific position, in this case president of the church. That sole person need not pay any attention to the council or voting of anyone in making any and all decisions. Certainly, the members of the church today have no right to be heard under this new organization. And technically, even the other church leaders, such as members of the Twelve, also have no legal right to have any effect on any decisions. Presumably in practice, the corporation sole, this sole proprietor of this new church, would counsel with others before making a decision, but there is no legal requirement that he do so.

It should be noted that the "corporation sole" feature of Utah law can no longer be used for any new organizations. This was not a "single use" statute, but almost.

This situation brings up the question as to why a church president would even want to become a dictator over all aspects of the church. Christ certainly did not seek any such power. Other charitable corporations require that there be at least three people with governing powers, as part of a committee or board of directors, but here the LDS church does not even recognize the wisdom of an ecclesiastical presidency or bishopric, or even the Godhead, for that matter, as it gives all earthly religious powers to a single person, exactly as is done by the Roman Catholic Church with its pope. That issue of concentration of power was also discussed elsewhere in this book.

That means that where the church members had a recurring opportunity to express themselves in a practical way as when choosing or re-authorizing a trustee, now their votes are of no significance whatsoever. It may be that public church voting has a ceremonial purpose so that it appears that church members can express themselves in ways that make a difference, but that is pure perception, not reality. If every person in the church voted against some proposal by the Church president, it would make no legal difference, although in that extreme case, the church leader might reconsider that particular decision, but only as a matter of public relations, not as a matter of legal requirement.

The church leaders have managed to take the original Gospel, in which those who were given the priesthood were held to the standard of "freely have ye received, freely give," and those leaders have changed everything so that nothing important is free, and all the higher ordinances must be paid for at an extravagant rate: 1/10 of a person's income for life. As a practical matter, this means that traditional Christian charity drops to near zero, since all the resources for performing that charity, the typical 10% of religious contributions, now all goes to the central church where those contributions are mostly wasted as far as accomplishing any typical early Christian goals of charity (which in our era should include improving the freedom and success of the entire society).

The money which is received mostly goes to salaries and travel costs and a small part of it ends up funding the construction of buildings. Perhaps $30 billion out of $1 trillion ($1,000 billion) received by the church over the last 120 years has gone to build chapels, with perhaps another $10 billion being devoted to building temples. None of those construction projects are required by the gospel program which Christ restored, so one must decide how much of this was spent for the proper benefit of the members and how much was spent as acts of pride by church leaders. Since the church would have been far more successful if those resources had all been devoted to Christian charity, it is possible that none of that spending was justified.

In summary, in the last 120 years the central church has used its paid-ministry-distorted preaching to extract about $1 trillion from the church members, and the bulk of that has been completely wasted. Some people have said that the church has about $100 billion in savings and investments, but that is all that is left of that $1 trillion which mostly went up in smoke. Perhaps that $100 billion could be reclaimed through some process and applied to charity purposes.

There is at least another $10 trillion which can be charged to a breach of fiduciary duty by the church leaders in the case of the church not promoting an alternate Social Security system when that would have been easy to do. The government made it very difficult for someone to simply avoid some kind of a pension system, and assuming that one could not avoid such a system, there was still the option to create a system on a private voluntary basis using parameters similar to the taxing parameters of the government-administered version of this new pension program.

If the church leaders had encouraged most of the church members to find a way to opt out of the government system and establish their own system, as many others did, by now that would have meant that church members would have received an extra $10 trillion in pension payouts over anything which the government system has provided. (That would be about 5 million church members each receiving an extra $2 million as part of their retirement package.) We might notice that that is enough money to pay the current budget of the church for about 1000 years, assuming that the current church budget is only about $10 billion a year. The main point is that this is a huge amount of money which would be free money to those who had retired, and it would have given them enormous possibilities for doing missionary work and charity work and doing other good things in the world on their own, completely outside of the controls of the central church organization.

Based on other church leader behaviors, one might wonder whether the church leaders made the actual calculation to avoid encouraging any such thing as an alternate social security system, simply because they did not want the church members to have the religious and economic freedom to take care of some of these things on their own. A highly active membership which was well-funded, might be a kind of embarrassment to the church leaders of today. Well-funded and enthusiastic church members might very well do things which the church leaders would prefer they didn't.

For example, the church leaders want to maintain a very bland presentation to all the generally corrupt leaders of the world, so that those corrupt leaders will welcome the church in on its preferred terms of being centrally directed itself, and if there were any church members who were actually promoting freedom in the world, it would make it far more difficult for the church to present itself as a very bland and passive organization (even while being monolithic). Presumably there are many members like myself who would take full advantage of this opportunity to make a difference in the world if they had the resources to do so. My activism would likely cause consternation among the highly control-minded church leaders who want to be able to operate without any competition from within. They don't want their decisions second-guessed or bypassed by enthusiastic members who are better Christians than the church leaders in their impulses.

As a quick review, we might notice that the central church took steps to disconnect itself from the church membership and make itself totally independent, without any legally enforceable duty to do anything to discover and carry out the views of the members. On numerous occasions, its self-selected impulse to operate above the U.S. Constitution and outside of US laws, sometimes actually cooperating with the political enemies of the US, is something it could not have done without consequence if it still had to maintain the approbation of the bulk of the membership.

Two possible insights into church thinking:
1. Starting with Wilford Woodruff, it is not possible to believe any statement made by the church and take it at face value. The brethren started lying on a grand scale at that point, and on a consistent basis, for their own economic benefit, so it is hard to winnow out the truth. One of the big problems is when they are deceptive about the reasons they do things, perhaps giving a convenient reason but not the true reason. That can present quite a difficulty for any historians trying to understand what was going on at the time.

For example, the case of the end of polygamy and the end of the endowment house seem to be one of these cases where the reasons given were not accurate or at least not complete. Whatever the church may have said, it appears that one of the goals of taking down the endowment house was to end the practice of handing out essentially free ordinances, making it so that people would then have to go to the temples, and at the temples they could eventually be excluded if they hadn't paid their full tithing to the central church offices.

Of course, at the same time, there was this political question of continuing the practice of polygamy. The main problem now is that whatever the church leaders may have said on this subject is immediately suspect because they were twisting and spinning things for their own economic advantage. Without digging very deeply into that piece of history, it is hard to know how much of that change was really assignable to the persecution of the federal government and how much of it was done simply as being convenient to the new church leaders, Wilford Woodruff and his co-conspirators. If the church could blame everything on the federal government and nothing on themselves, that would be the ideal situation, politically, even though it would not be the truth and therefore would damage anyone's understanding of the gospel and how the gospel would resolve many of these issues.

For example, there may have been other forces in play which would have allowed the territory of Utah to become a state without being forced to totally give up the concept of polygamy. The problem here is that it was extremely economically convenient for the church to join with the federal government to stamp out polygamy because at the same time they were monetizing temple ordinances and looking at a future stream of income of $1 trillion, as it turned out.

The completion of the intercontinental railroad in 1869, 27 years before Utah became a state, may have made it such that it was critical for outside interests to make Utah a state regardless of what happened on the issue of polygamy, and based on that calculation, statehood would have been available under almost any circumstances.

2. Today we have thousands of people who are trying to prove that Joseph Smith made a huge number of mistakes in trying to restore the church, so that he is to blame for all the problems we see today. However, that seems to be an error, a "tradition of the fathers", a narrative, that actually benefits the corrupt church leaders. This diversion keeps these complainers away from the actual truth which is far more damaging to the church than anything anyone could say about Joseph Smith. At least this particular popular narrative still seems to maintain that the current leaders are direct and legitimate priesthood descendants of Joseph Smith, even though they may not be.

The truth seems to be that people today look at the church as it is and find it greatly wanting, the management of money being one of the main avenues of attack. The church obviously does almost no charity work at all, and that is certainly not in keeping with the church which Christ restored during his life.

Rather than do the logical thing and blame the current leaders and their predecessors back to Wilford Woodruff, where almost all of these distortions began, people imagine that the church today is actually the same church which Joseph Smith restored, which it most certainly is not. The church today would hardly even be recognizable to Joseph Smith.

The thing which will be necessary is for people to look at the church today and see that it is wrong and realize that it has had all these distortions added since the time of Wilford Woodruff, not since the time of Joseph Smith, and then take the steps to correct it. Apparently admitting that the church has been distorted over the last 120 years is just too much for people to accept. It is apparently too much for them to even wonder about.

A lawsuit would be impractical

Since they have many billions of dollars they could spend in defending their current improper takeover of the LDS church, with its current policies and privileges and revenue flow, and they also apparently have control of the corrupt court system in Utah, it would make no sense at all to attempt to bring a court action against the church, since they have positioned themselves as being above the law. They would win by hook or crook, with no concern for the accuracy of any arguments. However, they are not above the court of public opinion, and that is where this "lawsuit" struggle needs to take place. Hurting them in the pocketbook by convincing people that they need to go somewhere else to get true religion, would probably offer the only possibility for bringing sanity to the current level of confusion and corruption at the church headquarters. Is anyone ready for a boycott? It would probably come as quite a shock to many church leaders that they are not authorized by the Scriptures to operate exactly as McDonald's does worldwide, avoiding all politics and other social influences and just "selling hamburgers," or, in the church setting, selling salvation by the pound or by subscription, by the month or year.

Another view of "breach of fiduciary duty" by the LDS church
The membership did not vote for that fraudulent takeover in 1923, which I call the "lawyers' coup." The old "one man, one vote, once" socialist trick was apparently the technique used by the church. That has led to "one man, no vote" as our current condition. This assumes there was a currently authorized trustee who exceeded his authority and decided to turn his temporary authority into permanent authority, as he imagined.

That process happens often enough in the political world where a would-be dictator uses democratic means to get dictatorial control over a nation. The church apparently used that Gadiaton Robber trick on the church itself, accomplishing a direct attack on freedom of religion.

Perhaps it is finally time to start over and reverse that lawyers' coup. Otherwise, the church will continue to be weak and lackadaisical and get even weaker as the pioneer spirit and heritage and population shrinks, since apparently only people from that tradition are willing to put up with this nonsense. No one else in the world is so foolish. Every other Christian in the world understands the actual gospel better than the LDS church does and is rightfully reluctant to join up with such a greedy church.
A breach of fiduciary lawyer explains fiduciary duty and consequences of breach
https://www.nyccriminallawyer.com/fraud-charge/investment-fraud/breach-of-fiduciary-duty/

Church gun control and other political pretensions
The church may have finally gone too far, far enough to cause a formal schism, something which hasn't happened for quite a long time. People have been leaving the church in large numbers, it seems, through resigning from the church, but very few of them have been starting their own separate churches. That may be about to change.

As I understand what is going on, Texas has passed a rule which allows and encourages concealed carry of weapons in almost every situation in the state, including in churches. Texas might have a good reason to do that since unarmed people in churches have been targets of mass killings, as have happened in every other place which someone might guess is a "gun free" zone.

So, without any very convincing evidence, using old cases that may or may not have anything to do with the new policy, the church has declared that as of the first week of August 2019, church members are not allowed to bring weapons of any kind to church, including concealed carry weapons.

The church claims that it will not put up any signs declaring its churches to be gun-free zones, but it has made announcements to that effect far and wide, so that no one need be in doubt, whether church member or potential terrorist.

This is a slightly ironic policy change since it used to be a requirement that all Protestant church members bring their weapons to church, partly as a way to ensure that they actually had a working weapon. The West was won, especially including the state of Utah, only because of a well-armed and well-prepared populace who would not tolerate hostile intervention by a federal Army. Without those weapons, it is quite possible that the church itself would not still be in existence.

Now we have the church welcoming in gays and telling patriots to stay home with their concealed carry weapons. In more "loaded" terms we might say that they have been recruiting gays and disinviting patriots or recruiting pagans and disinviting patriots.

This is one example of "jumping the shark," along with the building of a horrendously expensive temple in Rome, something which could be seen as another example of "jumping the shark," or catastrophically going too far. The church appears to be trying to keep up with the leftist movement in this country and other countries and it should not be too surprised if it finds that many people don't wish to go along with that ideological drift.

Recently it appointed itself our political representative, even though we have no say in or ability to elect any church leaders to act as our political representatives, and they have been giving away constitutional rights to gay activists as another ploy to keep up their membership by accommodating the demands of the insatiable political gays, the activists.

As I have suggested elsewhere, they are probably doing this partly to signal to the rest of the world that we as a church are pacifists and leftists so that no dictator need fear that any Mormon will resist their unrighteous dominion, whatever form it may take. That seems like a very bad precedent and policy to set. Certainly, it is very anti-Zion in spirit. One cannot have a Zion unless one has prepared a place legally and morally to be a Zion.

The church in essence is saying that it is superior to the U.S. Constitution, even where that constitution was incorporated by reference into the LDS Scriptures. Now it is explicitly rubbing out that aspect of LDS Scriptures and perhaps willingly saying goodbye to those people who actually believe fervently in the U.S. Constitution and its principles. Perhaps it is saying that the Pioneers, with their extreme emphasis on personal freedom, served their purpose, but we can throw them away too -- "throw them under the bus" so to speak, as the church surges forward into this brave new world of embracing leftism at every level.

The central church offices claim power to exclude people from local chapels and temples concerning firearms. But they may have finally gone too far. At one time all the chapels were owned locally, and only gradually were they transferred to the ownership of the central offices, mostly for convenience. That migration back to the local church organizations could begin as a result of the church imagining that it has more power than it actually has. Obviously, all the local churches were paid for by church members, not by the central offices. The central offices, like any government, can only transfer money from one place to another. They don't actually create any money, at least not enough to worry about.

Chapter 26

No time to relax. No "all is well in Zion"

I have often said that the LDS church leaders appear to have no idea what Zion would look like, and therefore most certainly have no idea of how to get there. They appear to be so embedded in today's statist systems at every level (more or less Satan-inspired) that thinking outside of that very constraining box is out of the question. I can hardly expect to remedy that lack of information and understanding in just a few pages, but even a brief outline might be helpful.

Getting to Zion, a gospel-based civilization, is really very simple. The U.S. Constitution, which is incorporated by reference into modern LDS Scriptures, sets the world standard for a government and a set of laws that define a free society. It is hard to imagine that anyone would argue that Zion could be Zion without incorporating complete political, economic, and religious freedom. Basically, just defining Zion as an aggressively free society would be enough.

There are thousands of attacks on US freedom every day, coming from inside and outside the United States. Simply organizing the thousands of activities necessary to counteract these constant attacks on freedom would be an excellent use of the church's resources. It needn't be initiated or managed by the central church at all. If church members were encouraged to use their own resources to resist these debilitating attacks, that would be good enough. In fact, it would probably have a much stronger and better effect than trying to coordinate these activities through the central church.

However, the church leaders, whether they know it or not (since the church staff lawyers seem to make all the most important policy decisions for the church), seem to have chosen to do as little as possible to defend freedom and the Constitution, and to care for the poor, which would result in positively changing the society we live in.

Unfortunately, the members are currently very much discouraged from undertaking any active changes to society, presumably on the theory that independent member actions could result in possible embarrassment to church leaders, nationally and internationally, even though that restriction interferes with members' freedom of religion. Any serious charity activity could also interfere with maximizing tithing income.

The church's refusal to take seriously its duties to care for the poor has left open to atheist secular governments the opportunity to institute enormous, wasteful, and corrupt tax-and-spend welfare systems whose very purpose is to displace and discredit the Christian religion. The church's abandonment of such activities basically to Satan's minions has been an enormous blow to the church and a boost to those minions.

The same is true of the church's abandonment of any meaningful influence on the nation's educational system, abandoning it to the corrupt worldly influences which have nearly taken over our entire nation, largely exactly because of corrupt atheistic influences on our children over generations.

The church leaders seem to have concluded that they will be most successful when they are almost invisible -- that the best way to promote the gospel is to not actively and openly promote it at all, however strange that plan may seem. The only way they are willing to join into public activity is to pretend to be just another example of a private business franchise system which is such a common feature of our business-oriented culture, something like McDonald's or Jiffy Lube, which provide a commonly needed service, but the church carefully avoids any statement or activity that might seem to indicate that they wish to change anyone's political or religious belief system or value system..

Nonpolitical

The church has made much of its claims to be nonpolitical, but it is a little difficult to understand why. The U.S. Constitution does not require American churches to be nonpolitical at all. From the very beginning, on issues related to the Revolutionary War, and later the Civil War, the churches had a major influence on society's opinions and actions.

I found it fascinating that in the lead-up to the Civil War, when proslavery and anti-slavery forces were skirmishing in Kansas (which included many of the proslavery forces from Missouri which was just next door, those proslavery forces being exactly the same ones who had previously run the LDS members out of Missouri), churches in New England sent wagon loads of "Beecher's Bibles" to the anti-slavery forces in Kansas to help make sure that the anti-slavery forces won the voting referendum there on the slavery issue. Some history on the topic:

> He (Henry W. Beecher) believed that the Sharps Rifle was a truly moral agency, and that there was more moral power in one of those instruments, so far as the slaveholders of Kansas were concerned, than in a hundred Bibles. You might just as well. ... read the Bible to Buffaloes as to those fellows who follow Atchison and Stringfellow; but they have a supreme respect for the logic that is embodied in Sharp's rifle. https://en.wikipedia.org/wiki/Beecher's_Bibles

> **Beecher Bibles** The Sharps rifle was a big innovation in firearms during the 1850s. It was highly sought after by men looking to gain political advantage in territorial Kansas. The unique weapon with its patented breech-loading and self-priming features offered quick loading, speed in firing, and accuracy in distance. https://www.kshs.org/kansapedia/beecher-bibles/11977
>
> The total number of Sharps that reached Kansas between 1854 and 1858 will probably never be known. Fragmentary records indicate somewhere around 900 to 1,000 Sharps were purchased for the border conflict. Https://civilwartalk.com/threads/beecher-bible-and-rifle-church-in-wabaunsee-kansas.152398/

The Sharp's rifle was legendary in its innovations. There was at least one Hollywood movie made about it, "Quigley Down Under" starring Tom Selleck. The rifle was somewhat akin to today's long-range sniper rifles, with a range of up to nearly a mile, with several different cartridges of varying powder loads available for it.

We should note that the U.S. Army which had been intentionally sent to Kansas to help turn Kansas into a slave state, and failed, probably partly because of the presence of Beecher's Bibles there, was the exact same Army which marched out to Utah in 1857 to try to turn Utah and California into slave states.

The Mormons in Utah at that time, including the leaders of the church, were hardly nonpolitical in their behavior. The 20,000 seasoned mountain men who then lived in Utah, about 10 times the number of regular soldiers in the army sent there, were not about to be driven out by this corrupt army, and they were not afraid to say what would happen to the army if it attacked, since it was obviously very isolated and far from any hope of resupply or reinforcement. I assume that army took the Mormons' threatening statements very seriously, and that is what kept things relatively peaceful.

The modern-day almost complete surrender to the concept of the church being "nonpolitical," even though the IRS's effort in trying to require churches to be nonpolitical is unconstitutional (but the IRS has so far avoided pressing hard enough to get a Supreme Court ruling on that issue) seems mostly aimed at keeping on good terms with the American federal government, specifically the IRS, so that the LDS church could do such things as stockpile $200 billion in unused contributions without any adverse political or economic consequences. Obviously, the federal government does not see the LDS church as any kind of threat. The LDS church today apparently wants to be seen as a completely loyal sub-organization to the federal government, perhaps even going so far as to operate as a virtual state church. This complete peace agreement and armistice may make life easier for the church leaders, but it almost completely torpedoes the actual mission of the church to change the society for the better.

Political
At the same time as it claims to be nonpolitical in one area, the LDS church has gone beyond its delegated authority from the members to get involved in political matters such as making political compromises at the state level with gay activists, weakening long-standing constitutional guarantees. Naturally, these political matters seem to only move in one direction by being in conformance with the typically constant leftward march of the federal government.

Zion and the Gathering
The doctrinal topic of the Gathering is the other side of the Zion coin. Zion is the gathering of those who desire freedom, and it is the very process of gathering into a major and formidable nation of freedom lovers that would allow them to have freedom. Their very size and homogeneity of ideology and values would allow them to enjoy and maintain freedom and to continually add to their strength by separating out the good people from Babylon, strengthening Zion and weakening Babylon.

In today's perverse situation, the church leaders REQUIRE that the members stay in one of the many Babylons where their lives are often miserable, and where they are unable to control and improve their own societies. At the same time, there is not even any place officially designated where they COULD gather to gain the autonomy that would allow them to enjoy freedom. Gathering together in small groups in hundreds of countries is never going to provide the critical mass to make a change in those societies, and the church would discourage it anyway. The church leaders have, in effect, joined with the exploiters of the world to maintain an unnecessarily low standard of freedom, apparently for no other reason than that it is in that condition that the central headquarters of the church can best justify its existence and its constant taking and consuming or wasting or stockpiling of massive sums of money from the members.

If the Saints were to break out and to spontaneously create their own Zion space, overruling central headquarters policy, and managed to combine all the saints together, the headquarters would quickly shrink in size since there would be no continuing need for expensive travel to and diplomacy with perhaps 200 different countries and governments. The saints would spontaneously take care of their own needs once gathered, and there would be no justification for an oversize administrative unit in Salt Lake City.

Rather than allow and encourage the gathering, which would make today's headquarters nearly unnecessary, the church prefers to keep hundreds or thousands of different church groups all separate and isolated just so it can spend vast amounts of money on staff and their travel to act as the coordinating body between them all, moving tithing money from some groups to others, etc., when, if left completely to their own devices, they would coalesce into one or a few places and spontaneously meet the needs of each other without any artificial church bureaucracy.

As it is, the central church bureaucracy essentially holds the members in all of these other Third World countries as both trophies and hostages, as ways to extract the maximum amount of contributions from its members in the First World. Freeing up those scattered members to build up Zion, presumably in the United States, would also free the First World members to direct their charitable contributions towards the highest social needs within the new Zion society.

In other words, the church today is actually as anti-Zion as it is anti-Gathering. This is a bizarre situation. One might even call it "antichrist" or anti-Christian, in the sense that Christ would not act to keep the Saints scattered when they all naturally and wisely desire to gather.

It is clear that the few million saints in the United States cannot control the political climate of the nation, and cannot even control the political climate of the State of Utah, which is far from an ideal Zion. However, if there were 100 million freedom-loving members gathered from around the world, where they probably learned to have a great love for freedom simply because they were systematically deprived of it, that 100 million members could have a profound effect on the culture in the United States and would ensure that righteousness and freedom was well supported there.

It seems remarkable that merely correcting this perverse structural situation -- consciously constructed by church leaders for their own purposes -- would almost automatically establish Zion, as the members around the world were allowed and encouraged to gather to the United States (and perhaps a few other places) and slowly build the society they would prefer. The central church would stop interfering with the natural good impulses of members to gather and establish and enjoy freedom, and Zion would happen spontaneously. That is supposed to be the effect of the Gospel on the world, and the leaders just need to stop interfering just for the purpose of rent-seeking, extracting money from the free members who are concerned about their less-free brothers and sisters, when the less-free are kept less-free by active church interference. This is a cynical, perverse behavior by the central church for the very purpose of manipulating members for the monetary gain of headquarters. The church is not growing now, and it is its own counter-gospel, counter-gathering policies and activities that keep the church from growing -- "we have met the enemy, and it is us."

I hear that the church finds it necessary to limit its expansion outside United States simply because, using current policies and practices, the amount of tithing received from the First World countries more than pays for First World costs, allowing the excess to be spent in Third World countries to accomplish the tasks and financial policies preferred by the Salt Lake City bureaucracy. But, obviously, there are limits on the net positive flow of tithing from First World countries, meaning that, to keep a proper financial balance, the church has to limit its growth and its preferred programs in Third World countries. This is a very artificial process which could end simply by encouraging the gathering from these Third World countries. Also, the operation of the church as designed by Christ was intended to allow it to move easily worldwide without these kinds of bureaucratic constraints. But, of course, there would be no profit in those methods, so they are not considered.

One case study of individual effect

One of my daughter's mission companions came to the United States from Poland. She naturally wanted to stay in the United States after her mission, but the church insisted she return to Poland and not attempt to move here. The logic was presumably that she should learn about the church here, and then go back to her native land and teach the Gospel there using her new experiences. However, it surely was clear to everyone involved that her life in Poland would be a poor shadow of what it could have been in the United States. She certainly had no reasonable expectation to change the corrupt culture of her home country all by yourself or with the help of a handful of members there.

The only practical, nondiscriminatory solution is to gather all those scattered and persecuted members to the US where they could enjoy full freedom and the benefits of living with millions of other saints, and then, sometime, perhaps when they have raised their children, perhaps either they or their children could return as privileged US citizens (like the privileges that church leaders enjoy as US citizens -- but are unwilling to do anything to protect) and influence their home countries to do better (perhaps after being weakened by losing many of their best and brightest to the homing beacon of the Gospel.) This sort of gathering would put the church actively on the side of freedom, and naturally would cause the church to be considered a negative force by the corrupt leaders of all these countries, and the church would be less able to act with its current policies in those countries. But I see that as a good thing, not a bad thing. Pandering to dictators all over the world and using church policy to strengthen the hand of those dictators is actually a way for the church to go against the Gospel and partially commit suicide by stopping its own growth in influence. The best people would gather themselves to Zion, and the world's societies would be changed by that activity, people voting with their feet for freedom and the Gospel.

The church apparently wishes to avoid offending the corrupt governments of the world by fostering a brain-drain of LDS members, but that is exactly what needs to happen to weaken Satan's grip on those places at this stage of working to change the world's societies toward a wide-spread Gospel civilization.

Some general history
Since 1896, when the practice began of the enforcing and consuming of tithing by church headquarters, the church leaders have collected about $1 trillion and wasted most of it on relatively frivolous activities. There might have been some benefits at the beginning of this worldwide expansion of a huge religious bureaucracy, but 100 years later there are nothing but problems. But far worse than the lost $1 trillion, by not allowing the Gospel to spread naturally, they have prevented at least $10 trillion, and probably much more, from being applied to Gospel purposes and the building up of Zion. They imposed an enormous 10% growth tax on church expansion for their own personal benefit, and, after a long decline in church growth rates, have finally completely killed any measurable church growth.

Had they allowed to the Gospel to spread naturally, the membership of the would be much larger now, and the members would have collectively spent trillions of dollars in the United States and elsewhere to advance the Gospel and to advance the societies in which they live, all moving the nations towards a Zion or a millennial condition. At least an extra $20 trillion in all would have been available to advance church work, including the $10 trillion that would have been available to retired church members if the church had encouraged the setting up of an alternate Social Security system which would have been many times more efficient than the corrupt wasteful tax-and-spend federal government version. Apparently, the church leaders planned a virtual ideological merger with the US government to minimize all conflict between organizations and make the lives of the church leaders more convenient.

The long and tortured trek toward Zion		
Date	Event	Consequences
1830	The LDS church is organized	This begins the trek toward Zion in earnest. Things go as planned for the first 66 years, during the presidencies of Joseph Smith, Brigham Young, and John Taylor, and the church is free and grows quickly. 90,000 converts come from Europe to bolster the process.
1896	Wilford Woodruff declares leadership salaries from church contributions	The church takes a terrible wrong turn and begins to suffer all the bad consequences of having a professional priesthood. Doctrines and practices are changed to maximize church income, not gospel influence for good on the world for the benefit of all members. The church consciously chooses to mimic the Roman Catholic Church. This creates the first financial class system in the church.
1923	The church creates a corporate structure which specifically separates the central offices from any control by the members	This makes it impossible for the church members to have any control over the money they contribute to the church, or even any knowledge of where it goes, and the church quickly begins to waste and hide the money it receives. According to plan, Christian charity gradually dies out and is replaced with law of Moses tithing and personal purity logic. $1 trillion is wasted and $10 trillion are kept from being applied to Zion projects, and the church ends up with $200 billion in sequestered assets.
1945 about	Church ends Relief Society independence	I believe Joseph Smith's vision was that the women should be spending on charitable projects nearly all the money which is now spent by church central offices for other things. (Women often managed charity in the New Testament.) That would ensure that we continued Christian charity as intended and not create a full-blown and wasteful law of Moses priestcraft system. The women were competing for church income, and that was "duplication," even though they were doing what they should.
1960 about	The church makes mandatory the payment of tithing before attending temples.	The successful monetizing of all higher ordinances sounds wonderful to church leaders who collect all the money, but the growth of the church takes a permanent downturn, heading towards zero, as we see today, because the members naturally do not agree with the leadership choices, and they shouldn't. In the United States, this means the average member must pay about $500,000 to maintain a lifetime membership in the church. Extra charity payments are strongly discouraged, as well as impractical. Charity can change society, and all such social change is discouraged. That individual tithing money is enough for a single person to build

		local meeting facilities for everyone if desired, with all the other money, the other 99%, going to Salt Lake to be consumed.
1977	The church officially ends the doctrinal policy of the Gathering	This step justifies central church leadership's keeping an enormous bureaucracy in Salt Lake City to travel to and coordinate among all the scattered members of the church, but it naturally further greatly slows the doctrinally required gathering and is the last nail in the coffin for any hope of establishing Zion in the United States or anywhere else. This makes permanent the international class system where the wealthier members in the United States pay for expensive (but unnecessary) architecture desired by leaders in foreign countries.
1978	The church allows priesthood ordinations for blacks	This was a necessary fairness development, and might have slightly assisted in the growth trajectory of the church. But this was probably not a profitable change for the church leaders, since most Third World countries consume more than they give in church contributions, so the leaders presumably tried to resist or contain that growth. On the other hand, if people can attend the temple, they are likely to pay more tithing, that being almost the entire business model of the LDS church today. This would logically mean that the tithing income from black members went up substantially with their receipt of temple privileges.

Chapter 27

Other Priestcraft Issues, Including Promoting One-World Government

Chapter topics:
1. The Correlation Function Of The LDS Church: The Ghost in the Machine? The Heart of Darkness?
2. How standard economic and legal trickery was used to turn a religion, with only unprofitable charitable volunteer activity, into a highly profitable business.
3. The Last Straw -- Unchristian Visions Of Worldly Grandeur

When I was first outlining this book, there were certain areas of study that I thought were just too unpleasant to even talk about. They present a "heart of darkness" that is probably more than most members are willing to believe of their church leaders. But now I fear that many readers will just gloss over the more general complaints mentioned here in this book until they realize what a priestcraft church is capable of doing to the gospel. The past gives us many clues about the future, but we are still left to speculate about where it all leads.

Obviously, we have 2000 years of history for the Roman Catholic Church to learn from as far as priestcraft is concerned, but we somehow imagine that we are fundamentally different from that ancient organization and the many misdeeds it has engaged in. However, basic human nature has not changed in 6000 years of history, so we should not assume that we are immune from many similar misdeeds of our own.

I see the church as taking conscious action to keep the effect of the gospel at about 2% of what it ought to be. That blocking function they are performing, all for the purpose of maximizing short-term church income, naturally upsets me. The current ideological corruption is very deep, although it is not obvious on the surface. The leaders must see every day the consequences of past policies, so that it is hard to imagine that they are not aware of these consequences and the policies behind them. They would naturally regularly have to review all past policies and all consequences before they could choose any new directions.

People always want to put off any potential bad consequences as long as they can. I think it's called "kicking the can down the road." The LDS church has been kicking that can down the road for 120 years, and it's time to straighten things out.

The Correlation Function Of The LDS Church: The Ghost in the Machine? The Heart of Darkness?

The LDS correlation committee is usually presented as a purely educational function of the church where all instructional materials that are sent out to the members are first examined by this correlation committee to make sure that they are in conformity with the scriptures and with all current church teachings and policies. Presumably that is indeed one of its functions.

However, it appears to me that the correlation committee would be better described as the puppet master for the entire church bureaucracy, setting and enforcing thousands of rules about interpretations of Scriptures and rules for the behavior of all the public faces of the LDS Church. The reason I say this is that the church, over the last 120 years, has deviated an enormous amount from the Gospel which Christ taught and which Joseph Smith taught. It has adopted many of the teachings and practices of men and has taken the church backward a giant step to enforce most of the concepts of the old law of Moses as though the church were deciding that it really didn't have the Christian answers anymore, and the best it can do is to revert to the original "schoolmaster." The church's current efforts concerning its new programs for children and youth, supposedly to get rid of the old checklist culture, the church program culture, actually highlights that it is at least partially aware of this "law of Moses" mindset and is trying to change it. That is laudable, but it must make a really major overhaul, including ending tithing, to really make a major and lasting change.

This law of Moses mindset that has been in place for nearly the last 100 years means that the teachings and behavior of the church today are far different from Christ's church. This presents a major problem since it probably happens all the time that the distinctions between the Scriptures, and the original Church of Christ, as compared to the current church, come up in many different settings, and someone must either try to justify those many differences or try to hide them. Part of that defense of the status quo includes telling lies about what the original Church of Christ was so that the new policies will be accepted as normal. This gets very complicated. As anyone knows who wants to put up an entire false front, riddled with untruths (something like the constant efforts of the current mainstream media to promote projects of the political left), it takes an enormous amount of thought and energy to keep this false story alive and plausible.

This means that we cannot have any general authorities speaking out of line, especially if they are advocating for parameters of the original Church of

Christ and, as a result, speaking against current policy. (This makes me think of the many hilarious comments of J. Golden Kimball, the "swearing elder," who was definitely "uncorrelated" most of the time. In his day, there were presumably no recordings and probably very few written transcripts, so strict central discipline was essentially impossible, and probably considered less necessary.) https://ldsblogs.com/11344/j-golden-kimball

One fairly recent example occurred when one lower-level general authority thought that there might be an easier way to solve the problem of getting church members around the world to be able to visit temples for their living ordinances without excessive travel expenses. As we know, it takes many years to get a temple authorized in a new country, and the costs for actually building the temple are also very large. This person suggested that an "endowment house" solution be used as a low-cost, quick-reaction way of providing access to saving ordinances around the world. (A similar earlier suggestion, which also died quickly, was to equip an airplane as a temple and send the airplane around the world periodically. That still seems like a genius idea.) After all, the members in Salt Lake City used the endowment house for essentially all of their ordinance work for 40 years while the Salt Lake Temple was being completed, so why would not that same solution work somewhere else? Obviously that solution would be catastrophic to the current church financing strategy and system which depends on strict control of recommends to keep people out of the temples (they helped fund) unless they have paid their tithing to the central offices. The other half of that monetizing proposition is that it has been declared that it is only elegant temples in which these ordinances can take place. Naturally, that church leader did not get to make that endowment house suggestion more than once, and it was quickly scrubbed from any written records.

Another interesting example is provided by Elder Thomas S. Monson, who had much to do with the building and use of the East German temple in Frieberg, Germany. After the wall went down between East Germany and West Germany, he expressed his gratitude that the East Germans were now free. However, the church policy is to never say anything in support of political freedom and to treat every government ideology as equal. In their minds it is perfectly rational to expect to be a good Mormon and a good communist at the same time, so talking about freedom being a good thing is considered a very bad thing for a general authority to say. He happened to make this comment at the very beginning of a general conference talk he was presenting. As fast as was humanly possible, his unscripted spontaneous comments, given as he began his talk, were quickly erased and do not appear in any videos or on any written versions of the talk he gave.

These are two examples out of presumably the tens of thousands which have occurred in the past where general authorities or public speakers might find themselves "off the ranch" as far as the current approved policies and attitudes about everything in the world.

As another example, one of the church attorneys made sure that the church conferences were not broadcast to any Arab countries lest some Arab governments be offended and some Arab members get imprisoned or killed. I see this as part of central church administrative paranoia. The truth is, that the church is much more worried about its own progress and freedom of action than it is about the lives of any members that may be impacted. Incidentally, we do have some Arab members, as in Lebanon.

There are many indicators that this single central church brain, this almost-alien force that has the LDS church in a powerful grip, enforcing thousands of tiny rules, is the real controlling force of the church. The top church leaders do have a fair amount of information and long-term continuity, but I believe it is simply impossible for any one of those men or all of them together to ever be able to examine every action and every potential misstep over a period of 120 years to make sure that the "cover story," and the established "narrative" is not breached, and the sham is not exposed.

A movie starring Tom Cruise entitled "Edge of Tomorrow" was very interesting to me. In that movie there was a single giant controlling alien intelligence which controlled millions of individual aliens and was even able to control time, allowing it to rerun any particular day so that any mistakes could be rectified so it could never lose a battle. The extreme level of control on every level, high and low, that it takes to keep the church on an even keel with a completely consistent internal and external message is certainly something that requires a superhuman effort. One small slip could expose the long-term fraud for what it is. This level of control is so great and so detailed that I find it frightening. That is why I say it is alien.

We have had government administrators such as the Italian Machiavelli who were able to manipulate governments and propaganda to reach certain results. But the difficulty of thinking of those strategies and then applying them on such a massive scale as to keep millions of people in the dark about what is really happening is truly impressive as well as disturbing. The level of secrecy maintained by the current church in its headquarters is remarkable, and that has to be part of this whole complex of information control and message control. Perhaps that is why the Church has felt so threatened by so-called "intellectuals" who dare to challenge any of the many assumptions on which the current church operates.

This whole system seems extremely fragile and therefore vulnerable, so it is very hard to see how we even got this far without a major gaffe, revealing the semi-sinister powers behind the throne. Perhaps we have finally reached the point where the evidence is overwhelming, and it is no longer possible for lies and manipulation to cover up the truth. If it is correct that the church has about $124 billion in reserve assets in one known collection, and many people think it is twice that amount if all sources are considered, then it is going to take some very serious long-term spinning to get rid of that obvious breach of fiduciary duty and put that question to bed.

How standard economic and legal trickery was used to turn a religion, with only unprofitable charitable volunteer activity, into a highly profitable business.

We start with the fact that Christ gave away for free all of his miracles and all of his ordinances. If the church leaders today followed that same example, as they did for at least the first 66 years after the church was organized by Joseph Smith, then it would be very hard to make a lot of money giving away religiously valuable goods and services. The obvious and time-honored way to move from a charitable service organization to a rent-seeking business is you have to find a way to charge a lot of money for something which should be free. One can do that by creating a legal monopoly so that the law demands that you pay a certain amount, regardless of the cost to produce, or you tell a big religious lie and then hammer it home over a generation until people finally accept the lie. The church has followed both courses of action to get to its highly lucrative business where the basic costs of its main product -- salvation, or, rather, peoples' subjective feeling that they are worthy of salvation -- has a near-zero cost to the dispensing organization. This is very much like today's consumer software business where having made one working copy of a program at great expense, the distribution of all other copies is nearly free.

The church has gone through several steps on its way to monetizing its ordinances. It went the government route of setting up a system within the state of Utah to authorize the formation of corporations of a certain sort, and then taking advantage of that corporation law to insulate the central church from the members. In essence, it used the fiction of the sovereign immunity of a state government to create a kind of sovereign immunity for the church organization itself. That was clearly inappropriate for a church to do, but was done anyway. "Secularization through incorporation" is one way to describe the process of partially corrupting a church. Really, it is only government organizations that can legitimately play the sovereign immunity game, but churches have found ways to trick people into believing the same thing about churches. A state church obviously fits that description where the two are formally merged. So, in Utah, the LDS church is more or less a state church. The Roman Catholic Church went through that process, and the Mormon church did the same, for the same reasons. Since the leaders of the church and of the state were basically the same people in Utah, they created the corporation sole as a feature of the Utah government and then adopted that for the church, making the leader of the church an absolute dictator on everything that has anything to do with the church. There is no group of people managing the church, where differing opinions can and need to be considered. There is only one man and he alone has absolute control.

Before that, the church was an unincorporated association which at least yearly needed to authorize a trustee to act on its behalf concerning property holdings. The great business weakness with that arrangement, for a church that wants to monetize its most valuable product, its ordinances, is that if the church members become irritated by the church leaders' misbehavior, they can vote for a different trustee. There is no particular reason for the yearly trustee to be the current head of the LDS church, otherwise typically known as the president and prophet. Someone else can fill that role. Or we might have the unseemly situation of people campaigning and competing to be the next trustee promising to operate with a different set of principles, as has happened before in LDS church history.

Going to the corporation sole format essentially squelched all member control options. Of course, what that means is that the trustee at the time, who allowed this process to go on to create a Corporation sole to control what had in the past been an unincorporated association, did indeed breach his fiduciary duty to the members of the church. But, this turncoat person, unauthorized do what he did unless he held a special member vote on that issue, would naturally be celebrated by those who were conspiring to take over the church and cut out all member influence on the management of the church and its resources. This was a "lawyers' coup." Apparently, after a few years of getting by successfully with this fraudulent move, then this strategic change became a fate accompli and everyone gave up and forgot.

On the "big lie" side of the takeover equation, people were told, at least by implication, that now that the central church owned all the resources, and the members owned nothing, and had no management control over anything, then the new owners of the church and its property and its copyrighted materials could have absolute control and they could therefore say who could attend the temples and who could not, since now all ownership of everything had been vested in this one autonomous and self-perpetuating totalitarian organization. That would have been a good time for a church revolution to stop this unprincipled takeover, but apparently it didn't happen, or it didn't happen with enough force to be effective.

So, then, gradually, members of the church were convinced that they were not worthy to go to the temple unless they did exactly what the new church leaders said, which mostly amounted to paying 10% of their income to the central offices, and giving up all control over that money. The church says that when some money passes into its hands, members have no control whatsoever over it. That means the leaders can spend it as they wish: they can waste it, they can hold it in reserve for pensions or perquisites, or whatever they want.

The really terrible part of this is that now essentially none of that money goes for the charitable purposes for which it had been used before, and which the church members would reasonably expect the church leaders to continue. But since there were now no legal or practical or economic constraints on that member money anymore, the church simply kept all the money and spent it as it saw fit, almost exclusively on itself. If there were new questions that came up, they could keep gradually tightening up the regulations so that there was no way out of paying the full tithe if one wanted to get access to saving ordinances which meant attending the temples.

The bad effects are many. All of the good intentions of members that their contributions be used to do good in the society are completely ignored and the church wastes or expends these resources any way it wishes with abandon and without responsibility.

One of the really worst parts of all this is that most societies are incapable of avoiding deterioration unless someone is willing to put in some idealistic effort and resources to keep the society from deteriorating. The true church is uniquely qualified and responsible to perform this task. It has certainly done so in the past, but at this point the church is part of the problem. If everyone is left completely to their own narrow self-interests, then it is not long until there are many people who lose out in the race of life, and there is no one to take care of their needs. One of the very important things to do is to maintain freedom in the society, and that will not be done by a rent-seeking church which avoids any kind of conflict with the world in efforts to maximize its short-term profits -- the death of idealism. Some conflict with the world is necessary to maintain the freedom of the people. Otherwise, the greedy totalitarians will gradually take over and crush out everyone, perhaps reaching the point where we have active slavery going again. Slavery is Satan's plan, and it can be achieved through many step-by-step processes. It is only the church, or at least religion and correct ideology, an active positive good, that can stop these constant deteriorating steps.

The church should be at the center for defending freedom, just as the Christian churches were the center for overcoming slavery during the Civil War. But here we have the church joining the forces of darkness to add their own form of economic bondage to the church members to extract money from them which the church is not entitled to get. When people who are supposed to be uplifting society become part of those groups that are destroying society, then the end is near. Alma 1:12 has an amazing statement which governs all societies. It is speaking of priestcraft, and we need to be wise enough to realize that priestcraft covers a multitude of sins concerning bondage, and the church is involved in many of those sins itself.

> Alma 1:12 ... and were priestcraft to be enforced among this people it would prove their entire destruction.

This is why there is no such thing as having priestcraft being a little bit okay. It is always the route to destruction of every society that adopts it -- the slippery slope. Since we have adopted it, our end is certain unless we can change direction, and we certainly cannot count on the LDS church to help the society change direction. The church will simply keep up their rent-seeking strategies until the whole societal structure goes up in smoke.

A better definition
It is certainly acceptable for a church member to spend money to advance the gospel mission. There can be no doctrinal complaint if that person decides to spend his own money in this way. But a problem can easily arise when someone tries in any way to convince a second person to supply the money the first person wishes to spend. What that first person cannot do is coerce another to supply him the money he wishes to spend, whether that involves direct temporal coercion using trickery or force, or using more subtle spiritual coercion. Spiritual coercion occurs when a theologian of priestcraft attempts to modify the doctrines of the gospel to justify and require payments to be made to an individual or corporate body in any other way than through personal, spontaneous, heartfelt, single, individual transactions each involving current free charitable intent. There can be no concept of debt or any enforceable repetitive payments or subscriptions. They must all be "arbitrary conveyances" or "arbitrary consecrations" in the wise words of John Selden. Otherwise, the result is unrighteous dominion and a corruption of the gospel's message of freedom and charity. Requiring a person to pay other men to gain his personal salvation is never a part of the gospel.

The Last Straw -- Unchristian Visions Of Worldly Grandeur

Once the heresy and temptation of priestcraft are accepted, the illusions and delusions of fame, money, and power seem to grow without limit, until the leaders imagine themselves as the rightful rulers of the world, God's viceroys overriding and including all other systems of human government, however absurd and wrong that result may seem in relationship to basic gospel principles. In fact, they may use gospel principles and opportunities to effectively become the Antichrist and accomplish the exact opposite of what was intended, persecuting the Saints using the gospel. Seeing these kinds of psychotic delusions being accepted and relished by the Church leaders should send shivers down the spines of all good members -- this is the heart of darkness, the mystery of iniquity.

In first creating a draft of this book, I tried to leave out this most sinister part of the consequences of the church deciding it's going to be the new one-world government, or at least part of it. But serious Christians need to know where all of this impulse to religious empire-building actually leads to in the fevered minds of ambitious church leaders.

The leaders seem to be unconstrained in what they can dream of and hope to do, all on the backs of their faithful Mormon tribalists, those tribalists having been prepared and conditioned by history to be willing to undertake very difficult activities if they are said to be necessary for the cause of Zion. But that willingness to sacrifice can be abused easily, as I believe it has already. However, "things which can't go on, don't," and the church leaders have definitely pushed things way too far in their search for power and prestige and glory. It is all a very prideful thing they do.

We might think of Ezra Taft Benson and his famous talk about pride. I have often wondered who he was talking about, and now I believe he was talking about the church leaders themselves, other than himself, who were hell-bent on world domination, Roman Catholic Church-style. This is psychotic, but still seems to drive at least a majority of church leaders. This is "Gadianton Robber" thinking, not the thinking of Christ. Christ would look to the needs of the one, not be willing to sacrifice individuals to the questionable plans for the greater glory of an illegitimate religious bureaucracy. When the church leaders think of themselves as the generals of a religious army, we are in deep trouble. Generals usually don't suffer the consequences of their errors, so they are often only too willing to sacrifice others.

There was a time within the church when it was considered a compliment for the church to be said to be "organized like the German army." The generals of the Third Reich, along with Hitler, probably imagined that they would be the rulers of the world and that they were so wise that they deserved such adulation and power. They were willing to sacrifice the lives of millions of people to reach the glories of a Third Reich. Luckily for everyone else in the world, they completely failed, but at a devastating cost in wholesale slaughter, something which Satan would have delighted in, regardless of whether his minions attained world domination.

The LDS church has not yet advocated for the sacrifice of individuals on the same scale, but they have come far too close, accepting in principle results that could be just as bad.

I know of about three instances when the church leaders have grossly stepped over the line, repudiating almost every aspect of the Gospel in their search for worldly power. They have not only failed and succumbed to the three temptations of Christ, but have done it with great gusto, imagining that the world owes them a living, a living which involves adulation and power. They wish to become the masters and haven't the slightest interest in being the servants of anyone. That puts them at war with the Church of God, even though they are supposedly the leaders of the Church of God.

The things I'm going to describe relate to times before, during, and after the active fighting in World War II, that being the great international convulsion of most recent memory. One would have to assume that there were many other instances where choices were made that were antithetical to the cause of the Gospel, with the leaders opting for the tantalizing route to temporal power, but most of those instances we would likely not know anything about. Only the largest and most outrageous events have made it to the point where they can be known publicly, slipping out of the darker recesses of church leadership strategy sessions and actions. Perhaps we need some more "wikileaks" on this important point, some filmed discussions of these highly damaging topics to get a better understanding of the values of our leadership class.

Before World War II actually began, the LDS Church declared itself to be neutral and pacifist. That seemed to be a very strange position to take. Did that tend to put ALL obedient church members in the position of a "fifth column" internal anti-freedom, antiwar movement, or did it only apply to the church headquarters itself? How did the members at the time resolve the issue? Did they support the church or did they support the nation? Captain Moroni would have figured out who the enemies of freedom were and would have focused all his energies on keeping them at bay or defeating them if they crossed a certain line. One might think that it would be important for the church leaders to want the church members to be politically free, at least in the United States, but, apparently, they have no concern about that issue.

If someone is going to be free, then someone has to pay the cost to maintain that freedom, and the church was declaring that it would not pay that cost, and, presumably, would not encourage its members to defend their own freedom. The church headquarters (perhaps accompanied by the members) became a free rider, depending on someone else, other people who were better Christians than they were, to maintain our freedom for us. Perhaps that's the way the church leaders felt -- that they were entitled to experience the benefits of freedom at no cost to themselves or to anyone they knew. But that is not the way it works in real life, as every adult understands.

It is a major problem already if anyone, the church included, is undecided about whether freedom is important or not. It is even worse to actively decide that one will never help the cause of freedom, that defense of freedom being inconsistent with the "will to power" of church leaders, where, for one person or group to gain power, someone else must give up power and freedom. (Many of the German leaders of the time admired the satanic "will to power" concept. Perhaps the church leaders of the time admired those German leaders and some of their philosophies.)

The church's pacifism was specifically helping the enemies of freedom, and, as we will see, the church often helped the enemies of freedom in more active ways. Today we have the twisted situation where the political left admires Islam for the very reason that it demands and maintains the obedience of the masses, as Islam repudiates nearly all the traditional principles of Western civilization.

In politics, often "the enemy of my enemy is my friend," meaning that for a civil government which wishes to take totalitarian control over its own citizens, those citizens become the enemy of this would-be dictatorial government, putting totalitarian Islam in the role of the government's friend while the citizens are the enemy. Islam helps the central government increase control over its people, without the central government necessarily getting all the blame for doing so.

It seems that we have a similar situation with the LDS church. The central headquarters sees the membership as "enemies" to be conquered and exploited. Any totalitarian government such as socialism or communism can thus be viewed as an assistant to the central church reaching its goals. This is very twisted thinking, but it seems to happen at church headquarters. There is a war going on between central headquarters and the members, but the goal is to keep the members from being aware that the central headquarters has declared war on them in its search for its own version of illegitimate world power.

This kind of deception and trickery may seem suicidal for a church headquarters, but that is only because we have not yet considered how the church central headquarters, as an entity, psychotically imagined that it could profit from World War II, no matter what the outcome might be. If the church leaders pridefully decided that their message and their political organization could and should survive no matter what the underlying ideology of any future government might be, only then would they make the foolish choice to try to stay above the fray, hoping to rule religiously over whatever was left after a military conflagration. As a practical matter, this would require the church headquarters to create an alliance with the expected future government, in this case the German Third Reich. A stable alliance between good and evil seems absurd, but the church leaders seemed to imagine that they could do the impossible.

Perhaps the church leaders were looking at the Roman Catholic Church as their model which manages to have church members in almost every kind of country where government ideologies of every sort are in power. We have the Russian Orthodox Church in Russia. We have the Catholic churches in South America which have adopted and incorporated local saints and miracles and beliefs into the basic religion. But what this means, of course, is that there are perhaps a hundred different versions of the Catholic Church in a hundred different countries, some more idolatrous than others, but none of them adopting the full Gospel of Christ. Perhaps the LDS leaders decided that if the Catholics could do it, then the Mormons could do it too, adjusting the Gospel parameters as needed at every different set of borders it crossed. But this is not the Gospel, this is nothing but opportunism. If every version of the Gospel is different and none of them match the original Gospel of Christ, then you have nothing but a big mess, with each country group being in its own varying stages of apostasy and deviation.

Save missionaries but not members
If the church felt that it needed to save the American missionaries who were sent to Germany, why would it not just as much try to save the German members in Germany? What exact kind of class system is the church trying to enforce here? Are the missionaries to be considered the diplomatic and military agents of the church central headquarters bureaucracy, and so they deserve special treatment over the regular members in Germany? Isn't every member a missionary? That seems like very bureaucratic thinking, not Christian thinking, especially if the church imagines that it operates above all worldly rules.

In those early times near the beginning of World War II, when everyone could see that there was going to be a great conflict, the LDS church at least took the action to remove its missionaries from Germany and other places in Europe. One might think that if the church were actually interested in doing the best thing for its church members no matter where they were, temporary missionaries or not, it would also have invited as many church members as possible to leave their soon-to-be war-torn countries, and sponsored their trips to the United States or to some other place where they would be safe from this coming hellish experience.

But the LDS Church did not do that. One might think that the LDS Church would be happy to welcome Jews, as part of the house of Israel to be gathered, especially those who had become church members who wished to leave Germany, seeing the handwriting on the wall that their fate was likely going to be very bad. (There is some historical mention that one of the church first presidency counselors at the time, J. Reuben Clark, had strong anti-Semitic feelings. That certainly does not well befit a member of the Mormon first presidency.)

One might especially think that Jews who had become Mormons would be especially vulnerable and therefore especially suitable for transporting out of Germany before the great conflicts began. But none of this happened. The church only brought its formal representatives home and gave no help whatsoever to any church members or any Jews who wished to leave that quickly-deteriorating place. Apparently, the church even specifically denied support for any requests for visas. As a result, many of the church members died from battle situations, and others, the most pitiful of all, killed their children and themselves rather than experience coming under the control of the invading Russian army or living under the control of the German army. In other words, the church behavior was responsible for numerous suicides of desperate church members who should have been aided in leaving that terrible place. (There were no romantic Mormon "Sound of Music" last-minute escapes from Germany and Austria that I know of.)

The logic seems to be, as I've hinted at above, that the Church wished to stay on good terms with the leaders of the Third Reich so that it could benefit from being allowed to have members remain after the battles were over. This seems to be assuming that the Third Reich would win. This almost puts the church in the situation of rooting for the Western Allies to fail. That meant doing things to individuals, sacrificing their interests, simply because sacrificing those individuals would prove to the Third Reich that the Mormons could be counted on as dependable citizen/slaves after the Third Reich took power. At this point, such thoughts seem to be total madness, and only in the fevered brains of "power at all costs" church leaders could this make an ounce of sense. I recall reading that there were a few minor cases where Mormons were given some small preferences by the German leaders based on their protestations of loyalty, even though one cannot reconcile the freedom-loving Gospel with the murderous dictatorship of the Third Reich where millions of people were killed simply because they preferred freedom and were not sufficiently obedient to the rising dictators.

If we move ahead to the time after the battles were over and Europe had been divided up between the Allied powers and the Russian army, and Germany had been divided into eastern and western sectors, then we see a continuation of this "diplomatic" pandering to the ruthless communist dictators which now controlled East Germany. It seems to me that all the events surrounding the building of the Freiberg Temple are not something to celebrate but should be repented of and atoned for.

To the extent possible, all of those church members in East Germany should have been assisted to get out of that satanic place. I don't know how much could have been accomplished before the Berlin wall went up, but it seems possible that large numbers of them could have escaped if they were assisted in some way. (Apparently the church leaders thought that it would be a feather in their cap to have some church members trapped in East Germany where they could theoretically act as a nucleus for spreading the church there later on.) But what a terrible cost the church headquarters seemed to expect these members in communist East Germany to pay to add power and prestige to the ambitious bureaucrats in Salt Lake City.

Perhaps when Ezra Taft Benson went to Germany right after the war and distributed aid to church members, that would have been a perfect time to get many of those church members out of that terrible place so that they could have lived normal lives. I am assuming that many of those people could have escaped before the Berlin wall made that impossible. (Can anyone imagine Captain Moroni making a deal with the Gadiaton Robbers or the Lamanites to put the church members in bondage to them? How could the church leaders consider selling church members into bondage as something they should be proud of?)

Certainly, after the Berlin wall was raised it would have been much more difficult to get those people out of that terrible place. But, the idea that the church could "make a deal" with the East German dictators to allow a temple to be built there to meet some of the religious needs of the members seems like a really terrible solution on many levels. (We might recall that expensive temples are really unnecessary by Gospel standards. Getting one built in this terrible place is really nothing but a prideful act, a tarnished trophy.)

First of all, it was recognizing the Russian dictators as a legitimate constitutional government, even though it was totally antithetical to everything that the Gospel stands for. The Communists were ruthless murderers and their Stasi secret police most likely harassed the Mormons as much as anyone else, and probably more.

Making that agreement and alliance of convenience with East German dictators and their Kremlin masters could do nothing but sully the Gospel and make any reasonable person wonder what the principles of the Gospel really were. Were they really to be just another layer of government added on top of whatever secular/atheist government might be operating there? So, we have a supposedly Christian government with its tithing taxes overlaying an atheist communist government with its taxes, widespread property confiscation, and ruthless controls? It is ideologically impossible to be a good communist and a good Mormon at the same time; those principles simply cannot coexist in the same brain or society coherently.

But, worst of all, the church was willing to use its influence in the United

States to hurt the freedom impulses and activities of the United States, hoping to curry favor with the corrupt dictators in East Germany and Russia, the church trading its influence over American society to weaken that society and strengthen the Communists. This seems simply unforgivable.

This all happened surrounding the MX missile issue. The United States had decided to build a vast series of missile storage facilities and missile silos interconnected by roads and railroad tracks. The idea being that one could hide hundreds of intercontinental ballistic missiles in perhaps a two-state area, and if those missiles were constantly on the move, the Russians could never know where all the missiles were. The idea was that no imaginable number of missiles shot from Russia could ever take out all of the US missiles, leaving a goodly number left for a return strike. This is the maximum version of the Mutually Assured Destruction strategy that the great powers were pursuing at the time.

Because these missiles were to be placed in Nevada and Utah, the LDS Church took it upon itself to do everything in its power to stop that missile complex from being built in the first place. Presumably the LDS Church was also acting as a negotiator with the East German government, promising to try to end or minimize this threat to Russian international power in exchange for being given permission to build a temple in East Germany. This is a terribly unbalanced bargain from any angle, and can't cannot be considered anything but treasonous to the interests of the United States by the LDS Church which appointed itself a fifth column movement to act on behalf of the Soviet government within the United States. As far as I know, the church never suffered for this disgusting anti-American activity, in pursuit of its tiny little corrupt interest in East Germany, but it should have. In the end, the church did stop the building of that giant missile complex in Utah and Nevada, and a much smaller number of missiles were placed in Wyoming, I believe, but they were far more vulnerable to a Soviet first strike than anything would have been in Nevada and Utah.

One of the strangest parts of this transaction is that we had Gordon B. Hinckley arguing that it would be terrible to have all of the construction workers coming into Utah to disrupt the people there. (This is nothing but a big lie, as is common in normal politics.) These presumably American construction workers were portrayed as being an evil and satanic influence of low morals who would greatly damage the state and its people. In fact, the more likely result would be that these were good people who would be coming here to do this complicated work, and many of them would likely become good church members when they came in contact with the church. That is the strategy today in the days of the expanding "Silicon Slopes" businesses in Utah. However, this foolish (and highly unchristian, even xenophobic) argument about the low quality of the workers was necessary to bolster the foolish argument against building a missile system in the first place. This scorn for all the outsiders was nothing but a very poor excuse for trying to stop the missile installations for what the church saw as its own long-term political interests in ruling the world -- one of Satan's temptations to Christ which the Savior naturally resisted.

One of the arguments proffered by Hinkley was that the church did not wish to have its headquarters unit anywhere near the potential blast zones for these missile systems. This "not in my backyard" attitude indicated that the Mormons were not willing to sacrifice anything to support the freedom of the United States. One might debate whether the missile system was the best solution to defending the United States, but that was not the issue the church raised. (Maybe the church could have allowed the missiles to be installed and then prayed that the heavens would intervene to make sure that the missile system was never needed, but that would not have matched with their long-term plans to merge with all other governments of the world.) It simply, in typical pacifist fashion, wanted nothing to do with any of these kinds of defensive systems. The real truth, of course, was that the church was negotiating away American freedom interests for its own selfish interests to remain a religious power in East Germany and presumably in Russia as well. I find this disgusting.

People may wonder why I am so adamant that any kind of priestcraft is bad, without exception. The problem is that as soon as anyone gets these foolish ideas in their heads of taking over the world, they start bending every principle of righteousness to achieve that disgusting goal. They want to do what Christ clearly avoided in every possible way, but He was extremely successful, nonetheless.

As a joke in a Beatles movie, there is a scene where two government scientists are saying that they are trying to "get a government grant to take over the world." This was intended to be funny, of course, but here we have the LDS church doing exactly the same thing, imagining that it can tax its own members enough, that, with clever diplomacy, it can become a world power, operating as just another ideological and practical level on top of all the corrupt secular governments which are already in place, which the church happily recognizes in any form, just so that it can be allowed to operate and extract another level of taxes and obedience out of the exact same people who are being exploited by the secular governments. (This kind of mixing of ideologies is obviously perfectly incoherent and impossible, but the church leaders saw no logical difficulty in carrying out this bizarre plan. Were they so ignorant concerning totalitarian governments that they imagined that they could become the state religion to an atheist communist Russia, replacing the centuries-old Russian Orthodox church which had already been completely subverted by the Russian Communists?).

There are so many things wrong with this that it's hard to even list them all. But the church does not seem to have changed its strategy at all from the World War II times. It would just as quickly forget about building "Zion on this American continent," and the principles of our Constitution, and every other principle of the Gospel, if by so doing it could gain some earthly power and wealth.

Why would any informed member want to be part of such a demented plan? This might even explain why some people leave the church, although they may not be able to clearly state their reasons. With this kind of absurd goals and reasoning driving the church, that is just another reason why the church has to keep all of its internal operations very secret, whether it is its long-term plans for "diplomacy" or its long-term plans to extract the maximum amount of money from the members to launch some of these ambitious diplomatic initiatives. A money horde of $200 billion is not enough to take over the world, but it might sound like a good start. This is a far more likely reason for the church's behavior in stockpiling this money. It is truly absurd for the church to be claiming that it is saving money for the second coming. That argument does not pass the laugh test, since all of its land titles and paper assets would probably disappear overnight in that cataclysmic situation.

I might mention that in the MX case the church claimed to be trying to defend its temple and its headquarters in Salt Lake City in its arguments against the missile complex. But, in truth, it was condemning itself and demonstrating its past corruptions of the Gospel by doing so. The church needs no central bureaucracy and needs no temples to operate. The church is intended to be worldwide, not a regional tribal Sanhedrin. It had already corrupted the Gospel by even setting up a huge bureaucracy and a fixed headquarters and defending a temple in the same way that the law of Moses priests defended the temple of Herod as the symbol of their power, or as any other pagan priests defended their temples and idols. There is nothing but corruption here.

Naturally the church wanted to defend the progress it had made in building its One-World religious government, but that is not something it should have been defending. It should never have constructed this bureaucracy and worldly government in the first place, so here it was using illegitimate means to protect something which was itself illegitimate. If people have very bad feelings about the church today, they have plenty of good reasons to have those feelings. The church has done terrible things and apparently will continue to do terrible things until the whole structure is torn down, just like the law of Moses was obliterated by the coming of Christ.

Notice now that the church leaders have recently decided to go along with the statists/Socialists and help attack the US Second Amendment by forbidding any concealed carry firearms in their facilities. The bad people will quickly learn that the LDS churches are now supposed to be gun free zones – and that always attracts murderous criminals. Many members may not care, some will willingly comply, while that may be the last straw for some people, and other people will simply ignore the new rule and continue with their concealed carry habits.

There will surely be a few far-left church members who will think it is a great idea to ban guns and help the anti-American socialists, but the pacifist, hate-America crowd is not really the group that I hope the church is trying to placate. I think it's interesting that a third or a half of the young people in the nation think that other countries in the world are better places to live than the United States. All that really does is show how completely ignorant and foolish they are. They know nothing about the rest of the world. They know nothing about our country in comparison to the rest of the world. This demonstrates that our secular civics lessons have been useless or worse. There is no adequate process in place to emphasize the importance of freedom and the place of the United States in maintaining freedom internally and in the world.

This constant US movement leftward is just another one of the catastrophes that are about to destroy this country, and the church cares nothing about it. They are simply trying to get along with the powers-that-be and keep collecting their money. This implies that the lawyers running the church don't believe in the gospel but do believe in collecting money through any means necessary, and they really don't care what happens later on. They will be like the dictators of Latin America as in the case where the president of Mexico simply stole $2 billion from the treasury when he left office as president of Mexico. It had a terrible effect on their currency, but he certainly did not care about that, and others had done it before him. This one person was going to be rich for life and he didn't care about anything else. I think the church leaders have about the same attitude, like the "presidents for life" around the world who loot their countries. We now seem to have pretty good proof that the church has hoarded at least $124 billion, and the real number may be closer to $200 billion. And this is all in cash, with all the real estate and other types of investments added on top of that for another unknown number of hundreds of billions of dollars.

Where is the church heading?
The epitome of the LDS strategy these days seems to be to become just like the Russian Orthodox Church. There are many state churches or semi-state Christian churches around the world that the LDS Church might use as examples of how they would like to operate, but the Russian Orthodox Church seems especially appropriate. The Russian Orthodox Church

became a state church under the Czar's and remained a state church under the atheistic Communists after the revolution and the overthrow of the Czars. Of course, the Communists, especially in the person of Stalin, tried to destroy the Russian Orthodox Church, blowing up hundreds of churches to try to rid the land of the scourge of religion (a competitor to his absolute power). However, in times of great distress as when the German army attacked Russia, it suddenly seemed convenient to have a church available around which to rally the citizens and the troops, mouthing calls to defend the church and the motherland and other such patriotic slogans. Asking people to defend the mass murderer Stalin and his atheist beliefs did not seem to stir up much enthusiasm among the populace.

Apparently even the most atheistic and brutal dictatorship such as the Russian government under Stalin finds it convenient sometimes to have a state religion component. Apparently, the claims of atheism and their promise of their communistic heaven on earth are not really very convincing on such eternal issues as death and the afterlife. The proletariat seems to still worry about the consequences of death and the nature of the afterlife. Apparently, having a state church available which provides a way to burn candles for the dead is a very useful social outlet for various kinds of anxieties.

Of course, the Russian Orthodox Church is completely compromised, being mostly staffed by Russian secret police operatives as opposed to actual monks from real monasteries. The LDS Church could expect to be as thoroughly compromised in any place where it plans to become the titular state church. Such a church must be thoroughly domesticated and compromised or it cannot coexist with Satan's minions in government.

The fact that the LDS Church is so foolish as to imagine that it could retain any more than a shadow of true Christianity and still function as the recognized state church in an atheist state indicates that the church leaders are extremely uneducated about the world and the workings of Satan. That alone would be a good enough reason to get rid of these misguided leaders who are trying to make themselves the new kings of the earth, as though they were authorized by Christ to do so.

Perhaps the LDS Church is thinking that as long as it has many millions or even billions of followers it can claim, then it doesn't really matter if the essence of the Gospel has been thoroughly corrupted and taken over and claimed by Satan's manipulative minions. Obviously, if the Church were to present this as their world strategy and request a sustaining vote from the members, they would get very few votes, especially in Utah where rugged individualism and freedom are still considered valuable goals and traits. In the one-worlder fever swamps of such places as Washington, DC or the

European Union headquarters in Brussels, Belgium they might get a few votes from the one-worlders gathered together there, some of whom might be DNA or cultural Mormons, but otherwise I think such a vote would only serve to clarify just how absurd our current church leadership has become.

It is hard to understand what President Nelson might mean by his "hinge point" rhetoric concerning the future of the Church as we commemorate the 200th anniversary of the restoration of the Gospel, but it seems highly likely that his vision is nothing more than to become a replacement and claimed upgrade to the Russian Orthodox Church and all similar pseudo-Christian churches seen around the world.

When the church leaders begin their planning logic for Church administration with the assumption that some kind of communism or communalism is a necessary part of the Gospel, they have already lost their way as they try to drag a few million Mormons along with them on this fool's errand. At this point, the fact that the church is still small becomes a blessing instead of a curse, since as long as the church is small it cannot do nearly as much damage as it might if it were larger. In a larger incarnation, it might provide even more protective coloration for the minions of Satan who wished to control the world, including choosing to rent or buy religious respectability as part of their machinations, and would appreciate being blessed in their evil projects by an organization which calls itself the true Church.

Part of this delusion is the church leaders imagining that their building up a giant international bureaucracy will somehow lead us to the situation where:

> "For out of Zion shall go forth the law, and the word of the Lord from Jerusalem." Isaiah 2:3

President Hinckley imagined that the law would eventually go forth from the new Conference Center in Salt Lake City, that being one of the reasons given to build that structure. But I believe he was delusional, since the "law" which is now going forth from the conference center, the ancient law of Moses, is a far cry from any message that Christ would like to see go forth.

Summary

Is it the mission of the Church to prepare many people to be good little citizen/slaves in a socialist or communist setting, the kind of world where Satan has almost complete control of everything, as seems to be their goal today? Or should they be preparing generations of Captain Moroni's who will do all in their power to maintain political freedom, if for no other reason than that free men can do more good with their lives than can slaves?

Chapter 28

LDS Church Grand Strategy: Past, Present, and Possible Future

Where are we? Where are we going?
What is the present state of the church, and where do we go from here? In recent times the net growth of the church has been very small, and we keep hearing of many people leaving the church, supposedly because of the Internet and the opportunity for members to hear many questions raised about the accuracy of the church history taught within the church system.

Perhaps it would be useful to list a sampling of some of the theories and opinions which have been suggested for why we find ourselves where we are, and where we think we are going. Jana Riess lists a few of these theories and opinions in her book *The Next Mormons*, and I have found a few others:

1. Catholic sociologist Thomas O'Dea, in his 1978 book *The Mormons*, based on his research from the 1950s, was pessimistic about the future of the LDS church arguing "among other things, that higher education would introduce such a strain of theological relativism to the LDS Church that it would decrease faithfulness among the religions brightest and best." But, as Riess points out in her book. "In fact, the opposite happened; ... it is often the best educated individuals who have the strongest ties to Mormon orthodoxy." Nonetheless, perhaps we can say that, in the end, Thomas O'Dea was correct in probably unknowingly anticipating the arrival of the Internet which has had the negative effect that he predicted for higher education, simply coming from a different source.[1]

2. Rodney Stark, an American sociology of religion professor, made some very optimistic projections in the 1980s which would put the church membership at 250 million by the year 2080. Actually, I think his rejections were reasonable based on the data he had. It simply seems that he did not anticipate that the LDS church would actively take steps to neutralize itself so that his projections were short-circuited. Many of those growth-destroying steps were taken in the 1960s and 1970s and apparently had not yet shown their full depressing effects.[2]

3. A survey of over 3000 individuals, done by a group of volunteers, and a

related summary and interpretive book completed in 2013, entitled *LDS Personal Faith Crisis,* seems to do a good job in describing many of the individual symptoms of faith crises, which have resulted in many of the best and brightest leaving the church. It points to the Internet and social media as the main disruptive forces, as they have quickly introduced large amounts of "uncorrelated" church history data to unprepared church members. However, it does not seem to offer any specific solutions to these problems, although it does express a sense of urgency about finding a good operational theory and solution. Nonetheless, there are hints that a much more comprehensive main church website might counter the many negative sites, but that appears to be a nearly impossible and Herculean feat at this point. In my opinion, that gigantic research and writing effort would be of limited value because it would not be addressing the main problem. Just expressing love and concern for those in faith crises seems to be the main proposed suggestion.[3]

4. David B. Ostler has experience as a stake president and mission president and has an MBA and has managed businesses focused on improving healthcare. He has written a book entitled *Bridges: Ministering to Those Who Question*. He does not seem to offer a theory about the reasons for the problems the church is having in gaining and retaining members. His emphasis seems to be mostly on finding ways to ease the mental and emotional pain of members who are feeling doubts and conflicts, with listening and seeking understanding as the main activities.[4]

5. John Gee is the William (Bill) Gay Research Professor in the Department of Asian and Near Eastern Languages at Brigham Young University. As expressed in an article in the online *Mormon Interpreter*, he thinks that Jana Riess is too pessimistic in her conclusions about the future of the church. He claims to have seen surveys that give more optimistic results for the future, but that optimism only seems to go so far as to indicate that the church is stable and will likely remain static. It appears that he would be perfectly happy if the church stayed stable and did not shrink, although in my opinion, if the gospel is as great as we claim, it ought to be growing quickly.[5]

6. Jana Riess is an American writer and editor, and a senior columnist for Religion News Service, who has written a book entitled *The Next Mormons: How Millennials Are Changing the LDS Church,* mentioned above. She chooses not to offer her own personal theory about Mormonism's future but favors the theory of Armand Mauss that "The LDS Church has accommodated change before, and it can do so again." That is a pretty thin and non-committal theory, not implying any particular direction to be taken, but at least it is mildly optimistic. My observation is that most past church changes have been driven mostly by economics, and one might expect future changes to follow the same pattern. Riess points out "that the literature about Mormonism and social science is so littered with failed theories that

anyone should be humbled by the prospect of adding one more tombstone to that graveyard."[6]

7. Of course, church leaders and speakers would typically say that everything today is just wonderful, "all is well in Zion," and that the 2019 completion of the magnificent temple in Rome should be seen as a "hinge point," presumably the beginning of a story of great success for the church in "gathering Israel," also approximately coinciding with the 2020 marking of the 200-year anniversary of the restoration of the church. My concern is that the 200-year mark is also typically the point at which a restoration of the gospel starts to fall apart as in 4 Nephi, and apparently as also seen in the Jerusalem church, to a lesser extent. I fear that is the more likely outcome, as things stand.

8. In the face of these fairly limited and unconvincing attempts to theorize about the problem, about where the church might or should go, or the attempts to simply ease the pain of the symptoms, without trying to discover and deal with the cause, I am surely going to seem excessively bold in pretending that I have a fairly comprehensive theory about the nature of the problem and the appropriate and specific plans to deal with it. Still, the project should be worth the effort and the risk since there should be a big practical payoff for the church and, especially, its members, in finding a workable theory and answer.

My theory in a nutshell

In the LDS church we have a supposedly Christian church that does not practice, or barely practices, the main tenet of Christianity as taught in the New Testament – CHARITY. 1 Cor. 13. Less than 1% of the money that goes to Salt Lake City is devoted to humanitarian aid or other social improvements. What does that tell us about the church's attitude about the doctrine of charity? This seems to explain essentially all the problems with today's church, and also implies a set of answers.

Introduction to the Three Phases of The Modern Dispensation

The church started out on the right path under Joseph Smith, and then, 66 years later, at the time of Wilford Woodruff, veered off the path of the gospel of Christ and gradually reintroduced the law of Moses nearly 100% as did the Roman Catholic Church as it later developed. The law of Moses today is no more inviting and exciting and uplifting or "salable" than it was at the time of Christ, and I believe that explains why the LDS church is barely expanding at all, or is actually static or even shrinking. If we wish to see the Gospel reestablish its growth rates and good influence on the world on the same scale that happened after Christ organized his church in the Jerusalem area, where remnants of that distorted church still eventually established Western civilization, then we will have to disassemble and reverse the new installation of the law of Moses and go back to how things were during the life of Christ and for about the first 300 years thereafter.

Three Phases of The Modern Dispensation		
1. Joseph Smith period (same as Christ's)	**2. Today**	**3. Future Zion-establishing church (suggested)**
•No tithing – No central collection of money, no paid central bureaucracy at all -- no professional priesthood. •No charge for any miracle or ordinance •Members were expected to take care of each other and perform other charitable works as wisdom dictated. •No requirement for chapels or temples, yet all higher ordinances were available locally, no need for expensive communication or travel. •With no building or travel or communication costs, all personal resources were available for charitable works.	•We have most of the ancient Old Testament law of Moses operating today even though Christ ended it completely at his time. •The law of Moses consisted of paying tithing to support a large professional priesthood who performed animal sacrifices. We have dropped the animal sacrifices, but still maintain many temple activities as just as necessary to salvation. We have the Sanhedrin, the large central bureaucracy. •To support this vast and unnecessary bureaucracy, we have essentially ended all charity, the heart of the gospel of Christ. •As under the Law of Moses, tithing and charity are mutually exclusive: if you have one you do not find the other. •The cost of membership is about $500,000 for a lifetime membership; we might think of each important temple ordinance as costing about $50,000.	•Establish the "New China Program" which is the same as the old Christian program. •End tithing again and encourage wise charitable behavior. •Replace statist tax-and-spend welfare programs with charity-based programs which are 2 to 5 times more efficient and they also encourage freedom in general. •Actively assert principles of freedom. •Actively counteract worldly philosophies including organic evolution. •Gather all freedom-loving people in one place for maximum mutual support. •Set up systems to employ up to $10 trillion a year in charity operations in the world to raise social standards to a millennial level.

Phase 1 economics

Under Christ and under Joseph Smith, joining the church cost nothing. All miracles and ordinances were free and available locally. It was hoped that church members would assist each other, and that would be their main financial commitment, although there was no specific requirement.

The Jerusalem Saints showed us that there was no religious requirement for building expensive chapels or the even more expensive temples, so that essentially all personal resources could be used for charity work. "Freely ye have received, freely give" is the rule on how to use priesthood power. Something similar applied to more worldly resources without any formal regulation. All saving ordinances should be free and locally administered, removing essentially all need for a paid central bureaucracy.

Until that crucial original policy can be restored, the LDS church will likely remain a mere tribal curiosity as was the Jewish church. The Law of Moses rules and practices could not serve any but the Jews, being completely unfit for worldwide consumption and application. The same is true of the LDS church today among the Mormons.

Phase 2 economics

As with the ancient law of Moses, today the central bureaucracy of the LDS church collects up essentially all charity from the members and spends it on itself, with less than 1% going out as humanitarian assistance or other social improvements. Most of the rest is spent on unnecessary things.

In today's LDS church world, the expected cost of a lifetime membership is around $500,000. That could mean that if a single person received one set of ordinances, their "endowment," that would be the total return to them on their $500,000. At the other extreme we might have a family with 10 children who were all married in the temple, implying a cost of about $50,000 per ordinance. For someone who did 100 ordinances for deceased relatives, that might bring the cost per ordinance down to $5,000 each. Again, under the rules of Christ's Church, or Joseph Smith's church, there would be no cost for any of those ordinances.

Consequences
Since 1896, when the church began collecting tithing centrally and authorizing it to be used for salaries for church leaders and employees, a rough estimate would be that the church has collected about $1 trillion from the church members to be spent mostly on salaries and travel and office facilities for church leaders and staff, with a small portion being devoted to chapels and temples, perhaps much less than 10% of the total. For example, if we assign a value of about $30 billion to the church's holdings of chapels, that $30 billion is only about 3% of the trillion dollars which has been collected over the past 120 years. (30,000 chapels at $1 million each would equal $30 billion.) Most of the rest of the $970 billion collected has apparently been spent for living expenses for church leaders and staff. That is $1 trillion which has been almost totally diverted out of the set of vital charity applications it was originally intended to be devoted to by the members who paid it in.

I think it is easy to imagine that if the church members had applied that trillion dollars effectively in charitable pursuits, instead of having essentially all of that money taken and consumed by church headquarters, those church members would have done a great deal of good in the world. People would see the good works of the members and would wish to join in themselves, having been shown how to be good Christians. That vast amount of individual charity work would probably be the most effective missionary work that anyone could ever do.

Some Important Events Along the Way to Establishing Phase 2		
Year	**Event**	**Significance**
1896	Church contributions declared available to be used for church leader salaries	Formal beginning of priestcraft and attempts to maximize headquarters income through new tithing channel to be developed. The goal was to monopolize and monetize all important ordinances. Federal persecution was used to the central church's advantage.
1899	Tithing re-invented and re-emphasized	The next step in maximizing headquarters income announced by Lorenzo Snow.
1923	Church incorporates as corporation sole	Church cuts off all member participation in church administration. Headquarters claims separate, complete, and even hostile ownership of all church assets and property.
1942	Church embraces pacifism for WW II	Church decides not to defend freedom in the United States or anywhere else. Considers itself above the U.S. Constitution.
1960 about	Church makes full central tithing mandatory for temple attendance	This was the formal end of Christian charity. Tithing and charity are mutually exclusive in practice.
1977	Doctrine of the Gathering abolished	Lowers general growth of church, but maximizes income from existing members. Foreign members are trophies and hostages to extract more money from more wealthy US members. 90,000 members came from Europe to Utah in the 1850s and 1860s to escape the bad conditions in their home countries and guaranteed church success in Utah. This vital growth process was officially ended.
1978	Blacks given priesthood	It is nice to have all men treated equally, but notice that with temple privileges came tithing "privileges," as well, making it sound like a revenue measure as much as a fairness measure. This would let the church grow in size, but even more in revenue.
1979	Abolish church patriarch position.	Finalize centralization, monopolization, and monetization of sealing ordinances. Stake patriarchs previously held all sealing powers, preventing central monetization.
2019	Ban guns from church facilities	Another blow to gospel freedom requirements. Shows willingness to degrade U.S. Constitution, not defend it, even though it is incorporated into LDS Scriptures.

In contrast, the church has essentially ended all charity work of any significance, and they send their missionaries out, the church's salesforce, for the main purpose of getting new people to send tithing money into the central church headquarters, where all of it is essentially wasted, regardless of the amount received.

I am going to assert as highly likely that this expenditure of a trillion dollars in high-quality charity work would have easily caused the church itself to be 10 times as large as it is now, having generated enormous amounts of goodwill by that Christian behavior. If we actually have 5 million serious and active members today, we would then have 50 million serious and active members. It is vital to realize that a very important aspect of this charity program is that it would create a complete social insurance system for its participants, the members, which could replace all of the extremely expensive, wasteful, and corrupt government tax-and-spend "charity" programs that are now in existence.

All of those resources which are now taken by taxation by greedy governments would be available to provide charity-based social insurance which would be at least 2 to 5 times as efficient as anything found available today. That very large amount of government tax money could be added to the church "tax" money, which the church calls "tithing," to represent a very large amount of money available for serious charity work. With that original 10-times increase in membership, and the creation of this very powerful positive upward spiral, by now we could have actually already reached another 10 times growth increment, possibly reaching a total of 500 million worldwide.

Besides providing a promise of overcoming death with a clearly described afterlife, the church could also promise to overcome suffering in this life, so that fear of death and fear of suffering could be greatly assuaged. Someone said that "a church which cannot save us temporally cannot save us spiritually," and I believe I have just briefly described how both can be achieved through correct teachings and policies.

I believe it would be sensible for the church to increase in size by 10 times every generation, which would mean by the end of the second generation, or sometime about now, the church could easily have an effective size of 200 million members or even 500 million members.

As another way to compute this, we might notice that when the federal Social Security program was proposed in the 1930s, there was an option to create an alternate nongovernment system to take care of the pension needs of citizens. Those who did take advantage of that alternate system option have done extremely well, with their pension payouts being in the range of 2.4 to 5 times as great as the government pension system can produce. In many cases, the retirees receive $2.5 million more than received by those in the government system, and that money is owned by the pensioner and he can spend it as he sees fit or pass it along to his children or devote it to charity or missionary work.

If church members had been encouraged to set up such systems 90 years ago, the typical retirees under those private systems would have reaped about $10 trillion more in pension benefits than they would have received under the single option of a government Social Security pension. That extra $10 trillion could have done a great deal to accomplish charity work and missionary work, far beyond what has actually been accomplished under the actual system accepted by the church and its members.

Precise calculations are a bit difficult, but it should be easy to see that if church members had had an extra $20 trillion to spend on charity work and missionary work over the past 90 years, 20 times what the church took to itself for its short-term purposes, it is not too much to expect that the church would have reached a 200 million membership level. The world is eagerly waiting for this kind of a gospel solution to all of life's problems, and millions would rush to join in.

As it is, with a membership lifetime cost of $500,000, that is an enormous net loss as compared to an additional increment such as the $2.5 million alternate Social Security system could provide.

The main point here is that by taking this money to itself, as a huge and almost prohibitive tax on church membership and growth, the church has greatly discouraged membership growth and has made essentially impossible the most effective kind of missionary work imaginable which is individual charity work on a very large scale.

Phase 3 economics (suggested)

China is the new Rome
China is the new Rome (but so is Russia, only on a much smaller scale). Blacks were given the priesthood so they could go to the temples, after paying tithing, which they now have an incentive to do, accomplishing the main church goal of increasing revenue. That action brought the blacks completely into the current system. In the Chinese case, they ought to be given old-style patriarchs who could bring them all of the sealing ordinances without the need for temples. That would be inventing a new system to bring the Chinese into. The same strategy should work just as well in Russia.

If someone were looking for a test bed to verify my claims here about how the gospel worked so successfully before, just after the life of Christ, and could do so again under the right conditions, all they would have to do is quickly create a very simple "China program" that was indistinguishable from the church at Christ's time. As under Roman rule, which fostered paganism as the state religion, in China there could be no visible LDS chapels and no temples to compete with the Chinese "state religion" of atheism, but all the saving ordinances, including all temple ordinances, could still be delivered there. Also, the comprehensive social insurance system that is an inherent part of a charity-based religious society would probably be very well received and would likely cause the church to grow explosively. The church would also find itself gently supporting freedom instead of trying to suppress freedom for its own financial benefit, as it does today in so many countries by explicitly supporting freedom-hostile regimes, as the current method of expanding gospel penetration into new areas.

India could be a similar trial ground, and the new program should be a lot easier to apply there, since the fanatically totalitarian communists do not have such a tight grip on that country. However, the temptation for the church to try to continue its law of Moses imposition in India as well, would probably doom that program to failure. Apparently, the original gospel of Christ can only work properly and reliably, on a long-term basis, in an authoritarian country like Rome or China. That is, we have the strange situation where an authoritarian government helps to enforce the correct version of Christianity, where a free country allows the priests to hornswoggle the members and set up their separate and destructive religious priestcraft systems, as in the U.S.

The authoritarian countries try to suppress all competing centers of influence and power, especially including outside religions that have not been certified as authentic "warlord religions" supporting dictatorships. The LDS church would apparently be willing to act as a convenient "warlord religion," but, thankfully, has not been very successful at it yet. For correct Christian religions to be successful in the context of a highly authoritarian government, it requires that those religions operate at least semi-underground so that there is at least no visible political and "hearts and minds" influence and ideological challenge to the reigning dictatorship.

Obviously, if this proposed China test were successful, it could show the absurdity of what the "free" West has been trying to do to the gospel, and with the gospel, by imposing a greedy professional priesthood to exploit and neutralize the natural charity-based Gospel for short-term financial gain.

Perhaps this suggested program is what is going on already in China, with the LDS commissariat having been forced to do what it would never do willingly and spontaneously. But this new China program would have to be kept more secret in the West that it is in China, since if anyone in the West knew that they could be active members in good standing without paying tithing to Salt Lake City, the entire current financing system would collapse. As it is, here we could have one authoritarian government (China) keeping another would-be authoritarian government (the LDS church) straight. There would be quite a bit of irony in that situation.

I believe the church normally demands that an adequate banking system be set up to collect and transfer money from foreign member locations to Salt Lake City before the church considers itself to have been established in some country. In the China case, there could be no import or export of tithing money, especially not through any official banking system, without putting the church, and especially the members, in harm's way, so that the churches there would have to be self-contained, as was intended to be true under Christ's church. Again, we would have made a "virtue of necessity," and accidentally got the right religious answer.

If members were to travel from China to Hong Kong, for example, to receive temple ordinances, they would immediately reveal their identity to the Chinese dictatorship and potentially cause themselves a great deal of trouble. However, if all ordinances could be administered in China, and done quietly, it would very definitely not be visible, and the Chinese government may not feel any need to intervene, especially since there would be no government profit in intervening. If everything is free, there is nothing to tax or extort, so there may be no reason to intervene as long as the members are not proposing revolution.

If members were able to migrate out of China as part of the Gathering, that could give even more Chinese people an incentive to associate with the church, and the process could collect the most freedom-loving people out of China and give them a better place to live and operate. A gradual brain-drain from China of the most freedom-loving people, leaving behind the "dregs," so to speak, could perhaps be a gentle reminder to the Chinese Communists that the way to a nation's greatest success is through establishing freedom-enhancing policies.

The attempt by the LDS church to add its extra governmental layer of revenue-producing religion over the top of a communist regime in East Germany, as part of the USSR, did not work out too well. Hopefully that was taken to demonstrate that Mormonism and communism cannot be made explicitly compatible, or even complimentary on a long-term cooperative basis, although they might be able to be peacefully overlapping in the same space for a short period until greater freedom arrives as with the fall of the Soviet Union.

The results of such experiments could reasonably mean that we eventually add 200 million members each in China, India, and Russia, plus another 200 million in the United States and Europe, and then, at perhaps 800 million members, we could actually claim to be a world church, having established a worldwide gospel-based civilization. This is what could reasonably happen if the church would get out of the way of gospel progress, and stop compulsively trying to milk a huge, even obscene profit on every single person who joins the church anywhere in the world.

Totally charity-based organizations (such as The Red Cross and Father Flanagan's Boys Home, now known as Boys Town -- both of which could probably be improved upon) can do very well in a free society, demonstrating that there is no need to monopolize religious ordinances and extort the members to get religious operating funds. It just requires an adjustment in thinking and an adjustment in how one presents projects worthy of member support. We have the totally non-religious "GoFundMe" or "Facebook Fundraiser" type of Internet mechanisms for assembling funds for good projects. Besides, with perhaps $200 billion in accumulated funds, the church could operate indefinitely without receiving another dime in tithing funds from anywhere in the world, although it might need to cut down on the number of structures built, which it probably ought to do anyway.

For some reason, the church has been afraid to use its $200 billion in reserves to use today's media outlets to prepare people to receive the gospel. That $200 billion is the same as about 200 presidential campaigns as far as being able to make people aware of what is going on and influence their thinking. A media blitz on a much smaller scale would be more than enough to prepare the way for missionaries so that there would be no need for them to behave as independent unsupported door-to-door salesman, but they could simply become "order takers" in a system for those who would like to join the church, empowering missionaries to bring in hundreds of people every year per missionary. Presumably, those techniques have not been used simply because the church wants to make no ideological or political ripples anywhere in the world and is perfectly happy with the current size of the church budget, so it sees no need to make its presence any better known.

This suggested charity-based technique or business model would allow the church to draw in hundreds of billions of dollars from sources outside of its current tithing extraction membership base. The church could become THE charity organization worldwide with multi-trillion-dollar budgets. Someone just needs to make the necessary changes in concept and direction.

NOTES

1. https://www.goodreads.com/book/show/2649810-the-mormons

2. https://en.wikipedia.org/wiki/Rodney_Stark

3. https://faenrandir.github.io/a_careful_examination/2013-faith-crisis-study/

https://faenrandir.github.io/a_careful_examination/documents/faith_crisis_study/Faith_Crisis_R28e.pdf

4. David B. Ostler, *Bridges: Ministering to Those Who Question* (Salt Lake City: Greg Kofford Books, 2019).

5. John Gee, "Conclusions in Search of Evidence." *Interpreter: A Journal of Latter-day Saint Faith and Scholarship* 34 (2020): 161-178; https://journal.interpreterfoundation.org/conclusions-in-search-of-evidence/

6. Jana Riess, *The Next Mormons: How Millennials Are Changing the LDS Church* (New York: Oxford University Press, 2019), pp. 233-5

Chapter 29

Can Humans Become Gods?

It seems like almost everyone wants to grow up to be a Levite, supported on some religious or government payroll for life, rather than striving to become an independent, generous, charitable man or god. I don't see how self-centered Levites, who add nothing to the economy, including the charitable economy, can ever learn how to be gods.

Where did this idea come from in our time concerning humans becoming gods? Presumably it came from the same place it came from in all prior times – the prophets and the scriptures.

On these issues, the LDS have their scriptures and their history:

1. Ps. 82:6 I have said, Ye are gods; and all of you are children of the most High.

2. John 10:34 Jesus answered them, Is it not written in your law, I said, Ye are gods?

3. D&C 76:58 "Wherefore, as it is written, they are gods, even the sons of God –"

4. From Joseph Smith:

> If men do not comprehend the character of God, they do not comprehend themselves.[1]
>
> From his King Follett Discourse:
>
> God himself was once as we are now, and is an exalted man, and sits enthroned in yonder heavens![2]

5. The famous Lorenzo Snow couplet, presumably based on Joseph Smith's earlier teachings:

> As man is, God once was; as God is, man may become.[3]

6. Another evidence of this idea being embedded in our culture comes from Hymn number 171, "With Humble Heart," which has a sacrament theme, where the ending phrase is

"And grow, dear Lord, to be like thee."

7. God told Moses about His philosophy and plans, and in that indirect way tells us what he would like to be able to do for us, and, by extension, what we can eventually do for others, assuming we take the steps to qualify ourselves to be part of the "family business" of advancing souls in the eternities:

> Moses 1:39 For behold, this is my work and my glory – to bring to pass the immortality and eternal life of man.

> Moses 7:56 and the Saints arose, and were crowned at the right hand of the Son of Man, with crowns of glory;

We seem happy to accept all the largess presented to us by God, but apparently it never occurs to us that the only way we can be as he is, is to be just as happy and joyful to give those blessings to others. If that is not our goal, then it is hopeless that we might ever become like God. We may benefit from his generosity, but our lack of generosity will make us unfit. I believe if our main focus is on benefiting from others, accepting a portion of what Satan's plan was, then we are doomed, as far as this godhood thing is concerned.

This expansive doctrine, that man can become a God, or be like god, and should actually want to, was proudly declared by Joseph Smith and others of his generation.

Joseph Smith also supplied a more action-oriented version of his general philosophy:

> "A man filled with the love of God is not content with blessing his family alone, but ranges through the whole world, anxious to bless the whole human race." -- Joseph Smith, Jr.[4]

Joseph Smith's philosophy of blessing the whole human race sounds like a good one, if a man seriously wanted to learn how to become a God, since that is what we imagine our Heavenly Father is doing with His time. Perhaps not by chance, this philosophy matches rather well with the importance placed on individual acts of charity in the New Testament. Wouldn't it be wonderful if everyone in the world put a large amount of effort into raising everybody else up, instead of so many people exploiting other people to get gain. That constant "raising up" seems like a nice way to think of heaven.

But notice that this philosophy of generosity matches rather badly with the Old Testament concept of mandatory tithing. That Old Testament philosophy invites self-centeredness, focusing on personal "purity," whatever that may be, with charity towards others being an impediment to that feeling of personal "purity" or superiority and importance.

Joseph Smith made many other important statements on this general topic. He was asked continually what the requirements were for joining his church.

> In the afternoon I answered the questions which were frequently asked me ... as printed in the *Elders Journal*, Vol. I, Number II, pages 28 and 29, as follows:
>
> > ...Sixth "Do the Mormons believe in having all things in common?"
> > No.
> > ...Twelfth "Do the people have to give up their money when they join his Church?"
> > *No other requirement than to bear their proportion of the expenses of the Church, and support the poor. (emphasis supplied)*
> > ...I published the forgoing answers to save myself the trouble of repeating the same a thousand times over and over again. HC 3:28 29. May 8, 1838, Far West.

We might notice that he makes no mention of paying tithing in this publication, but does mention a general duty of charity. By definition, charity is not enforceable, and is not required in payment for other gospel blessings such as priesthood ordinances. A church would not be modeling charity very well if it demanded generous payment for every benefit it conferred.

The concept of "paying it forward" is another term for charity that is occasionally heard today that suspends the typical tightly-managed quid pro quo way of doing business in the world.

There are other places we can look for interesting philosophies on this general point. People have argued forever about the inherent nature of man. He might be a noble savage to some, or an evolved ape to others. Some might try to construct a "new Soviet man," or a "new Gospel man," using force or stratagem, based on whatever their preferred ideologies might require. But God's description of man is that man is a god in embryo, a literal son of god, even though he may not know that because of the world into which he is born. The purpose of the gospel is to set man's goals as high as possible, not to try to make him of no eternal consequence as most worldly philosophers seem to do.

The theme of the writings of the philosopher Jacques Rousseau, as in his 1762 book *The Social Contract*, is that "Man is born free, but he is everywhere in chains." That theme has apparently been interpreted in many different ways, including the "notion that man, at his core, is good, and that he is inevitably corrupted by society." I would say that if men are indeed trapped in their culture and cannot think of the grand things which God would like them to think about, it is the purpose of the gospel to raise their sights. It is hard to think of a higher goal and purpose than for men to become like God.

The grand idea fades away

It seems like as soon as Joseph Smith died, all the other prominent church members and leaders began to be slightly obsessed with the idea that it was mandatory that some members must pay money into the church system and others need not. It took a while before the idea fully developed of using required tithing to pay church leader salaries, but things kept moving in that direction until Wilford Woodruff made it official in 1896. Some of this detailed economic history is described in D. Michael Quinn's June 1996 *Sunstone* article entitled "LDS Church Finances From The 1830s To The 1990s." One interesting story involves a patriarch who made a nice living by charging one dollar for each blessing given, while encouraging people to seek out multiple blessings. Where he had little income before, he now made a nice living offering this religious service. [p.21][5]

Strangely, what was once a fairly clear doctrine about the possibility of man becoming like God has more recently become a source of confusion and embarrassment to the church leaders. President Hinckley, among others, has publicly said, paraphrasing, that "we don't know much about that." The problem with "not knowing much about that" is that without that exalted concept of God and man, on earth and in heaven, the LDS church becomes just another Catholic/Protestant church, following something like the original Nicene Creed, without actually admitting it – worshiping an unknowable, incomprehensible, non-anthropomorphic God, etc. Certainly, that god of the old creeds is not a creature that men would even think of trying to become like. The concept of heaven changes from being a place where people are busily helping others to advance, and instead deteriorates into nothing more than a place where people sit on fluffy clouds and play harps forever, thinking only of themselves and not actually helping anyone else. They don't even imagine that they *could* help anyone else there.

In Ether 3, the brother of Jared has the unique opportunity of seeing the spirit body of Christ in the exact form in which He will appear during his mortal ministry on earth. One might guess that the brother of Jared fully understood that God intended this particular man, the brother of Jared, having great faith, and having been forgiven of his sins, to eventually become exactly like God. It's nice to have the Book of Mormon, as evidence that the restoration occurred, and that man can become like God, but if we don't believe and practice what is in the Book of Mormon, as we clearly don't, and apparently have forgotten, then we really have nothing important to distinguish us. We simply have more scriptures to condemn us in our ignorance and misbehavior than do many other churches.

I want to insert here a small side issue: The church leaders today do supply us with many words to influence our religious behavior, but only at an excessive financial and spiritual cost, in my opinion. Are the contents of the conference talks really worth $40,000 for each word, as it seems to cost? As a curiosity, I want to compute the cost per word of the instructions we receive from church leaders, over and above the cost of our personal scriptures.

The April 2020 conference talks, published in the May 2020 *Ensign,* amount to 132 pages containing 79,646 words. If we assume that the church receives about $10 billion in income each year, and we triple the number of words in one conference to account for a second conference edition plus other teaching materials, we end up with a formula of $10,000,000,000/240,000 words = $41,667 per word. We might rearrange those numbers to say that 1 million people could each receive $10,000 in aid or 4 million people could each receive $2500 in aid. I am assuming that most of this aid would be in the form of capital investments in education, tools, working capital, etc. I assume that proper investments in charity would have a long-term exponential effect and would result in extreme expansions in what I will call the charitable economy. We ought to have the goal of spending at least $100 billion each year on valuable charitable projects, with money coming from many different sources, wisely administered by LDS members. We might wonder whether those spoken and printed words by church leaders are a good trade-off for the influential charitable and uplifting actions that might otherwise be taken.

A broader view of the question

In most of the world, the question of "whether humans can become gods" is an almost unthinkable question. The answer is now resoundingly "No" everywhere, even in Utah. There was a short time when the LDS church was the only church on the planet that taught such a thing, and even that single "Yea" vote has been silent for a long time. Like all the topics in this book, this topic deserves a book-length treatment, but all that can be managed here is a quick overview, hoping to quickly encapsulate the essence of the current situation.

Based on my limited understanding of Eastern religions, I believe that some of them go so far as to claim that a person can eventually merge with the divine in the universe, while others postulate that the highest form of existence is nonexistence – annihilation, the end of all desires and passions. Certainly, neither of those depressing ideas contemplate a human seeking for and gaining godlike powers and status. Why would a person with such beliefs even want to or attempt to? It appears that these Eastern religions have fully accepted Satan's doctrine about what should happen to everyone in the universe except himself – subjugation, slavery, or annihilation.

We might notice that the Protestants and Catholics have certainly given up on anything like men becoming gods. Their version of the reality of the universe is that men are hopelessly fallen sinners and the idea of ever becoming like God is either laughably foolish or blasphemy. Christ was crucified by Old Testament thinkers on the charge of blasphemy for claiming he was God or the son of God. Today, anyone making the same claims would likely receive the same treatment, at least in sentiment. It doesn't matter that wanting to be a God is a good thing, not a bad thing, assuming you have the correct understanding of God in the first place.

For many, this typical "man is nothing but a hopelessly fallen sinner" language is a copout, an excuse for being irresponsible, including minimizing charity and societal uplift. They tend to say that Christ has done everything, so that they don't have to do anything, and they couldn't do anything good and useful even if they tried, so there is no need to even try. This is a long way from the active force for good which was epitomized by the Good Samaritan.

The original LDS God was famous for his mighty works, with worlds coming and going at his command. Moses 1:35-40. But the Catholics and Protestants want no part of that "works" mentality, or any potential associated responsibility to take action. The grace of God means to them that no works by men are necessary. In fact, exercising originality may do more harm than good, so being passive is good. At some point, this pessimistic pacifism starts to look like Buddhism, which, as we noted above, is basically the opposite point of view from men attempting to become gods for the very purpose of performing powerful works for good. We might notice that the LDS church adopted pacifism during World War II, apparently using much the same logic as the Buddhists, and little has changed doctrinally since, as far as I know.

We have heard that people will sometimes say "the devil made me do it," but we also have some people who would say "God made me do it" in the sense of the predestination taught by the Calvinists. Here we have people glorying in the impossibility of becoming God, since, in their view, a person can never be anything more than a choiceless and unthinking dependent tool of God (or of the state).

Pacifism might be interpreted as not wanting to get involved, for good or ill. I see that as a self-centered attitude which also tends to avoid charitable actions simply to save money for oneself while attempting to not take sides. Is the LDS god a god who does not take sides, and is "nonpolitical," or is he a distant, passionless, Deist-style god, for whom good and evil are all the same? That reading doesn't fit well with the scriptures and the scriptural prophets.

There is naturally a political effect to this kind of "man is nothing" thinking, and that thinking is promoted exactly and exclusively for that intended political effect. If ambitious priests or philosophers can convince people that those people are totally dependent on Christ, and they are unable to do anything themselves to help themselves in this life or in the hereafter, that, conveniently, promotes the idea that each individual ought to feel totally dependent on any claimed (often self-appointed) representatives of God, whether in religious organizations or governmental organizations. The end effect is that people accept the idea that slavery, or being part of a caste system, is the way the universe ought to be, as their overlords continually tell them.

In contrast, the concept that man can become like God should have a very positive effect on the world's cultures, encouraging respect for all humans and inspiring constant efforts to help each other be successful.

There are several possible impulses operating here. Religion is often, and perhaps even universally, used as a means of confusing and subduing people, Satan-like, by teaching them that they are really nothing, and so their accomplishments, their pain, despair, or death have no meaning to the universe. This "religion-backed" view happens to match with the atheist view as well, with the atheists just brutally skipping all the fake religious overlays and explanations and going straight to the law of the jungle. So, if we have religionists and atheists basically teaching the same doctrine, that might make someone a little bit suspicious of claimed "religious" teachings.

This is the "warlord religion" concept which appears to me to be currently totally victorious over all other original religions. It is so successful because it has such a practical purpose to would-be dictators and would-be human "gods" in the mold of Satan himself.

In the past, protestants often wanted to be fiercely independent and free, religiously, politically, and economically, but they are gradually being worn down to mostly be good little dependent slaves of various exploitative governments.

To complicate things, even a genuine altruistic urge to help others, which urge may often be poorly defined, will be exploited mercilessly by the evil one. That evil being urges and argues for altruism, and then exploits it mercilessly, if possible. It seems that hardly anyone can balance all these factors correctly, especially with every conceivable method of confusion and distortion being thrown at them.

It is my opinion that only by a lifetime of attempted charitable activity can a person learn all the principles and practices of doing good without doing more harm than good, the excesses of do-gooder bleeding-heart liberals versus the too-limited help for others, and engaging in other such delicate balancing acts.

Those who claim to be gods already
Of course, on the issue of men becoming gods, there are the exceptions for the cult of personality situations where men such as an Egyptian Pharaoh might claim to be God, or a God, but the pattern that particular human is usually following is to use Satan's definition of godhood where there is only one being who is allowed to think and act independently, and all the others are enslaved and must do and think exactly as he says. The Christian God would say there is only one God, but that one God delights in the freedom, independence, and creativity of all other beings in the universe. It is his goal to maximize the power and experience of others. This, of course, is the exact opposite of Satan's concept of the perfect universe.

Another example of a godly man
We seem to forget that there is a good reason why some of the Western religions are considered Abrahamic religions – Judaism, Christianity, and Islam. Although many godly men went before him, including Adam and many other great leaders, apparently Abraham was another ideal man who would be God, and we just happen to know a little more about him than we do about many of the others. He was as intelligent and wise and free and independent as any human could be in this life. He very consciously did good everywhere he could. As close as is humanly possible, he is a model for men who would become gods in heaven. Unfortunately, but seemingly as part of a larger plan, his posterity gradually became slaves in Egypt, where they grew greatly in numbers, and their miraculous return to complete freedom, or at least all the freedom they could tolerate, is the great story of the Old Testament – their great exodus from Egypt, from slavery to freedom. Against constant prophetic counsel, those Israelites finally insisted on having a king, and through that route became almost as enslaved as they were in Egypt. Bound down by a burdensome law of Moses religion, with its professional Levites and priests taking at least 1/10, combined with a burdensome all-powerful state, as under kings David and Solomon, which took most of the rest of their personal resources, they learned to exploit each other and came to consider that to be the normal state of affairs.

When Christ came to free them from their sins and their foolishness and self-slavery, many wanted to keep the old ways, and their lucrative religious income, while many others embraced freedom.

Today, we are almost back to where the whole thing started at the time Christ was born, with a burdensome and self-centered priestly class demanding that they are entitled to our resources and our obedience, while giving back nothing in return except a fraudulent/counterfeit sense of being saved.

Can men who are habitually uncharitable become gods?
When we learn that the church leaders today have at least $100 billion stashed away in liquid assets for some unspecified rainy day, obviously ignoring everyone's rainy days except their own, it is hard to believe that they agree with the sentiment expressed by Joseph Smith about men becoming gods. If they were to focus regularly on Joseph Smith's philosophy, as expressed in statements appearing above, the contrast between his philosophy of generosity and their philosophy of avoiding charity whenever possible might become inconveniently obvious. This seems to explain why abundant acts of charity disappear at the same time that the doctrine disappears that men can become like God. Those two ideas seem to be bound closely together, and they appear and disappear together. I believe we can say that the requirement of tithing paid to headquarters, before priesthood blessings can be accessed, is completely inconsistent with the promotion of individual charity and individual godhood. The fictional Three Musketeers declared their mutual loyalty to each other with the motto "All for one and one for all." The church leaders seem to accept the first part of the motto from the members and the rest of society, but skip the last part.

Notes

1. History of the Church, 6:303
https://www.calledtoshare.com/2018/01/05/10-powerful-quotes-from-joseph-smith-the-prophet/

2. https://emp.byui.edu/jexj/new/talks/talks/JS%20KingFollettDiscourse.pdf
The Being and Kind of Being God Is; The Immortality of the Intelligence of Man. Joseph Smith, April 7, 1844, History of the Church, 6:302-317

3. https://www.mrm.org/status-of-lorenzo-snow-couplet
"Does Lorenzo Snow's famous couplet no longer have a functioning place in LDS theology?"
https://www.mrm.org/snow-couplet#:~:text=%E2%80%9CFrom%20President%20Snow%E2%80%99s%20understanding%20of,Presidency)%20General%20Conference,%20October%201964

4. *History of the Church,* 4:227.
"Anxious to Bless the Whole Human Race"
https://www.churchofjesuschrist.org/study/ensign/1999/04/anxious-to-bless-the-whole-human-race?lang=eng

5. D. Michael Quinn, "LDS Church Finances From The 1830s To The 1990s," *Sunstone*, June 1996, pp. 17-29. http://followtheprophets.com/wp-content/uploads/2017/09/LDS-Finances-to-1990s.pdf

Chapter 30

The Fund For Zion Project

By purchasing this book, you will be contributing a small amount to The Fund for Zion Project (TFFZ) which is intended to do all those things which the LDS Church has failed to do for the last 100 years -- all the missed opportunities to influence our nation and world to be better than they are. The project will then go on to plan what should be done for the next 100 years, and take the appropriate actions. Other contributions will also be gladly accepted and carefully devoted to the purposes of The Fund for Zion Project. These extra funds will be directed according to donor intent to the extent practicable.

Just a few of the many potential projects will be listed here: 1) Better showing the world and its many religions and ideologies the errors of their ways, as compared to Christ's Gospel, and helping them with their plans to become more in line with Christ's Gospel. 2) The alarming number of abortions in the world come to mind as a denial of that aspect of the gospel plan which calls for spirits to come to the earth to gain a body and learn about morality and how the gospel applies in mortality. 3) Repair our broken education systems so that gospel principles and values are taught first and foremost as a way to evaluate our world and all that goes on within it. 4) Take action to repair our broken and corrupt political and legal systems so that justice is always recognized and done. 5) Our nation's news media and entertainment systems are a major factor of confusion and corruption and need to be countered by major systems that teach and operate on gospel principles. 6) Greatly improve social insurance and welfare systems, emphasizing flexible charity solutions rather than statist tax-and-spend methods. 7) And so on, as funds allow.

It appears that the LDS Church has collected perhaps $1 trillion over the last 124 years, but instead of applying it all to Christian charitable activities and attempting to influence the nation and the world to live by the right principles and do the right things, it has mostly focused on the narrow financial interests of the corporation of the president and the bureaucracy it represents. Its bad practical advice concerning government ideologies and practices have cost the church members another $10 trillion in lost retirement income, much of which might have been directed to highly beneficial charitable acts – spontaneous acts and projects done under the greatly expanded religious freedom opportunities thus afforded to wise and experienced church members.

The Fund for Zion – mission statement

Maximize religious freedom for LDS church members, and any other charity-minded people who wish to participate, by creating a democratically-managed organization to carry out charitable works consistent with the teachings of Christ. This might legally be considered or established as a church or a parachurch or other tax-exempt organization depending on what is practically required to achieve its mission.

Chapter 31

Epilogue

In order to offer an adequate overall theory within limited space, this current book only makes a short presentation for each of the important topics it covers. It is barely more than an outline of all that is needed. To do an adequate job on all the topics presented, including some important topics which are barely mentioned or hinted at here, there would need to be a separate book for almost every chapter in this book. And then, going beyond that, there should be another book applying all of the same principles to each of the approximately 9 other world religions that underlie the world's various civilizations.

These various world religions have generally wandered even further off the gospel path than has the LDS church, although the forces pulling them off that path are probably generally the same, operating in about the same sequence. The LDS church is just the most recent example. Perhaps this whole meta-process is the "mystery of iniquity," spoken of by the apostle Paul. 2 Thes.2:7.

All of these tasks need to be done, but the question is who has the time and expertise to do all of that work? That all remains to be seen. It would be ideal if the hundreds or thousands of people who are qualified researchers and writers on Mormon topics could take on these topics and create the completely new library of studies which are needed.

Bibliography

An explanation of sources
The modern-day LDS Scriptures are extremely important to the study. Either the doctrines they teach are controlling, or they are not. This mostly explains my reference to "A Constitutional Approach." I spent a great deal of time and practical effort comparing the teachings and practices of the church today with the teachings and practices found in the LDS Scriptures, and I found that there are many major mismatches. For example, Christ ended tithing, and taught and practiced charity with almost unimaginable generosity, and the early Christians likewise paid no tithing and aggressively practiced charity. Today we pay tithing in conformance with the law of Moses and practice very little charity. Capt. Moroni spent his life defending the freedom of the Nephites, but today we do nothing to defend freedom. We are mere consumers of freedom rather than suppliers and supporters. This is the level of mismatch that I am talking about. There are no documentary sources of authority I can cite for these major principles. It is simply my personal observations I am spelling out. Apparently, no one has studied and publicly written about these matters in the last 200 years.

Similarly, the other four books I have written are themselves a major source of documentation for the positions I assert. At this point I am largely building upon the exploratory work of my earlier studies. Those books and their contents are an important part of my bibliography, and they also contain bibliographic references to many other general sources, especially in my book *Creating the Millennium*.

There are a few other books I quote from and cite, including materials found on the Internet which are not otherwise generally available to a lone researcher. These sources can be seen in the text of my book. I could repeat them here in the bibliography, but repeating just a few of those items here would make them appear to have far too much importance as compared to the mass of information sources which are not listed here.

In summary, this book is mostly the product of my 79 years of life's observations, all the information I have examined and processed during that period. That makes it a kind of autobiography or memoir. There are a few books I can point to which give some useful information on the topics of the book. However, the bulk of the observations, analysis, and comments come from my own experience, and cannot be found written in other places. Personal, painful, and expensive research is at the base of most of the most important insights offered here. Other materials have been collected to clarify and expand on those seminal personal experiences and observations.

Index

Author's Biography

Kent W. Huff is an attorney and a computer consultant. He grew up in Utah Valley, attended Brigham Young University, married Suzanne Snow from Los Angeles, and has six children. At BYU he studied political science, mathematics, and engineering. He has two law degrees from George Washington University in Washington, D.C., which were focused on government regulation and taxation.

His work took him and his family to our nation's capital, where he was employed by ten U.S. Government agencies in technical work related to their largest computer systems. One example is the Treasury disbursing system which makes 600 million payments a year totaling the entire federal government budget. He later worked in the capital cities of three other countries: Riyadh, Saudi Arabia; Mexico City, Mexico; and Moscow, Russia.

Abroad, he worked with the Saudi government on computer processing related to gathering and analyzing government statistics, implementing government social insurance programs, and international shipping, inventorying and selling of petrochemicals. At the large U.S. embassies in Mexico City and Moscow he assisted with internal computer hardware and software needs, plus the international communications systems.

After retiring from the U.S. Department of State, he assisted in the Y2K upgrading of US Airways airline reservation and accounting systems. He then assisted Bell Atlantic (now Verizon) in the programming and testing of its gigantic Event Processing System which handles all computer processing relating to telephones for most of the East Coast population. He has since been granted a computer software patent as the result of research concerning more efficient Internet processing of worldwide genealogy data. He has held numerous church positions in the US and abroad.

He has published three previous books on complex LDS-related topics: *Joseph Smith's United Order: A Non-Communalistic Interpretation* (1988), *Brigham Young's United Order: A Contextual Interpretation* (1998), and *Creating The Millennium: Social Forces and Church Growth in the 21st Century (2004).* The interplay of many religious, social, political, legal, and economic factors is a common theme in all these books. Email address: huffkw@juno.com.

www.ingramcontent.com/pod-product-compliance
Lightning Source LLC
Chambersburg PA
CBHW031123090426
42738CB00008B/956